Hana-Kimi
For You in Full Blossom

3

story and art by
HISAYA NAKAJO

HANA-KIMI
For You In Full Blossom
VOLUME 3

STORY & ART BY HISAYA NAKAJO

Translation/David Ury
English Adaptation/Gerard Jones
Touch-Up Art & Lettering/Gabe Crate
Design/Izumi Evers & Judi Roubideaux
Editor/Jason Thompson

Managing Editor/Annette Roman
Editor-in-Chief/Alvin Lu
Production Manager/Noboru Watanabe
Sr. Director of Acquisitions/Rika Inouye
VP of Marketing/Liza Coppola
Executive VP/Hyoe Narita
Publisher/Seiji Horibuchi

Hanazakari no Kimitachi he by Hisaya Nakajo © Hisaya Nakajo 1997
All rights reserved. First published in Japan in 1998 by HAKUSENSHA, Inc., Tokyo. English
language translation rights in America and Canada arranged with HAKUSENSHA, Inc., Tokyo.
New and adapted artwork and text © 2005 VIZ, LLC. The HANA-KIMI logo is a trademark of
VIZ, LLC. The stories, characters and incidents mentioned in this publication are entirely fictional.

Printed in Canada

Published by VIZ, LLC, P.O. Box 77010, San Francisco, CA 94107

Shôjo Edition
10 9 8 7 6 5 4 3 2

First printing, July 2004
Second Printing, May 2005

CONTENTS

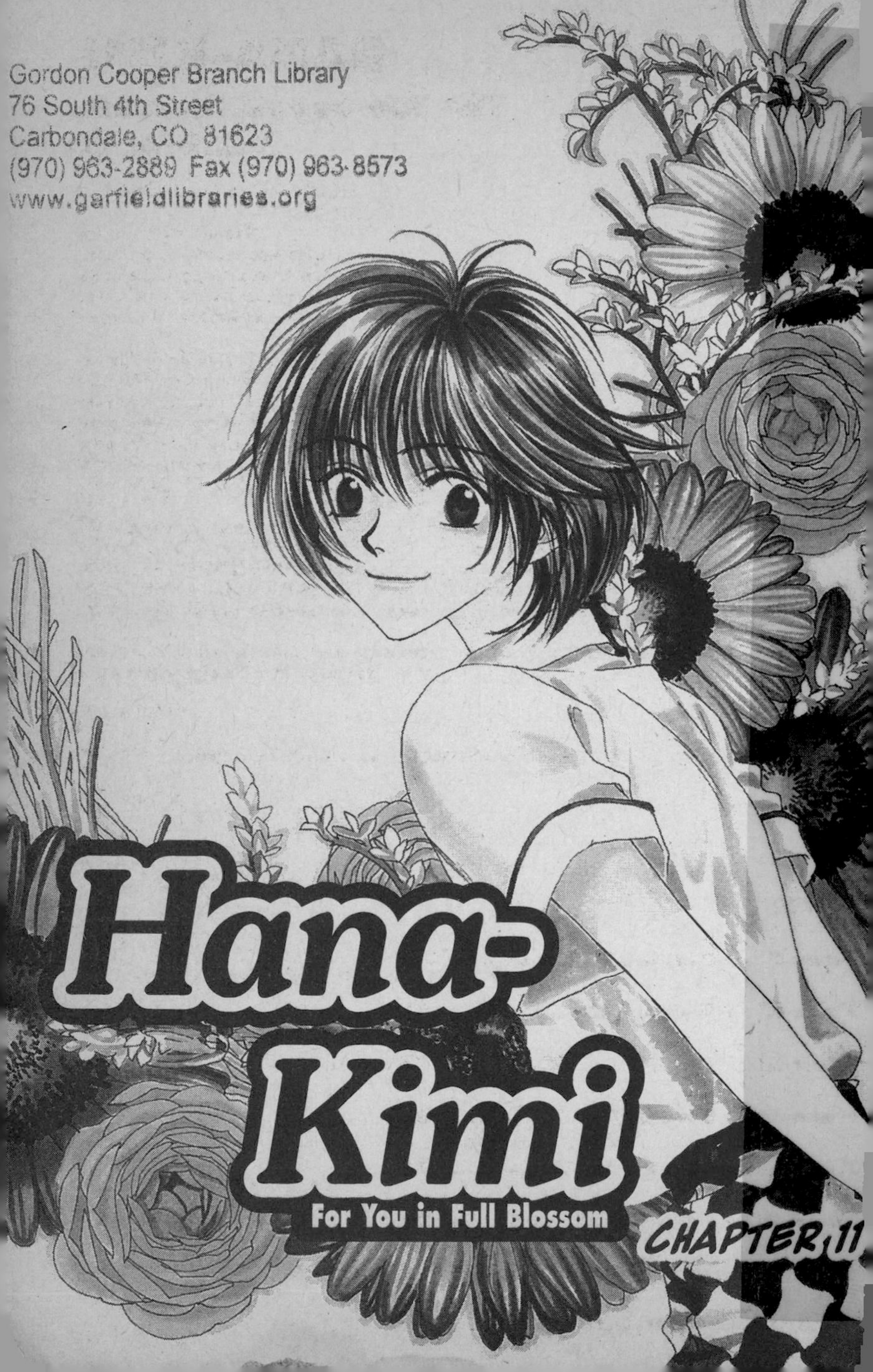
Hana-Kimi
For You in Full Blossom
CHAPTER 11

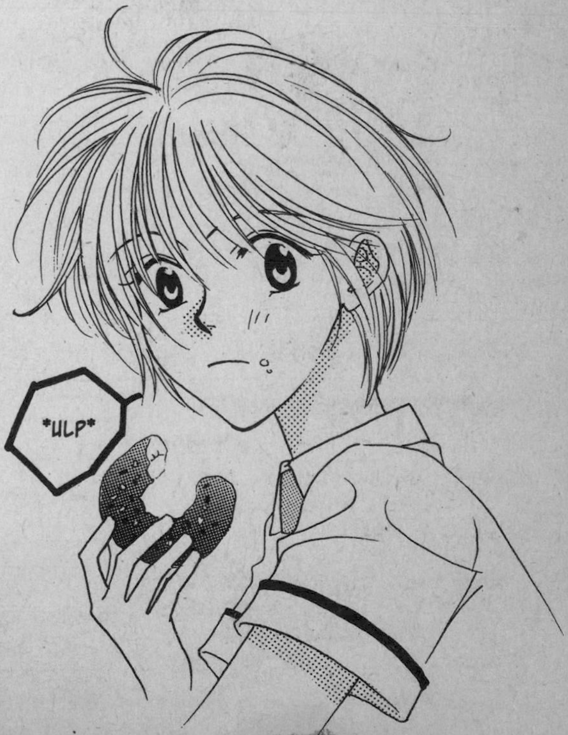
ULP

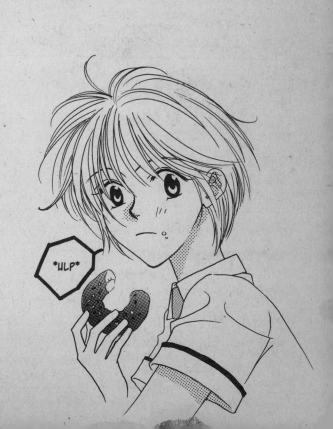

DING DONG
OKAY, TIME'S UP.
DING DONG
PHHHHEW!
IT'S OVER...
WIPED OUT
Every-one bring your test for-ward.
OSAKA
OSAKA HIGH SCHOOL IS KNOWN FOR ITS STRENGTH IN BOTH ACADEMICS AND ATHLETICS.
THE FINAL EXAMS REFLECT ITS HIGH STAN-DARDS.
NOW I'LL PASS OUT THE RESULTS OF YESTERDAY'S ENGLISH TEST.
BLEHH
Agh, this sucks!
I don't wanna know the results.

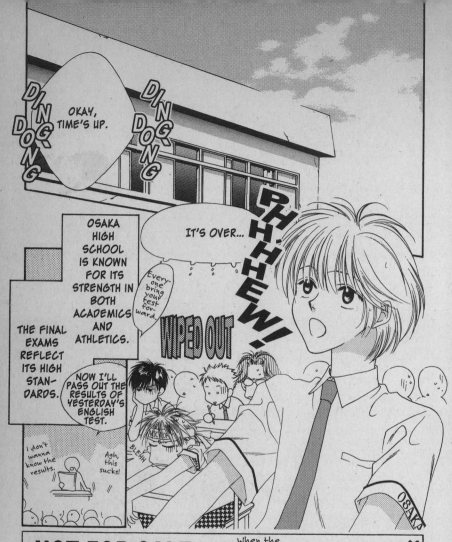

NOT FOR SALE...

I MADE UP MIZUKI'S ALARM CLOCK--IT DOESN'T EXIST IN THE REAL WORLD. ALTHOUGH I THINK IT WOULD BE COOL IF IT DID. EVERYONE'S ALWAYS ASKING, "WHERE DO THEY SELL THOSE?" I GUESS IT WOULD DO PRETTY WELL! (HA-HA!)

When the egg is raised up, that means the alarm is set.
12
9
3
6
The alarm goes "Pi pi pi pi pi".
The color is metallic white, no glare.

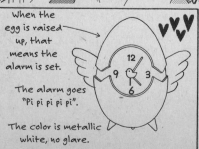

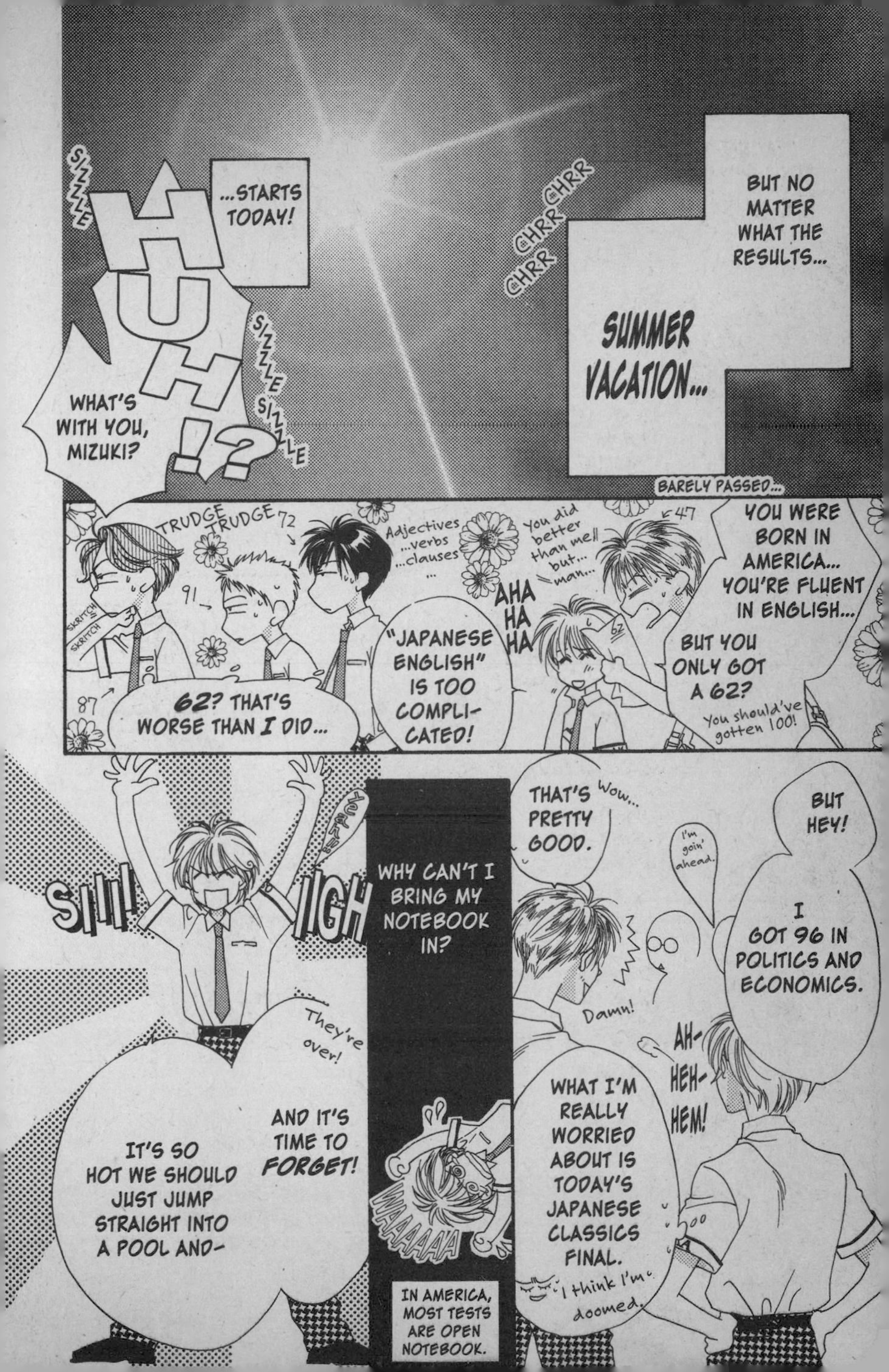
BUT NO MATTER WHAT THE RESULTS...
SUMMER VACATION...
CHRR CHRR CHRR CHRR
...STARTS TODAY!
SIZZLE
HUH!?
SIZZLE SIZZLE SIZZLE
WHAT'S WITH YOU, MIZUKI?
BARELY PASSED...
YOU WERE BORN IN AMERICA... YOU'RE FLUENT IN ENGLISH...
BUT YOU ONLY GOT A 62?
You should've gotten 100!
47
You did better than me! but... man...
AHAHAHA
62
"JAPANESE ENGLISH" IS TOO COMPLICATED!
72
Adjectives ...verbs ...clauses ...
TRUDGE TRUDGE
91
SKRITCH SKRITCH
87
62? THAT'S WORSE THAN I DID...
BUT HEY!
I GOT 96 IN POLITICS AND ECONOMICS.
I'm goin' ahead.
THAT'S PRETTY GOOD.
Wow...
Damn!
AH-HEH-HEM!
WHAT I'M REALLY WORRIED ABOUT IS TODAY'S JAPANESE CLASSICS FINAL.
I think I'm doomed.
WHY CAN'T I BRING MY NOTEBOOK IN?
WAAAAAA
IN AMERICA, MOST TESTS ARE OPEN NOTEBOOK.
Yeah!!
SIIIIGH
They're over!
AND IT'S TIME TO FORGET!
IT'S SO HOT WE SHOULD JUST JUMP STRAIGHT INTO A POOL AND-

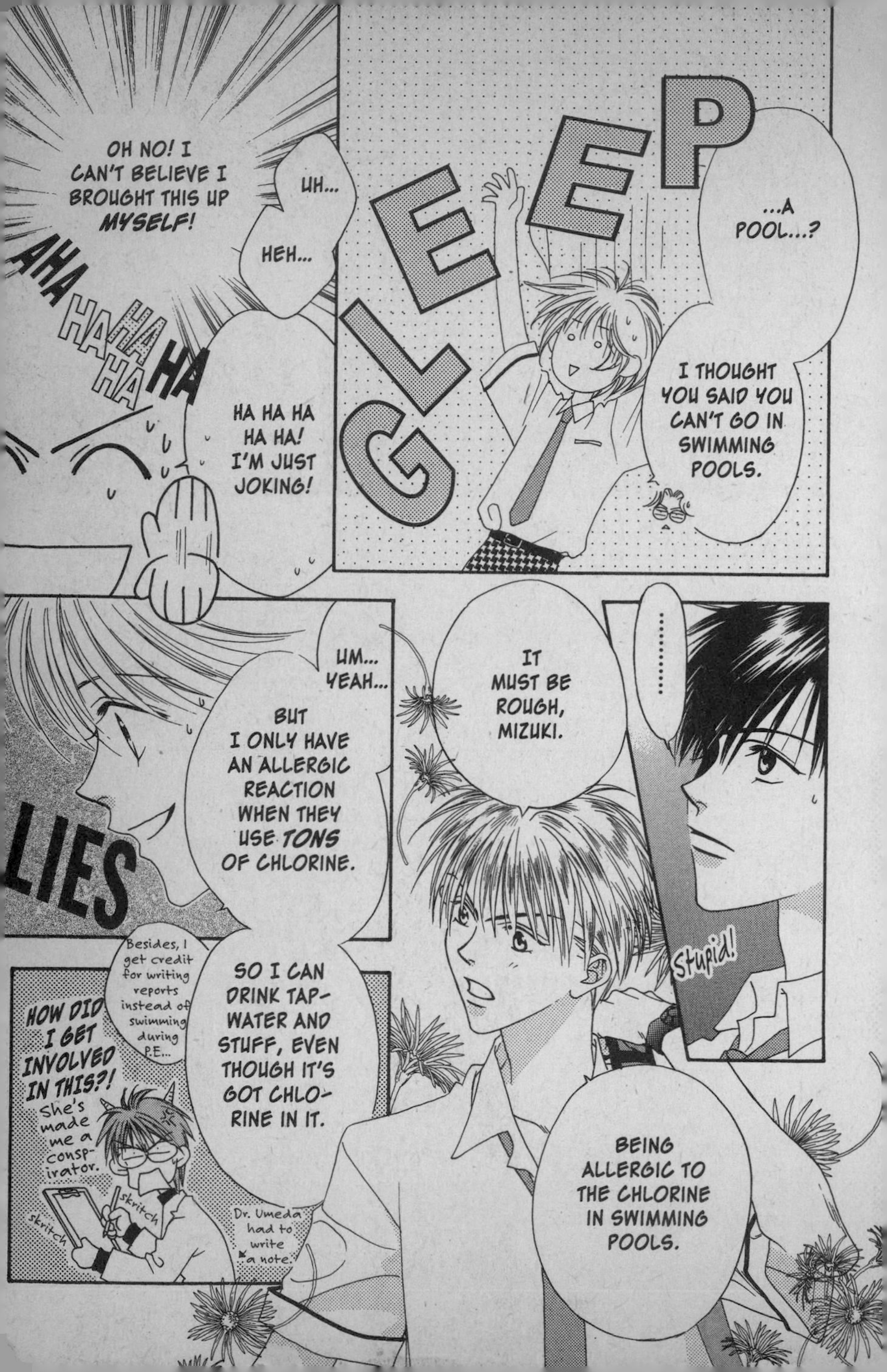
...A POOL...?
I THOUGHT YOU SAID YOU CAN'T GO IN SWIMMING POOLS.
GLEEP
UH...
HEH...
OH NO! I CAN'T BELIEVE I BROUGHT THIS UP *MYSELF*!
AHA HAHA HA HA HA
HA HA HA HA HA! I'M JUST JOKING!
....
Stupid!
IT MUST BE ROUGH, MIZUKI.
BEING ALLERGIC TO THE CHLORINE IN SWIMMING POOLS.
UM... YEAH...
BUT I ONLY HAVE AN ALLERGIC REACTION WHEN THEY USE *TONS* OF CHLORINE.
LIES
SO I CAN DRINK TAP-WATER AND STUFF, EVEN THOUGH IT'S GOT CHLORINE IN IT.
Besides, I get credit for writing reports instead of swimming during P.E...
HOW DID I GET INVOLVED IN THIS?!
She's made me a conspirator.
skritch
skritch
Dr. Umeda had to write a note.

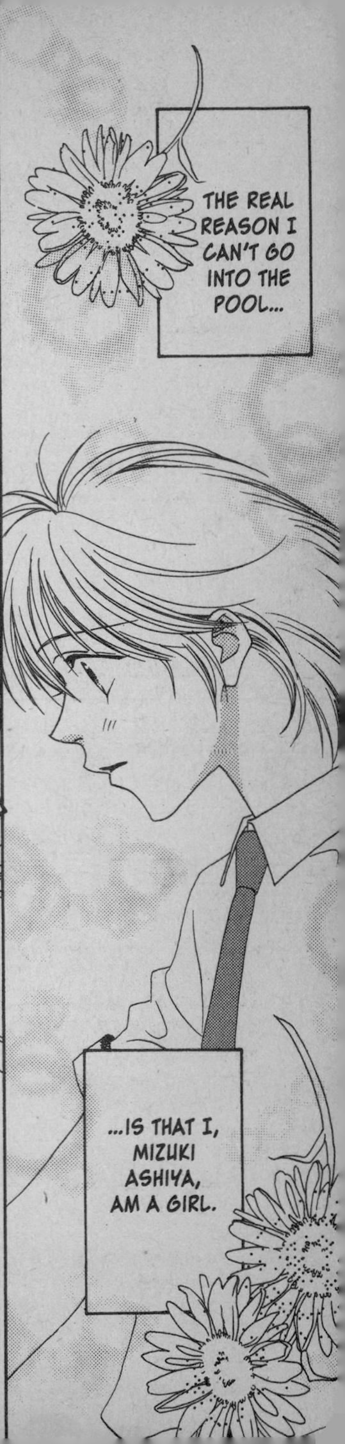
THE REAL REASON I CAN'T GO INTO THE POOL...
...IS THAT I, MIZUKI ASHIYA, AM A GIRL.

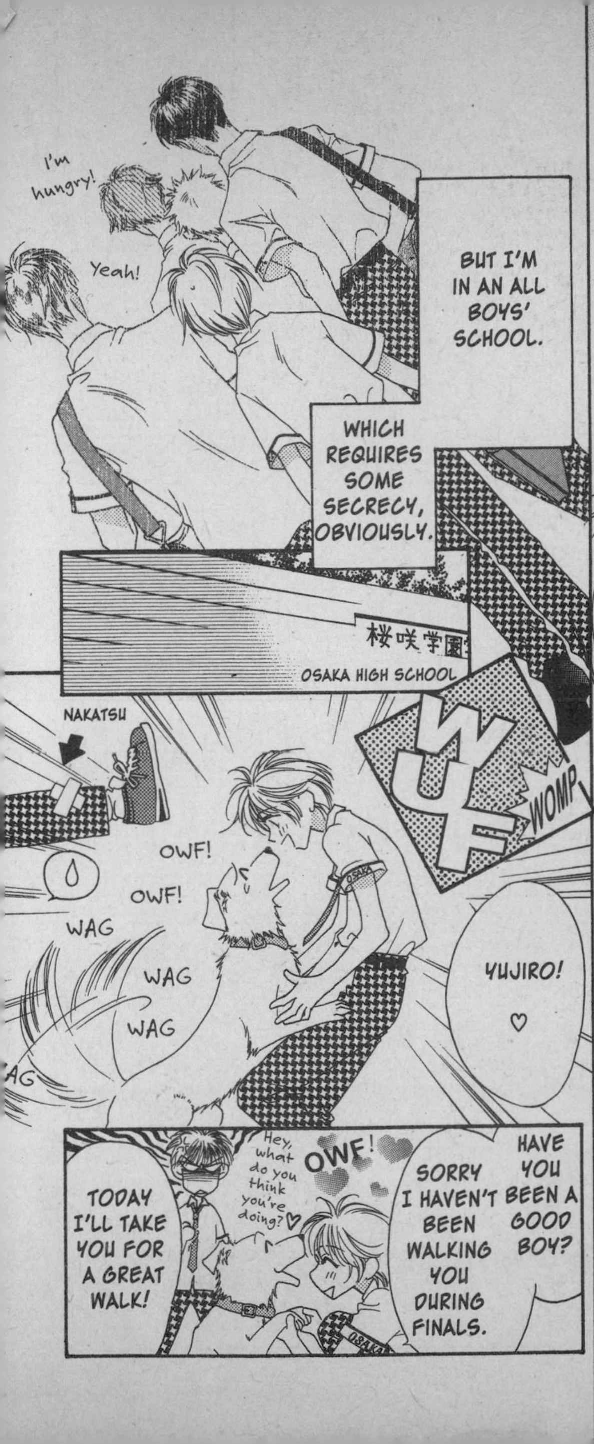
BUT I'M IN AN ALL BOYS' SCHOOL.
I'm hungry!
Yeah!
WHICH REQUIRES SOME SECRECY, OBVIOUSLY.
桜咲学園
OSAKA HIGH SCHOOL
WUF
WOMP
YUJIRO! ♡
NAKATSU
OWF!
OWF!
WAG
WAG
WAG
AG
HAVE YOU BEEN A GOOD BOY?
SORRY I HAVEN'T BEEN WALKING YOU DURING FINALS.
OWF!
Hey, what do you think you're doing? ♡
TODAY I'LL TAKE YOU FOR A GREAT WALK!

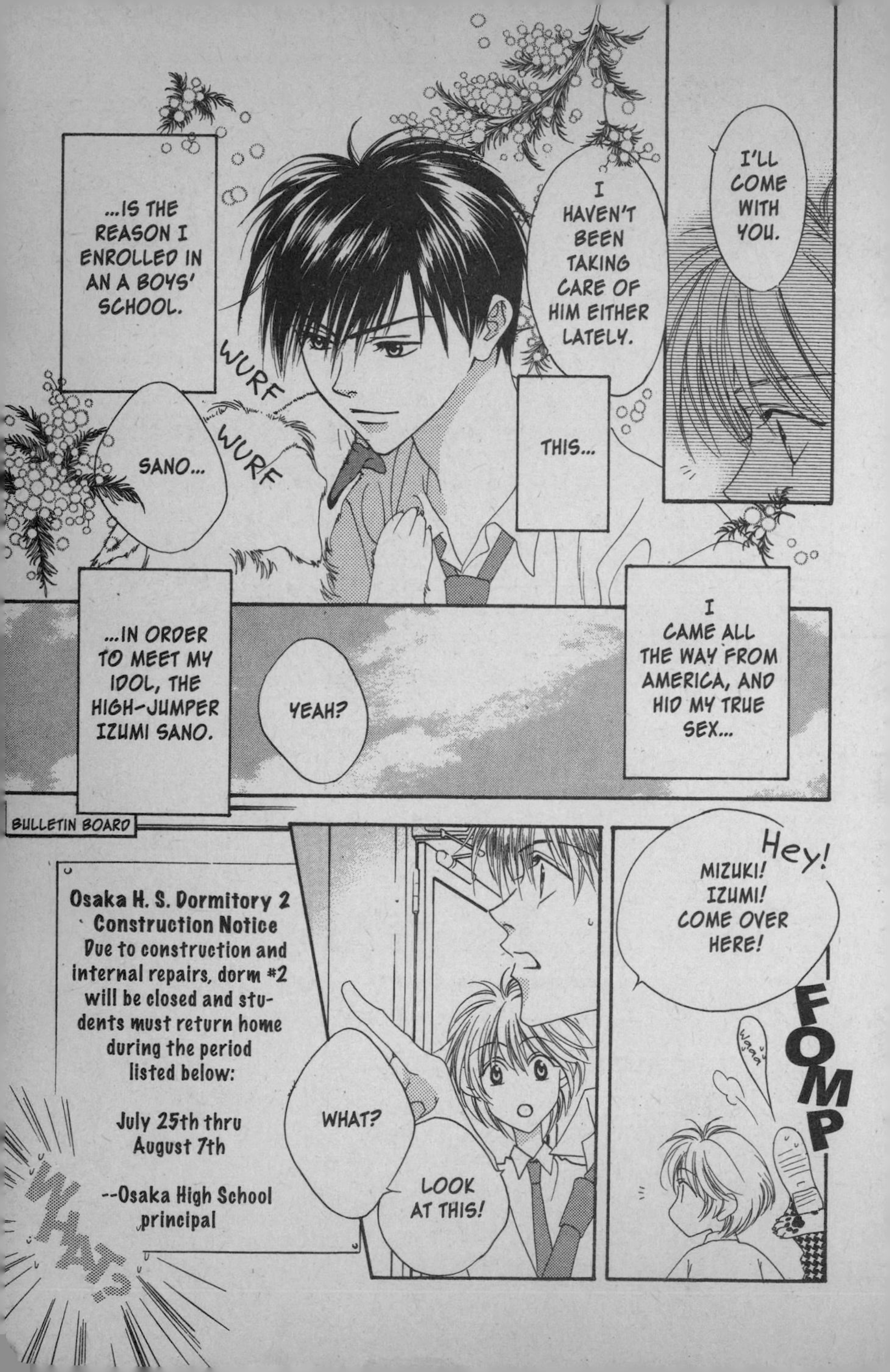
I'LL COME WITH YOU.
I HAVEN'T BEEN TAKING CARE OF HIM EITHER LATELY.
THIS...
...IS THE REASON I ENROLLED IN AN A BOYS' SCHOOL.
WURF WURF
SANO...
I CAME ALL THE WAY FROM AMERICA, AND HID MY TRUE SEX...
YEAH?
...IN ORDER TO MEET MY IDOL, THE HIGH-JUMPER IZUMI SANO.
BULLETIN BOARD
Hey!
MIZUKI! IZUMI! COME OVER HERE!
FOMP
WHAT?
LOOK AT THIS!
Osaka H. S. Dormitory 2 Construction Notice
Due to construction and internal repairs, dorm #2 will be closed and students must return home during the period listed below:
July 25th thru August 7th
--Osaka High School principal
WHAT?!

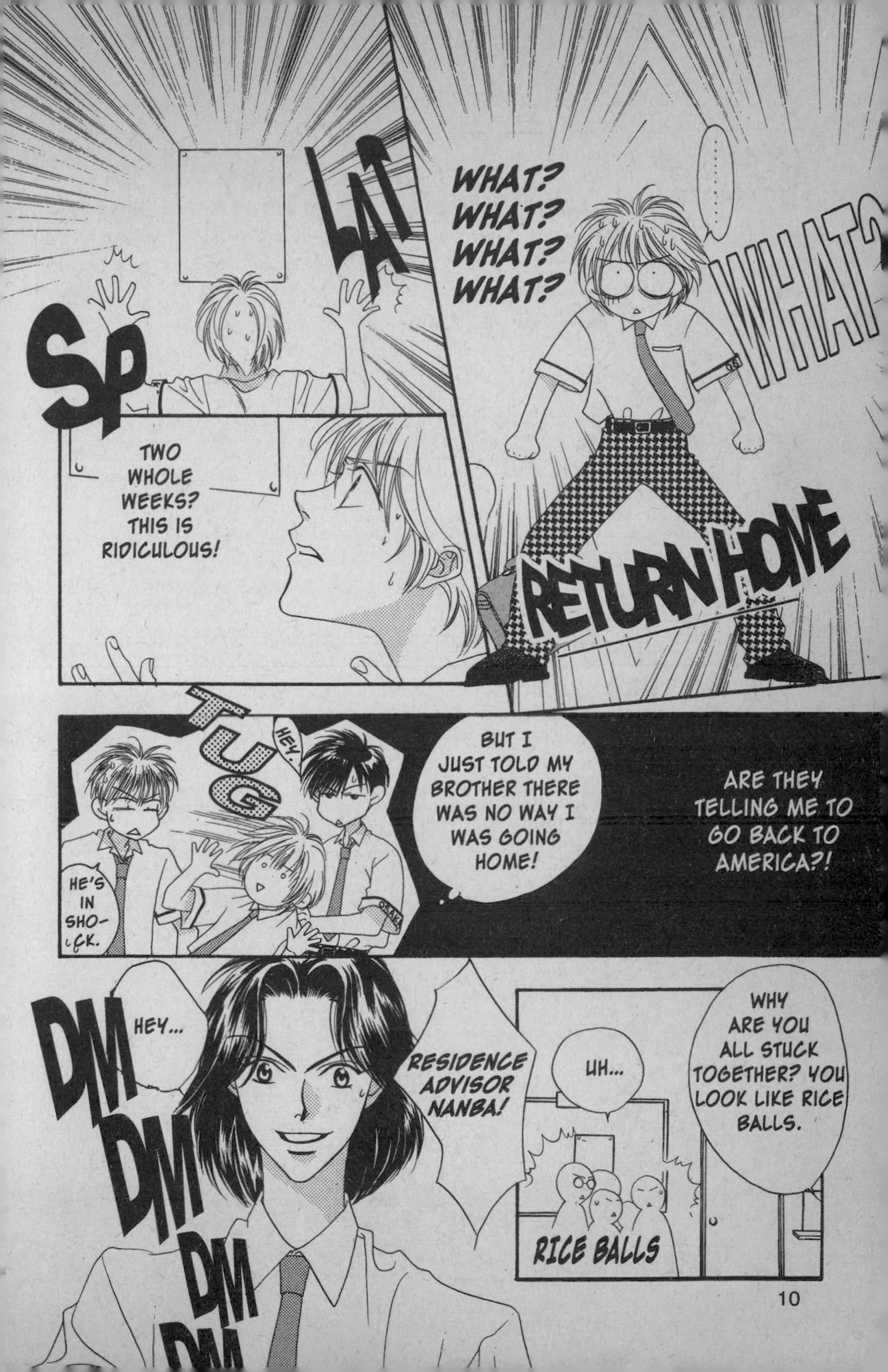
......
WHAT?
WHAT?
WHAT?
WHAT?
WHAT?
RETURN HOME
LAT
SP
TWO WHOLE WEEKS? THIS IS RIDICULOUS!
ARE THEY TELLING ME TO GO BACK TO AMERICA?!
BUT I JUST TOLD MY BROTHER THERE WAS NO WAY I WAS GOING HOME!
HEY.
TUG
HE'S IN SHO-CK.
WHY ARE YOU ALL STUCK TOGETHER? YOU LOOK LIKE RICE BALLS.
UH...
RICE BALLS
RESIDENCE ADVISOR NANBA!
HEY...
DM
DM
DM

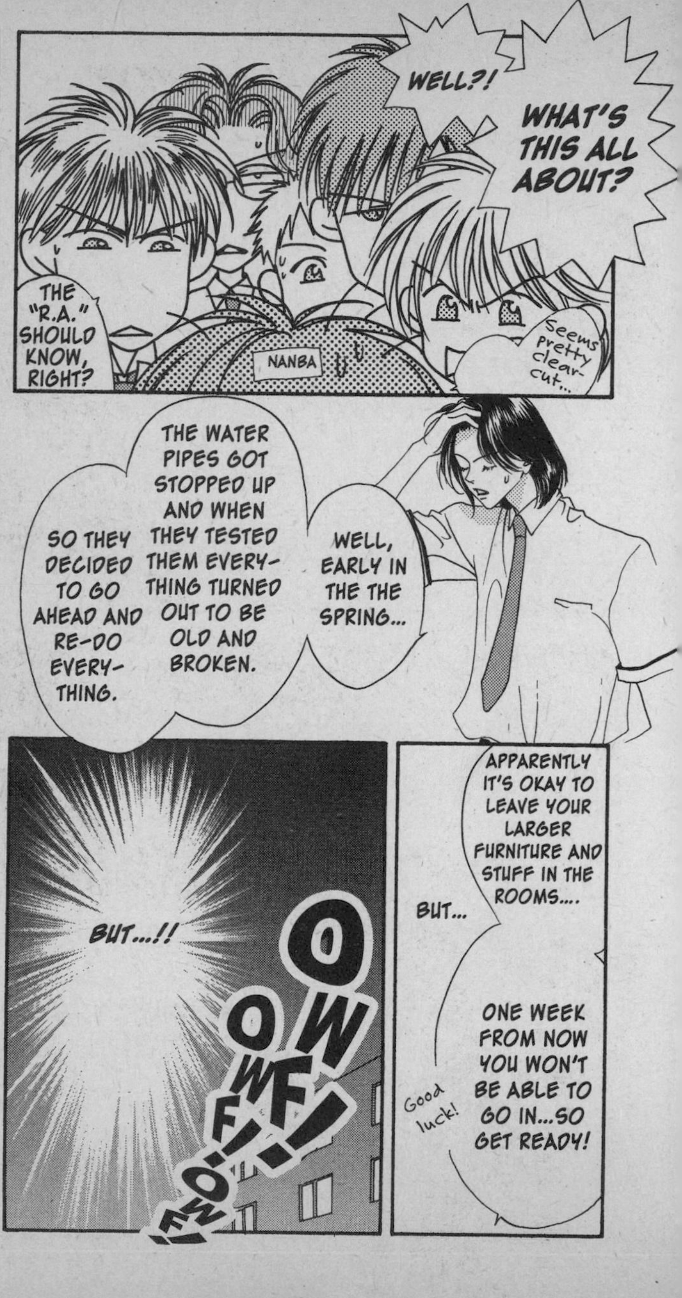
WELL?!
WHAT'S THIS ALL ABOUT?
Seems pretty clear-cut...
THE "R.A." SHOULD KNOW, RIGHT?
NANBA
WELL, EARLY IN THE THE SPRING...
THE WATER PIPES GOT STOPPED UP AND WHEN THEY TESTED THEM EVERYTHING TURNED OUT TO BE OLD AND BROKEN.
SO THEY DECIDED TO GO AHEAD AND RE-DO EVERYTHING.
APPARENTLY IT'S OKAY TO LEAVE YOUR LARGER FURNITURE AND STUFF IN THE ROOMS....
BUT...
ONE WEEK FROM NOW YOU WON'T BE ABLE TO GO IN...SO GET READY!
Good luck!
BUT...!!
OWF! OWF! OWF!

GREETINGS!

WELCOME TO THE THIRD BOOK OF "HANA-KIMI." I DREW THIS ONLY FIVE MONTHS AGO (NOW IT'S NOVEMBER)...SO WHY DO I FEEL SO EMBARRASSED WHEN I LOOK AT THESE DRAWINGS? I CAN'T TELL YOU EXACTLY WHAT'S CHANGED BUT SOMEHOW IT'S DIFFERENT. YEAH, PART OF IT IS THAT I GOT USED TO DRAWING THE CHARACTERS. AND MAYBE I'VE IMPROVED A LITTLE...? ANYWAY, I'D BETTER BUY A REFERENCE BOOK ON DOGS FOR YUJIRO. LATELY, I'VE BEEN FEELING LIKE I SHOULDN'T JUST RELY ON MY MEMORY.

GASP!

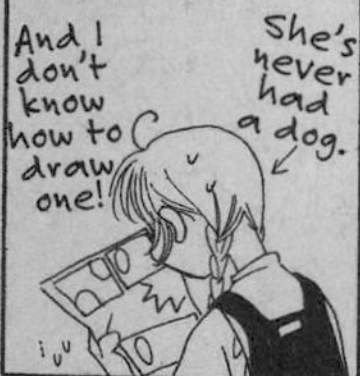
She's never had a dog.
And I don't know how to draw one!

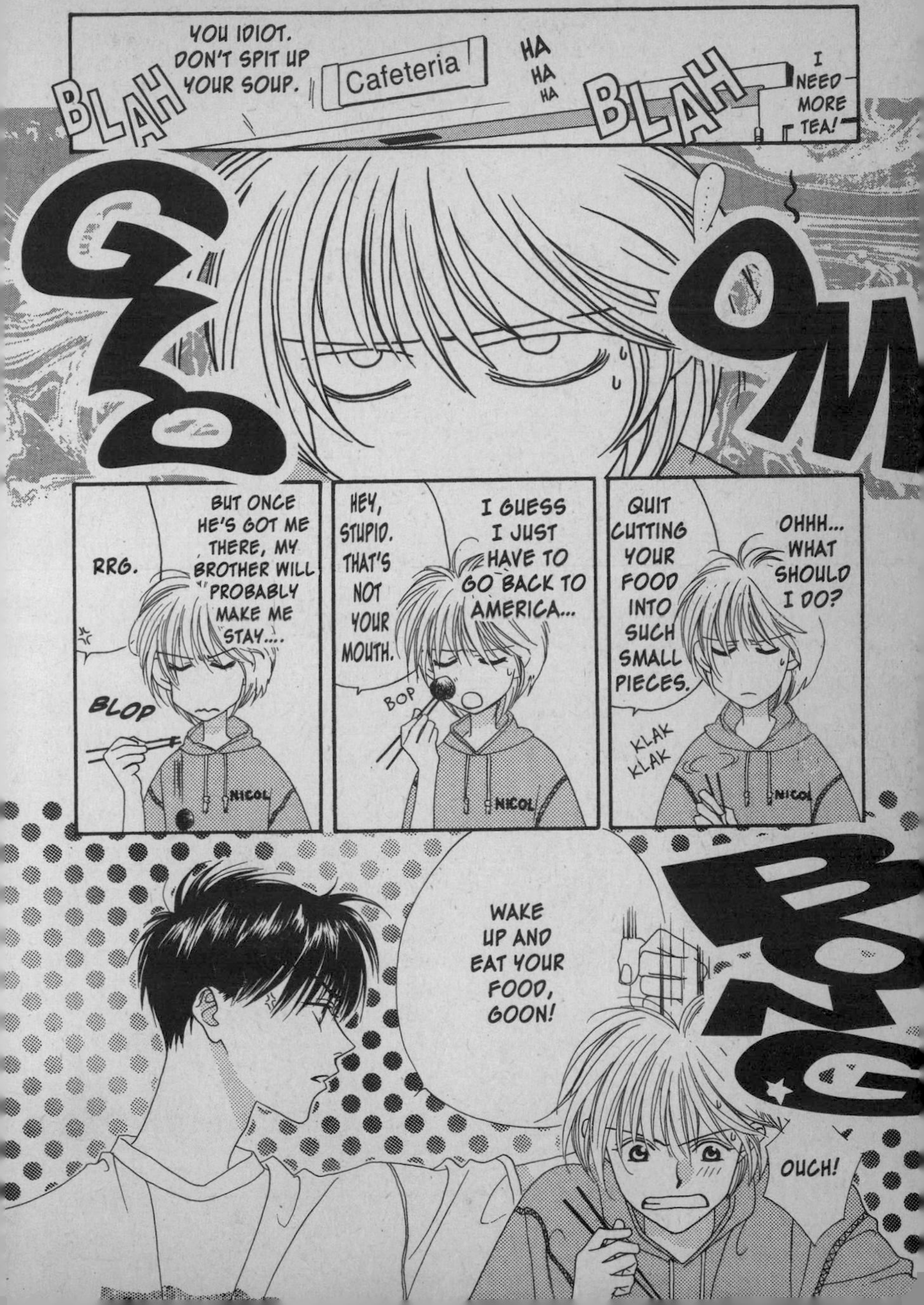
BLAH
I NEED MORE TEA!
HA HA HA
Cafeteria
YOU IDIOT. DON'T SPIT UP YOUR SOUP.
BLAH
OHHH... WHAT SHOULD I DO?
QUIT CUTTING YOUR FOOD INTO SUCH SMALL PIECES.
KLAK KLAK
NICOL
I GUESS I JUST HAVE TO GO BACK TO AMERICA...
HEY, STUPID. THAT'S NOT YOUR MOUTH.
BOP
NICOL
BUT ONCE HE'S GOT ME THERE, MY BROTHER WILL PROBABLY MAKE ME STAY....
RRG.
BLOP
NICOL
BONG
OUCH!
WAKE UP AND EAT YOUR FOOD, GOON!

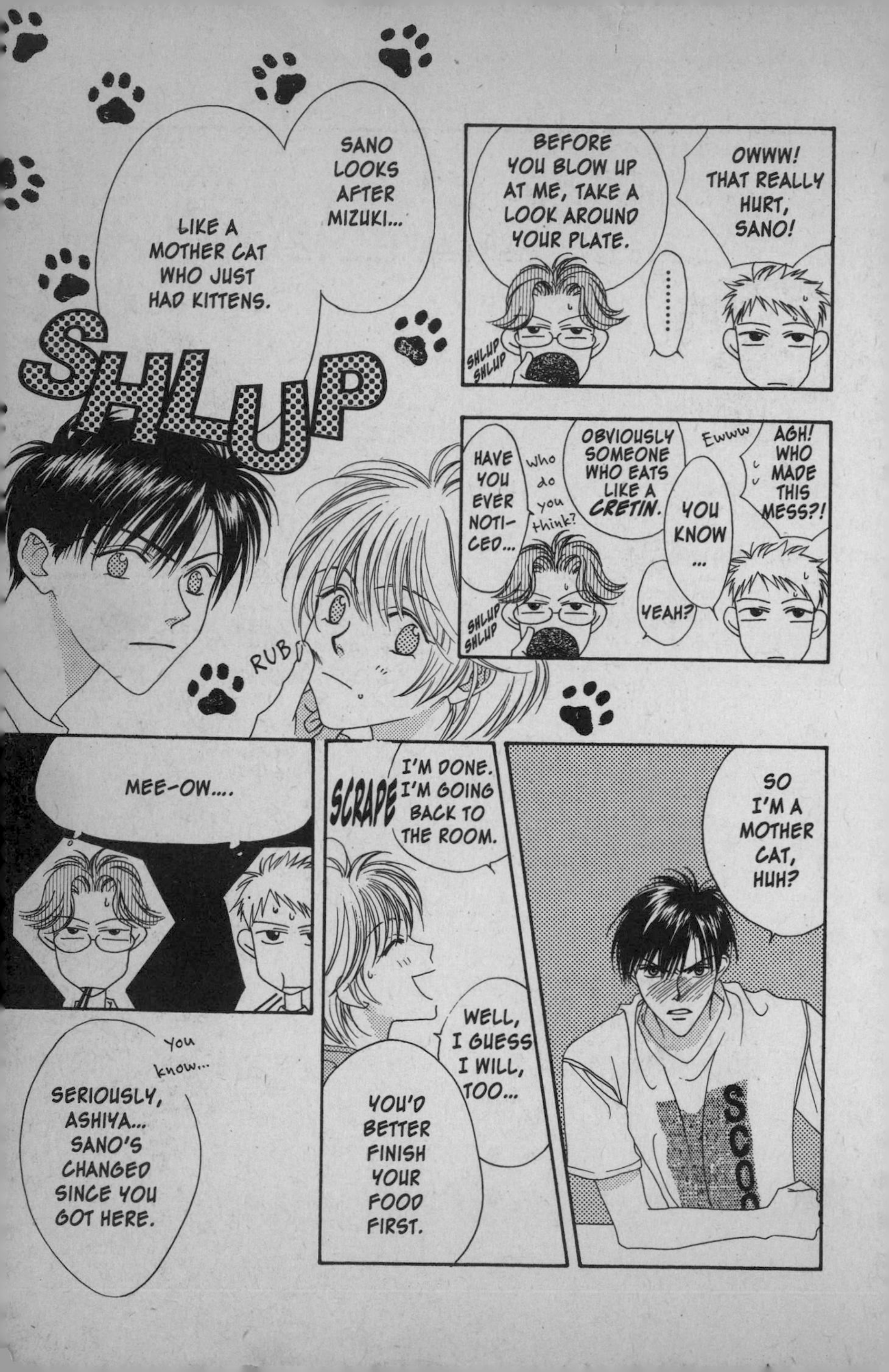
OWWW! THAT REALLY HURT, SANO!
BEFORE YOU BLOW UP AT ME, TAKE A LOOK AROUND YOUR PLATE.
......
SHLUP SHLUP
AGH! WHO MADE THIS MESS?!
Ewww
OBVIOUSLY SOMEONE WHO EATS LIKE A CRETIN.
YOU KNOW ...
who do you think?
HAVE YOU EVER NOTICED...
YEAH?
SHLUP SHLUP
SANO LOOKS AFTER MIZUKI...
LIKE A MOTHER CAT WHO JUST HAD KITTENS.
SHLUP
RUB
SO I'M A MOTHER CAT, HUH?
SCRAPE
I'M DONE. I'M GOING BACK TO THE ROOM.
WELL, I GUESS I WILL, TOO...
YOU'D BETTER FINISH YOUR FOOD FIRST.
MEE-OW....
You know...
SERIOUSLY, ASHIYA... SANO'S CHANGED SINCE YOU GOT HERE.

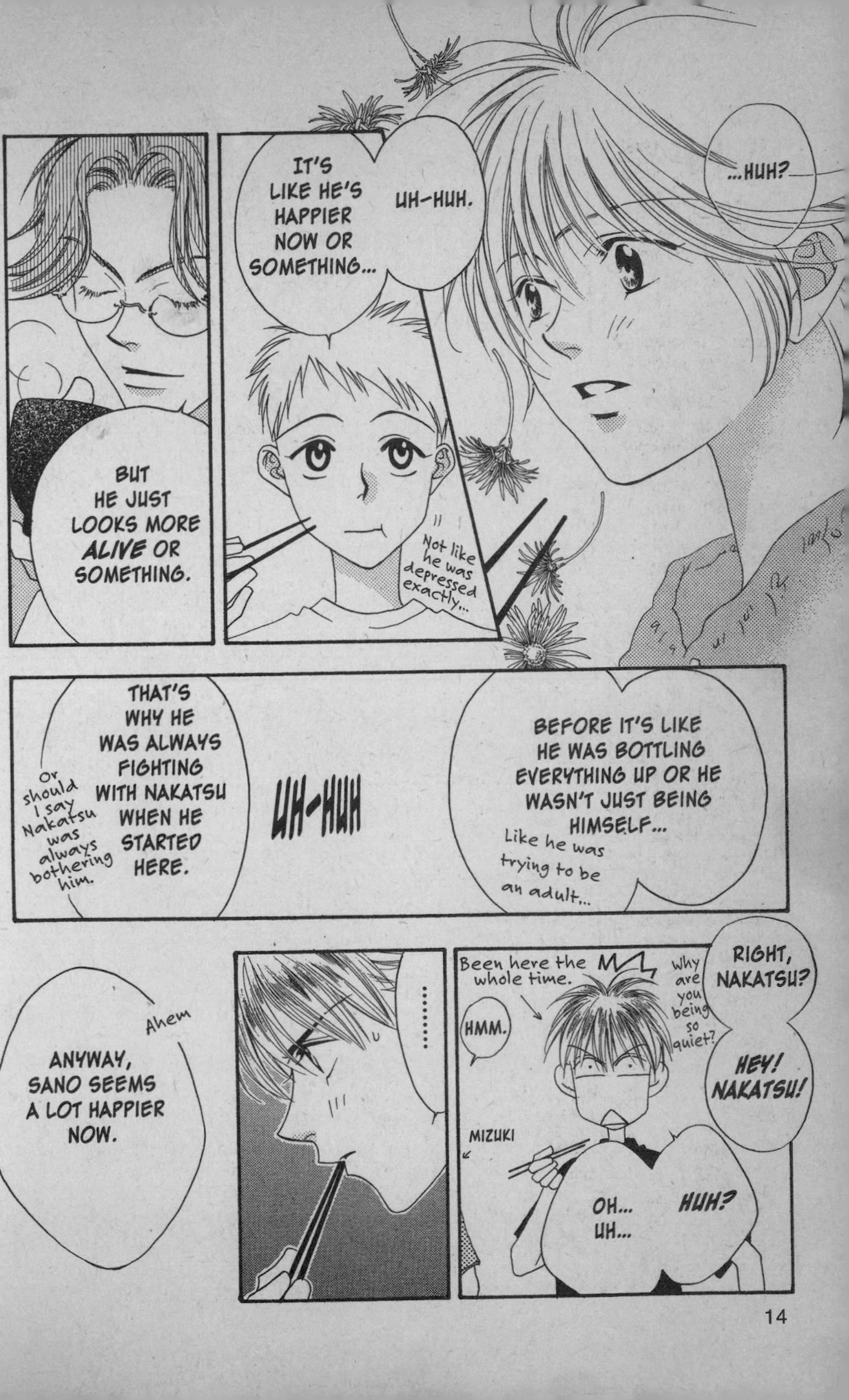
...HUH?
IT'S LIKE HE'S HAPPIER NOW OR SOMETHING...
UH-HUH.
Not like he was depressed exactly...
BUT HE JUST LOOKS MORE *ALIVE* OR SOMETHING.
BEFORE IT'S LIKE HE WAS BOTTLING EVERYTHING UP OR HE WASN'T JUST BEING HIMSELF...
Like he was trying to be an adult...
UH-HUH
THAT'S WHY HE WAS ALWAYS FIGHTING WITH NAKATSU WHEN HE STARTED HERE.
Or should I say Nakatsu was always bothering him.
RIGHT, NAKATSU?
HEY! NAKATSU!
Why are you being so quiet?
Been here the whole time.
HMM.
HUH?
OH... UH...
MIZUKI
....
Ahem
ANYWAY, SANO SEEMS A LOT HAPPIER NOW.

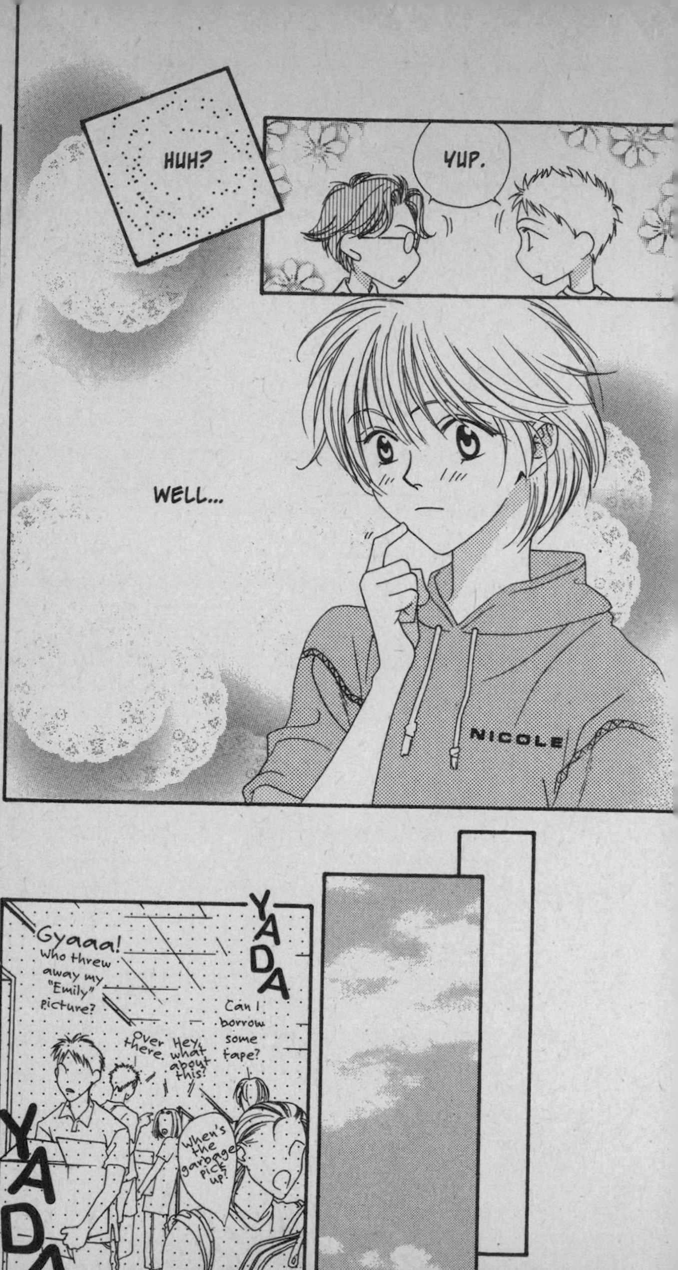
HUH?
YUP.
WELL...
NICOLE
YADA
Gyaaa! Who threw away my "Emily" picture?
Can I borrow some tape?
Hey, what about this?
Over there.
When's the garbage pick up?
YADA
YADA

WHISPERED SECRETS

MIZUKI ASHIYA

BIRTHDAY: MAY 2ND
AGE: 17
BLOOD TYPE: O
SIGN: TAURUS
HEIGHT: 160CM
FAVORITE FOODS: PEACH, JELLY, MARINATED SEAFOOD
FAVORITE MUSICIANS: SPITZ, BONNIE PINK, KINK...ETC.
FAVORITE MOVIES: FIELD OF DREAMS, PHILADELPHIA
FAVORITE BRANDS: NONE IN PARTICULAR. ANYTHING THAT MAKES ME LOOK LIKE A BOY.
FAVORITE SPORT: EVERYTHING
FAVORITE PET: I LIKE ALL ANIMALS. RIGHT NOW, I LIKE YUJIRO BEST.
FOODS I HATE: PICKLED PLUMS, WASABI, HOT THINGS (I HAVE A SENSITIVE TONGUE).
FLOWER: DAISY

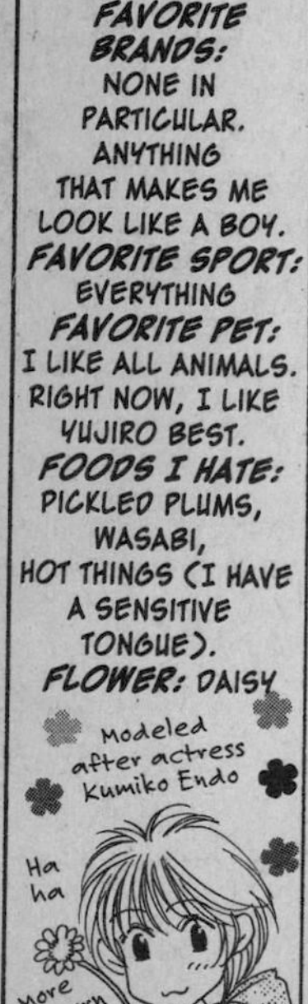
Modeled after actress Kumiko Endo
Ha ha
More stubborn than she looks.

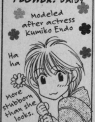

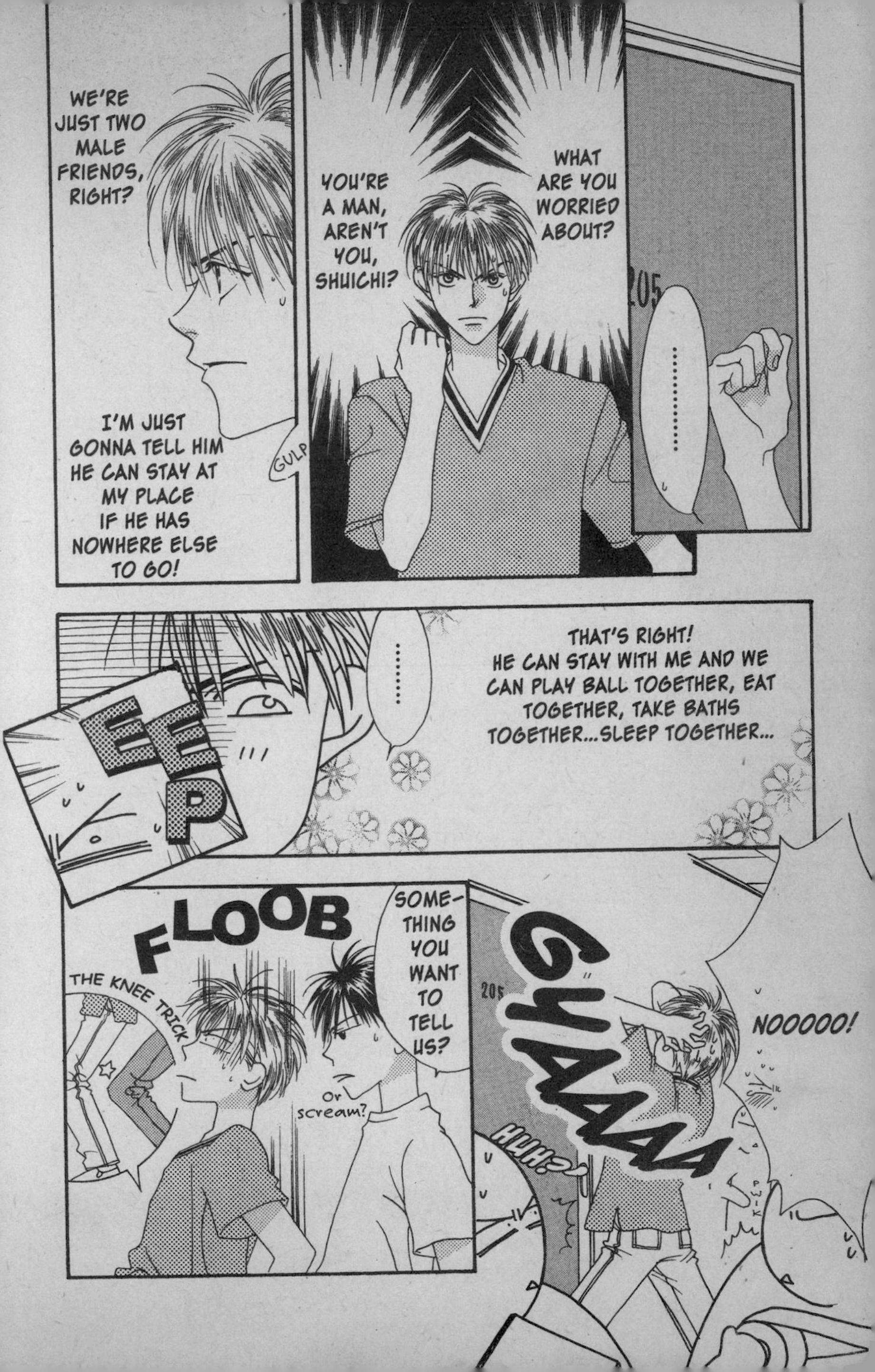
205
......
WHAT ARE YOU WORRIED ABOUT?
YOU'RE A MAN, AREN'T YOU, SHUICHI?
WE'RE JUST TWO MALE FRIENDS, RIGHT?
GULP
I'M JUST GONNA TELL HIM HE CAN STAY AT MY PLACE IF HE HAS NOWHERE ELSE TO GO!
THAT'S RIGHT! HE CAN STAY WITH ME AND WE CAN PLAY BALL TOGETHER, EAT TOGETHER, TAKE BATHS TOGETHER...SLEEP TOGETHER...
......
EEP
NOOOOO!
GHAAAA
HUH?
PWIK
205
SOME-THING YOU WANT TO TELL US?
Or scream?
FLOOB
THE KNEE TRICK

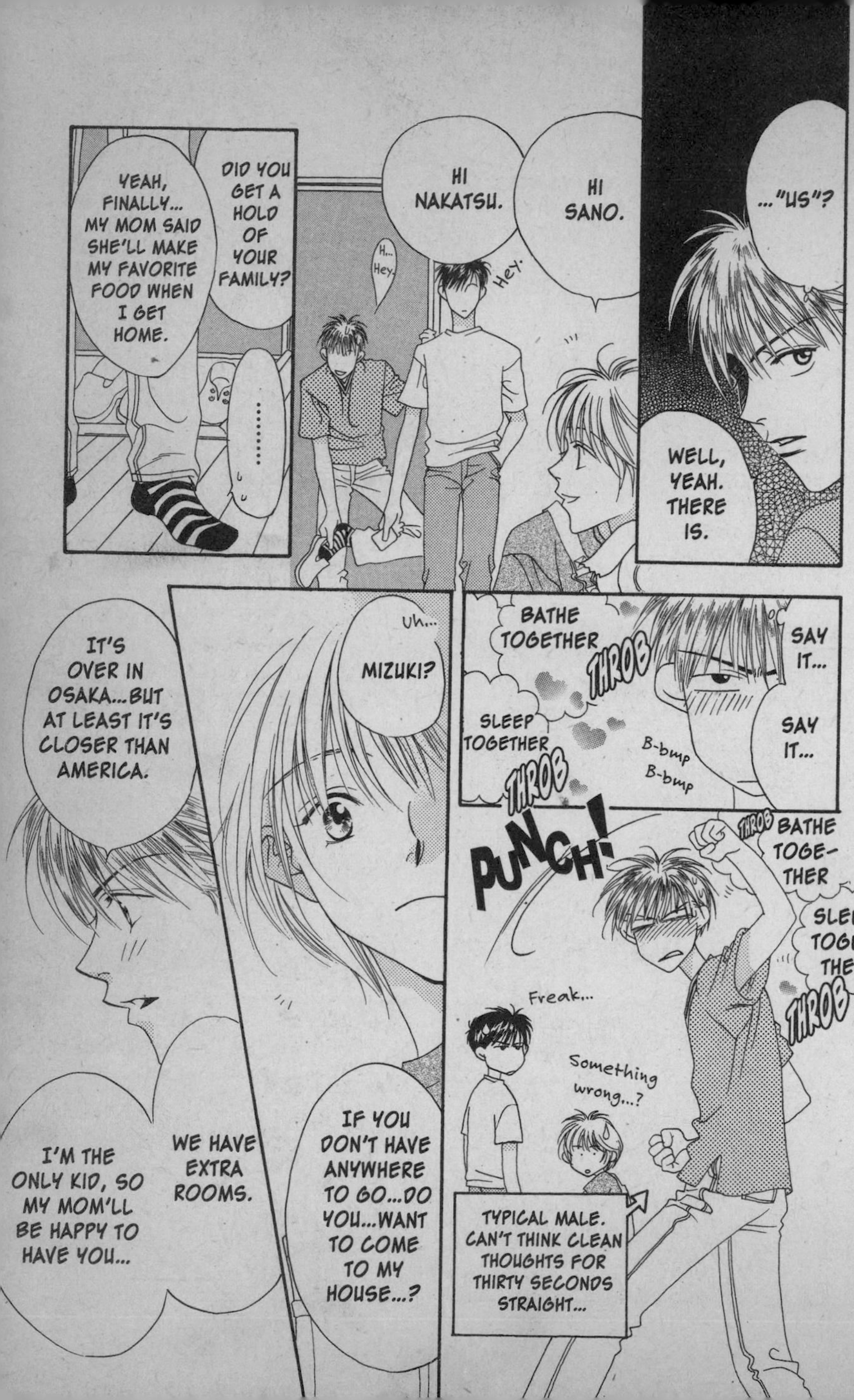
..."US"?
WELL, YEAH. THERE IS.
HI SANO.
HI NAKATSU.
Hey.
H... Hey.
DID YOU GET A HOLD OF YOUR FAMILY?
YEAH, FINALLY... MY MOM SAID SHE'LL MAKE MY FAVORITE FOOD WHEN I GET HOME.
......
SAY IT...
SAY IT...
BATHE TOGETHER
THROB
SLEEP TOGETHER
THROB
B-bmp B-bmp
THROB
BATHE TOGE-THER
SLEEP TOGE-THER
THROB
PUNCH!
Freak...
Something wrong...?
TYPICAL MALE. CAN'T THINK CLEAN THOUGHTS FOR THIRTY SECONDS STRAIGHT...
Uh...
MIZUKI?
IF YOU DON'T HAVE ANYWHERE TO GO...DO YOU...WANT TO COME TO MY HOUSE...?
IT'S OVER IN OSAKA...BUT AT LEAST IT'S CLOSER THAN AMERICA.
WE HAVE EXTRA ROOMS.
I'M THE ONLY KID, SO MY MOM'LL BE HAPPY TO HAVE YOU...

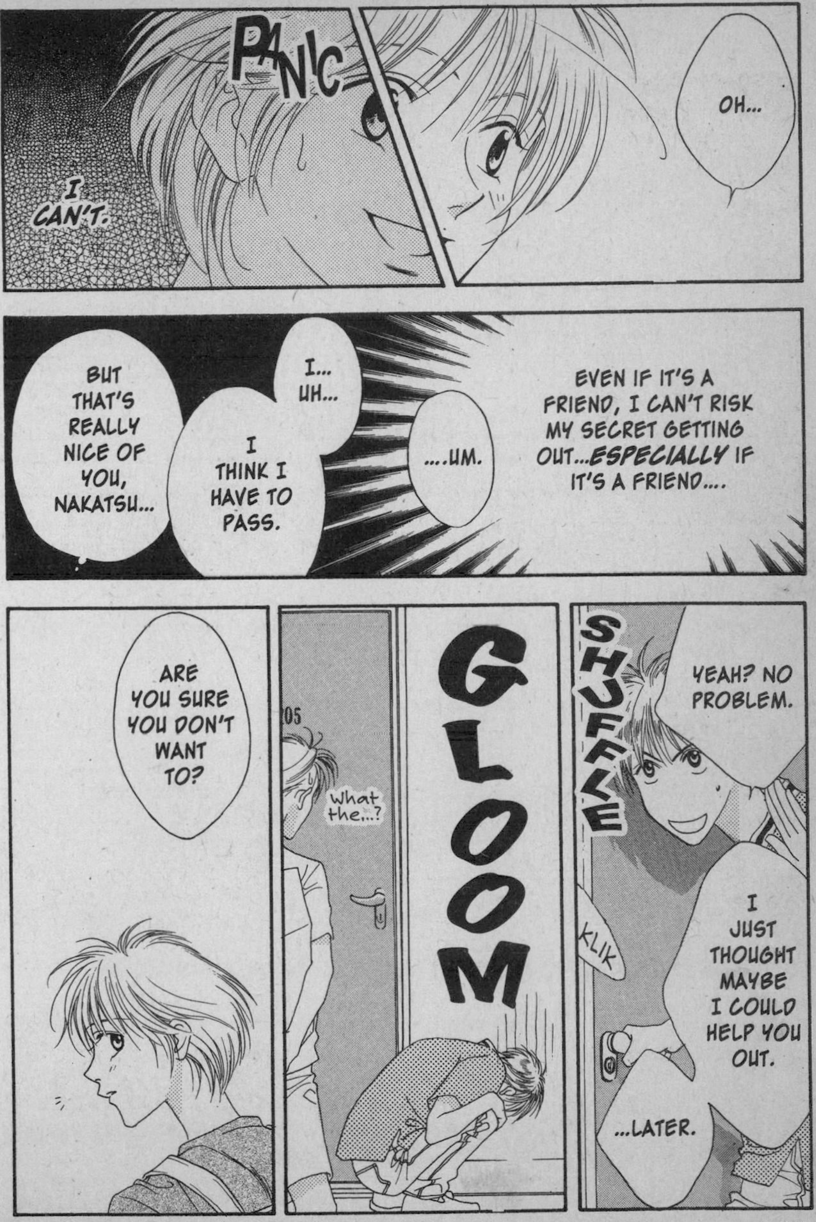
OH...
PANIC
I CAN'T.
EVEN IF IT'S A FRIEND, I CAN'T RISK MY SECRET GETTING OUT...ESPECIALLY IF IT'S A FRIEND....
....UM.
I... UH...
I THINK I HAVE TO PASS.
BUT THAT'S REALLY NICE OF YOU, NAKATSU...
SHUFFLE
YEAH? NO PROBLEM.
I JUST THOUGHT MAYBE I COULD HELP YOU OUT.
KLIK
...LATER.
GLOOM
What the...?
ARE YOU SURE YOU DON'T WANT TO?

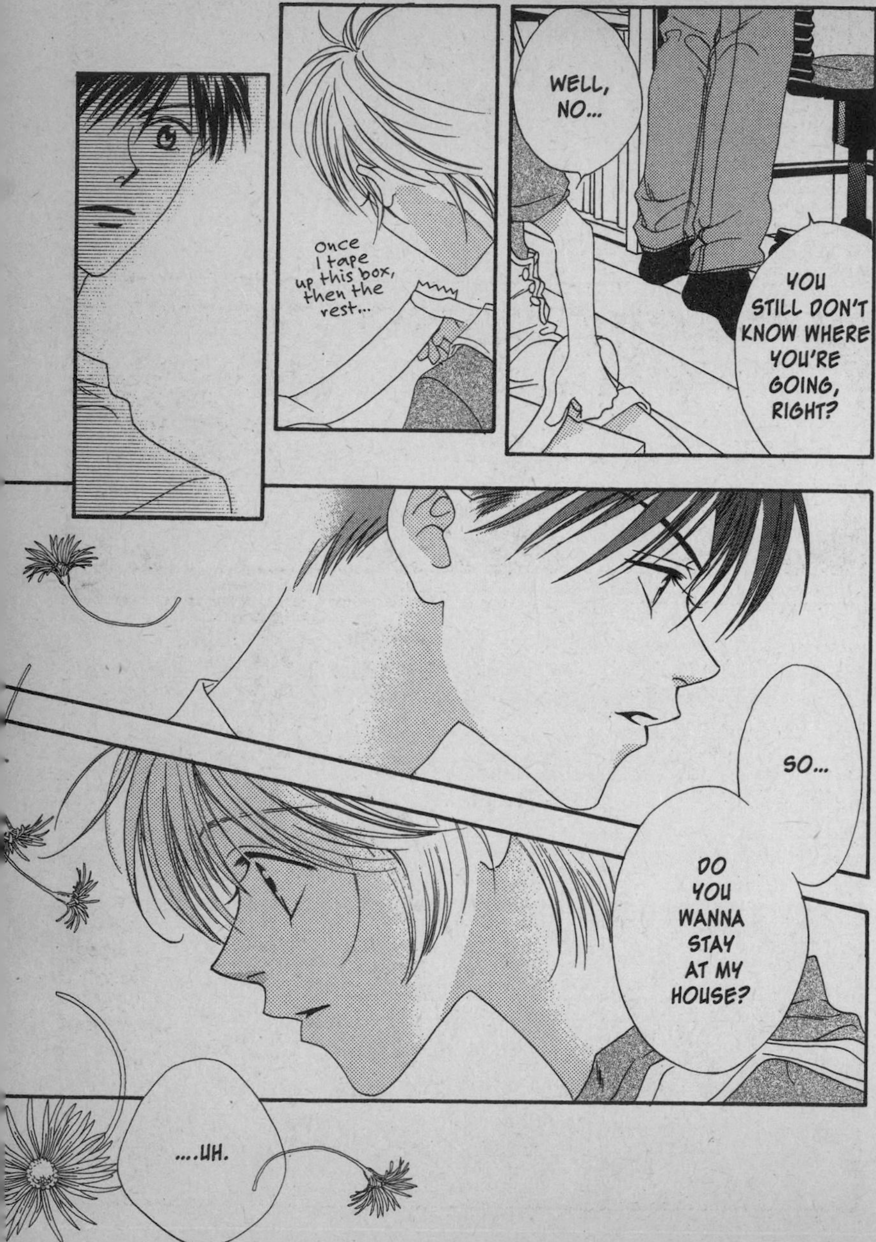
YOU STILL DON'T KNOW WHERE YOU'RE GOING, RIGHT?
WELL, NO...
Once I tape up this box, then the rest...
SO...
DO YOU WANNA STAY AT MY HOUSE?
....UH.

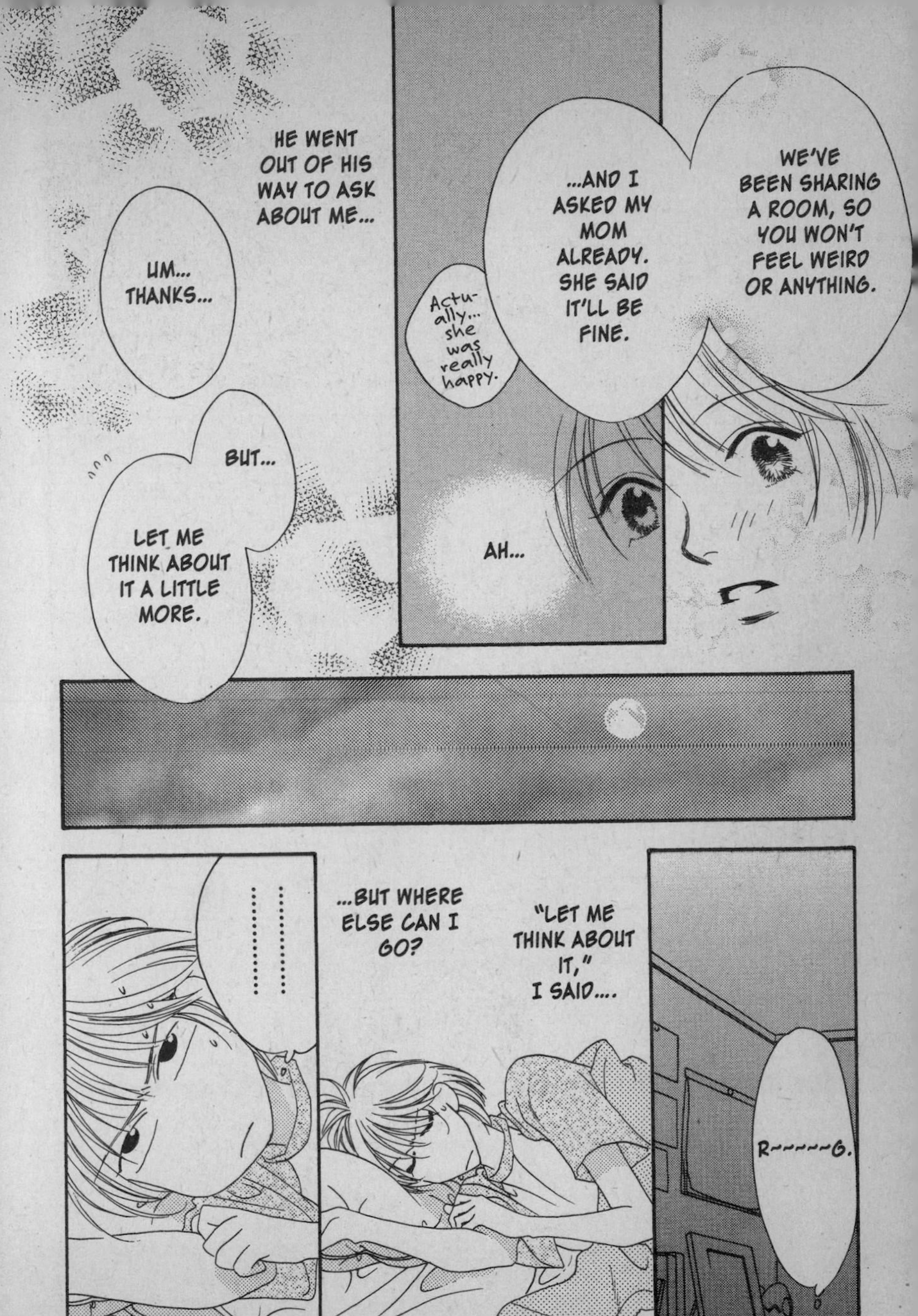
WE'VE BEEN SHARING A ROOM, SO YOU WON'T FEEL WEIRD OR ANYTHING.
...AND I ASKED MY MOM ALREADY. SHE SAID IT'LL BE FINE.
Actu-ally... she was really happy.
AH...
HE WENT OUT OF HIS WAY TO ASK ABOUT ME...
UM... THANKS...
BUT...
LET ME THINK ABOUT IT A LITTLE MORE.
R~~~~G.
"LET ME THINK ABOUT IT," I SAID....
...BUT WHERE ELSE CAN I GO?
......

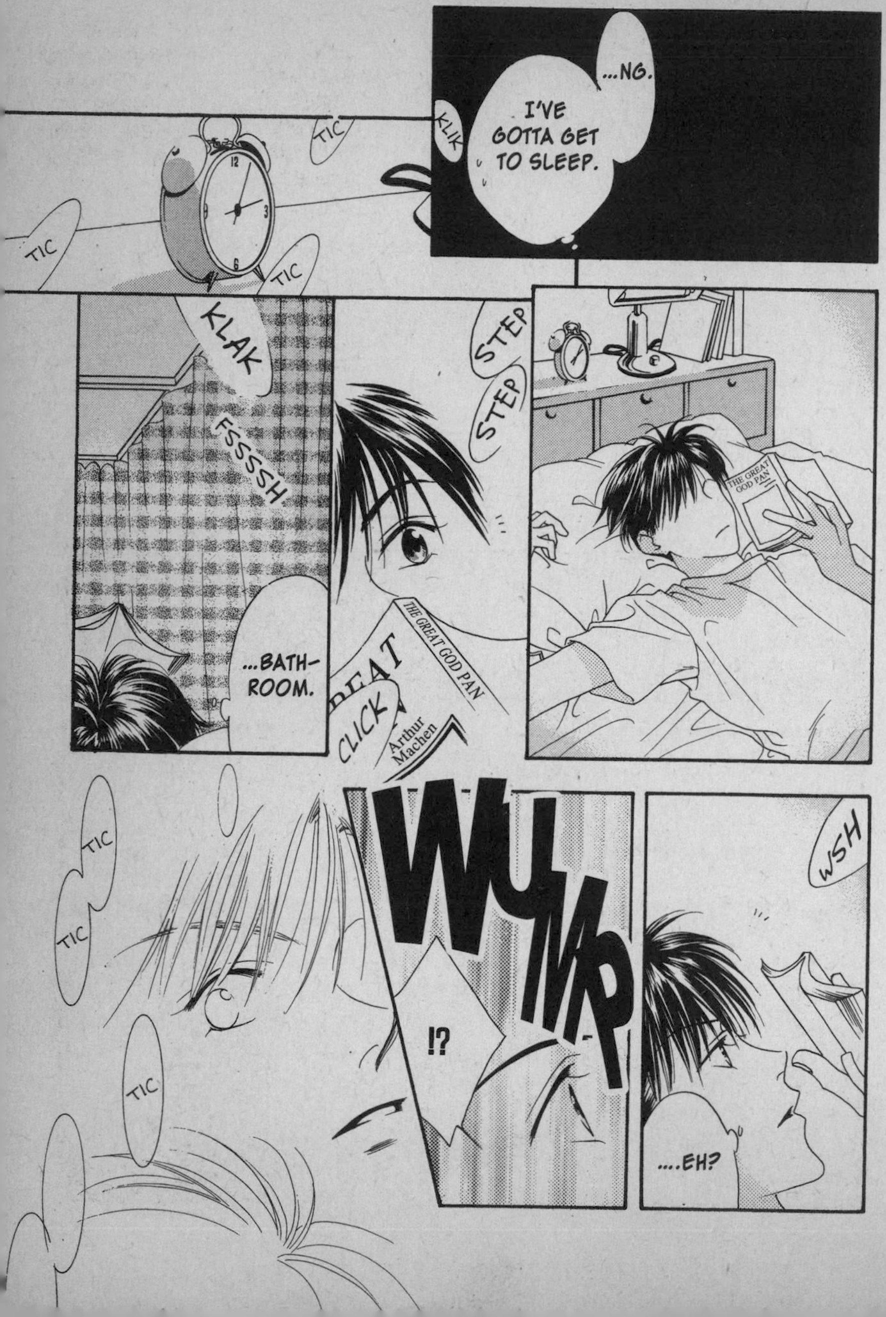
...NG.
I'VE GOTTA GET TO SLEEP.
KLIK
TIC
TIC
TIC
THE GREAT GOD PAN
STEP
STEP
THE GREAT GOD PAN
Arthur Machen
CLICK
KLAK
FSSSSSH
...BATH-ROOM.
WSH
....EH?
WUMP
!?
TIC
TIC
TIC

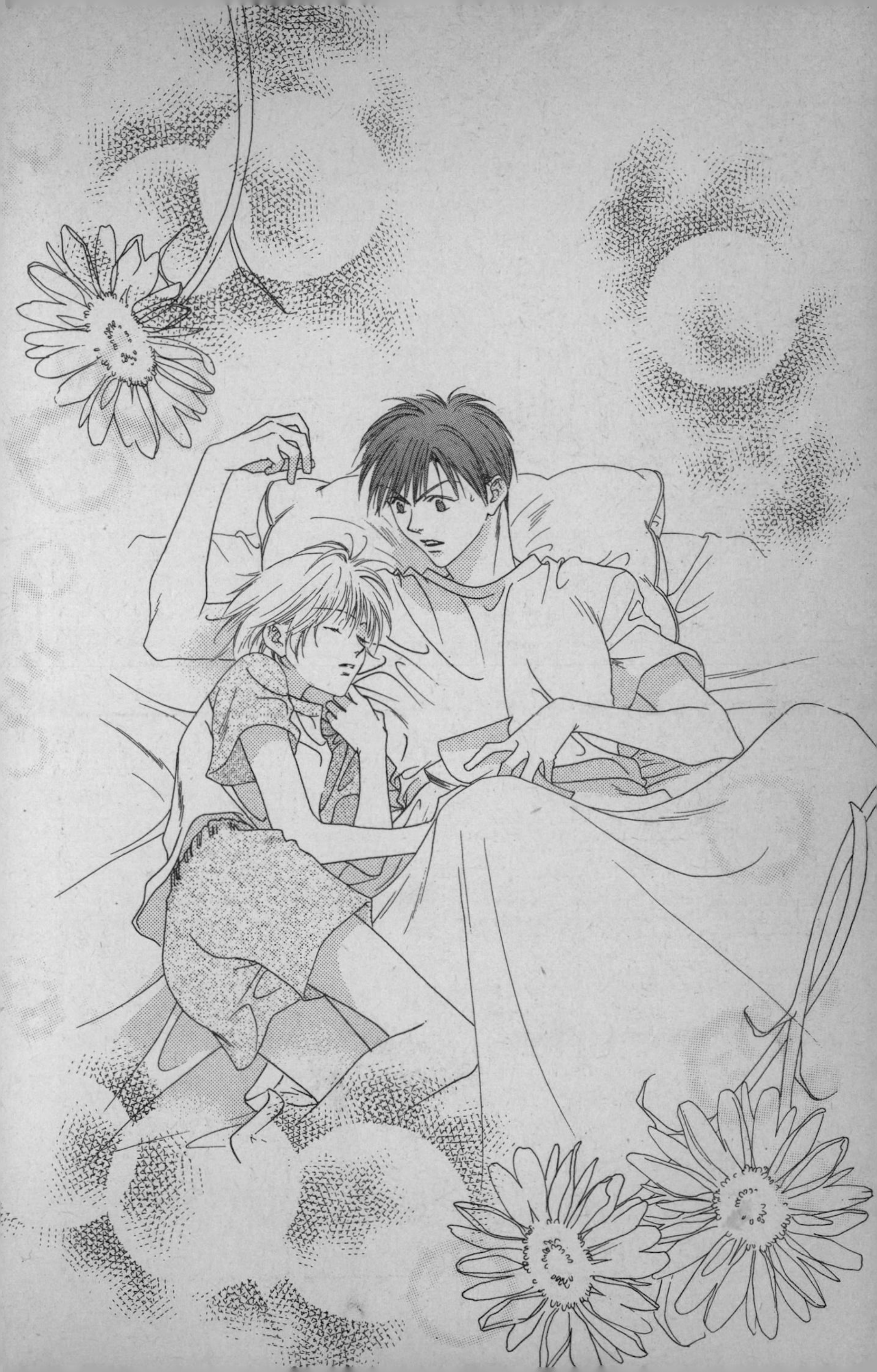

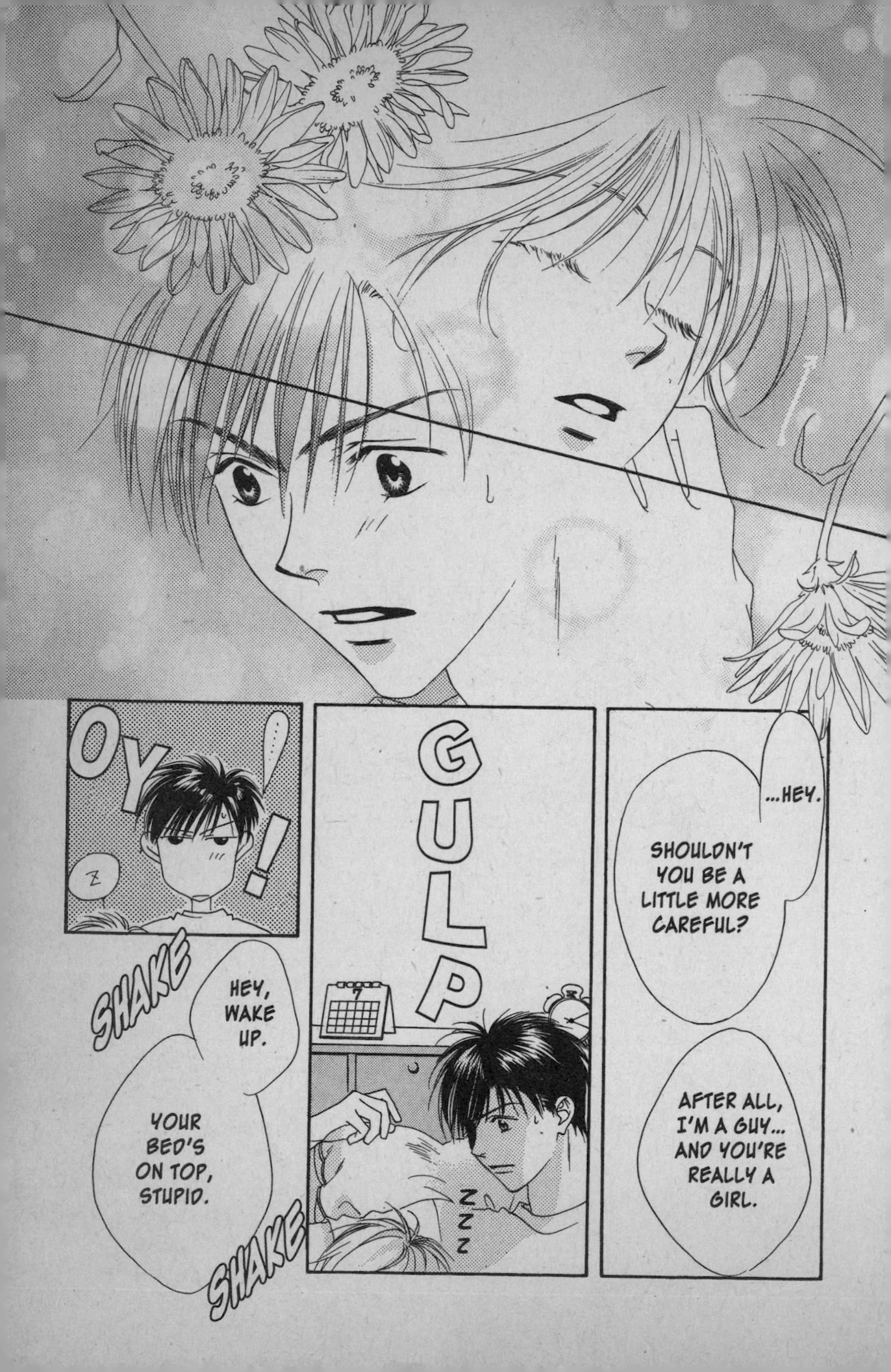
...HEY.
SHOULDN'T YOU BE A LITTLE MORE CAREFUL?
AFTER ALL, I'M A GUY... AND YOU'RE REALLY A GIRL.
GULP
ZZZ
OY
...!
Z
!
SHAKE
HEY, WAKE UP.
YOUR BED'S ON TOP, STUPID.
SHAKE

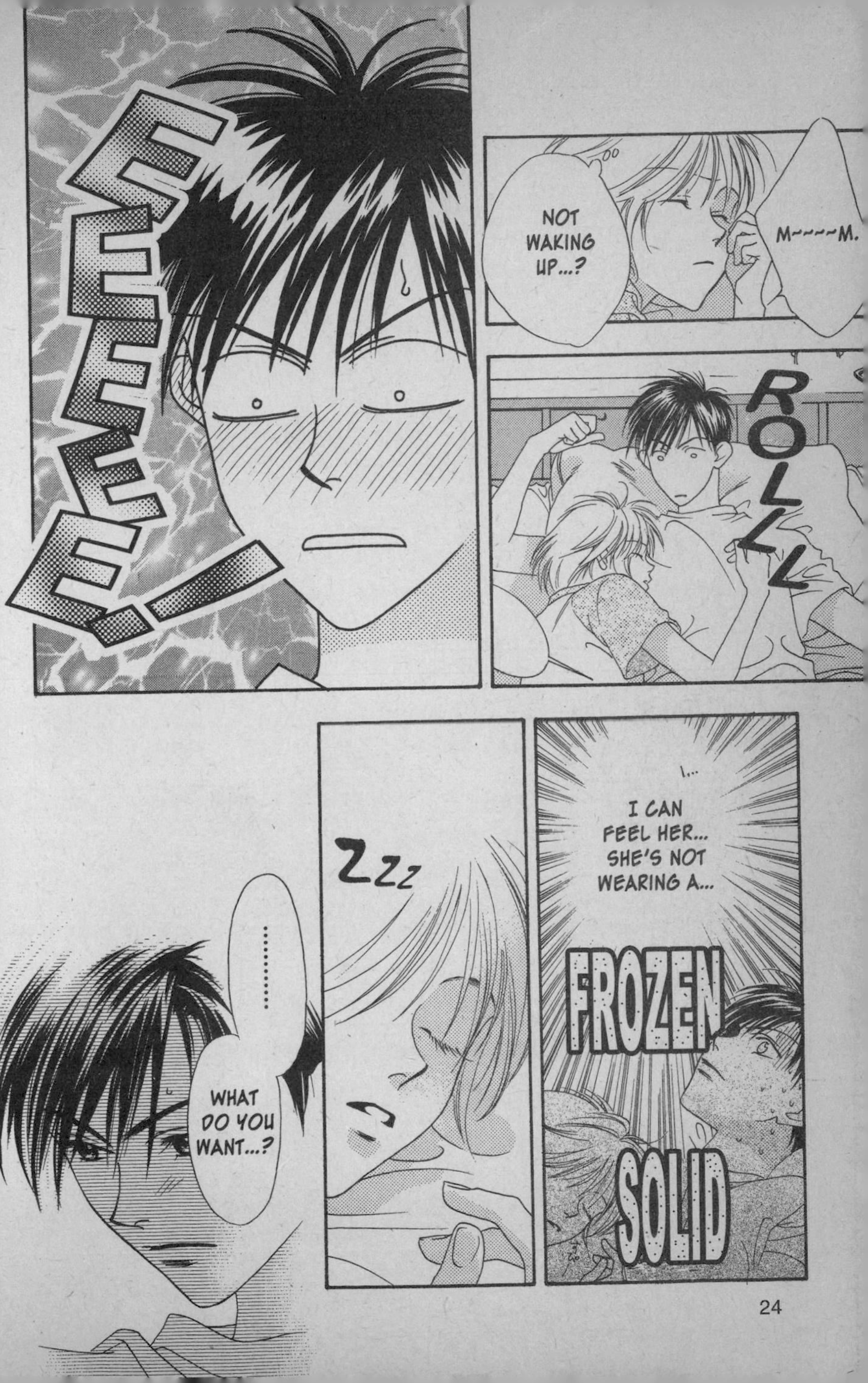
M~~~~M.
NOT WAKING UP...?
ROLL
EEEEE!!
I...
I CAN FEEL HER... SHE'S NOT WEARING A...
FROZEN
SOLID
ZZZ
......
WHAT DO YOU WANT...?

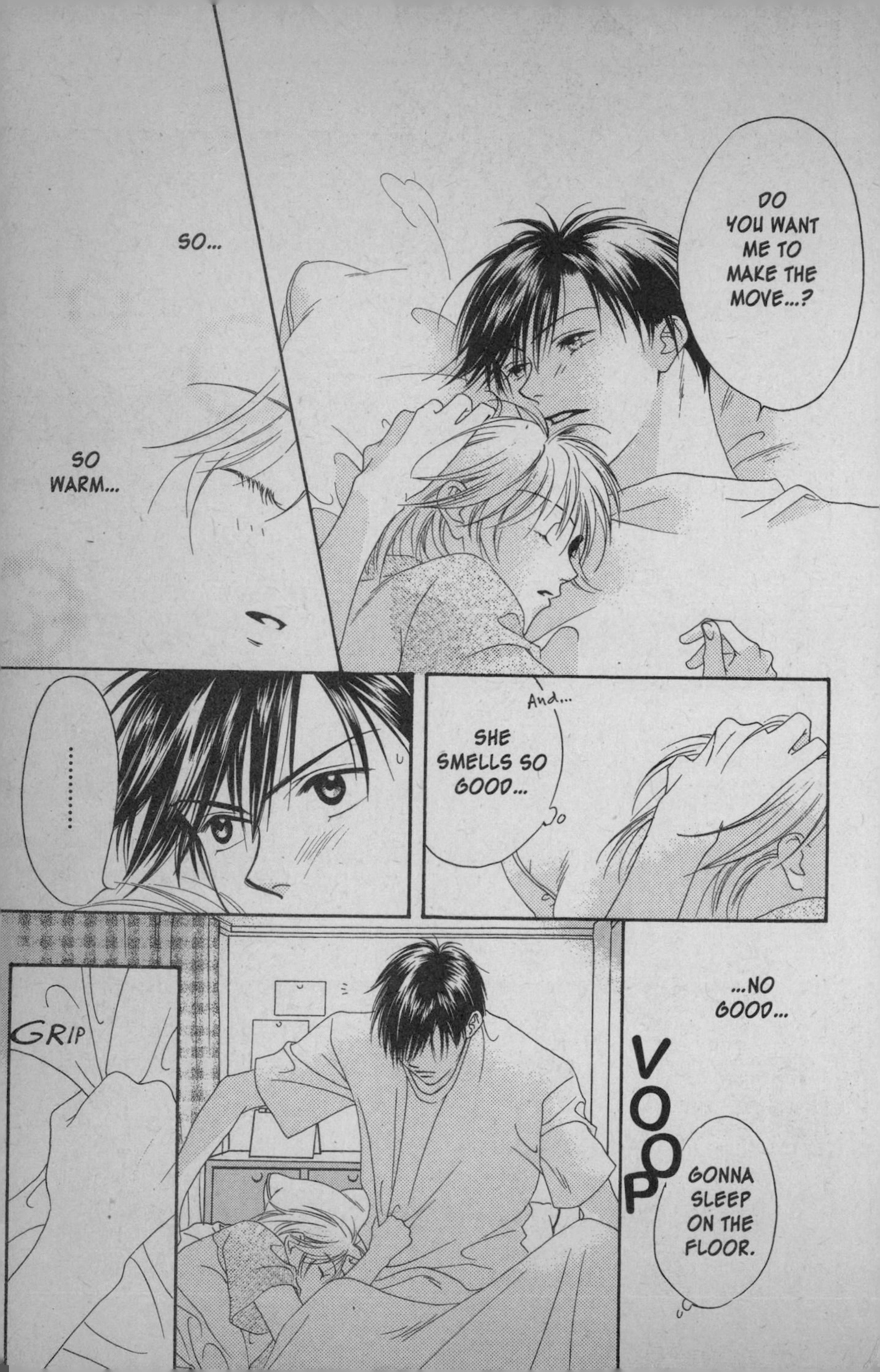
DO YOU WANT ME TO MAKE THE MOVE...?
SO...
SO WARM...
And...
SHE SMELLS SO GOOD...
....
...NO GOOD...
VOOP
GONNA SLEEP ON THE FLOOR.
GRIP

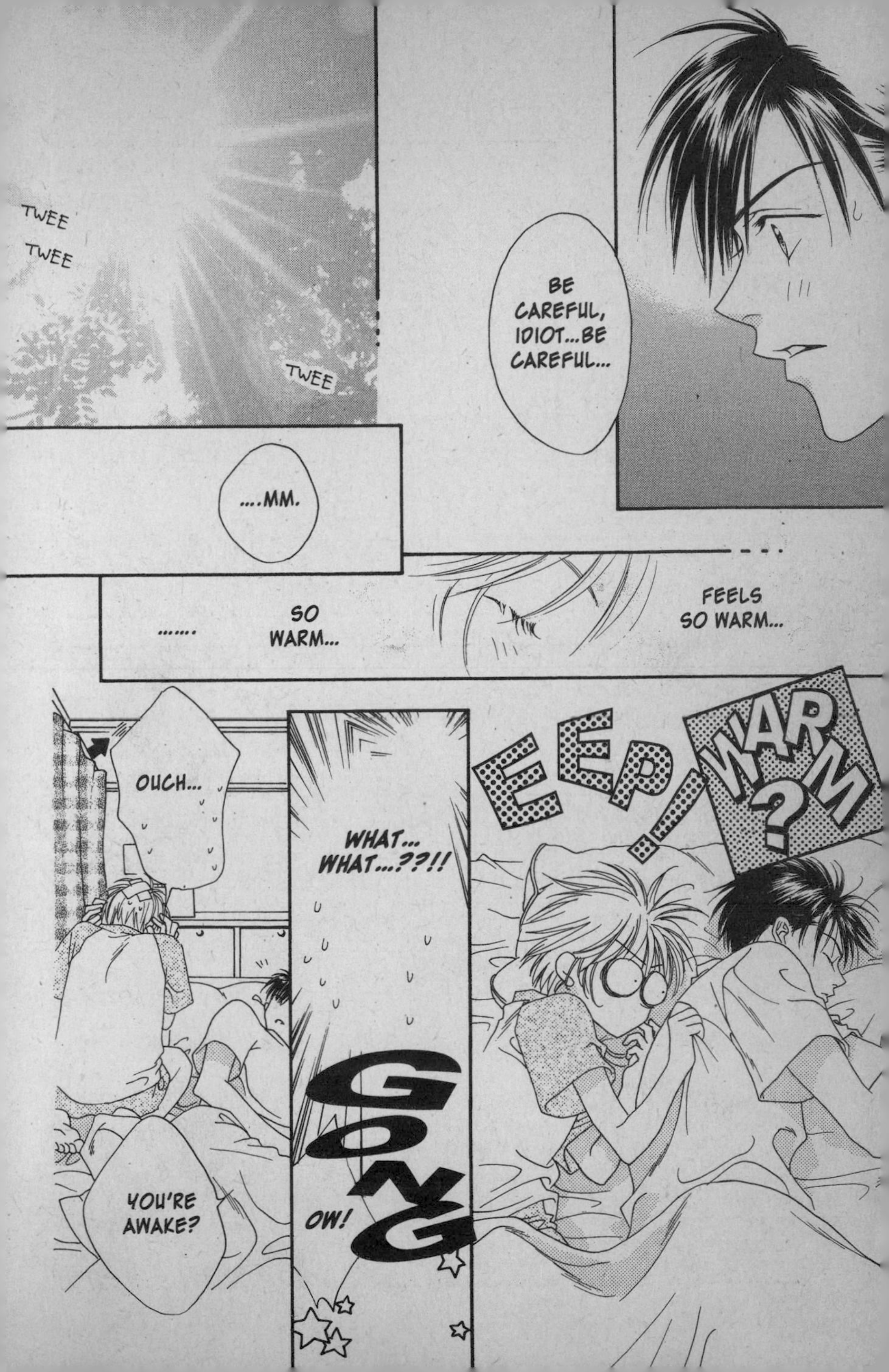
BE CAREFUL, IDIOT...BE CAREFUL...
TWEE
TWEE
TWEE
....MM.
FEELS SO WARM...
SO WARM...
....
WARM?
EEP!!
WHAT... WHAT...??!!
GONG
OW!
OUCH...
YOU'RE AWAKE?

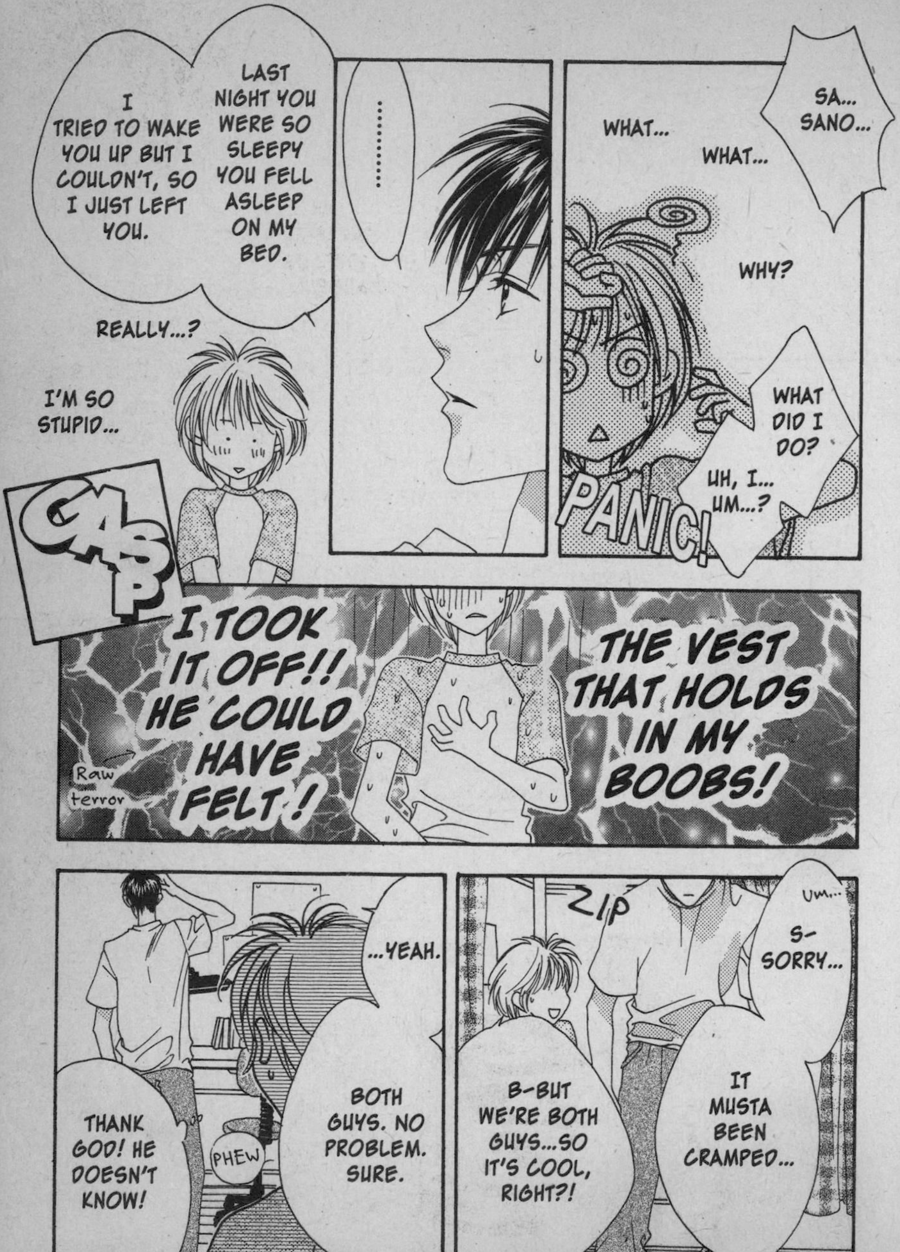
SA... SANO...
WHAT...
WHAT...
WHY?
WHAT DID I DO?
UH, I... UM...?
PANIC!
......
LAST NIGHT YOU WERE SO SLEEPY YOU FELL ASLEEP ON MY BED.
I TRIED TO WAKE YOU UP BUT I COULDN'T, SO I JUST LEFT YOU.
REALLY...?
I'M SO STUPID...
GASP
THE VEST THAT HOLDS IN MY BOOBS!
I TOOK IT OFF!! HE COULD HAVE FELT!
Raw terror
ZIP
UM...
S-SORRY...
IT MUSTA BEEN CRAMPED...
B-BUT WE'RE BOTH GUYS...SO IT'S COOL, RIGHT?!
...YEAH.
BOTH GUYS. NO PROBLEM. SURE.
PHEW
THANK GOD! HE DOESN'T KNOW!

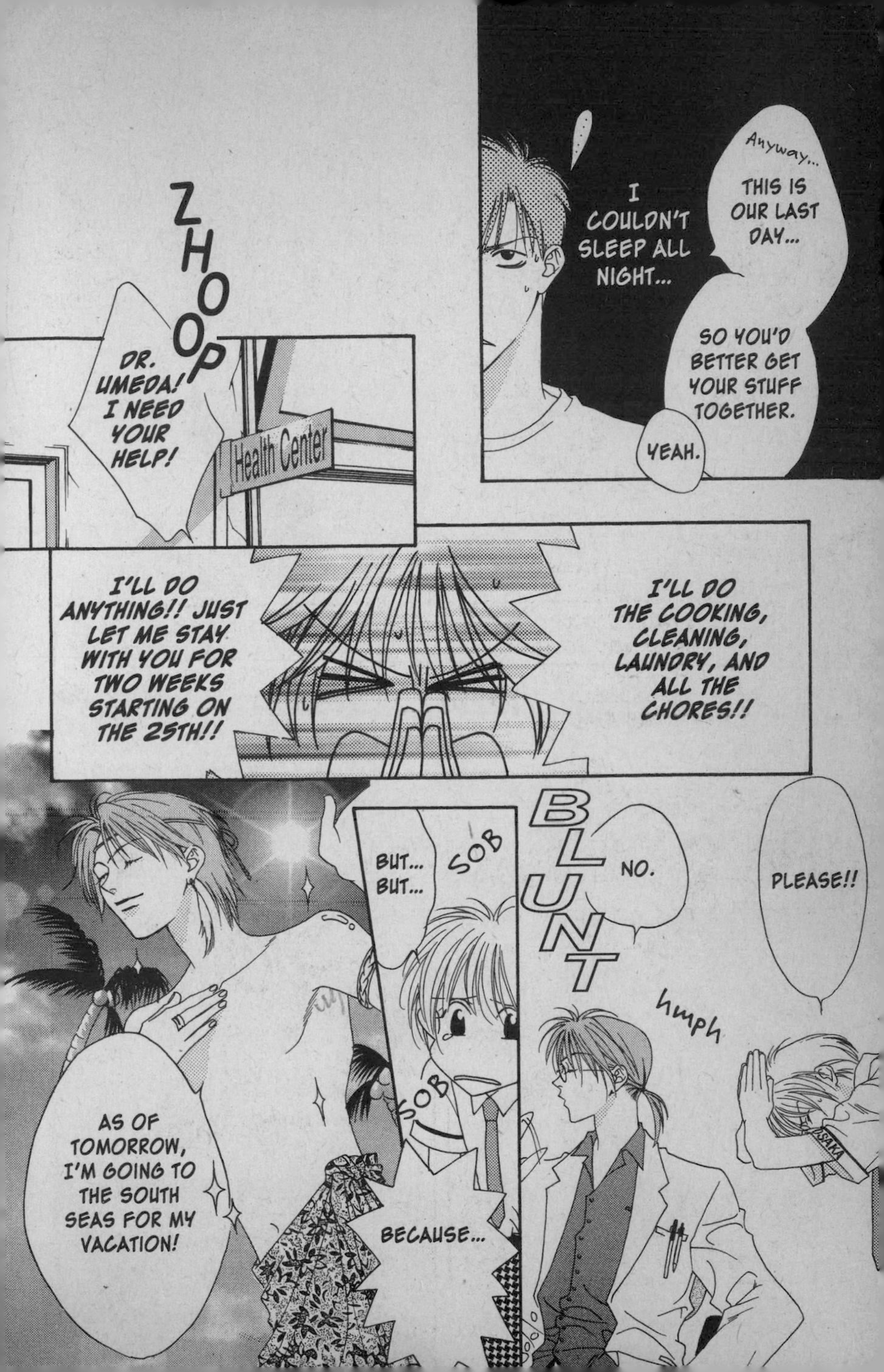
Anyway...
THIS IS OUR LAST DAY...
I COULDN'T SLEEP ALL NIGHT...
SO YOU'D BETTER GET YOUR STUFF TOGETHER.
YEAH.
ZHOOP
Health Center
DR. UMEDA! I NEED YOUR HELP!
I'LL DO THE COOKING, CLEANING, LAUNDRY, AND ALL THE CHORES!!
I'LL DO ANYTHING!! JUST LET ME STAY WITH YOU FOR TWO WEEKS STARTING ON THE 25TH!!
PLEASE!!
BLUNT
NO.
hmph
SOB
BUT... BUT...
SOB
BECAUSE...
AS OF TOMORROW, I'M GOING TO THE SOUTH SEAS FOR MY VACATION!

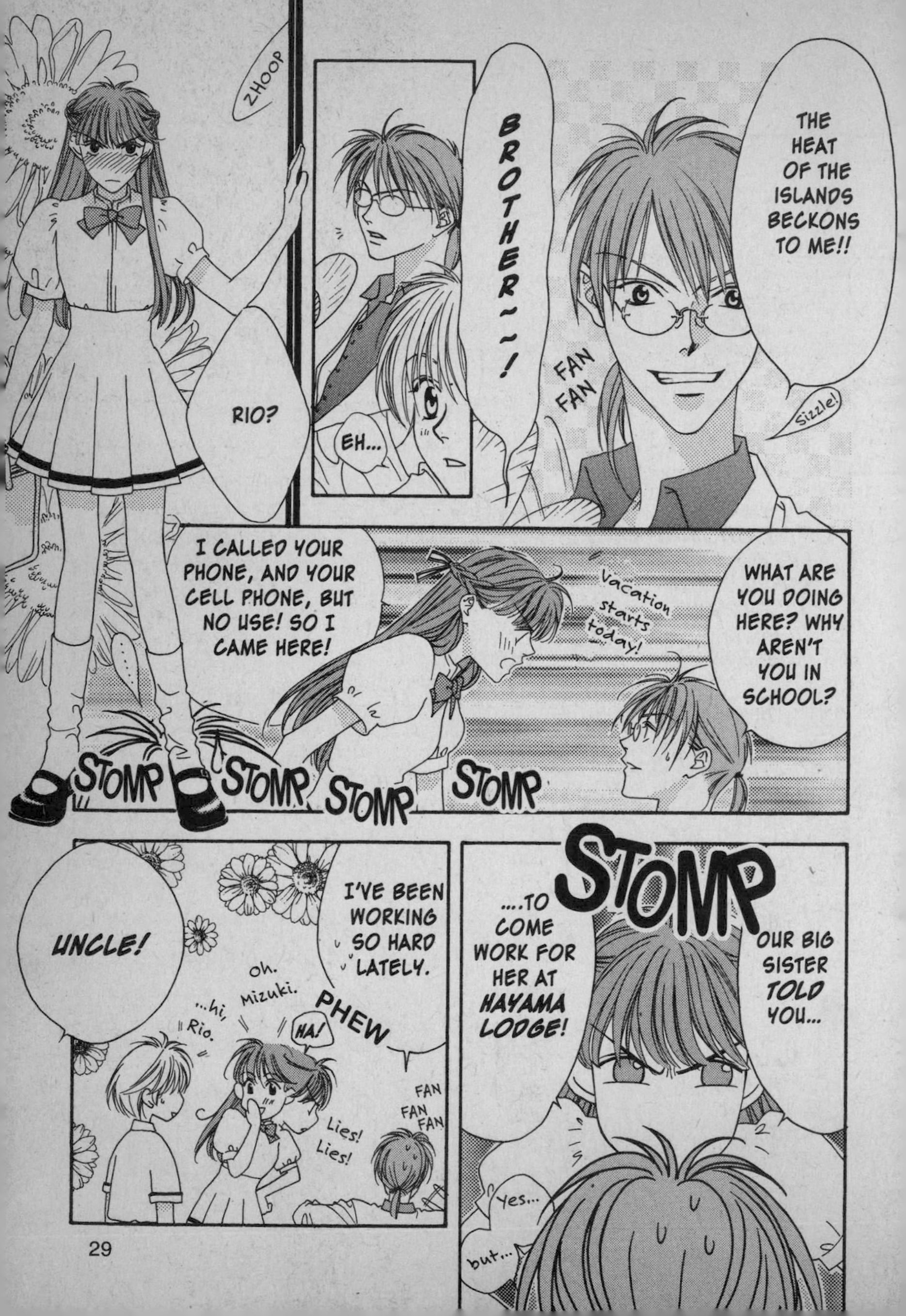
THE HEAT OF THE ISLANDS BECKONS TO ME!!
Sizzle!
FAN FAN
BROTHER~~!
EH...
ZHOOP
RIO?
WHAT ARE YOU DOING HERE? WHY AREN'T YOU IN SCHOOL?
Vacation starts today!
I CALLED YOUR PHONE, AND YOUR CELL PHONE, BUT NO USE! SO I CAME HERE!
STOMP
STOMP
STOMP
STOMP
STOMP
OUR BIG SISTER TOLD YOU...
....TO COME WORK FOR HER AT HAYAMA LODGE!
Yes...
but...
I'VE BEEN WORKING SO HARD LATELY.
UNCLE!
PHEW
HA!
oh. Mizuki.
...hi, Rio.
FAN FAN FAN
Lies! Lies!

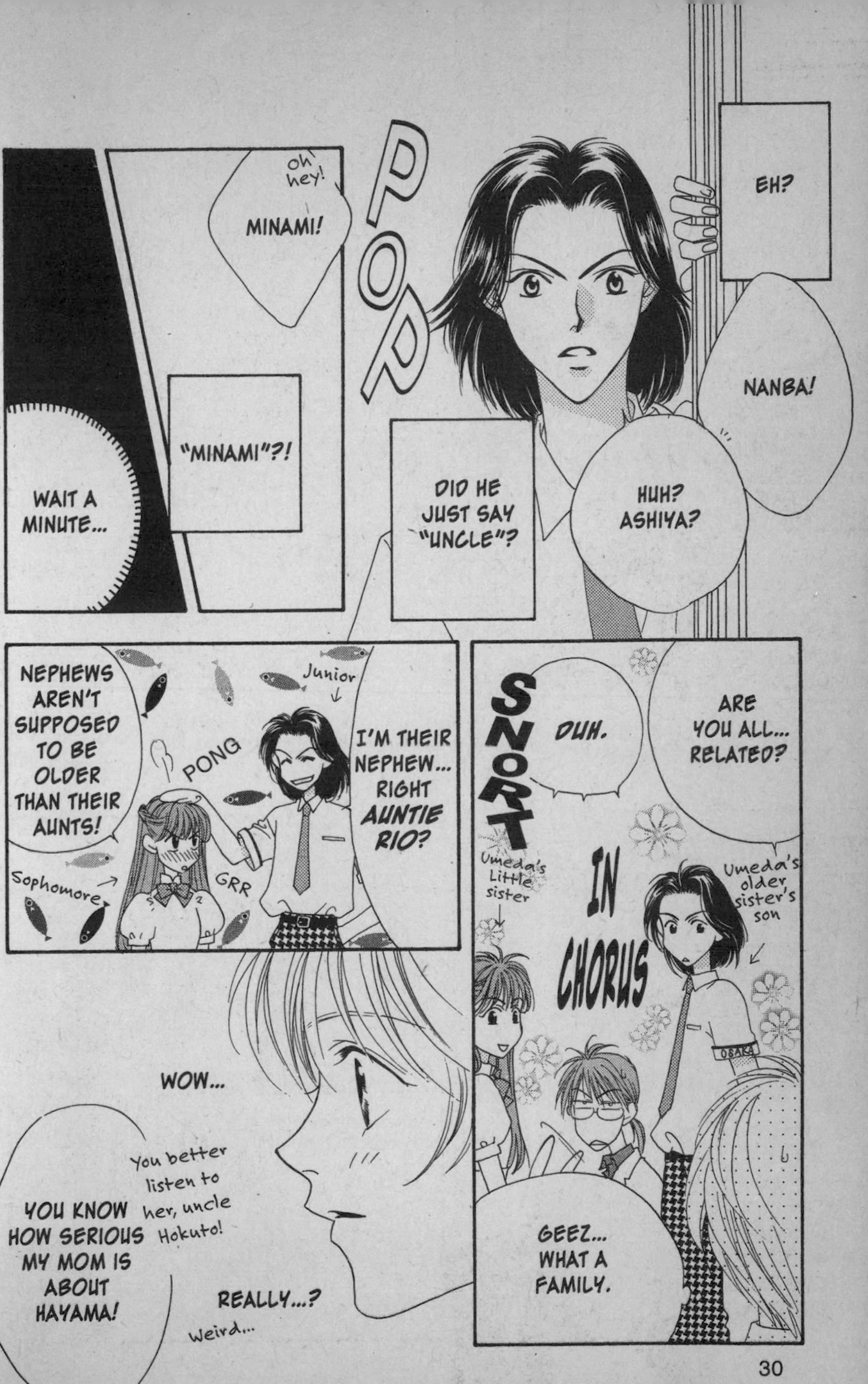
POP
EH?
NANBA!
HUH? ASHIYA?
DID HE JUST SAY "UNCLE"?
oh hey!
MINAMI!
"MINAMI"?!
WAIT A MINUTE...
ARE YOU ALL... RELATED?
DUH.
SNORT
IN CHORUS
Umeda's older sister's son
Umeda's Little sister
GEEZ... WHAT A FAMILY.
I'M THEIR NEPHEW... RIGHT AUNTIE RIO?
Junior
PONG
NEPHEWS AREN'T SUPPOSED TO BE OLDER THAN THEIR AUNTS!
GRR
Sophomore
WOW...
REALLY...?
Weird...
You better listen to her, uncle Hokuto!
YOU KNOW HOW SERIOUS MY MOM IS ABOUT HAYAMA!

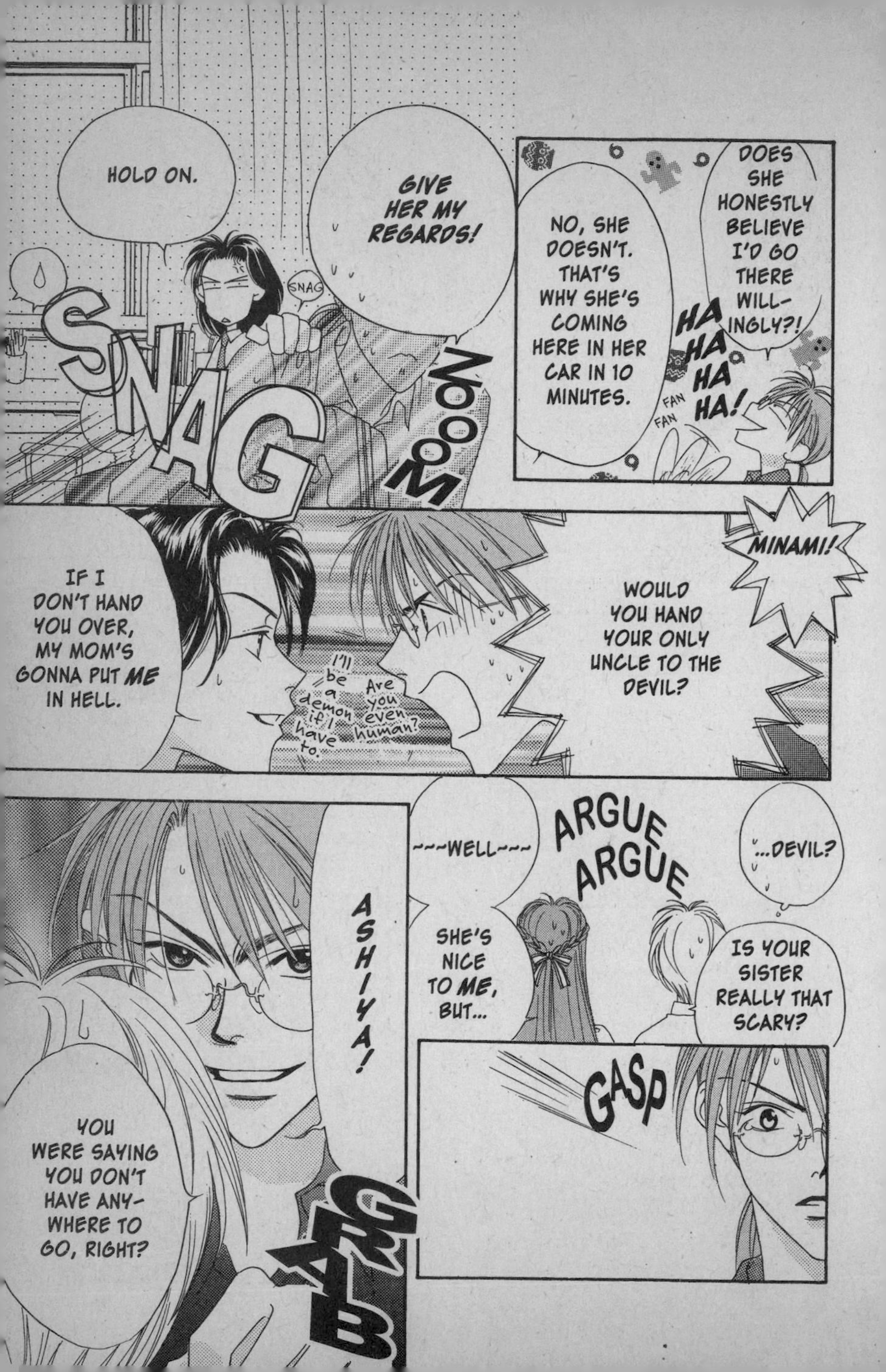
DOES SHE HONESTLY BELIEVE I'D GO THERE WILL-INGLY?!
HA HA HA HA!
FAN FAN
NO, SHE DOESN'T. THAT'S WHY SHE'S COMING HERE IN HER CAR IN 10 MINUTES.
GIVE HER MY REGARDS!
ZOOOOM
SNAG
HOLD ON.
SNAG
MINAMI!
WOULD YOU HAND YOUR ONLY UNCLE TO THE DEVIL?
Are you even human?
I'll be a demon if I have to.
IF I DON'T HAND YOU OVER, MY MOM'S GONNA PUT ME IN HELL.
...DEVIL?
IS YOUR SISTER REALLY THAT SCARY?
ARGUE ARGUE
---WELL---
SHE'S NICE TO ME, BUT...
GASP
ASHIYA!
YOU WERE SAYING YOU DON'T HAVE ANY-WHERE TO GO, RIGHT?
GRAB

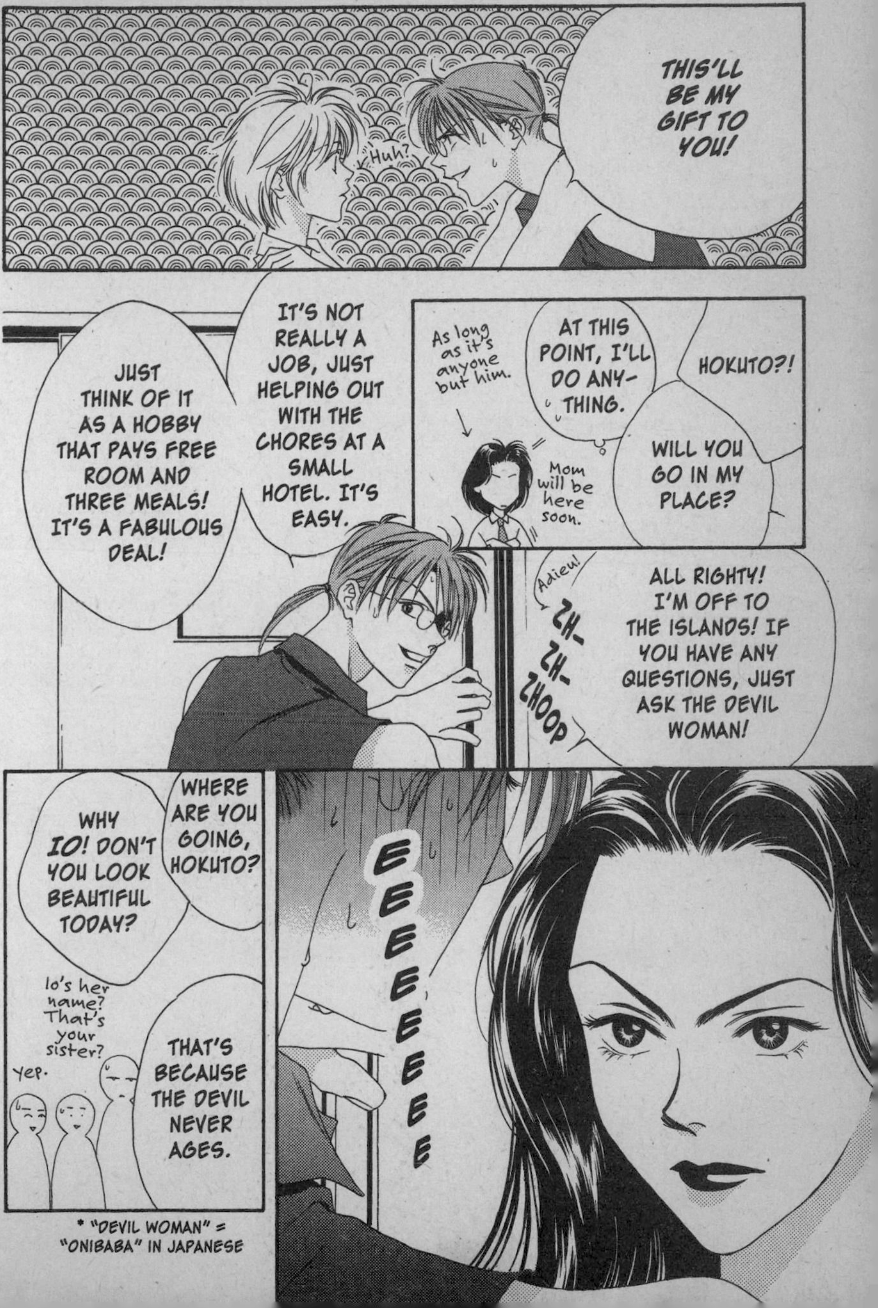
THIS'LL BE MY GIFT TO YOU!
Huh?
HOKUTO?!
WILL YOU GO IN MY PLACE?
AT THIS POINT, I'LL DO ANYTHING.
As long as it's anyone but him.
Mom will be here soon.
IT'S NOT REALLY A JOB, JUST HELPING OUT WITH THE CHORES AT A SMALL HOTEL. IT'S EASY.
JUST THINK OF IT AS A HOBBY THAT PAYS FREE ROOM AND THREE MEALS! IT'S A FABULOUS DEAL!
ALL RIGHTY! I'M OFF TO THE ISLANDS! IF YOU HAVE ANY QUESTIONS, JUST ASK THE DEVIL WOMAN!
Adieu!
ZH-ZH-ZHOOP
EEEEEEEEE
WHERE ARE YOU GOING, HOKUTO?
WHY *IO!* DON'T YOU LOOK BEAUTIFUL TODAY?
THAT'S BECAUSE THE DEVIL NEVER AGES.
Io's her name? That's your sister?
Yep.

* "DEVIL WOMAN" = "ONIBABA" IN JAPANESE

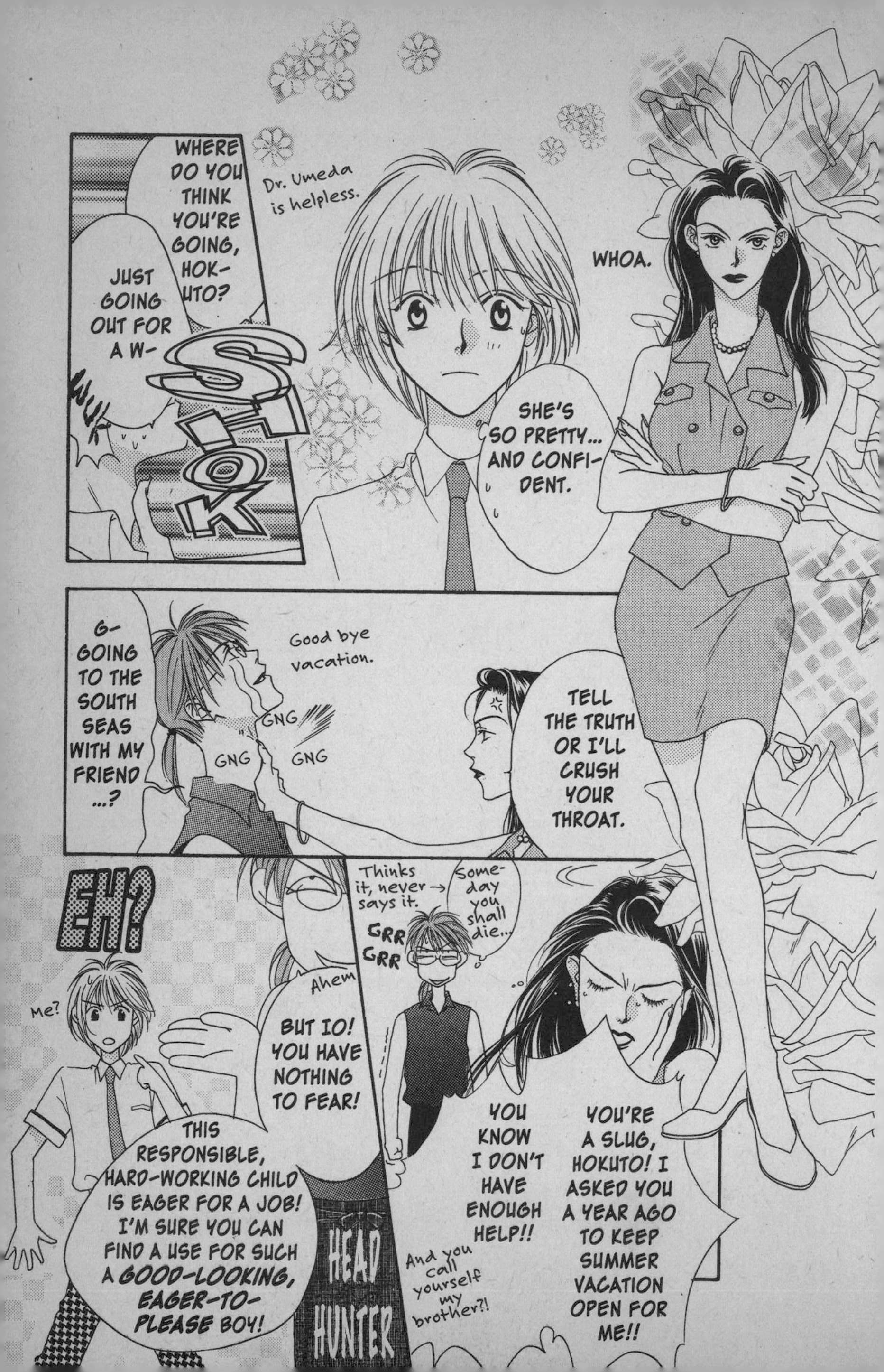
WHOA.
Dr. Umeda is helpless.
SHE'S SO PRETTY... AND CONFIDENT.
WHERE DO YOU THINK YOU'RE GOING, HOKUTO?
JUST GOING OUT FOR A W-
SHOK
TELL THE TRUTH OR I'LL CRUSH YOUR THROAT.
GNG
GNG
GNG
G-GOING TO THE SOUTH SEAS WITH MY FRIEND ...?
Good bye vacation.
YOU'RE A SLUG, HOKUTO! I ASKED YOU A YEAR AGO TO KEEP SUMMER VACATION OPEN FOR ME!!
YOU KNOW I DON'T HAVE ENOUGH HELP!!
Someday you shall die...
Thinks it, never says it.
GRR GRR
And you call yourself my brother?!
HEAD HUNTER
Ahem
BUT IO! YOU HAVE NOTHING TO FEAR!
THIS RESPONSIBLE, HARD-WORKING CHILD IS EAGER FOR A JOB! I'M SURE YOU CAN FIND A USE FOR SUCH A GOOD-LOOKING, EAGER-TO-PLEASE BOY!
EH?
Me?

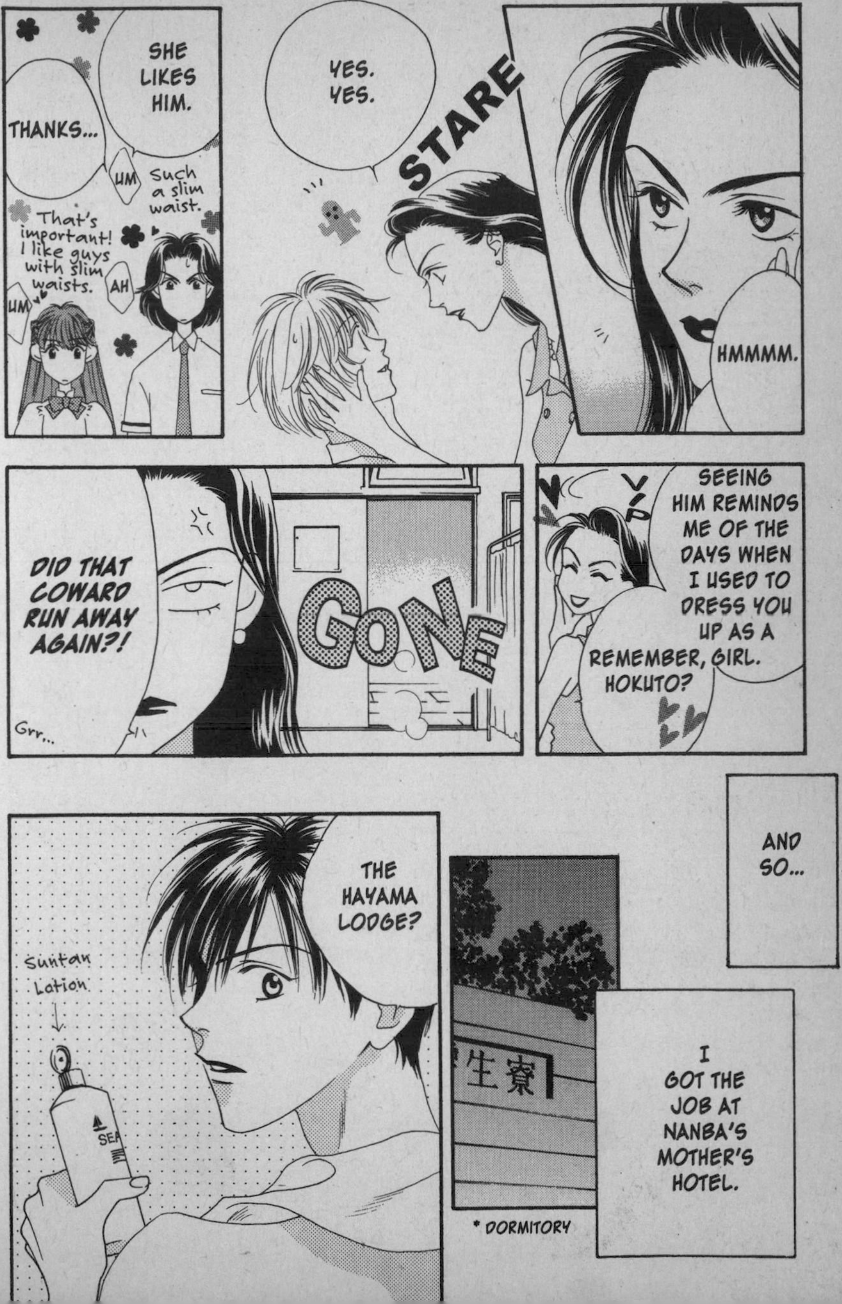
HMMMM.
STARE
YES. YES.
SHE LIKES HIM.
THANKS...
UM
Such a slim waist.
That's important! I like guys with slim waists.
AH
UM
VIP
SEEING HIM REMINDS ME OF THE DAYS WHEN I USED TO DRESS YOU UP AS A GIRL.
REMEMBER, HOKUTO?
DID THAT COWARD RUN AWAY AGAIN?!
GONE
Grr...
AND SO...
I GOT THE JOB AT NANBA'S MOTHER'S HOTEL.
生寮
* DORMITORY
THE HAYAMA LODGE?
Suntan Lotion
SEA

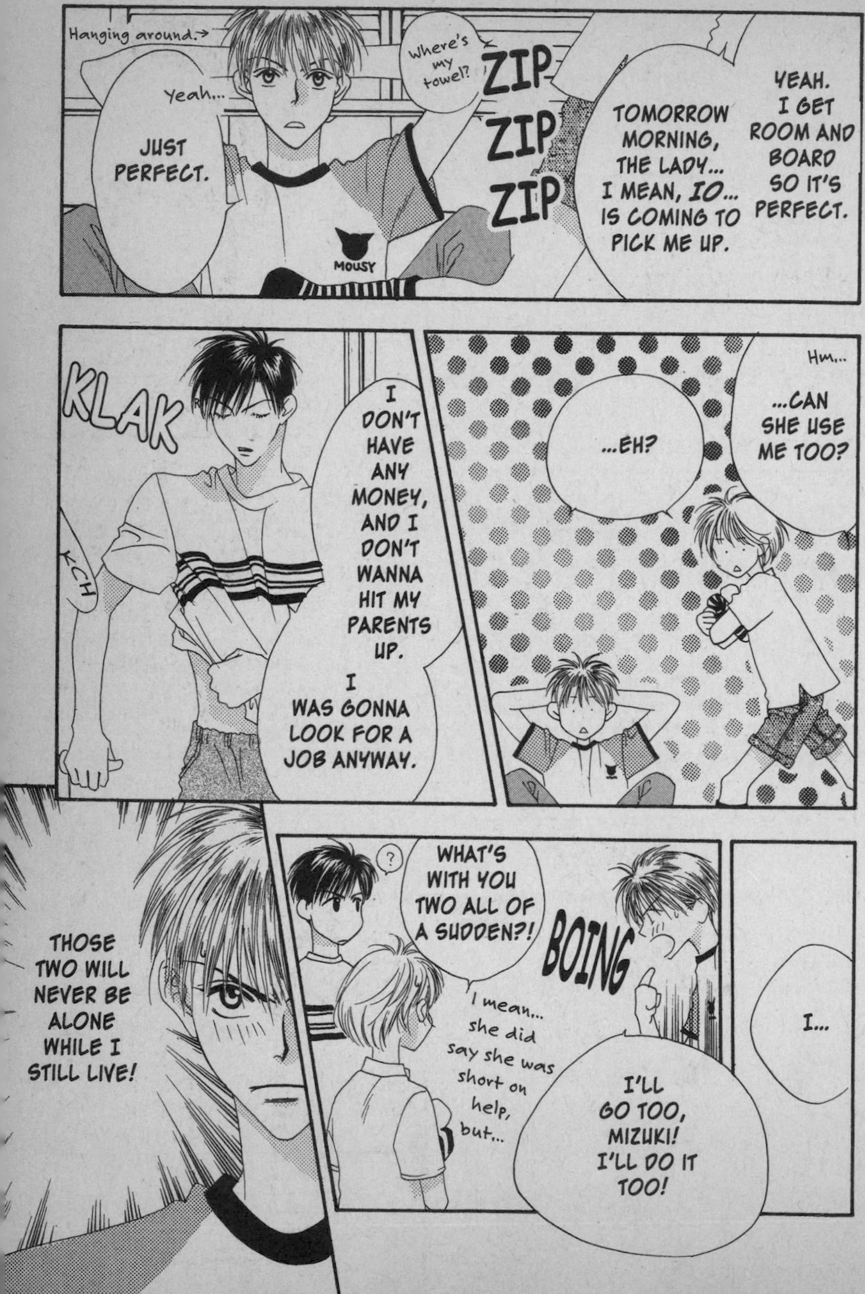
YEAH. I GET ROOM AND BOARD SO IT'S PERFECT.
TOMORROW MORNING, THE LADY... I MEAN, *IO*... IS COMING TO PICK ME UP.
ZIP ZIP ZIP
Where's my towel?
Yeah...
JUST PERFECT.
Hanging around.→
Hm...
...CAN SHE USE ME TOO?
...EH?
I DON'T HAVE ANY MONEY, AND I DON'T WANNA HIT MY PARENTS UP.
I WAS GONNA LOOK FOR A JOB ANYWAY.
KLAK
KCH
I...
BOING
I'LL GO TOO, MIZUKI! I'LL DO IT TOO!
WHAT'S WITH YOU TWO ALL OF A SUDDEN?!
?
I mean... she did say she was short on help, but...
THOSE TWO WILL NEVER BE ALONE WHILE I STILL LIVE!

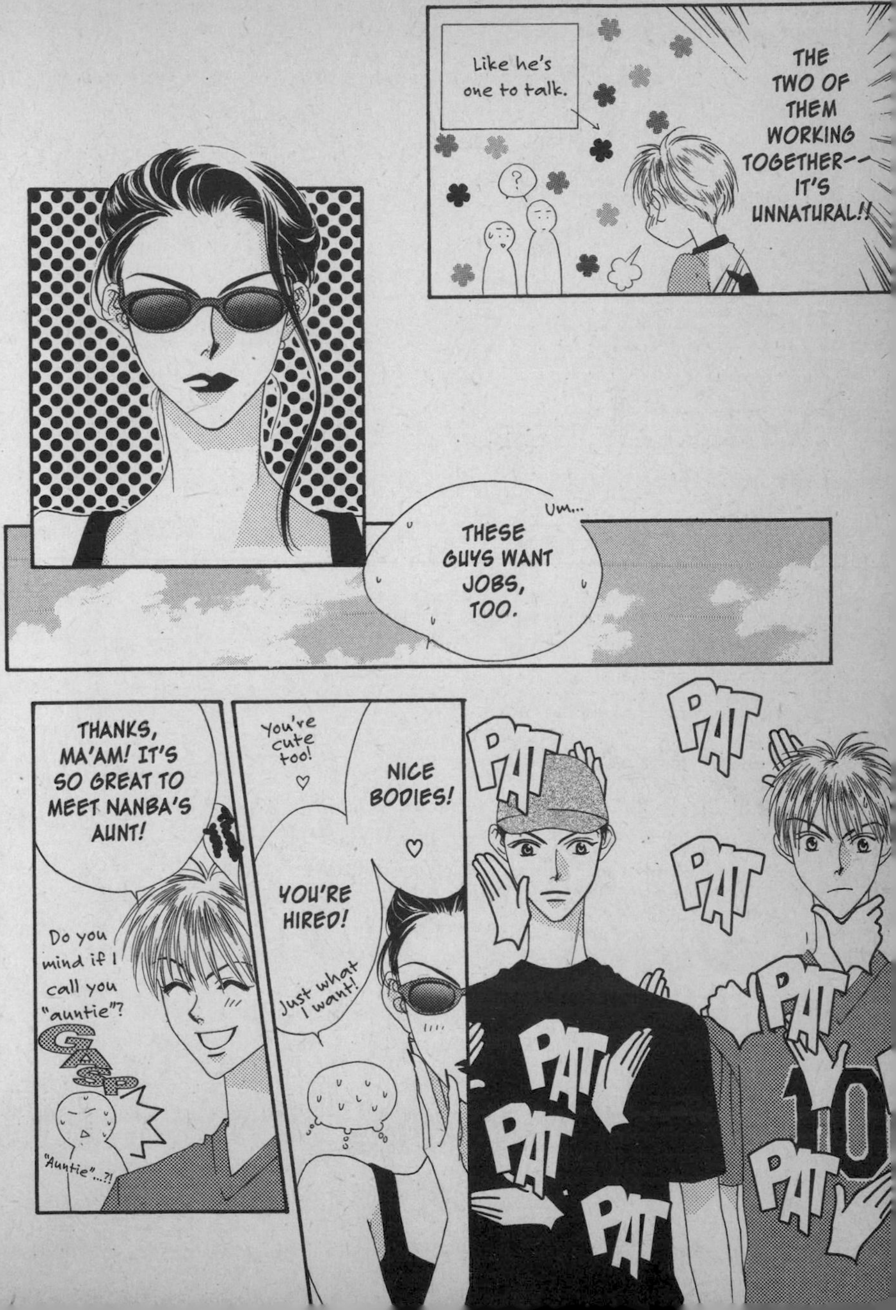
THE TWO OF THEM WORKING TOGETHER-- IT'S UNNATURAL!!
Like he's one to talk.
?
Um...
THESE GUYS WANT JOBS, TOO.
PAT
PAT
PAT
PAT
PAT
PAT
PAT
PAT
NICE BODIES!
You're cute too!
YOU'RE HIRED!
Just what I want!
THANKS, MA'AM! IT'S SO GREAT TO MEET NANBA'S AUNT!
Do you mind if I call you "auntie"?
GASP
"Auntie"...?!

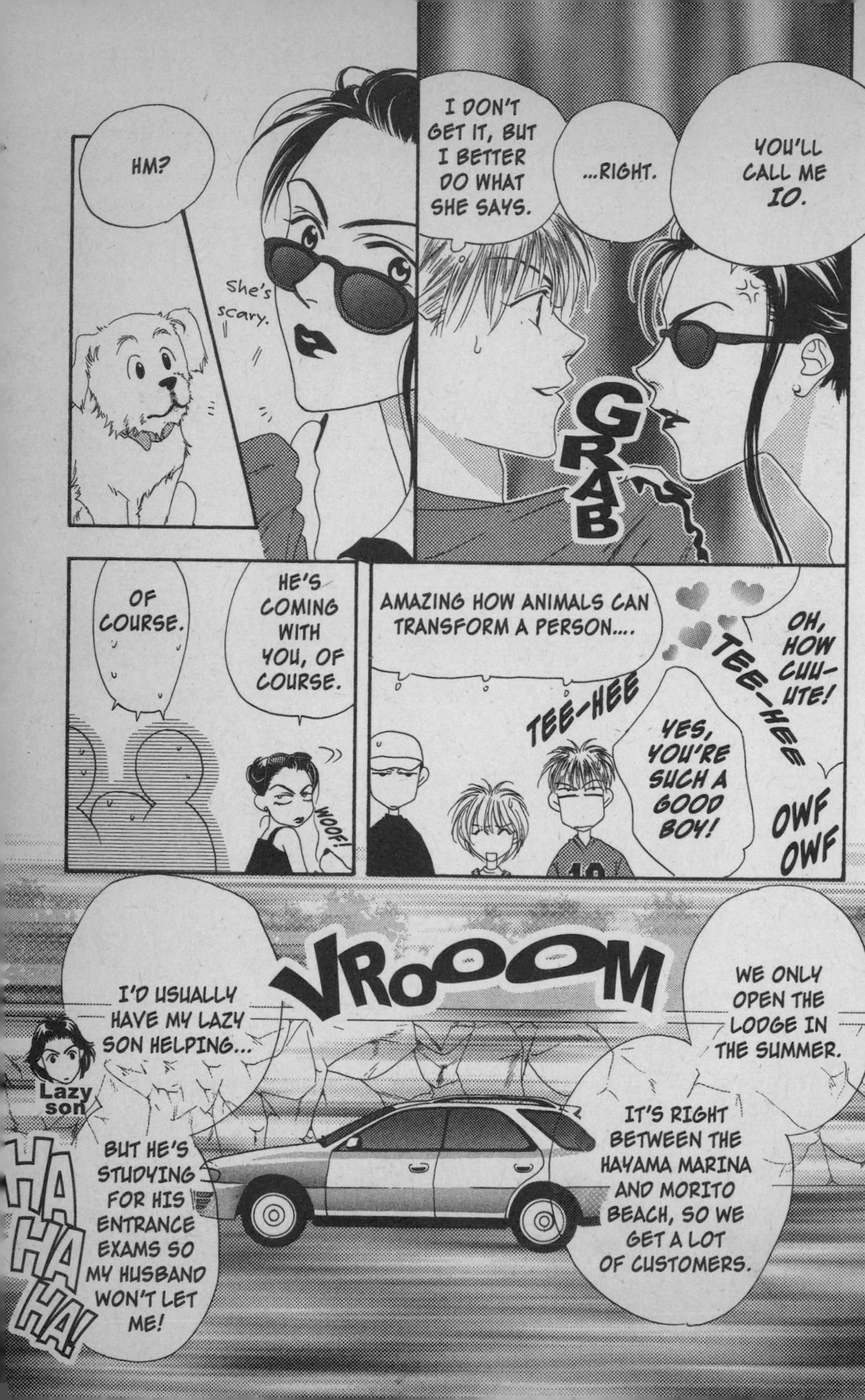

YOU'LL CALL ME IO.
...RIGHT.
I DON'T GET IT, BUT I BETTER DO WHAT SHE SAYS.
GRAB
HM?
She's scary.
OH, HOW CUUUTE!
TEE-HEE
TEE-HEE
YES, YOU'RE SUCH A GOOD BOY!
OWF OWF
AMAZING HOW ANIMALS CAN TRANSFORM A PERSON....
HE'S COMING WITH YOU, OF COURSE.
OF COURSE.
WOOF!
WE ONLY OPEN THE LODGE IN THE SUMMER.
IT'S RIGHT BETWEEN THE HAYAMA MARINA AND MORITO BEACH, SO WE GET A LOT OF CUSTOMERS.
VROOOM
I'D USUALLY HAVE MY LAZY SON HELPING...
Lazy son
BUT HE'S STUDYING FOR HIS ENTRANCE EXAMS SO MY HUSBAND WON'T LET ME!
HA HA HA HA!

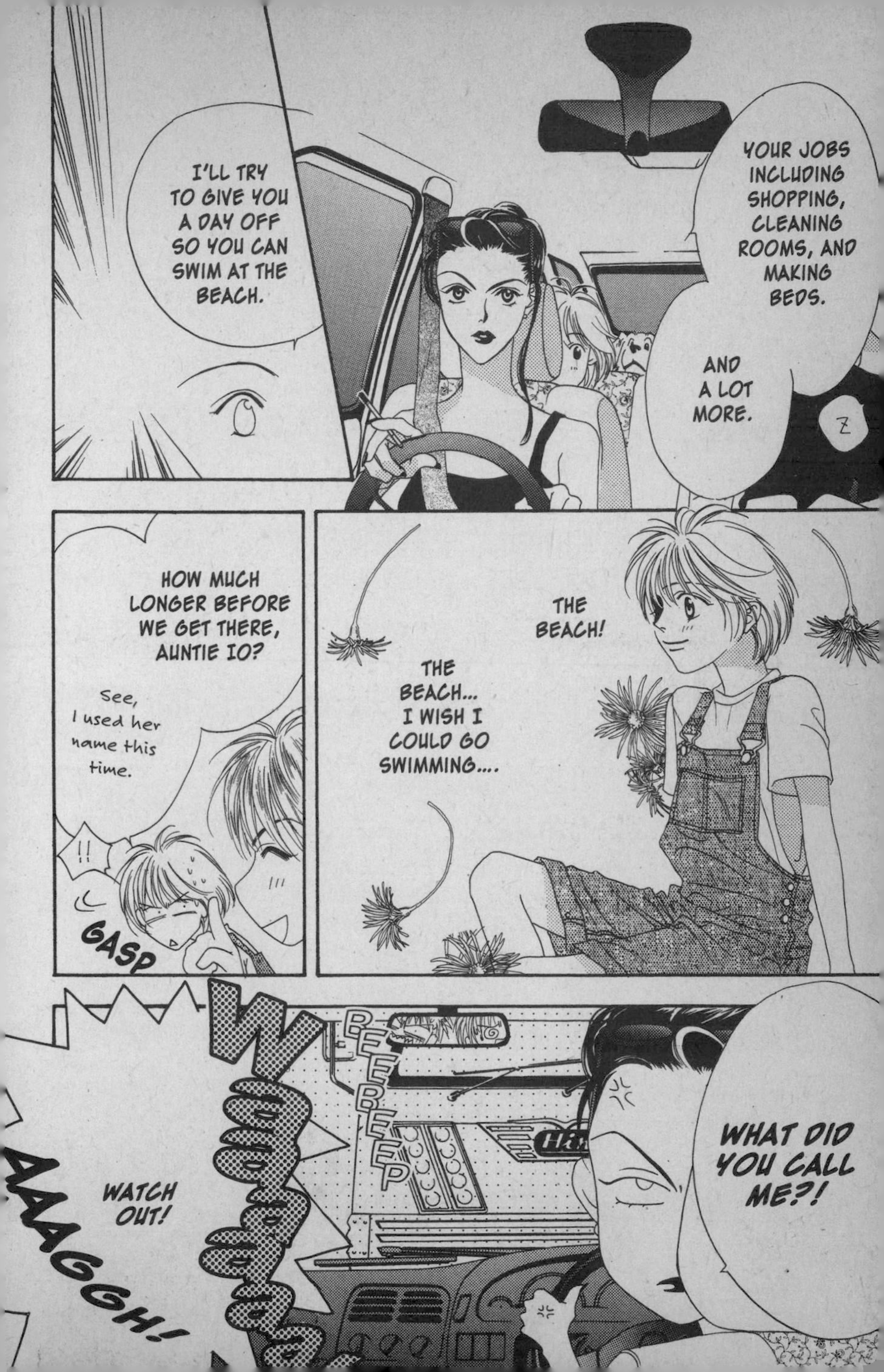
YOUR JOBS INCLUDING SHOPPING, CLEANING ROOMS, AND MAKING BEDS.
AND A LOT MORE.
Z
I'LL TRY TO GIVE YOU A DAY OFF SO YOU CAN SWIM AT THE BEACH.
THE BEACH!
THE BEACH... I WISH I COULD GO SWIMMING....
HOW MUCH LONGER BEFORE WE GET THERE, AUNTIE IO?
See, I used her name this time.
!!
GASP
WHAT DID YOU CALL ME?!
BEEBEEP
WATCH OUT!
AAAGGH!

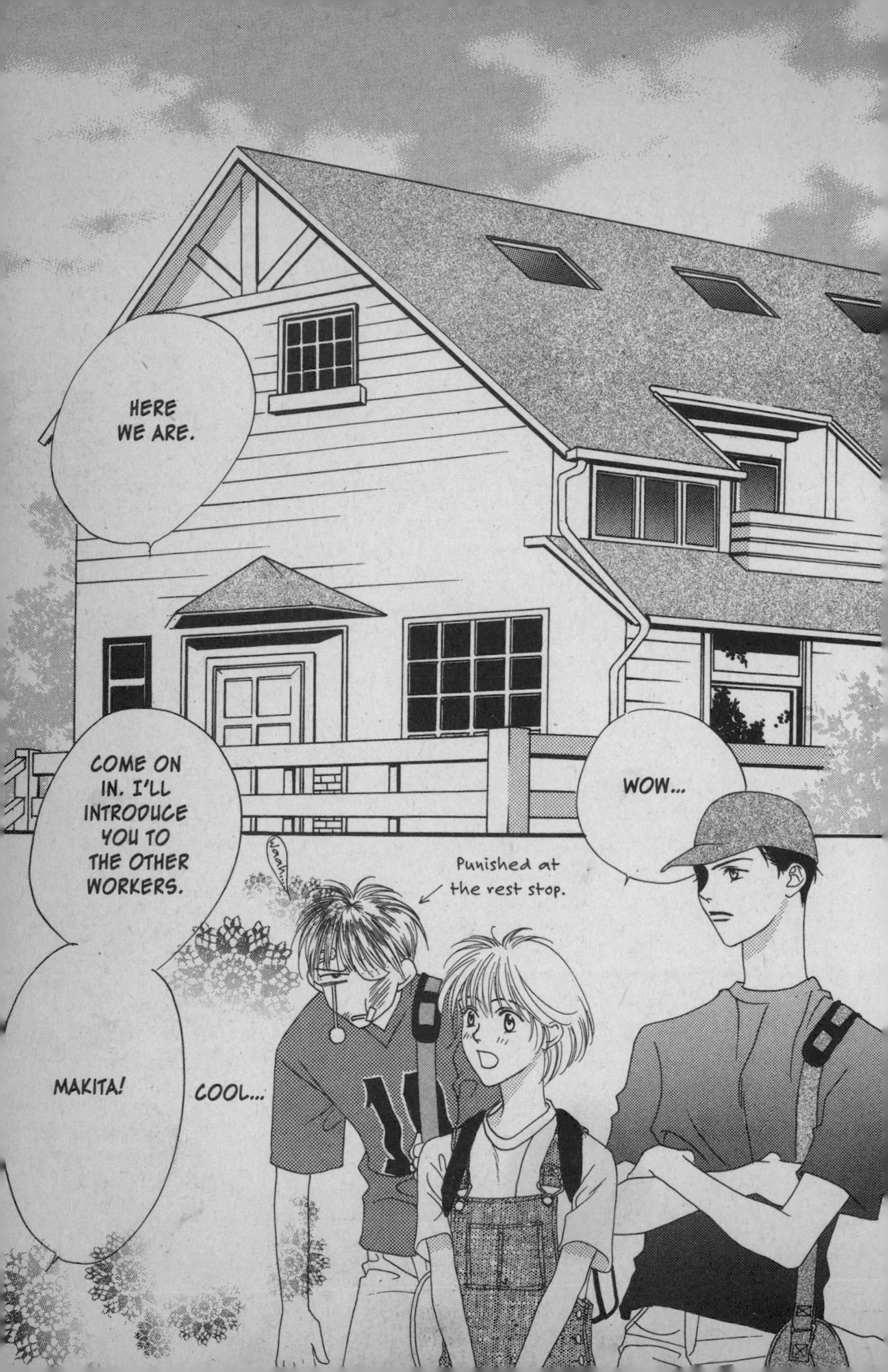
HERE WE ARE.
WOW...
Punished at the rest stop.
COME ON IN. I'LL INTRODUCE YOU TO THE OTHER WORKERS.
Waah...
COOL...
MAKITA!

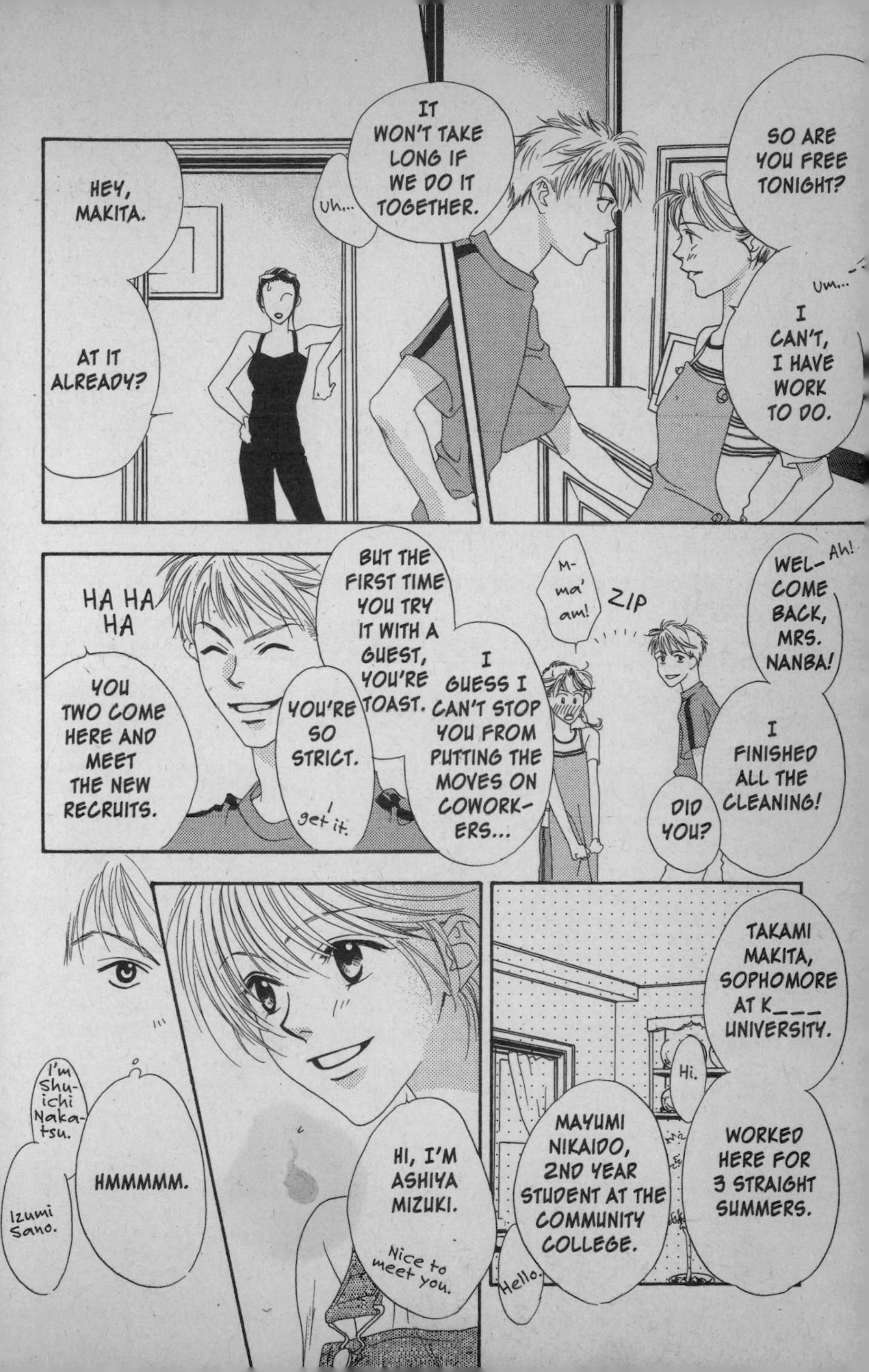
SO ARE YOU FREE TONIGHT?
Um...
I CAN'T, I HAVE WORK TO DO.
IT WON'T TAKE LONG IF WE DO IT TOGETHER.
Uh...
HEY, MAKITA.
AT IT ALREADY?
WEL-COME BACK, MRS. NANBA!
Ah!
I FINISHED ALL THE CLEANING!
DID YOU?
M-ma'am!
ZIP
I GUESS I CAN'T STOP YOU FROM PUTTING THE MOVES ON COWORK-ERS...
BUT THE FIRST TIME YOU TRY IT WITH A GUEST, YOU'RE TOAST.
YOU'RE SO STRICT.
I get it.
HA HA HA
YOU TWO COME HERE AND MEET THE NEW RECRUITS.
TAKAMI MAKITA, SOPHOMORE AT K___ UNIVERSITY.
Hi.
WORKED HERE FOR 3 STRAIGHT SUMMERS.
MAYUMI NIKAIDO, 2ND YEAR STUDENT AT THE COMMUNITY COLLEGE.
Hello.
HI, I'M ASHIYA MIZUKI.
Nice to meet you.
HMMMMM.
I'm Shuichi Nakatsu.
Izumi Sano.

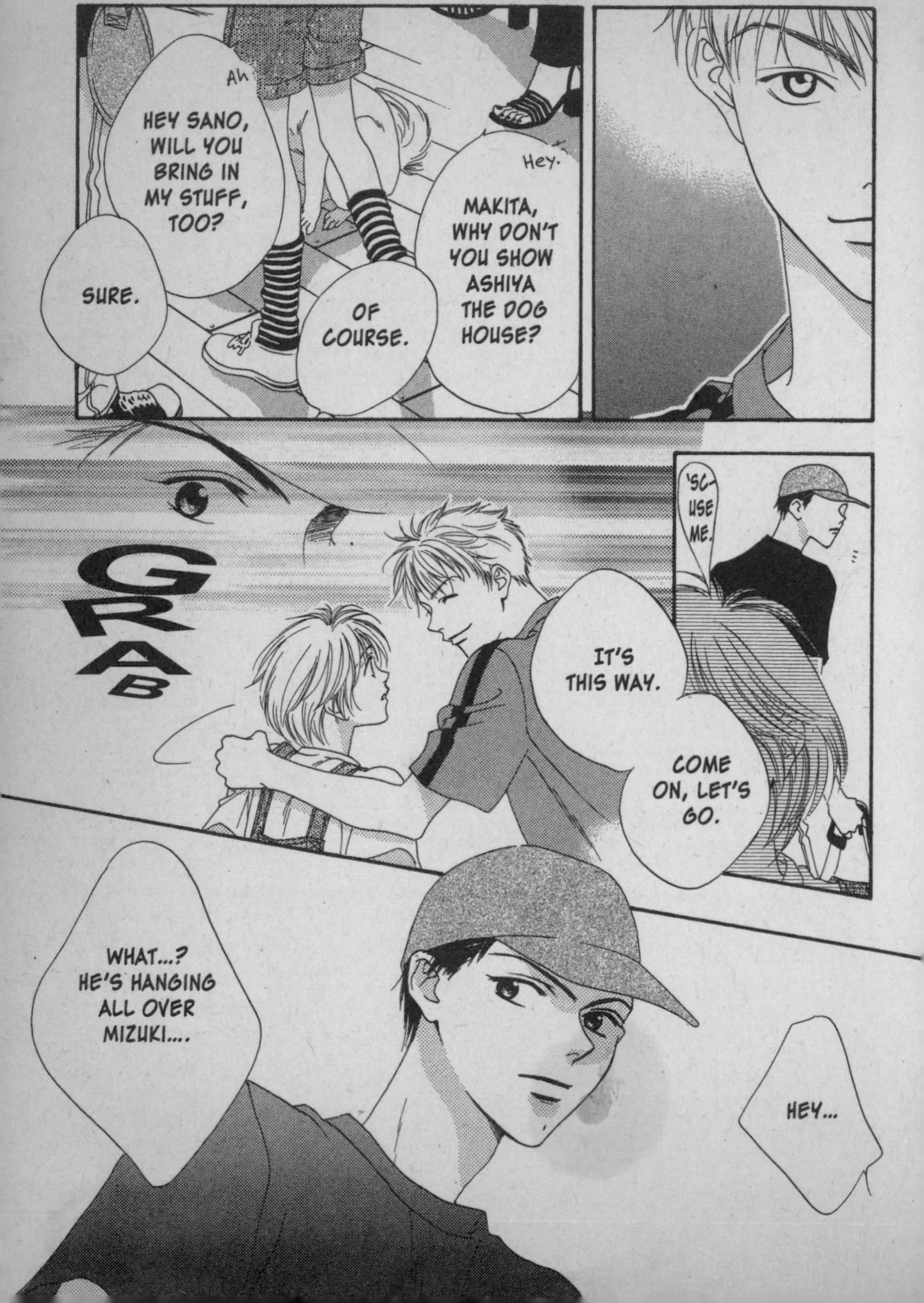
Hey.
MAKITA, WHY DON'T YOU SHOW ASHIYA THE DOG HOUSE?
Ah
HEY SANO, WILL YOU BRING IN MY STUFF, TOO?
OF COURSE.
SURE.
'SC-USE ME.
IT'S THIS WAY.
COME ON, LET'S GO.
GRAB
HEY...
WHAT...? HE'S HANGING ALL OVER MIZUKI....

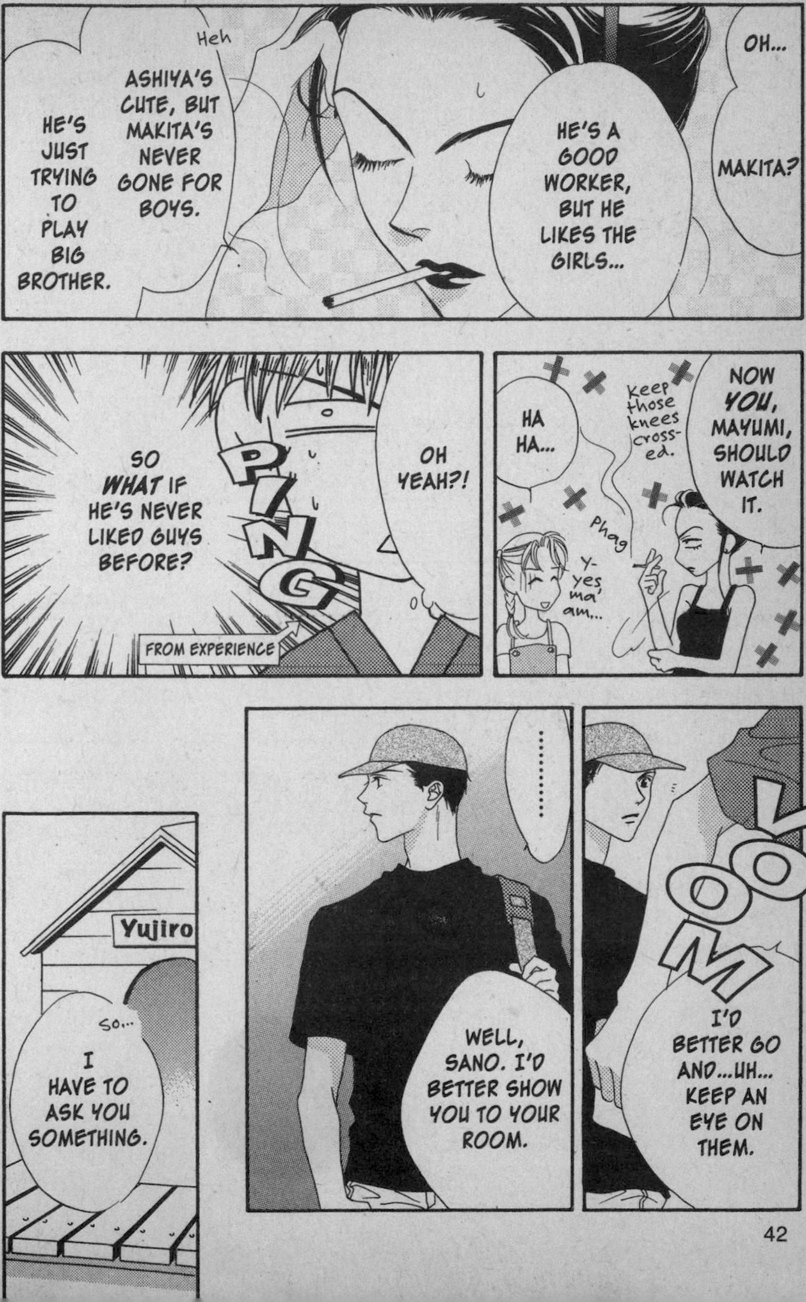
OH... MAKITA?
HE'S A GOOD WORKER, BUT HE LIKES THE GIRLS...
Heh
ASHIYA'S CUTE, BUT MAKITA'S NEVER GONE FOR BOYS.
HE'S JUST TRYING TO PLAY BIG BROTHER.
NOW YOU, MAYUMI, SHOULD WATCH IT.
Keep those knees cross-ed.
HA HA...
Phag
Y-yes, ma'am...
OH YEAH?!
PING
SO WHAT IF HE'S NEVER LIKED GUYS BEFORE?
FROM EXPERIENCE
VOOM
I'D BETTER GO AND...UH... KEEP AN EYE ON THEM.
....
WELL, SANO. I'D BETTER SHOW YOU TO YOUR ROOM.
Yujiro
So...
I HAVE TO ASK YOU SOMETHING.

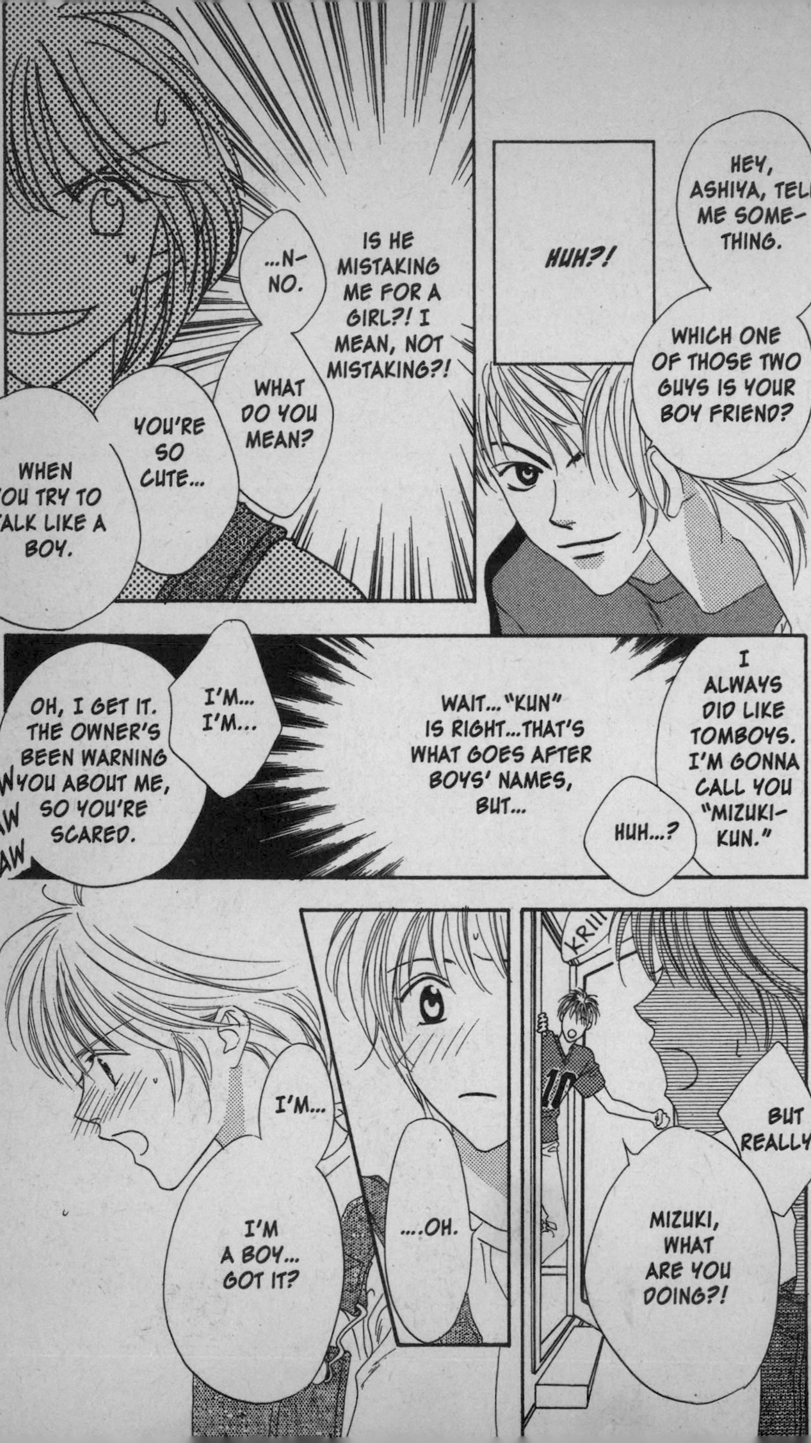
HEY, ASHIYA, TELL ME SOME-THING.
WHICH ONE OF THOSE TWO GUYS IS YOUR BOY FRIEND?
HUH?!
IS HE MISTAKING ME FOR A GIRL?! I MEAN, NOT MISTAKING?!
...N-NO.
WHAT DO YOU MEAN?
YOU'RE SO CUTE...
WHEN YOU TRY TO TALK LIKE A BOY.
I ALWAYS DID LIKE TOMBOYS. I'M GONNA CALL YOU "MIZUKI-KUN."
HUH...?
WAIT... "KUN" IS RIGHT...THAT'S WHAT GOES AFTER BOYS' NAMES, BUT...
I'M... I'M...
OH, I GET IT. THE OWNER'S BEEN WARNING YOU ABOUT ME, SO YOU'RE SCARED.
HAW HAW HAW
KRIII
BUT REALLY...
MIZUKI, WHAT ARE YOU DOING?!
....OH.
I'M...
I'M A BOY... GOT IT?

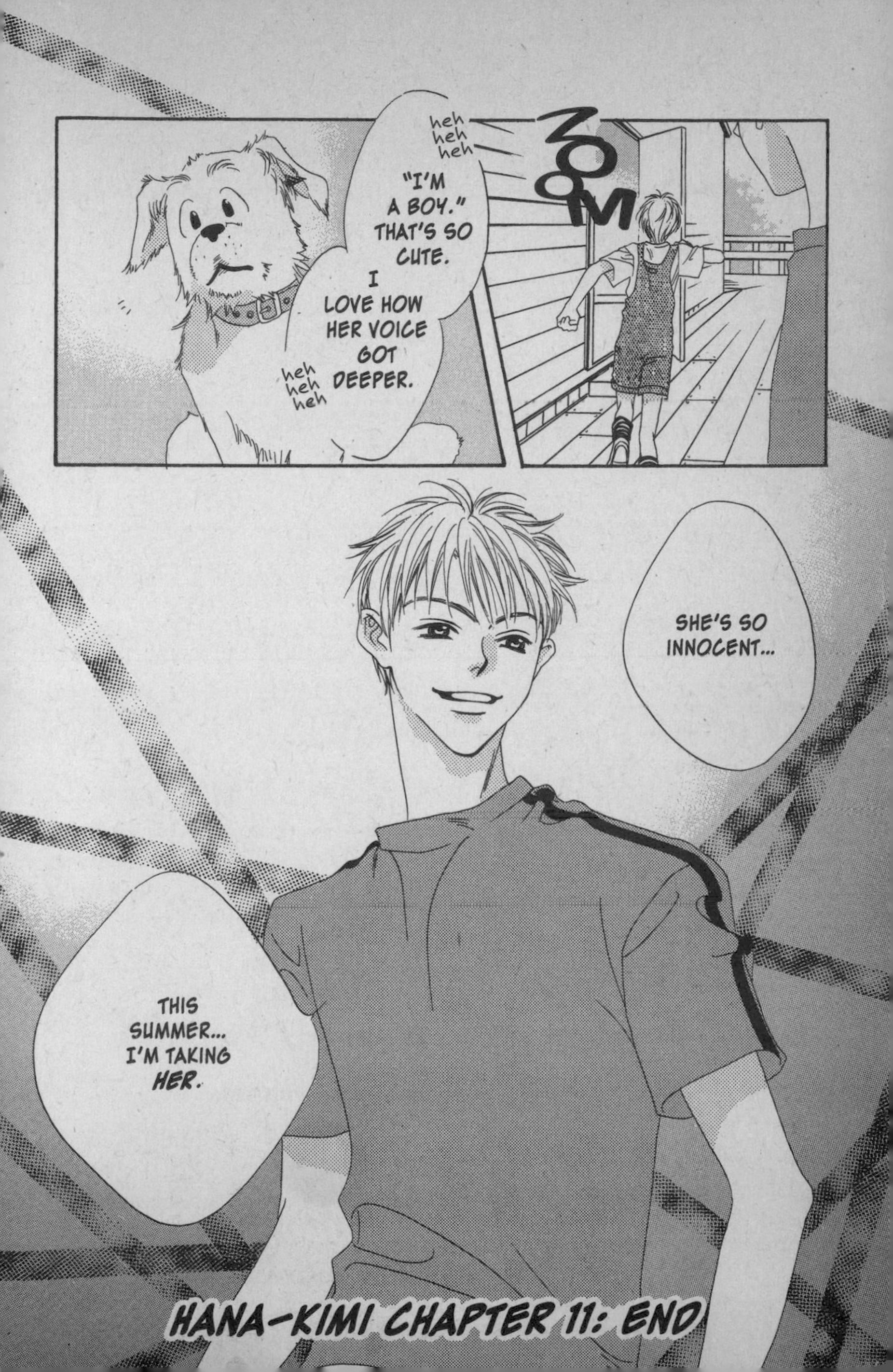
ZOOM
heh heh heh
"I'M A BOY." THAT'S SO CUTE.
I LOVE HOW HER VOICE GOT DEEPER.
heh heh heh
SHE'S SO INNOCENT...
THIS SUMMER... I'M TAKING *HER*.
HANA-KIMI CHAPTER 11: END

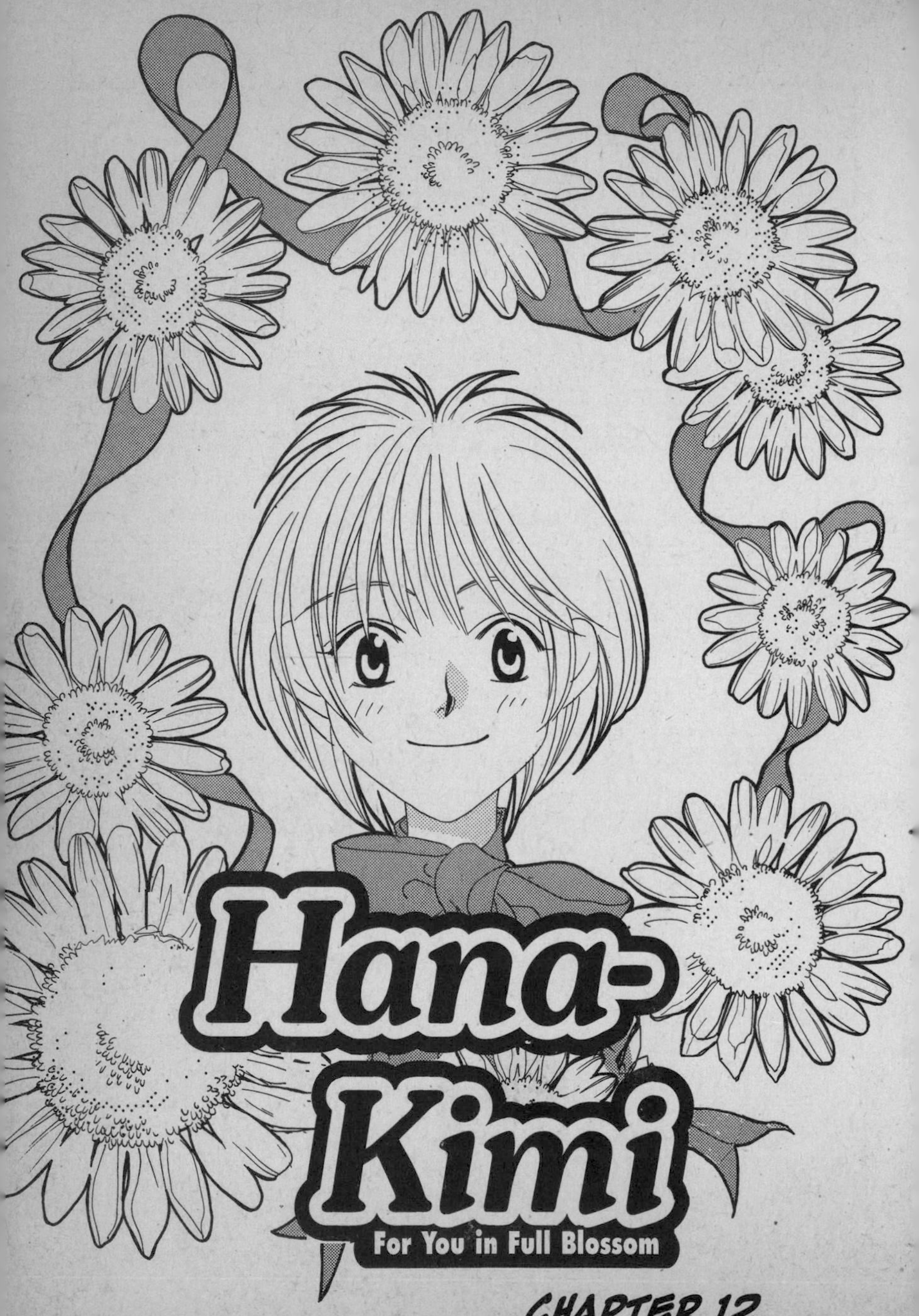
Hana-Kimi
For You in Full Blossom
CHAPTER 12

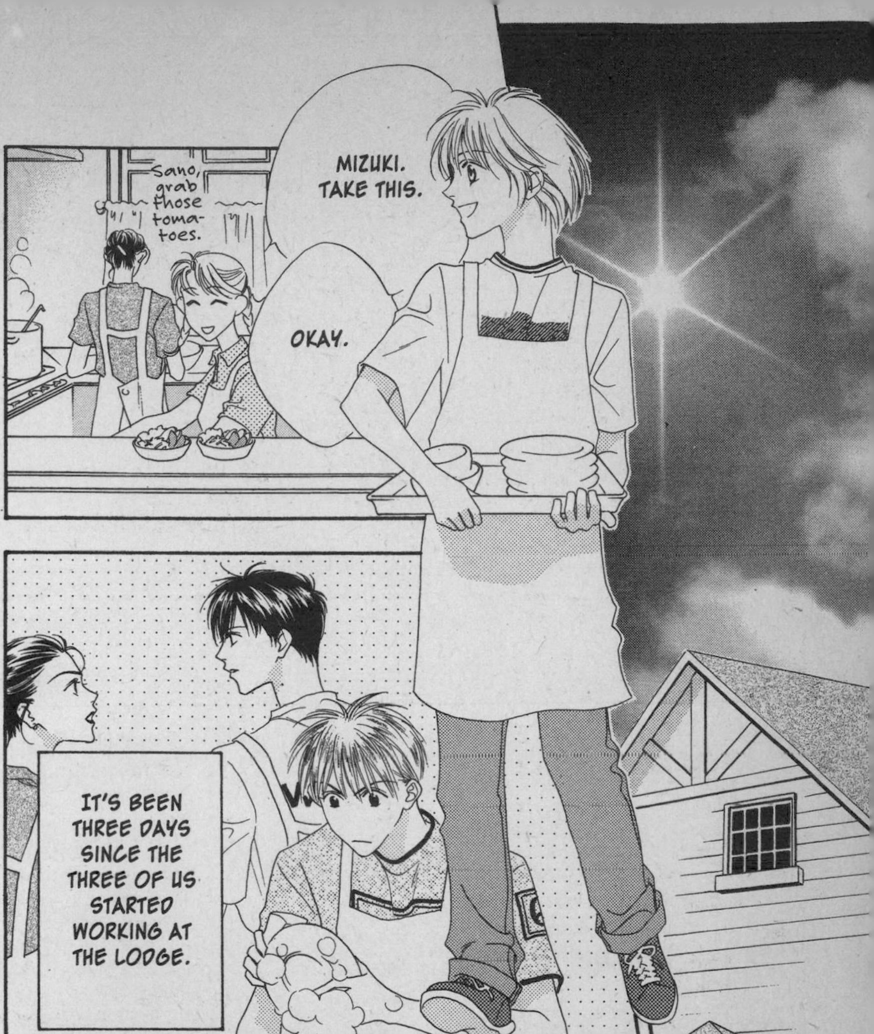
MIZUKI. TAKE THIS.
OKAY.
Sano, grab those tomatoes.
IT'S BEEN THREE DAYS SINCE THE THREE OF US STARTED WORKING AT THE LODGE.

HORROR NOVELS

THE BOOK THAT SANO WAS READING IN CHAPTER 11, "THE GREAT GOD PAN," IS ACTUALLY A CLASSIC HORROR NOVEL. JUST BECAUSE IT SAID "PAN" THAT DOESN'T MAKE IT MYTHOLOGY. (HA-HA) HE'S JUST READING IT TO KILL TIME, HE'S NOT A HORROR JUNKIE. HE'S JUST OKAY WITH SCARY STORIES. WHEN IT COMES TO FOREIGN WRITERS, HE READS KING, LOVECRAFT, AND MACHEN. I LIKE THEM, TOO! AS FAR AS JAPANESE WRITERS GO, I GUESS HE READS KOJI SUZUKI.

I heard that David Cronenberg is making a new movie. "Rasen" is gonna be made into a movie too. "Ring" was scary enough... Lately, I haven't been able to handle the scary movies.

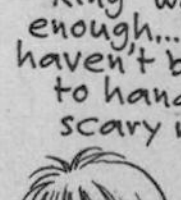

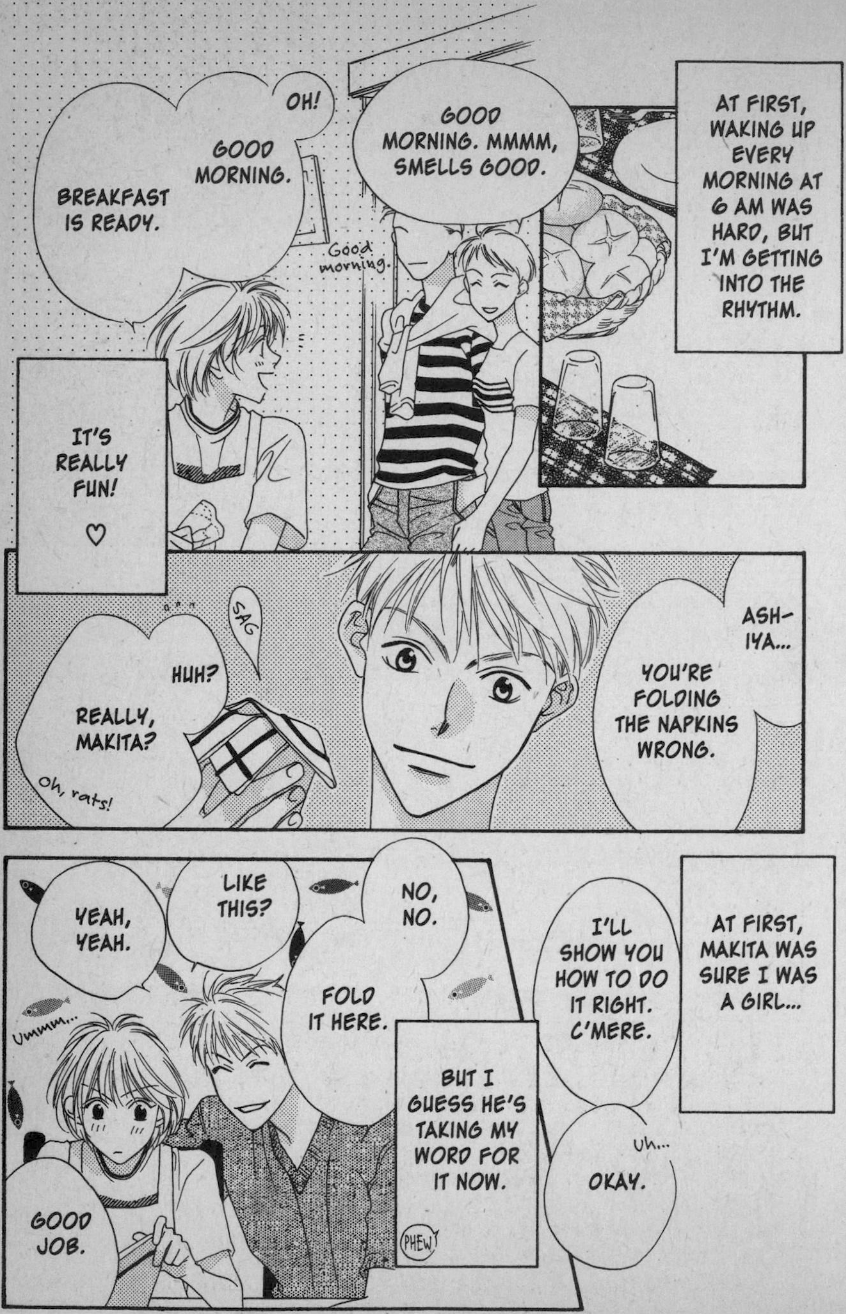
AT FIRST, WAKING UP EVERY MORNING AT 6 AM WAS HARD, BUT I'M GETTING INTO THE RHYTHM.
GOOD MORNING. MMMM, SMELLS GOOD.
Good morning.
OH!
GOOD MORNING.
BREAKFAST IS READY.
IT'S REALLY FUN! ♡
ASH-IYA...
YOU'RE FOLDING THE NAPKINS WRONG.
SAG
HUH?
REALLY, MAKITA?
oh, rats!
AT FIRST, MAKITA WAS SURE I WAS A GIRL...
I'LL SHOW YOU HOW TO DO IT RIGHT. C'MERE.
Uh...
OKAY.
NO, NO.
FOLD IT HERE.
BUT I GUESS HE'S TAKING MY WORD FOR IT NOW.
PHEW
LIKE THIS?
YEAH, YEAH.
Ummm...
GOOD JOB.

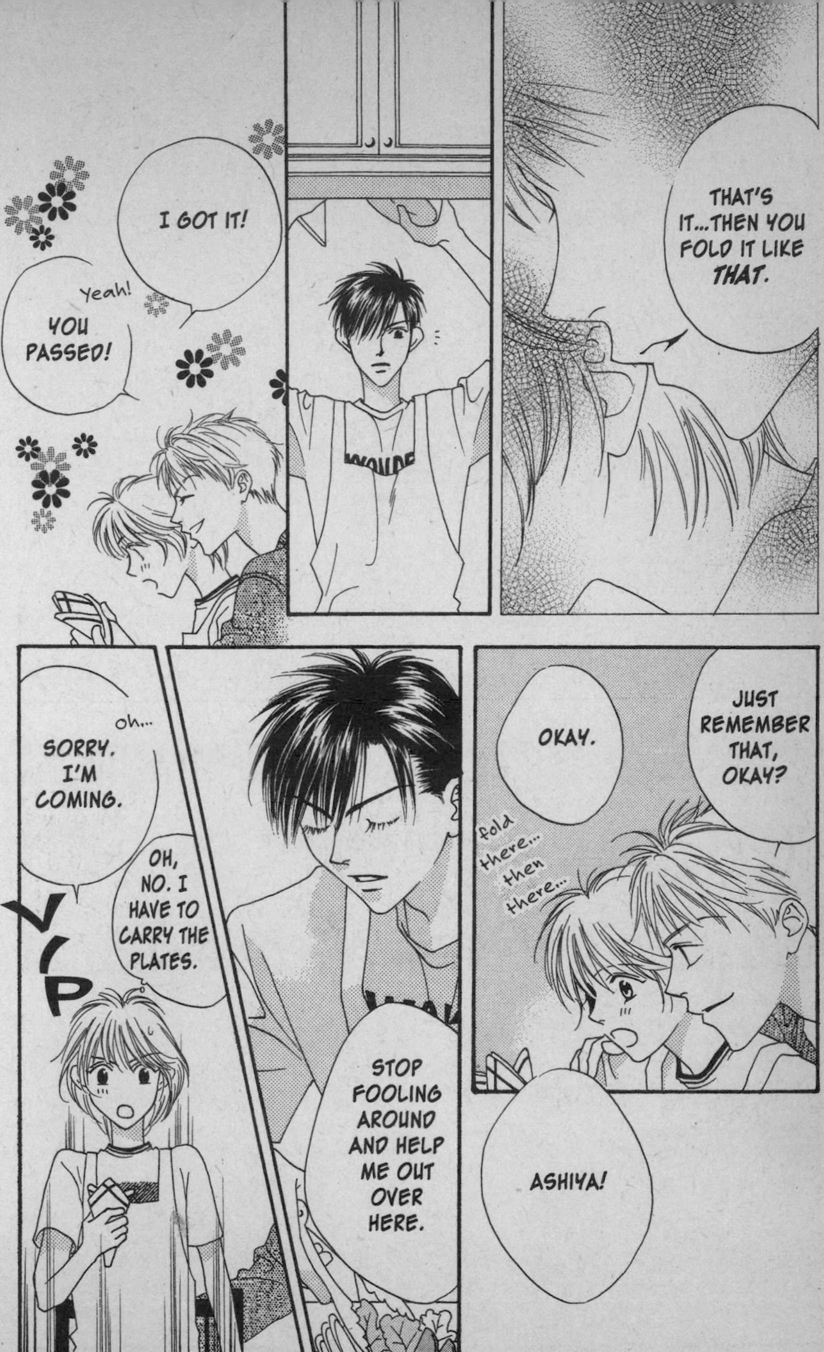
THAT'S IT...THEN YOU FOLD IT LIKE THAT.
I GOT IT!
Yeah!
YOU PASSED!
JUST REMEMBER THAT, OKAY?
OKAY.
fold there... then there...
ASHIYA!
STOP FOOLING AROUND AND HELP ME OUT OVER HERE.
oh...
SORRY. I'M COMING.
OH, NO. I HAVE TO CARRY THE PLATES.
VIP

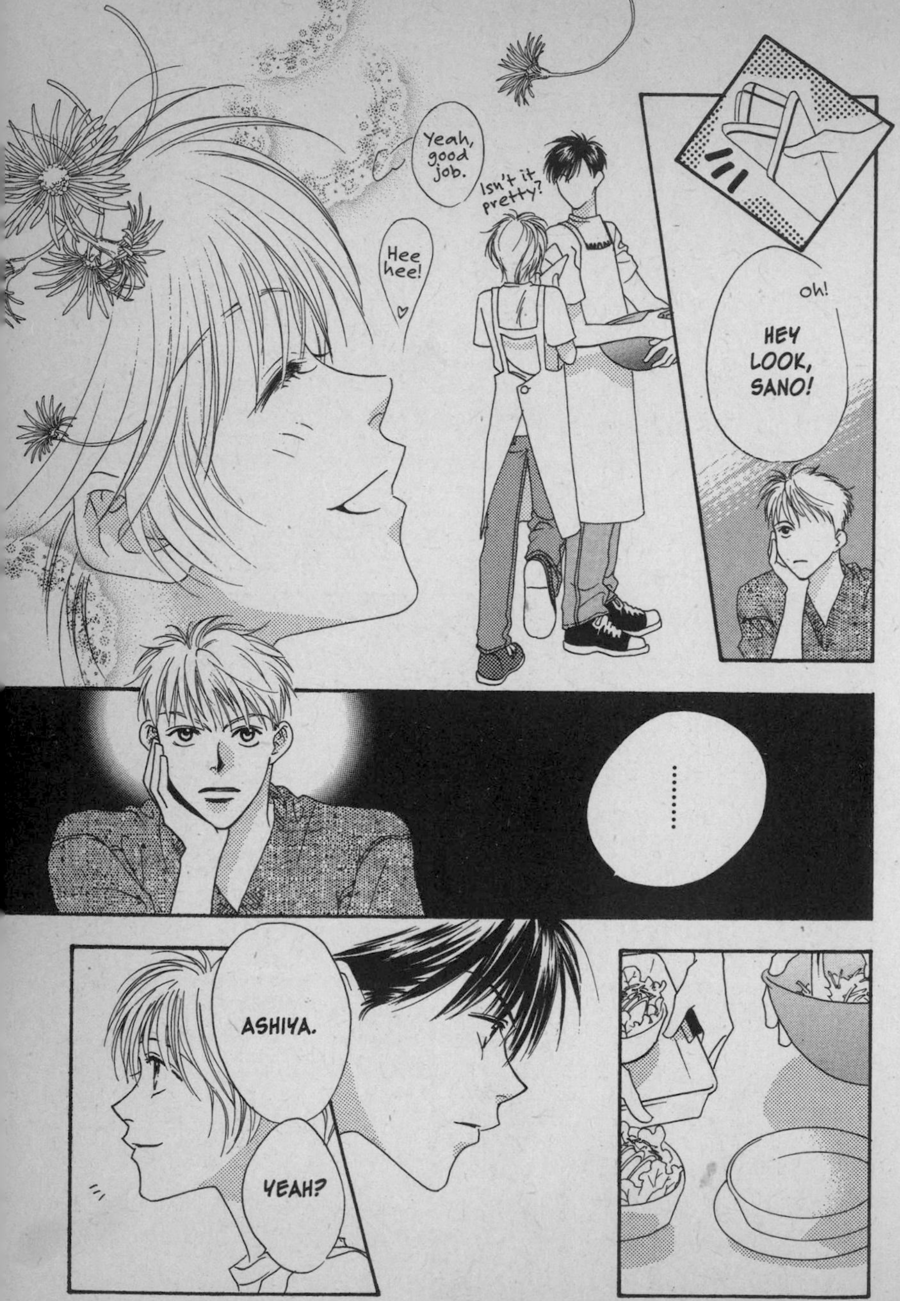
Oh!
HEY LOOK, SANO!
Isn't it pretty?
Yeah, good job.
Hee hee!
……
ASHIYA.
YEAH?

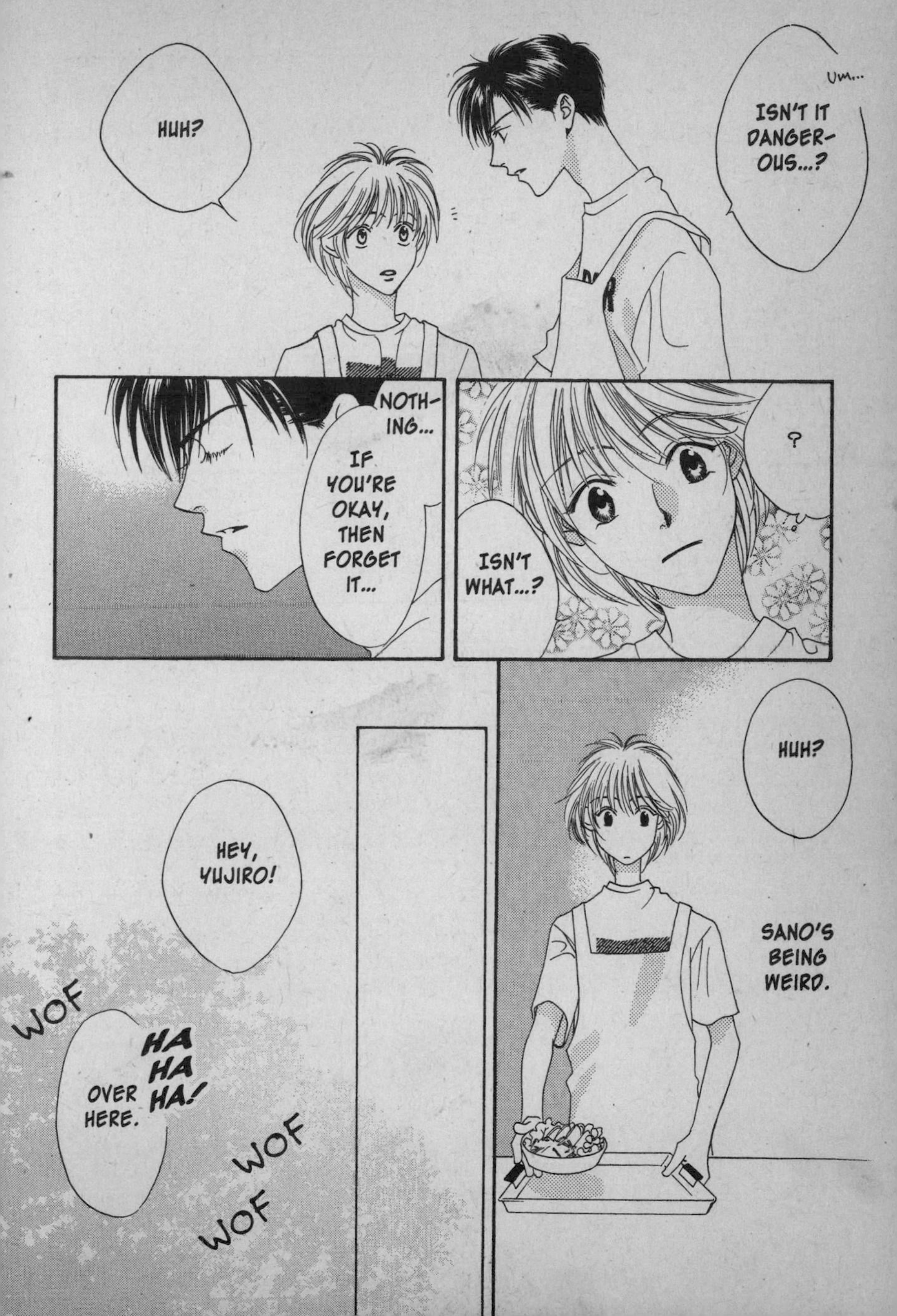
Um...
ISN'T IT DANGER-OUS...?
HUH?
?
ISN'T WHAT...?
NOTH-ING...
IF YOU'RE OKAY, THEN FORGET IT...
HUH?
SANO'S BEING WEIRD.
HEY, YUJIRO!
WOF
HA HA HA!
OVER HERE.
WOF
WOF

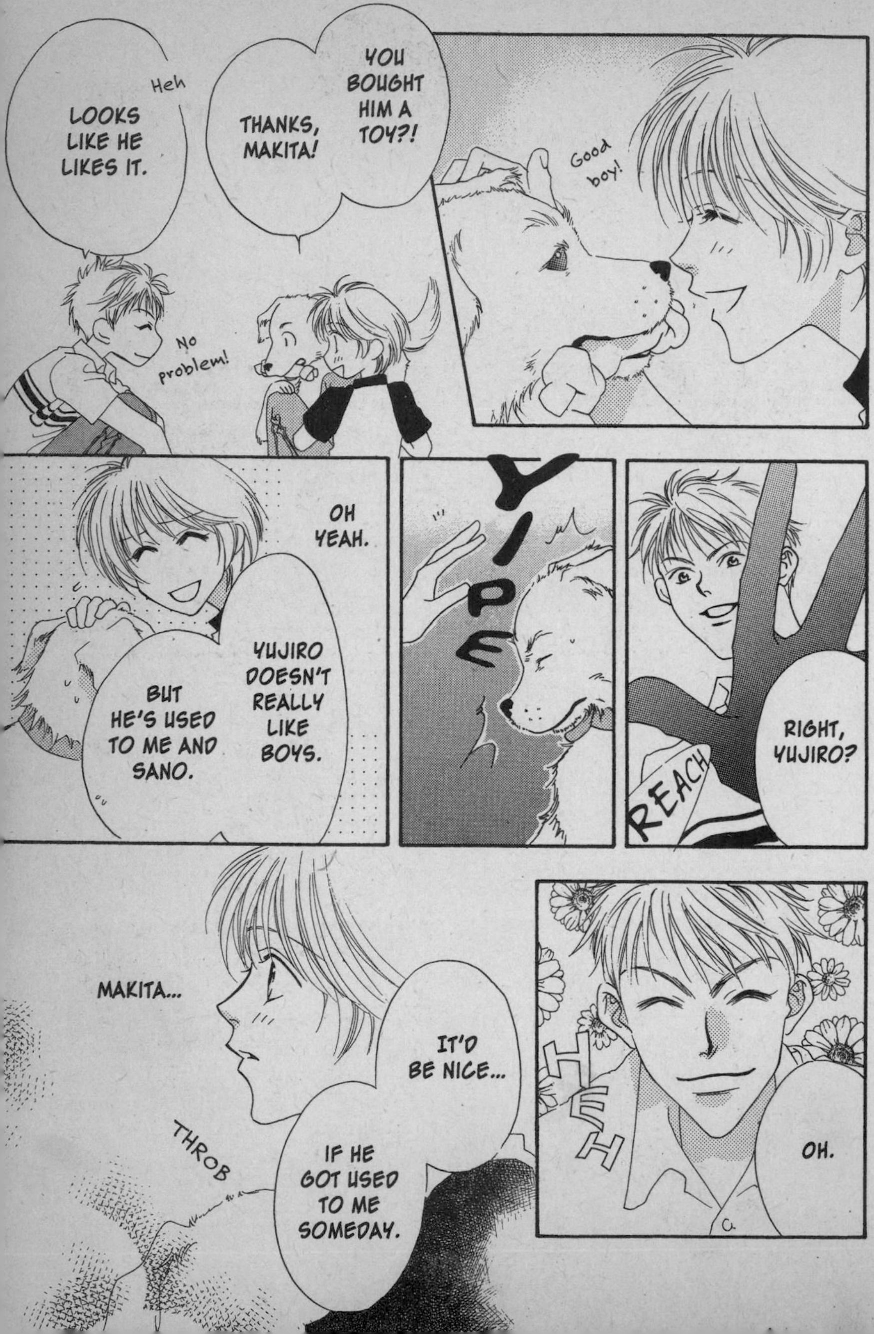
Good boy!
YOU BOUGHT HIM A TOY?!
THANKS, MAKITA!
Heh
LOOKS LIKE HE LIKES IT.
No problem!
RIGHT, YUJIRO?
REACH
YIPE
OH YEAH.
YUJIRO DOESN'T REALLY LIKE BOYS.
BUT HE'S USED TO ME AND SANO.
HEH
OH.
IT'D BE NICE...
IF HE GOT USED TO ME SOMEDAY.
MAKITA...
THROB

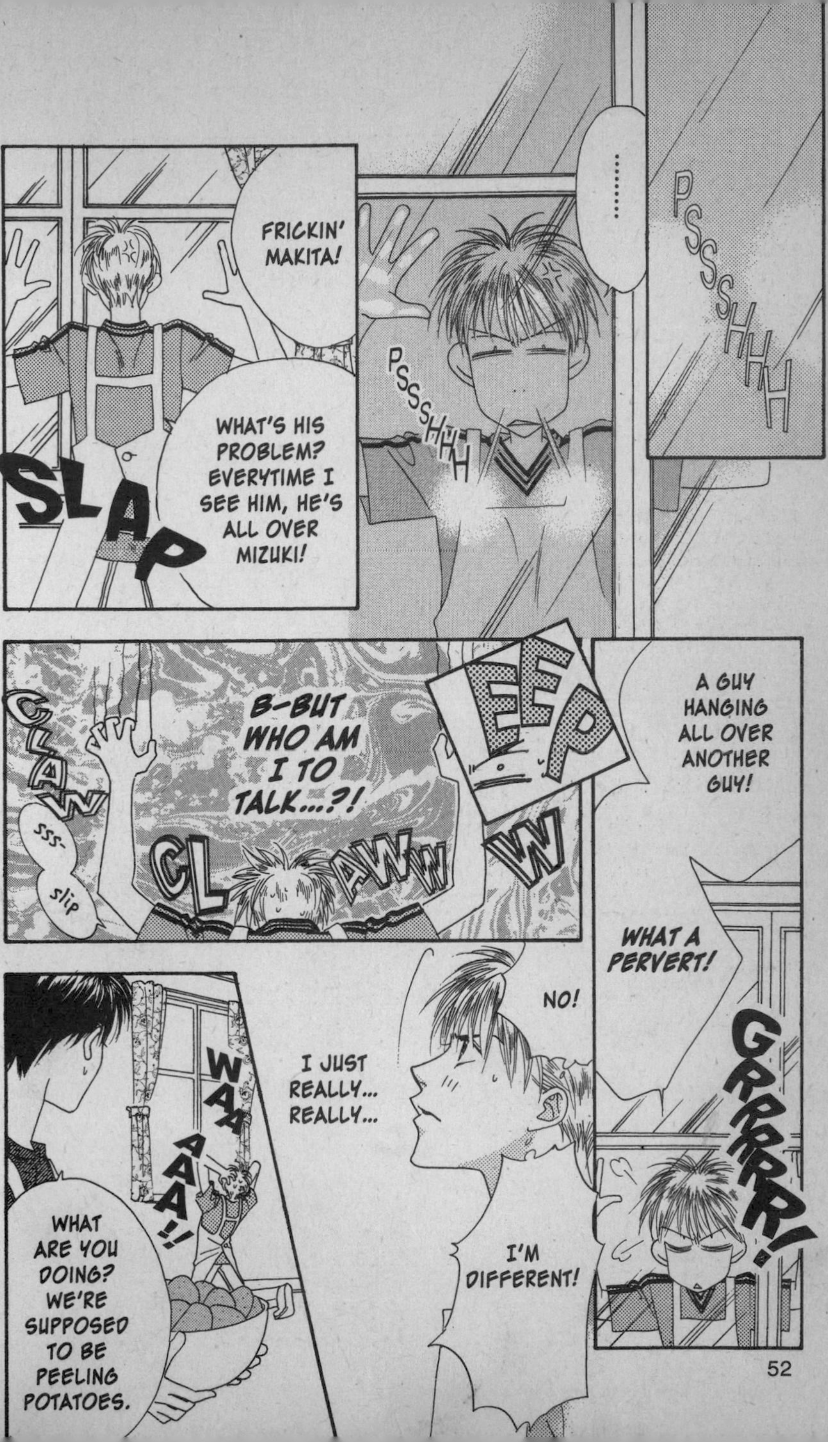
......
PSSSHHHH
PSSSHHHH
FRICKIN' MAKITA!
WHAT'S HIS PROBLEM? EVERYTIME I SEE HIM, HE'S ALL OVER MIZUKI!
SLAP
A GUY HANGING ALL OVER ANOTHER GUY!
EEP
B-BUT WHO AM I TO TALK...?!
CLAWWW
CLAW
sss-slip
WHAT A PERVERT!
GRRRRR!
NO!
I JUST REALLY... REALLY...
I'M DIFFERENT!
WAAAAA!!
WHAT ARE YOU DOING? WE'RE SUPPOSED TO BE PEELING POTATOES.

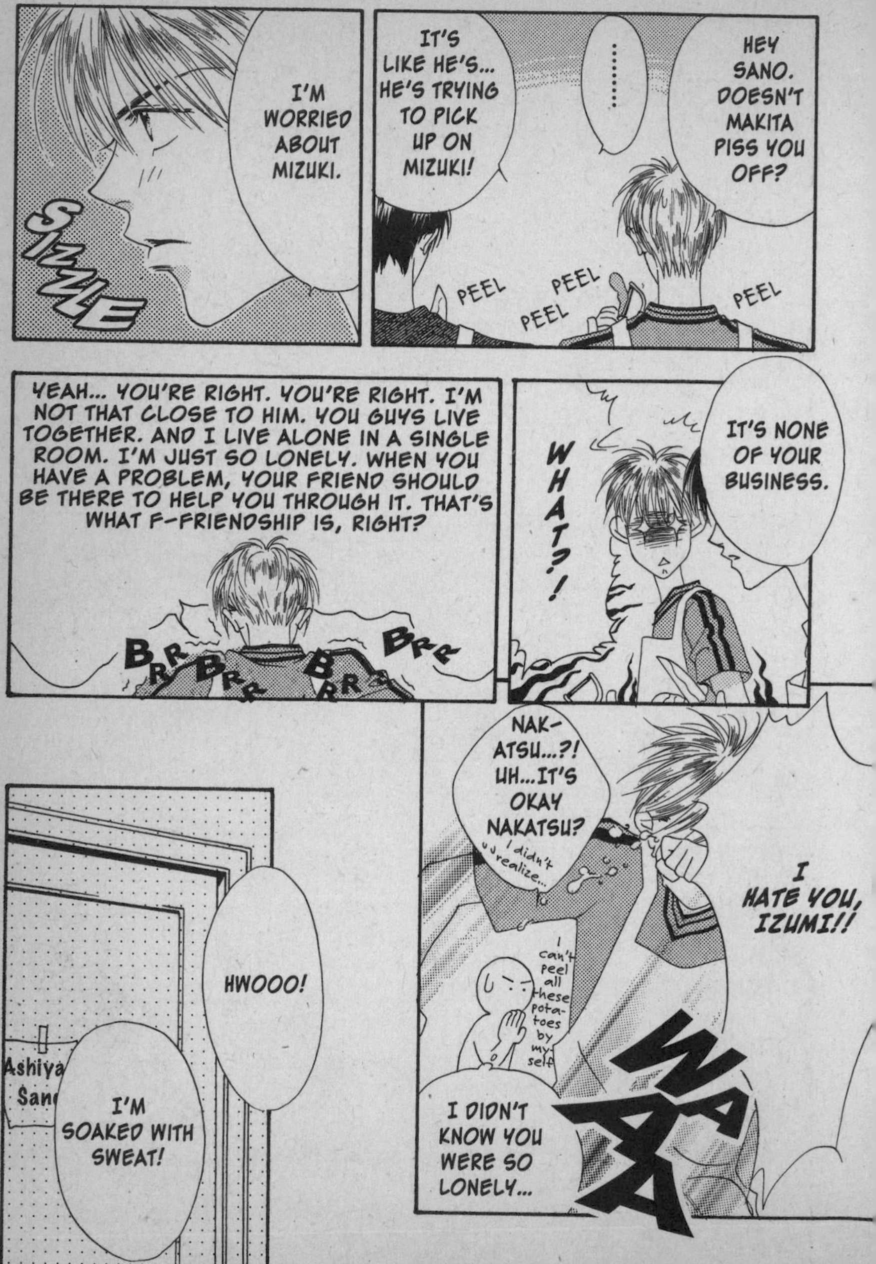

HEY SANO. DOESN'T MAKITA PISS YOU OFF?
......
IT'S LIKE HE'S... HE'S TRYING TO PICK UP ON MIZUKI!
PEEL
PEEL
PEEL
PEEL
I'M WORRIED ABOUT MIZUKI.
SIZZLE
IT'S NONE OF YOUR BUSINESS.
WHAT?!
YEAH... YOU'RE RIGHT. YOU'RE RIGHT. I'M NOT THAT CLOSE TO HIM. YOU GUYS LIVE TOGETHER. AND I LIVE ALONE IN A SINGLE ROOM. I'M JUST SO LONELY. WHEN YOU HAVE A PROBLEM, YOUR FRIEND SHOULD BE THERE TO HELP YOU THROUGH IT. THAT'S WHAT F-FRIENDSHIP IS, RIGHT?
BRR
BRR
BRR
BRR
I HATE YOU, IZUMI!!
NAKATSU...?! UH...IT'S OKAY NAKATSU?
I didn't realize...
I can't peel all these potatoes by myself
I DIDN'T KNOW YOU WERE SO LONELY...
WAAA
HWOOO!
I'M SOAKED WITH SWEAT!
Ashiya

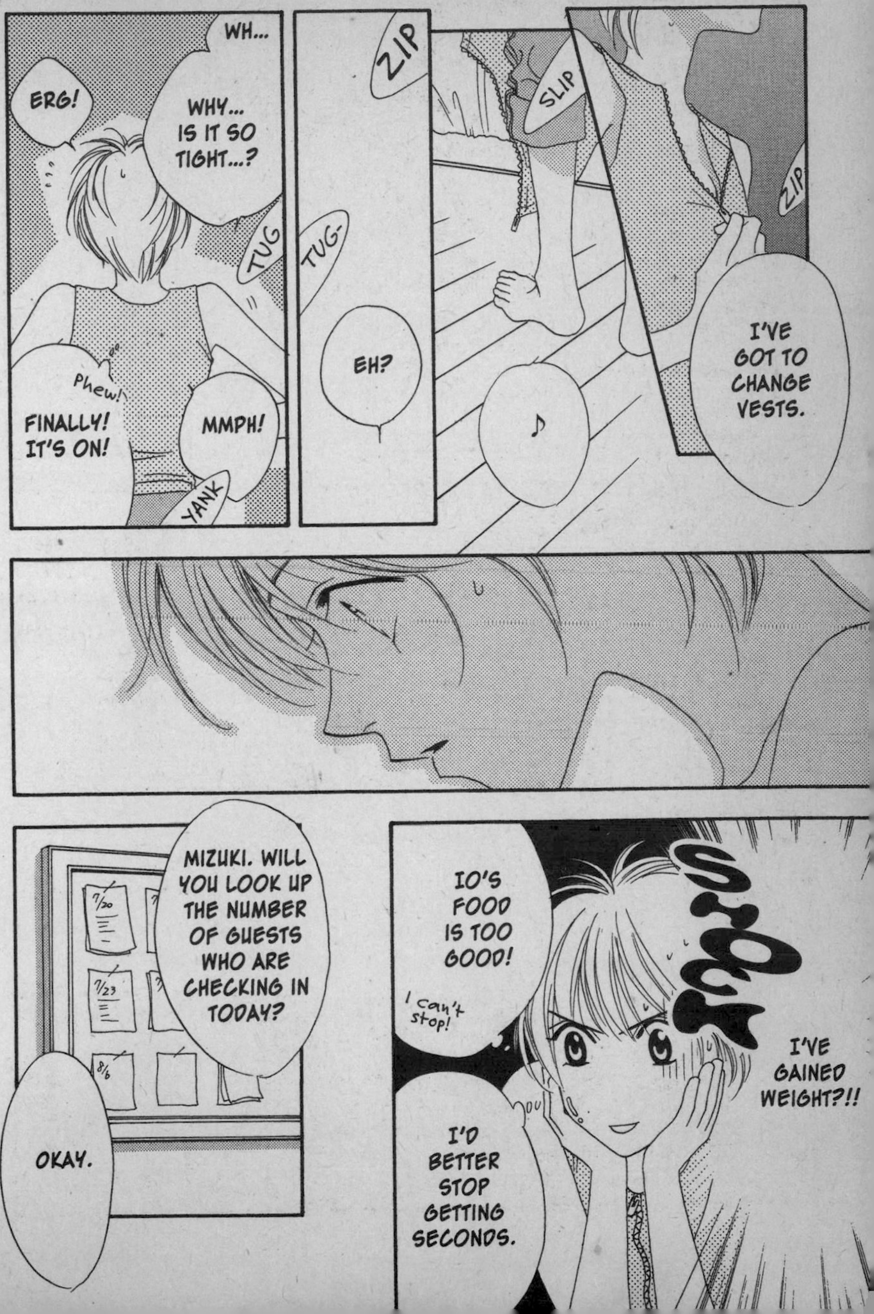
SLIP
ZIP
I'VE GOT TO CHANGE VESTS.
♪
ZIP
TUG-
EH?
WH...
WHY... IS IT SO TIGHT...?
ERG!
TUG
Phew!
MMPH!
FINALLY! IT'S ON!
YANK
I'VE GAINED WEIGHT?!!
IO'S FOOD IS TOO GOOD!
I can't stop!
I'D BETTER STOP GETTING SECONDS.
MIZUKI. WILL YOU LOOK UP THE NUMBER OF GUESTS WHO ARE CHECKING IN TODAY?
OKAY.

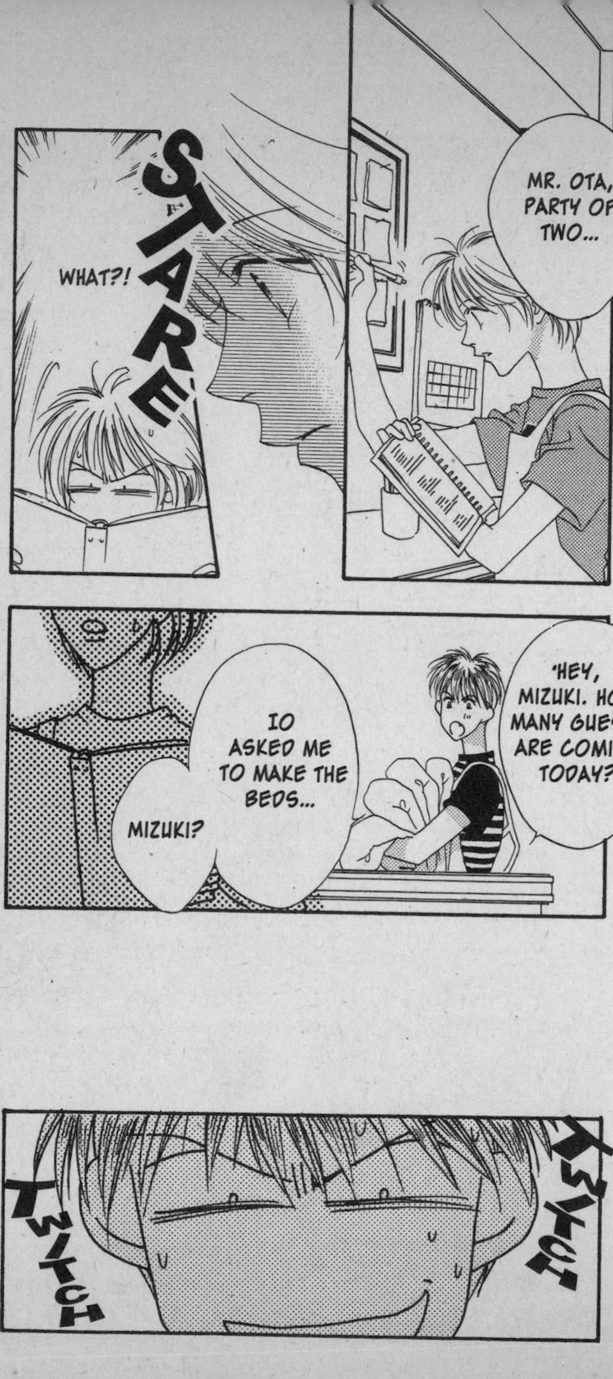
MR. OTA, PARTY OF TWO...
STARE
WHAT?!
'HEY, MIZUKI. HOW MANY GUESTS ARE COMING TODAY?
IO ASKED ME TO MAKE THE BEDS...
MIZUKI?
TWITCH
TWITCH

WHISPERED SECRETS

IZUMI SANO

BIRTHDAY: DECEMBER 24TH
AGE: 17
BLOOD TYPE: O
SIGN: CAPRICORN
HEIGHT: 180CM
FAVORITE FOODS: BOILED FISH, TEMPURA, ODEN
FAVORITE MUSICIANS: NONE IN PARTICULAR
FAVORITE MOVIES: STAR TREK SERIES, BLADE RUNNER, DEAD POETS SOCIETY
FAVORITE BRANDS: NONE IN PARTICULAR, BUT HE LIKES NIKE.
FAVORITE SPORT: HIGH JUMP
FAVORITE ANIMAL: PROBABLY DOGS
FOODS HE HATES: SWEETS (EVEN THE SMELL MAKES HIM SICK)
FLOWER: CALLA LILY

He likes baths just like Shizuka from Doraemon.

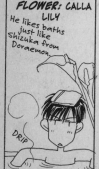

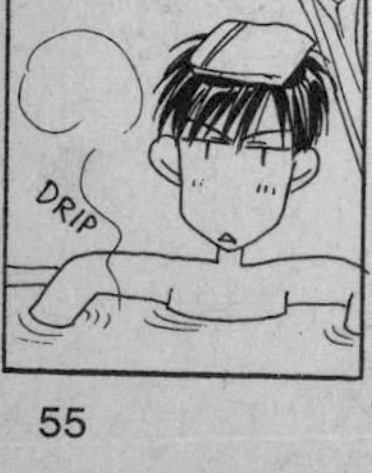
DRIP

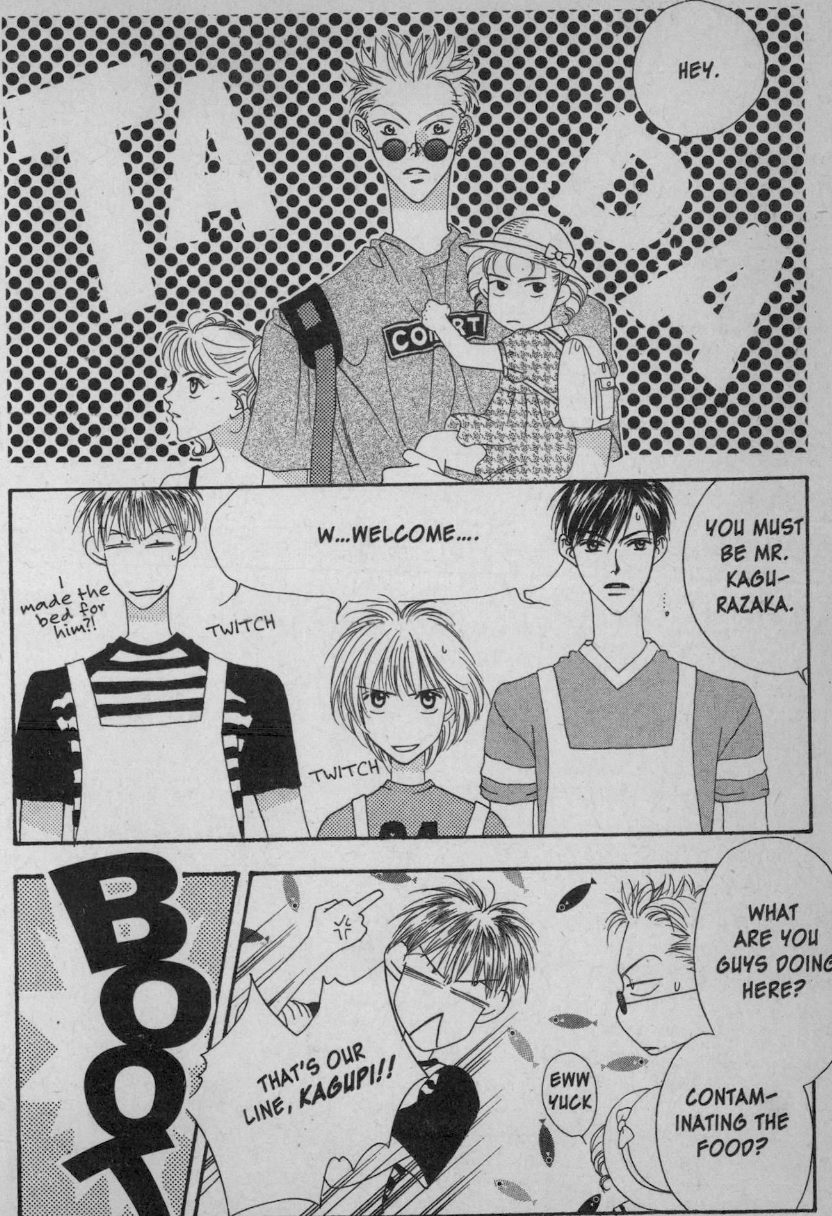
HEY.
TADA
YOU MUST BE MR. KAGU-RAZAKA.
...
W...WELCOME....
TWITCH
I made the bed for him?!
TWITCH
WHAT ARE YOU GUYS DOING HERE?
CONTAM-INATING THE FOOD?
EWW YUCK
THAT'S OUR LINE, KAGUPI!!
BOOT

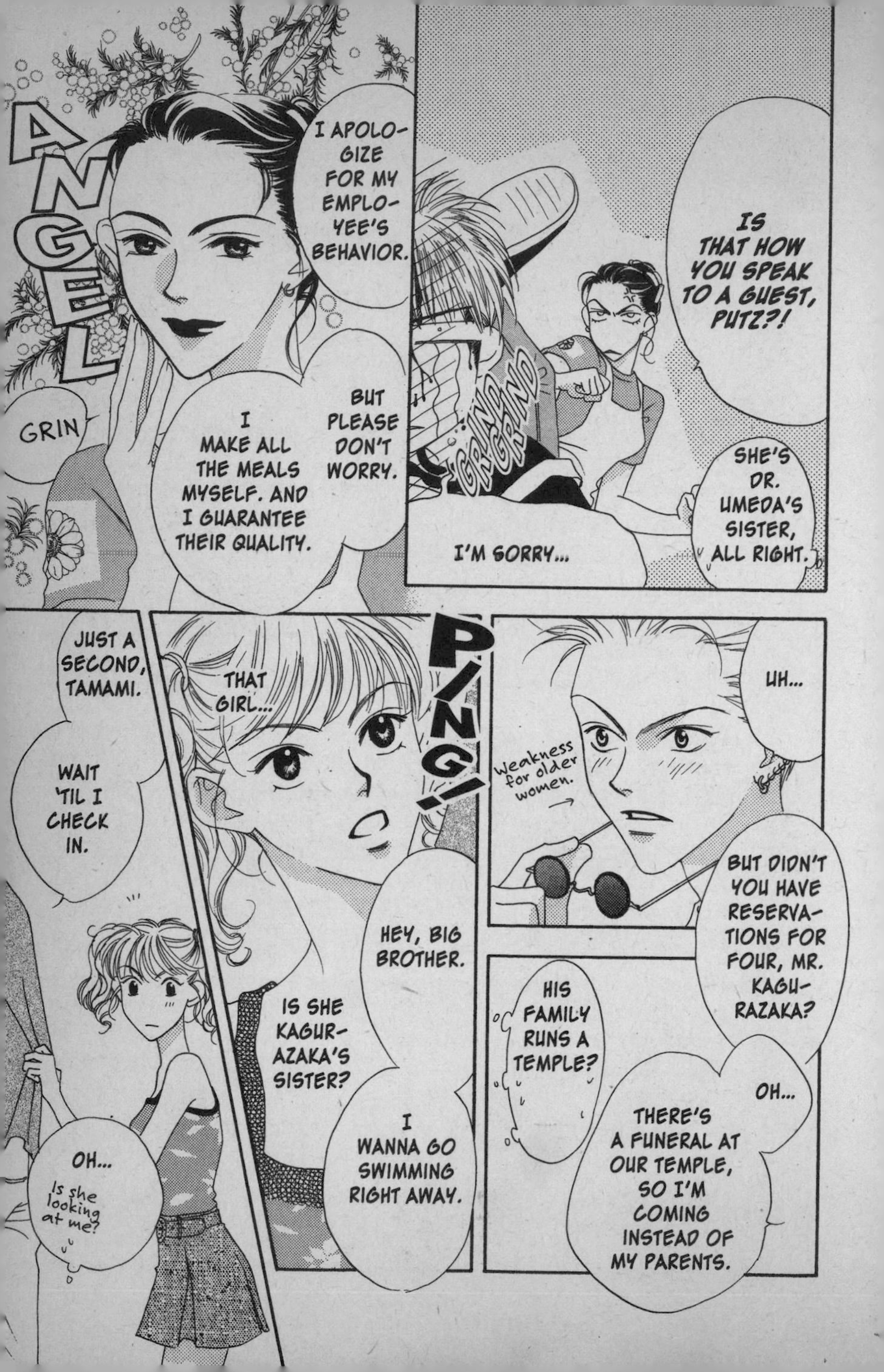
IS THAT HOW YOU SPEAK TO A GUEST, PUTZ?!
GRIND GRIND
SHE'S DR. UMEDA'S SISTER, ALL RIGHT.
I'M SORRY...
ANGEL
I APOLOGIZE FOR MY EMPLOYEE'S BEHAVIOR.
BUT PLEASE DON'T WORRY.
I MAKE ALL THE MEALS MYSELF. AND I GUARANTEE THEIR QUALITY.
GRIN
UH...
Weakness for older women.
BUT DIDN'T YOU HAVE RESERVATIONS FOR FOUR, MR. KAGURAZAKA?
OH...
THERE'S A FUNERAL AT OUR TEMPLE, SO I'M COMING INSTEAD OF MY PARENTS.
HIS FAMILY RUNS A TEMPLE?
PING!!
THAT GIRL...
HEY, BIG BROTHER.
IS SHE KAGURAZAKA'S SISTER?
I WANNA GO SWIMMING RIGHT AWAY.
JUST A SECOND, TAMAMI.
WAIT 'TIL I CHECK IN.
OH...
Is she looking at me?

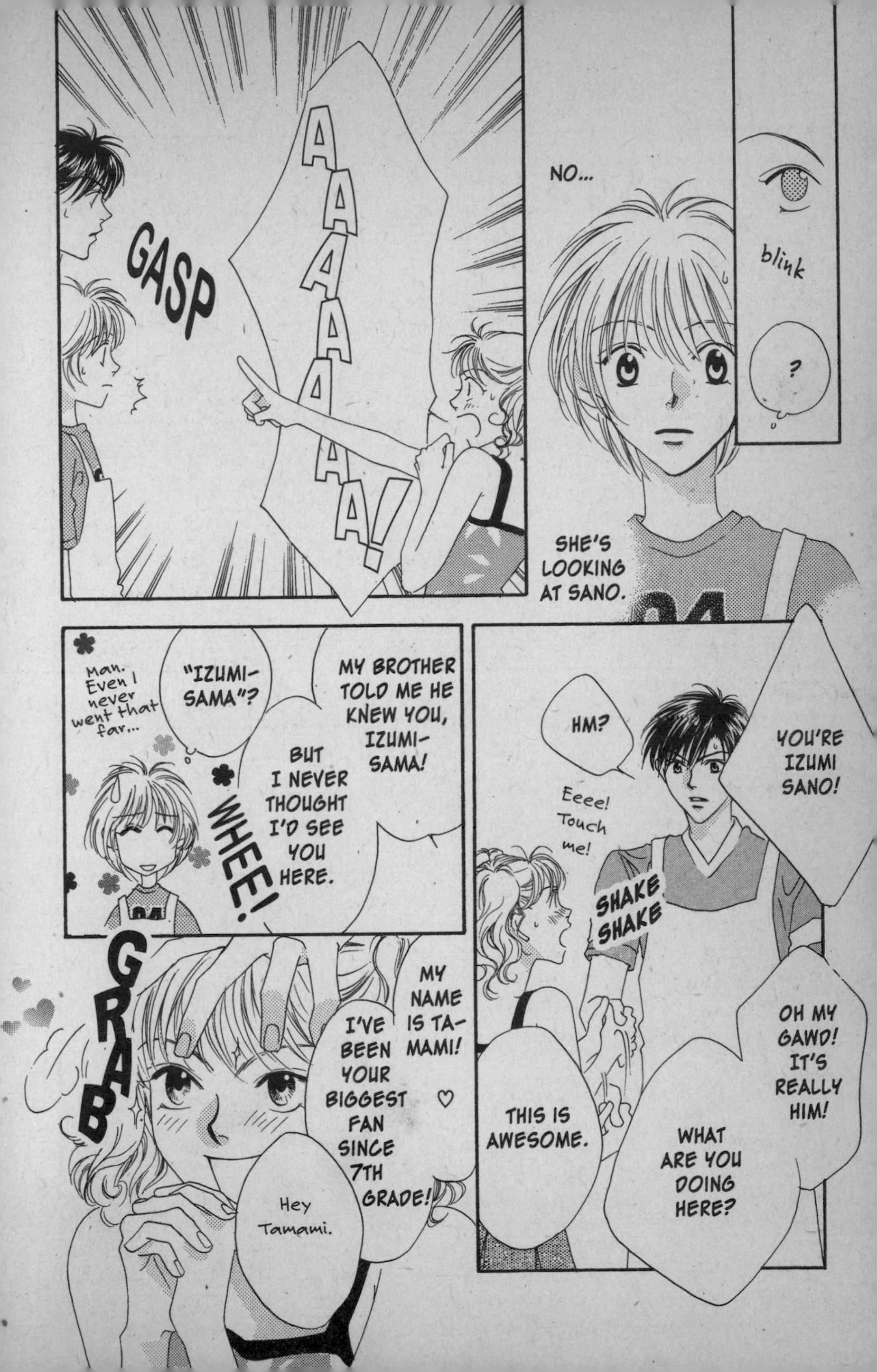
blink
?
NO...
SHE'S LOOKING AT SANO.
GASP
AAAAAAA!
YOU'RE IZUMI SANO!
HM?
Eeee! Touch me!
SHAKE SHAKE
OH MY GAWD! IT'S REALLY HIM!
WHAT ARE YOU DOING HERE?
THIS IS AWESOME.
MY BROTHER TOLD ME HE KNEW YOU, IZUMI-SAMA!
BUT I NEVER THOUGHT I'D SEE YOU HERE.
WHEEE!
"IZUMI-SAMA"?
Man. Even I never went that far...
MY NAME IS TA-MAMI!
I'VE BEEN YOUR BIGGEST FAN SINCE 7TH GRADE! ♡
GRAB
Hey Tamami.

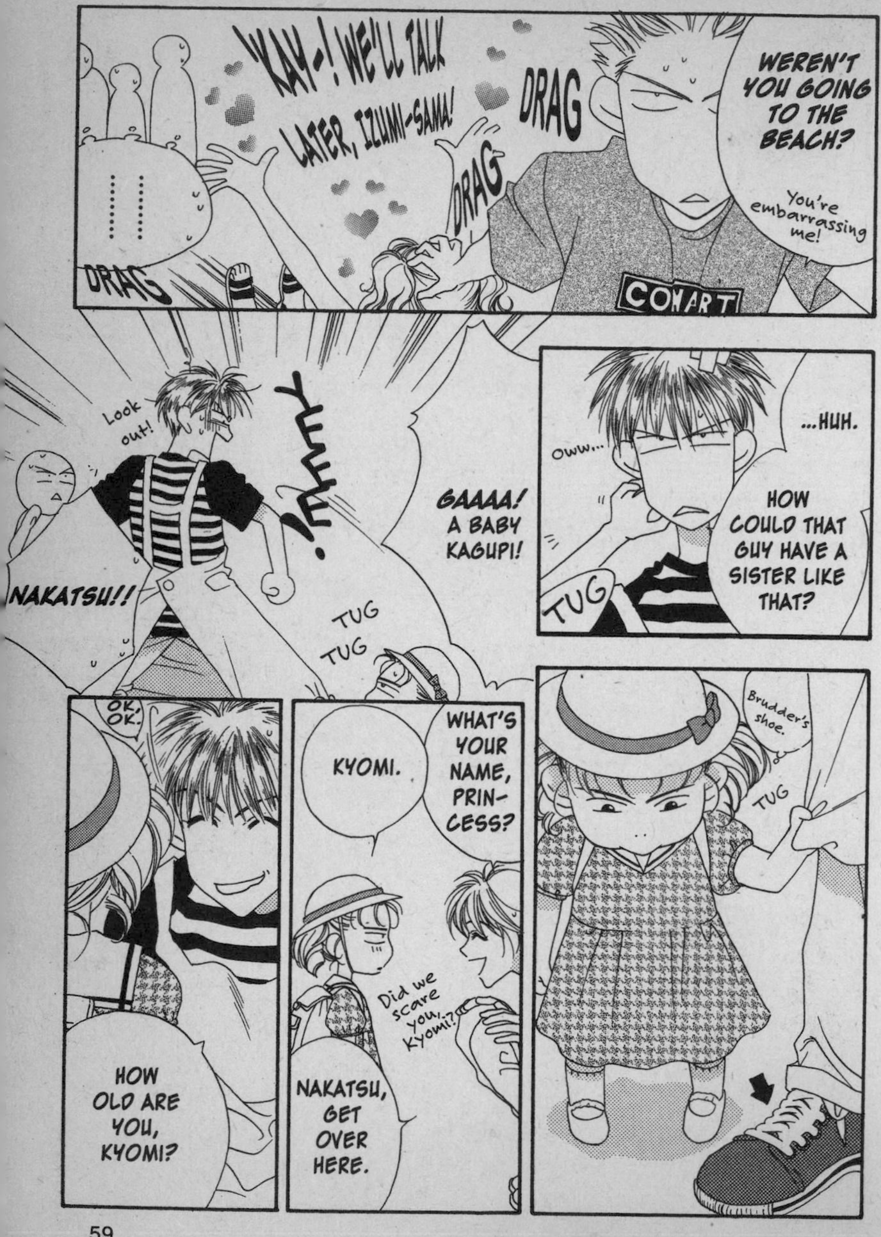
WEREN'T YOU GOING TO THE BEACH?
You're embarrassing me!
DRAG
DRAG
'KAY-! WE'LL TALK LATER, IZUMI-SAMA!
......
DRAG
...HUH.
Oww...
HOW COULD THAT GUY HAVE A SISTER LIKE THAT?
TUG
GAAAA! A BABY KAGUPI!
YEEEE!
Look out!
NAKATSU!!
TUG TUG
Brudder's shoe.
TUG
WHAT'S YOUR NAME, PRINCESS?
KYOMI.
Did we scare you, Kyomi?
NAKATSU, GET OVER HERE.
OK, OK.
HOW OLD ARE YOU, KYOMI?

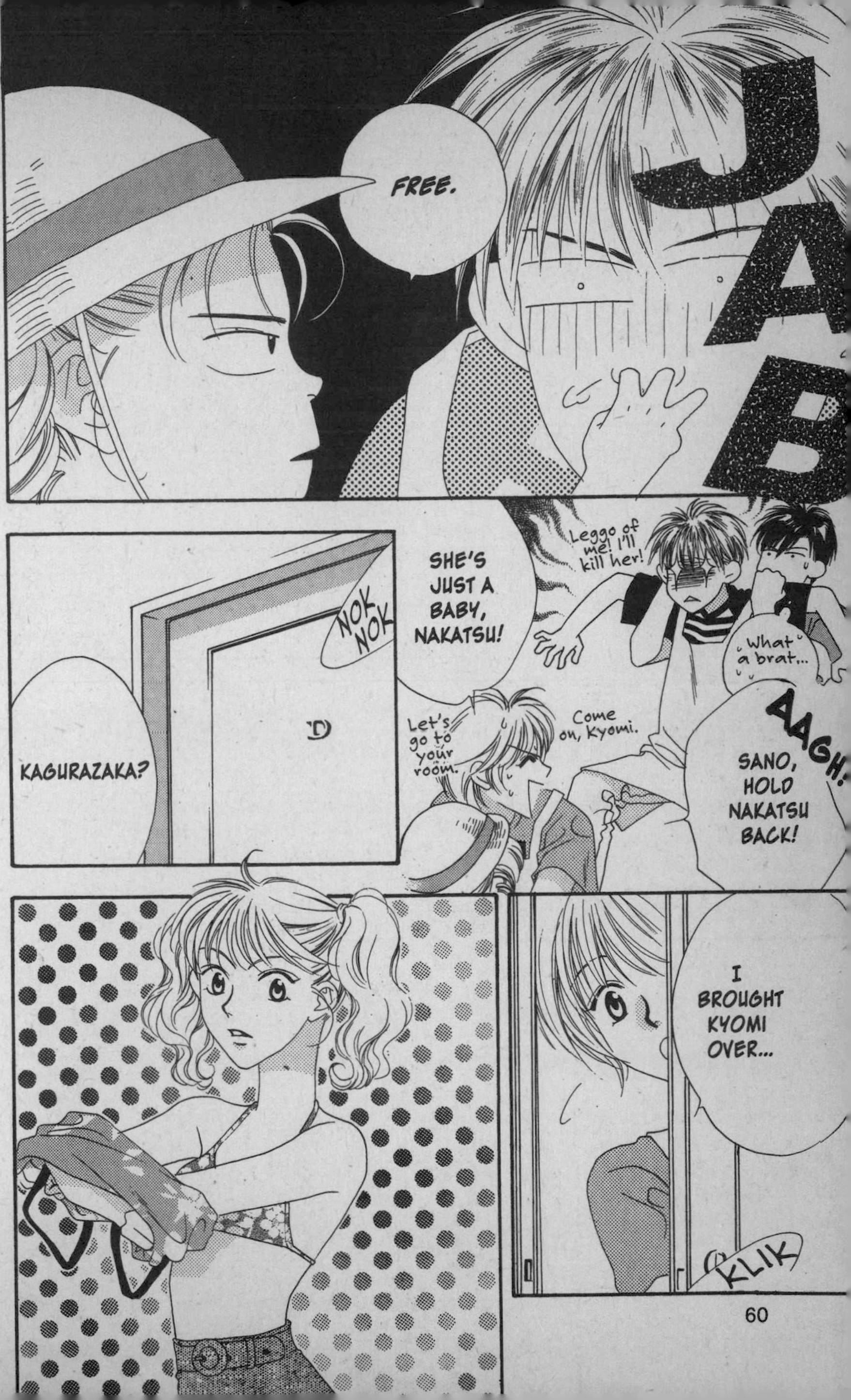
JAB
FREE.
Leggo of me! I'll kill her!
What a brat...
AAGH!
SANO, HOLD NAKATSU BACK!
SHE'S JUST A BABY, NAKATSU!
Come on, Kyomi.
Let's go to your room.
NOK NOK
KAGURAZAKA?
I BROUGHT KYOMI OVER...
KLIK

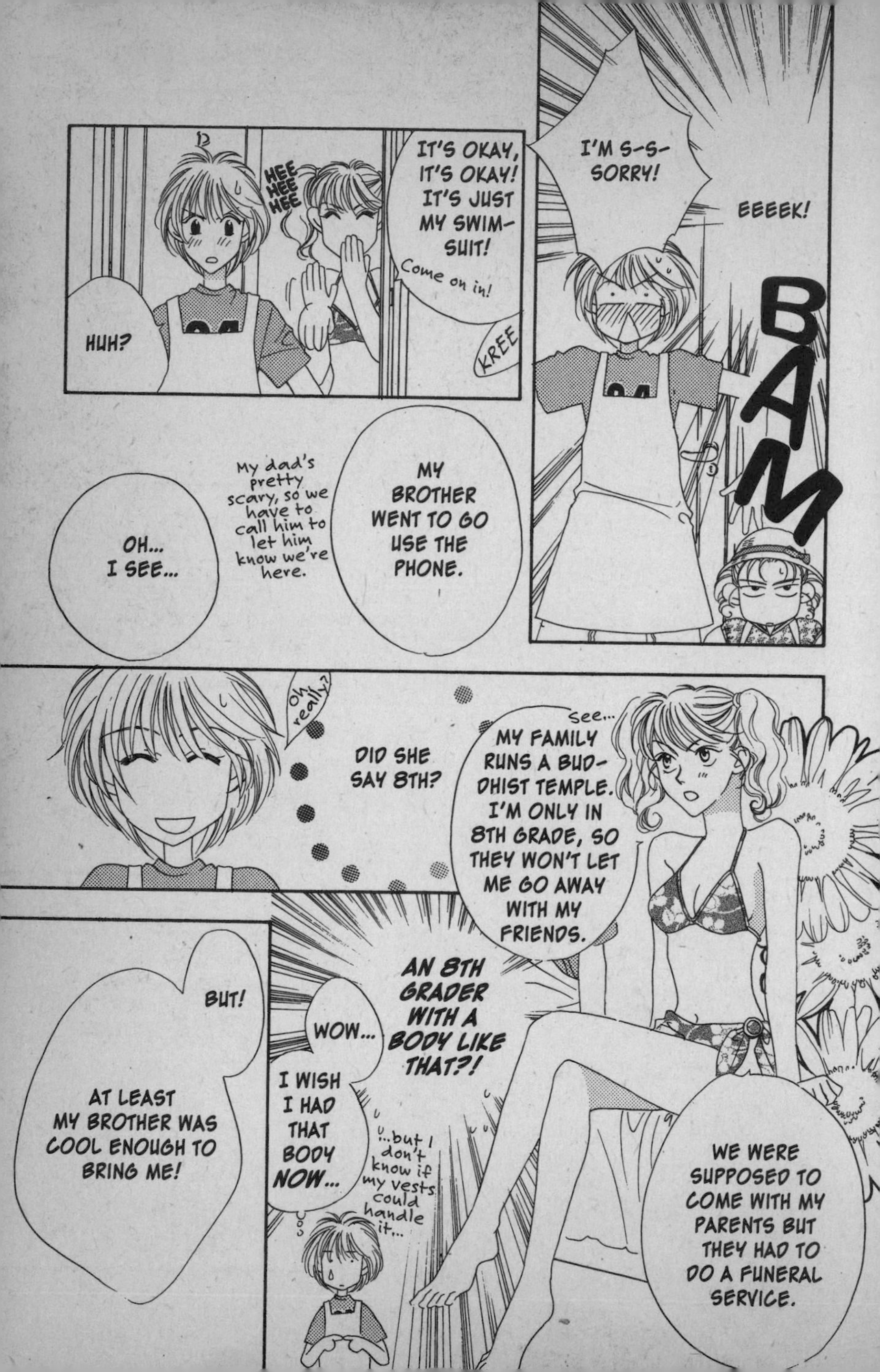
EEEEK!
I'M S-S-SORRY!
BAM
KREE
IT'S OKAY, IT'S OKAY! IT'S JUST MY SWIM-SUIT!
Come on in!
HEE HEE HEE
HUH?
MY BROTHER WENT TO GO USE THE PHONE.
My dad's pretty scary, so we have to call him to let him know we're here.
OH... I SEE...
see...
MY FAMILY RUNS A BUD-DHIST TEMPLE. I'M ONLY IN 8TH GRADE, SO THEY WON'T LET ME GO AWAY WITH MY FRIENDS.
DID SHE SAY 8TH?
Oh really?
WE WERE SUPPOSED TO COME WITH MY PARENTS BUT THEY HAD TO DO A FUNERAL SERVICE.
AN 8TH GRADER WITH A BODY LIKE THAT?!
WOW...
I WISH I HAD THAT BODY NOW...
...but I don't know if my vests could handle it...
BUT!
AT LEAST MY BROTHER WAS COOL ENOUGH TO BRING ME!

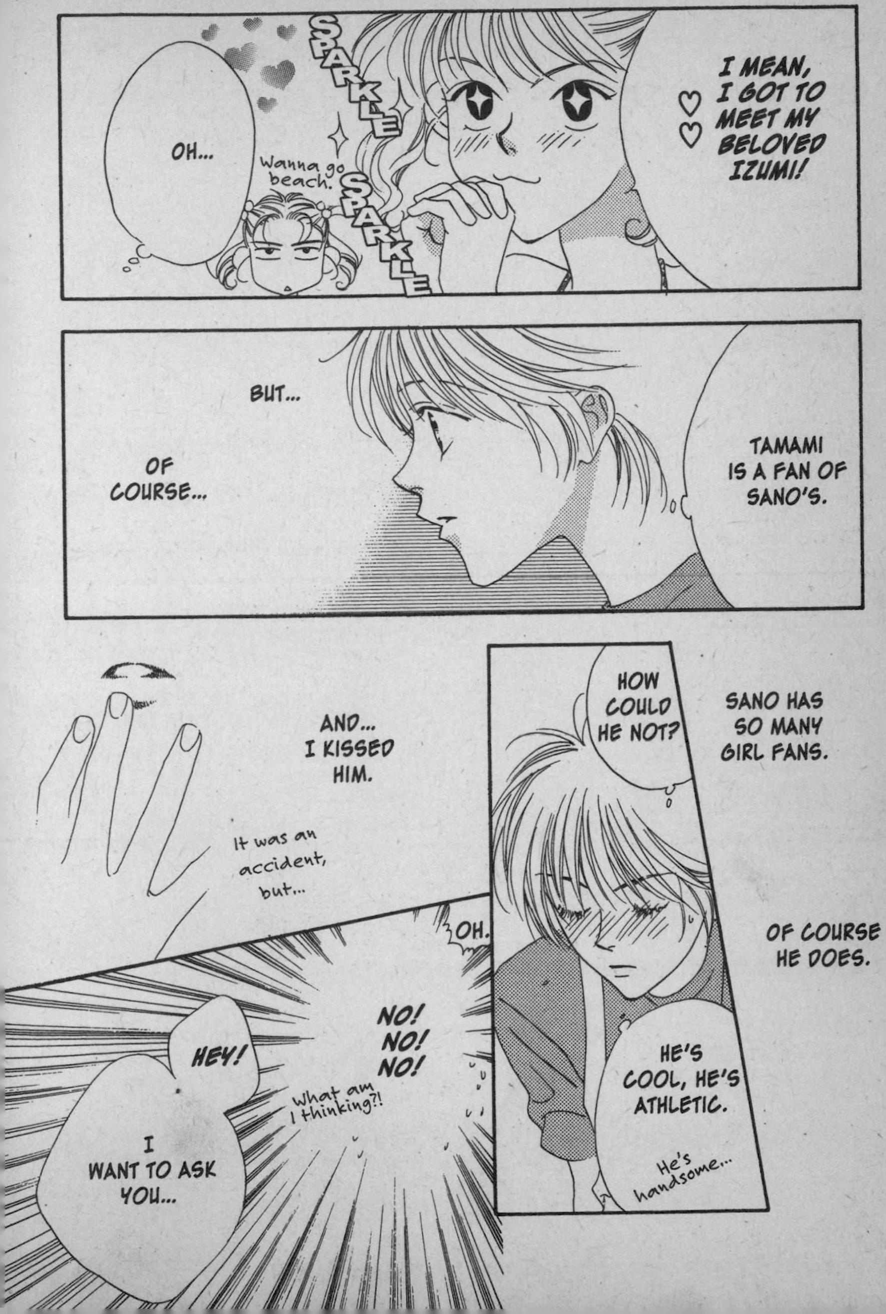
I MEAN, I GOT TO MEET MY BELOVED IZUMI! ♡ ♡
SPARKLE
SPARKLE
Wanna go beach.
OH...
TAMAMI IS A FAN OF SANO'S.
BUT...
OF COURSE...
SANO HAS SO MANY GIRL FANS.
HOW COULD HE NOT?
OF COURSE HE DOES.
HE'S COOL, HE'S ATHLETIC.
He's handsome...
AND... I KISSED HIM.
It was an accident, but...
OH.
NO! NO! NO!
What am I thinking?!
HEY!
I WANT TO ASK YOU...

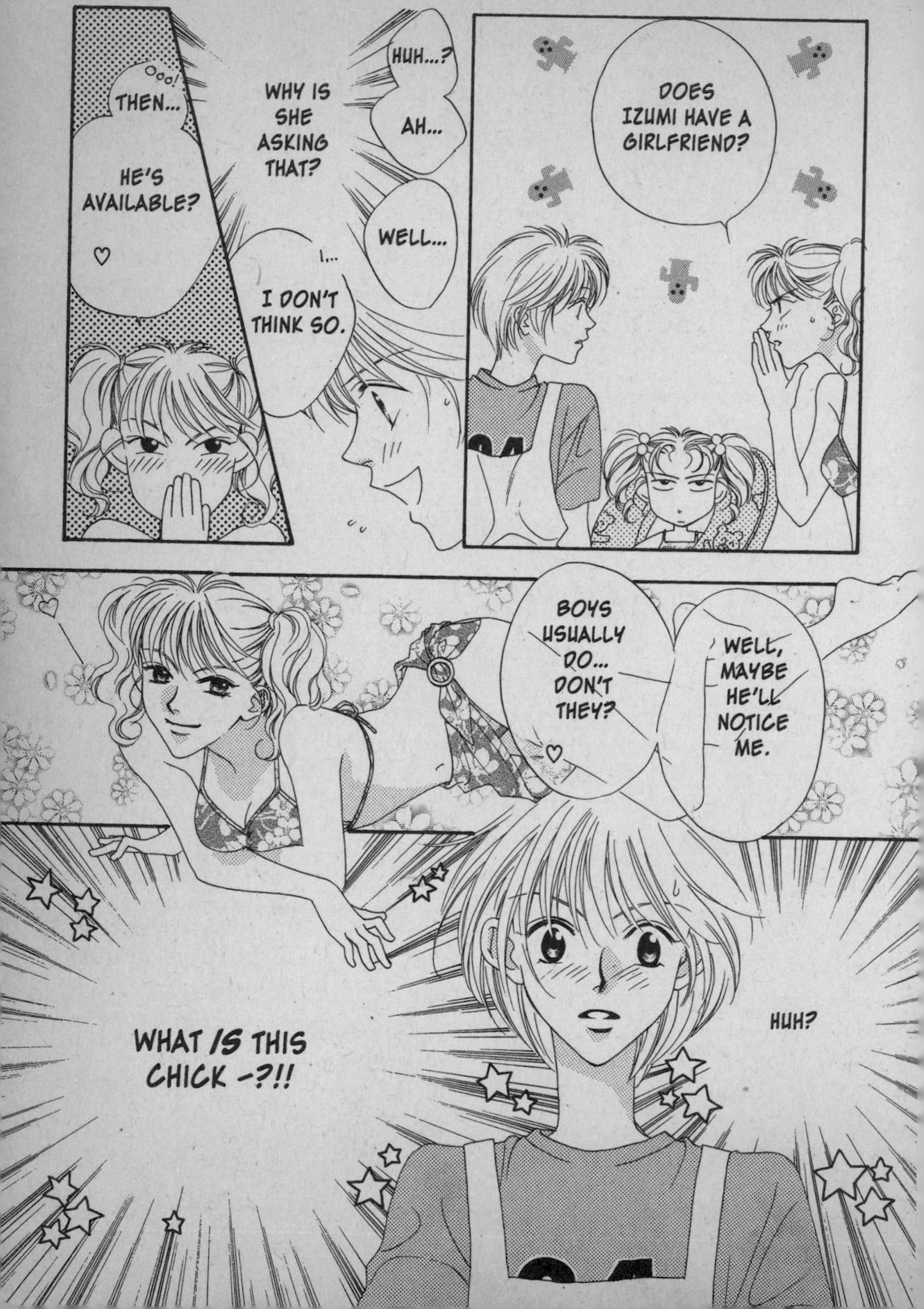
DOES IZUMI HAVE A GIRLFRIEND?
HUH...?
AH...
WELL...
I...
I DON'T THINK SO.
WHY IS SHE ASKING THAT?
OOO!
THEN...
HE'S AVAILABLE?
♡
WELL, MAYBE HE'LL NOTICE ME.
BOYS USUALLY DO... DON'T THEY?
♡
HUH?
WHAT *IS* THIS CHICK -?!!

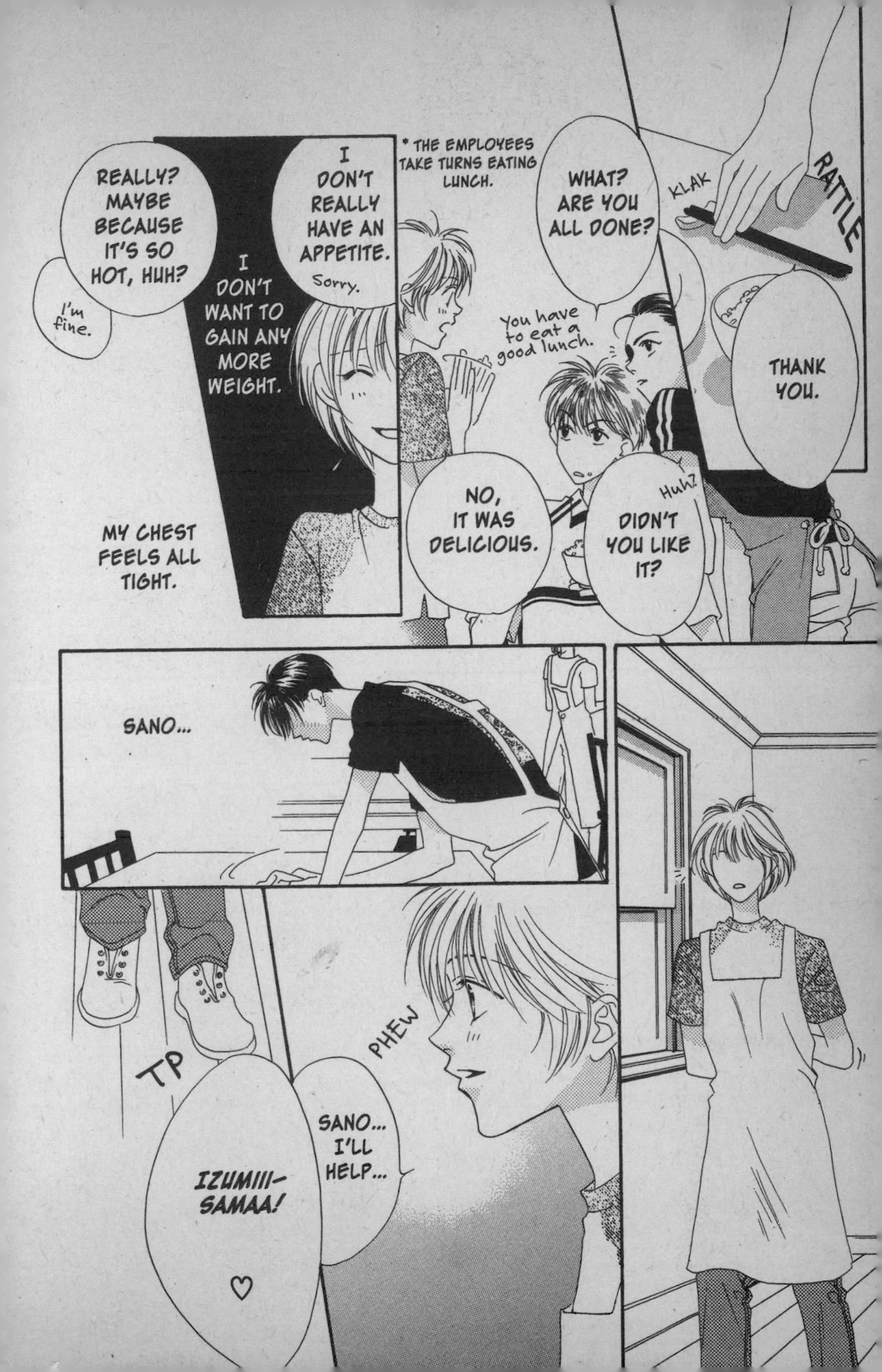
RATTLE
KLAK
THANK YOU.
WHAT? ARE YOU ALL DONE?
You have to eat a good lunch.
Huh?
DIDN'T YOU LIKE IT?
NO, IT WAS DELICIOUS.
* THE EMPLOYEES TAKE TURNS EATING LUNCH.
I DON'T REALLY HAVE AN APPETITE.
Sorry.
I DON'T WANT TO GAIN ANY MORE WEIGHT.
REALLY? MAYBE BECAUSE IT'S SO HOT, HUH?
I'm fine.
MY CHEST FEELS ALL TIGHT.
SANO...
PHEW
SANO... I'LL HELP...
TP
IZUMIII-SAMAA!
♡

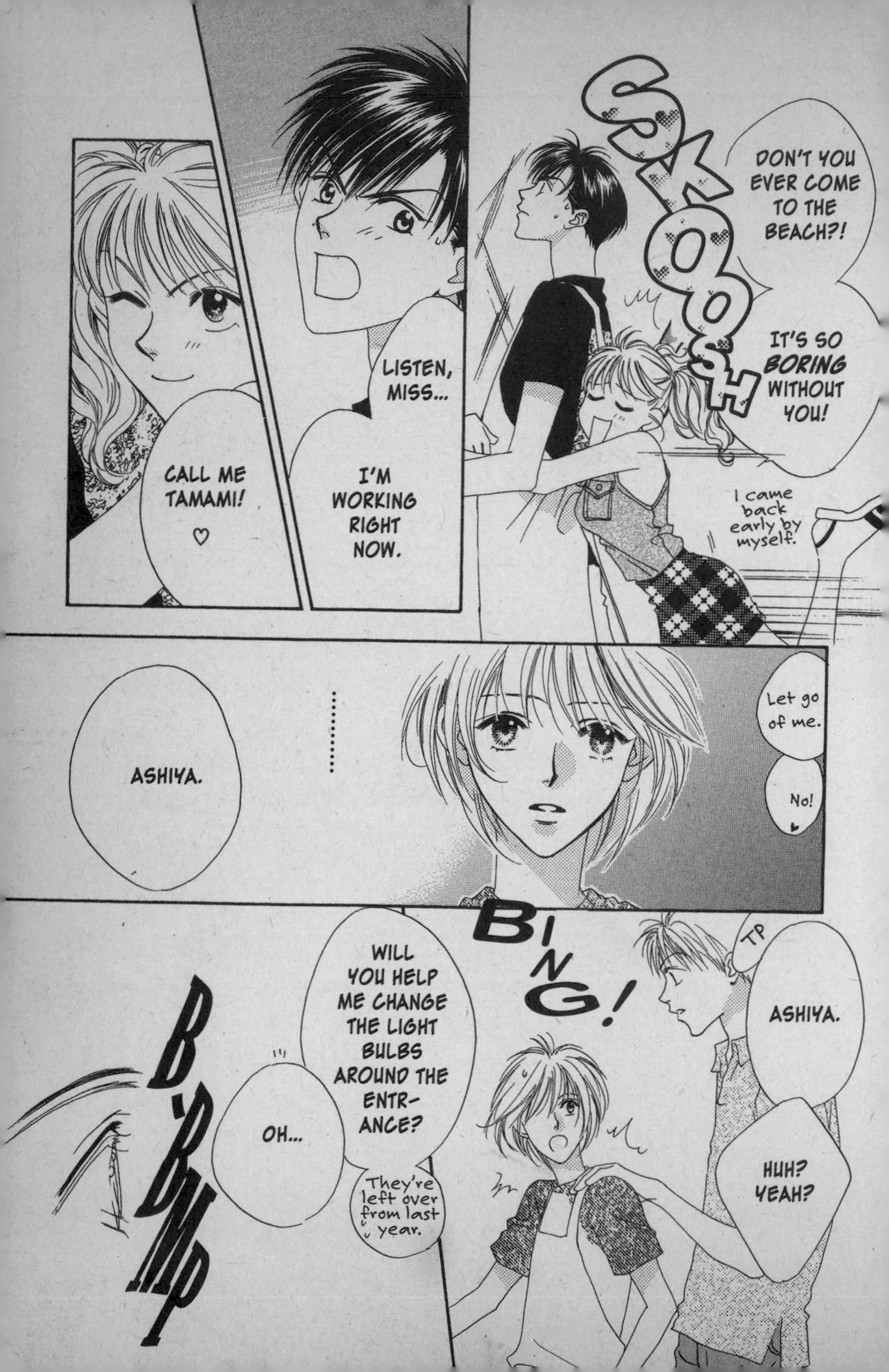
DON'T YOU EVER COME TO THE BEACH?!
SKOOSH
IT'S SO BORING WITHOUT YOU!
I came back early by myself.
LISTEN, MISS...
I'M WORKING RIGHT NOW.
CALL ME TAMAMI! ♡
Let go of me.
No!
......
ASHIYA.
TP
ASHIYA.
BING!
HUH? YEAH?
WILL YOU HELP ME CHANGE THE LIGHT BULBS AROUND THE ENTR-ANCE?
They're left over from last year.
OH...
B-BMP

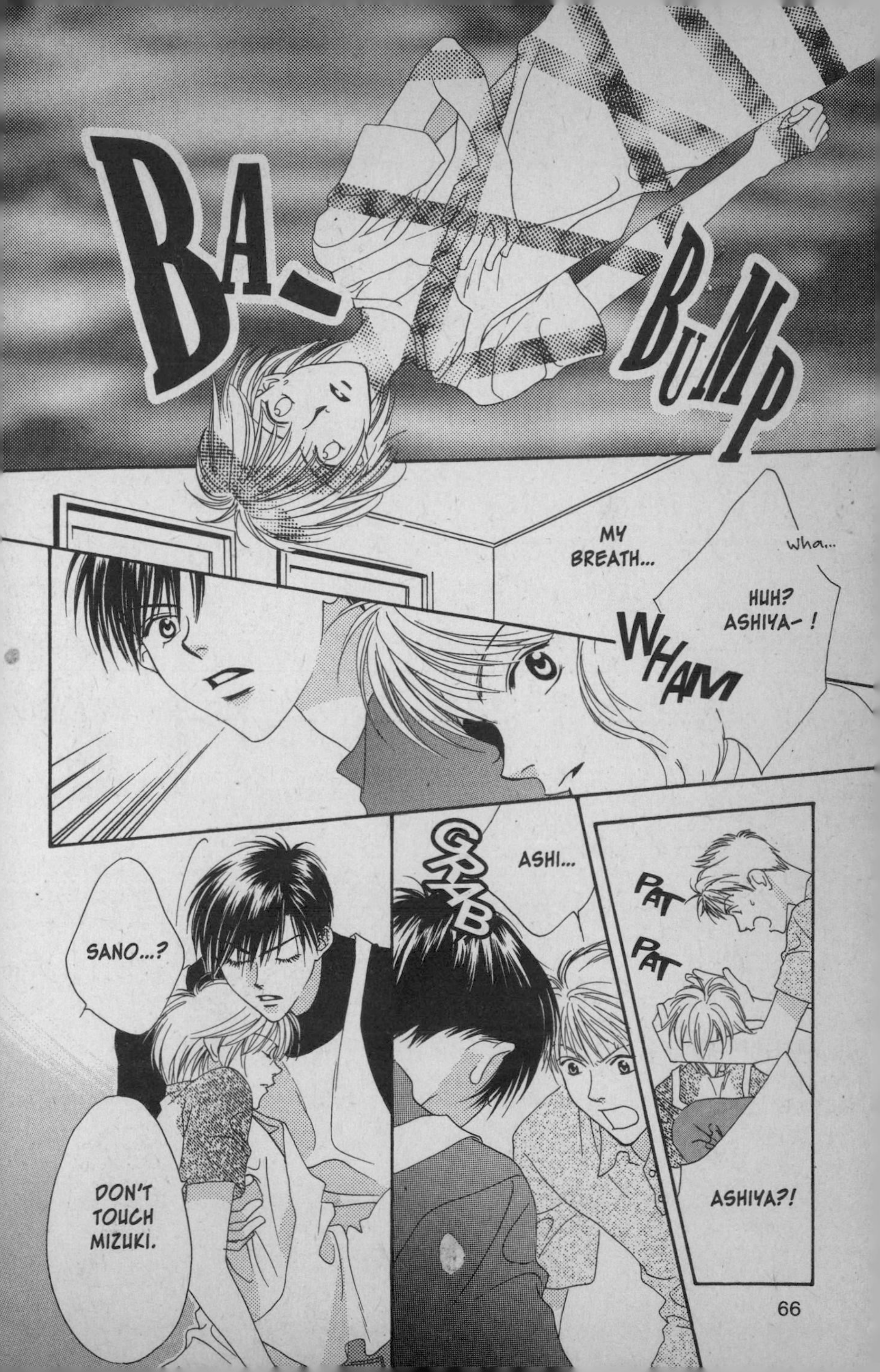
BA-BUMP
wha... HUH? ASHIYA- !
MY BREATH...
WHAM
PAT PAT
ASHIYA?!
GRAB
ASHI...
SANO...?
DON'T TOUCH MIZUKI.

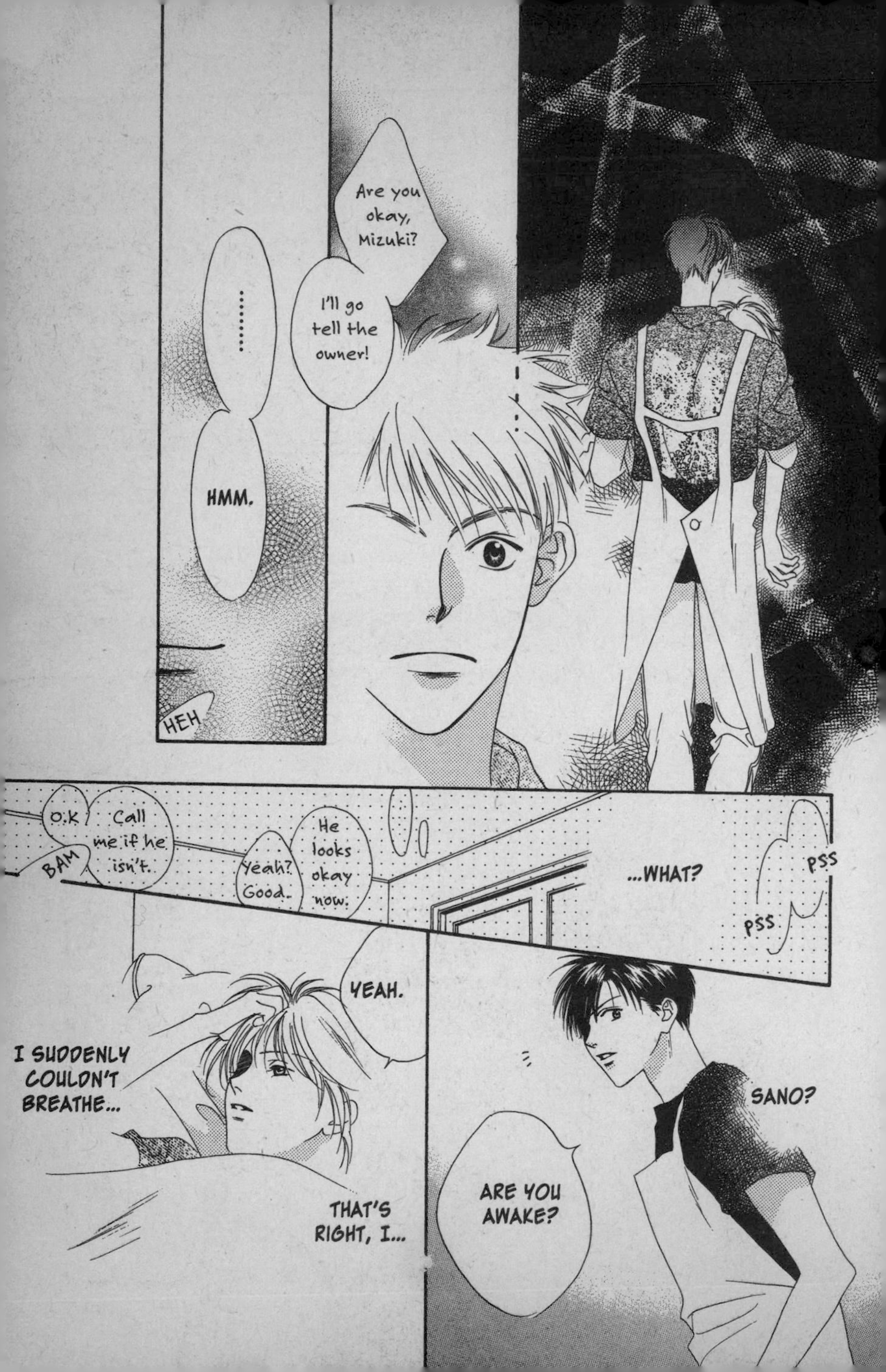
Are you okay, Mizuki?
I'll go tell the owner!
......
HMM.
HEH
PSS
PSS
...WHAT?
He looks okay now.
Yeah? Good.
Call me if he isn't.
O.K
BAM
SANO?
ARE YOU AWAKE?
YEAH.
THAT'S RIGHT, I...
I SUDDENLY COULDN'T BREATHE...

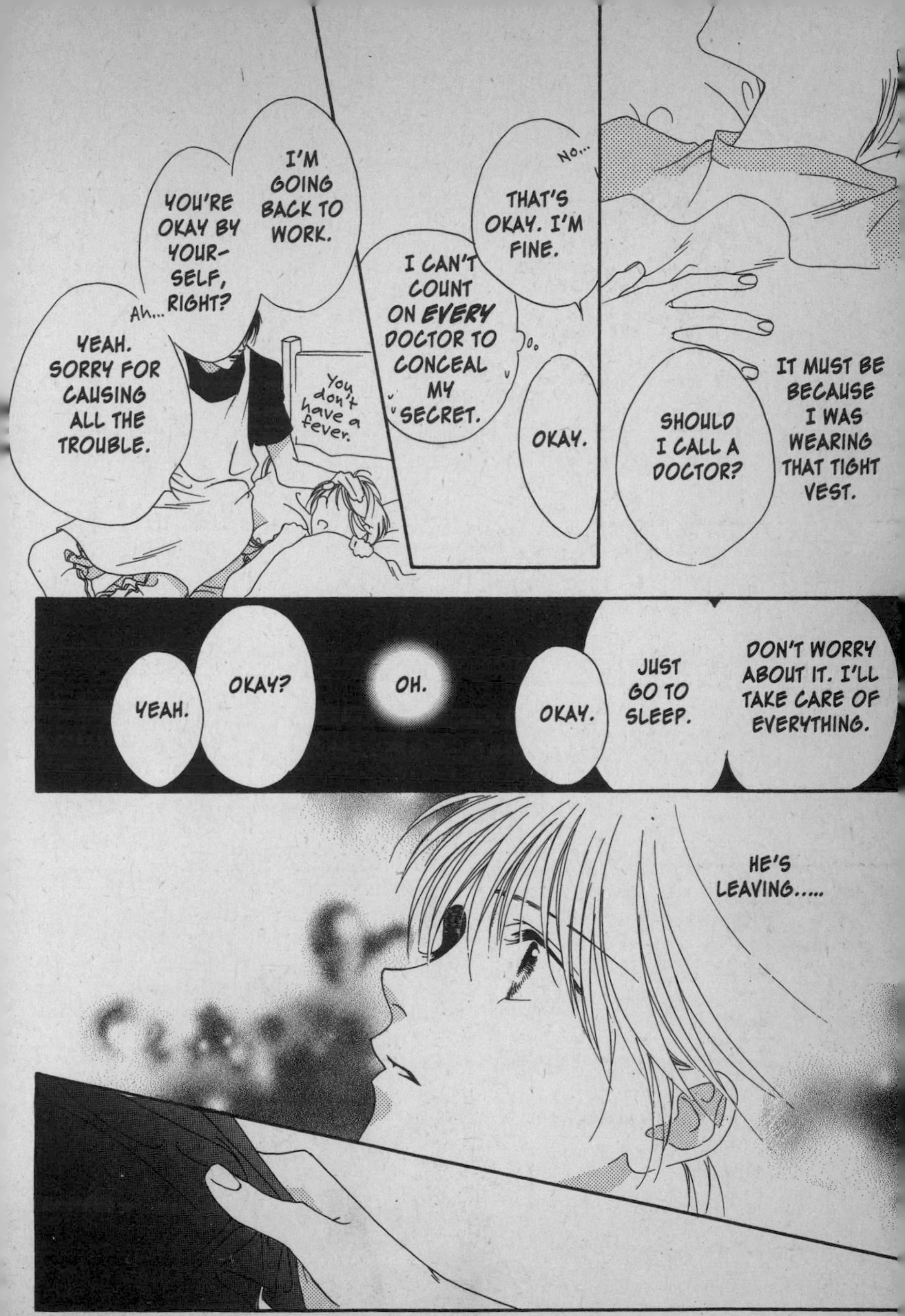
IT MUST BE BECAUSE I WAS WEARING THAT TIGHT VEST.
SHOULD I CALL A DOCTOR?
No...
THAT'S OKAY. I'M FINE.
I CAN'T COUNT ON *EVERY* DOCTOR TO CONCEAL MY SECRET.
OKAY.
You don't have a fever.
I'M GOING BACK TO WORK.
YOU'RE OKAY BY YOURSELF, RIGHT?
Ah...
YEAH. SORRY FOR CAUSING ALL THE TROUBLE.
DON'T WORRY ABOUT IT. I'LL TAKE CARE OF EVERYTHING.
JUST GO TO SLEEP.
OKAY.
OH.
OKAY?
YEAH.
HE'S LEAVING.....

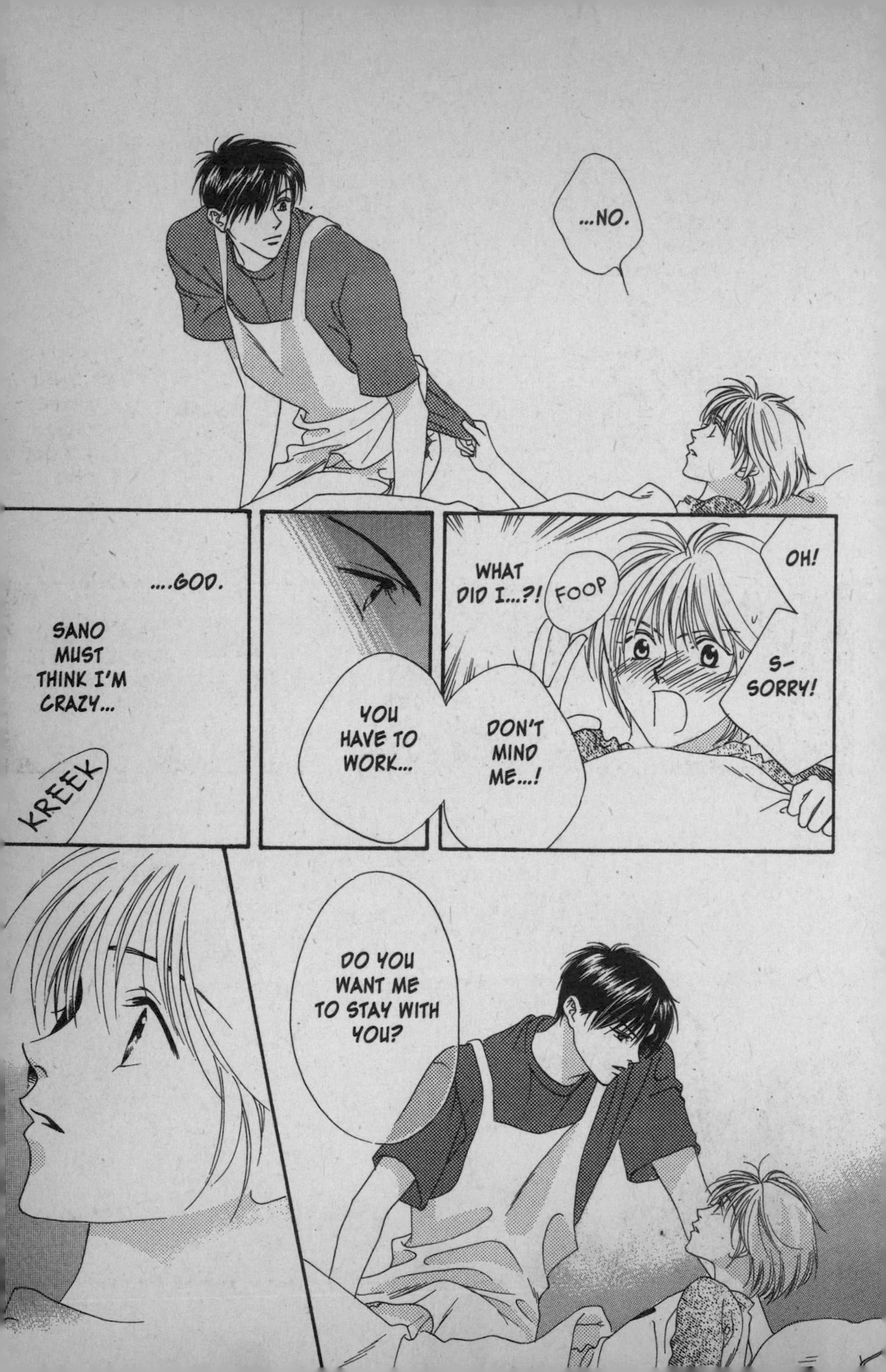
...NO.
OH!
S-SORRY!
WHAT DID I...?!
FOOP
DON'T MIND ME...!
YOU HAVE TO WORK...
....GOD.
SANO MUST THINK I'M CRAZY...
KREEK
DO YOU WANT ME TO STAY WITH YOU?

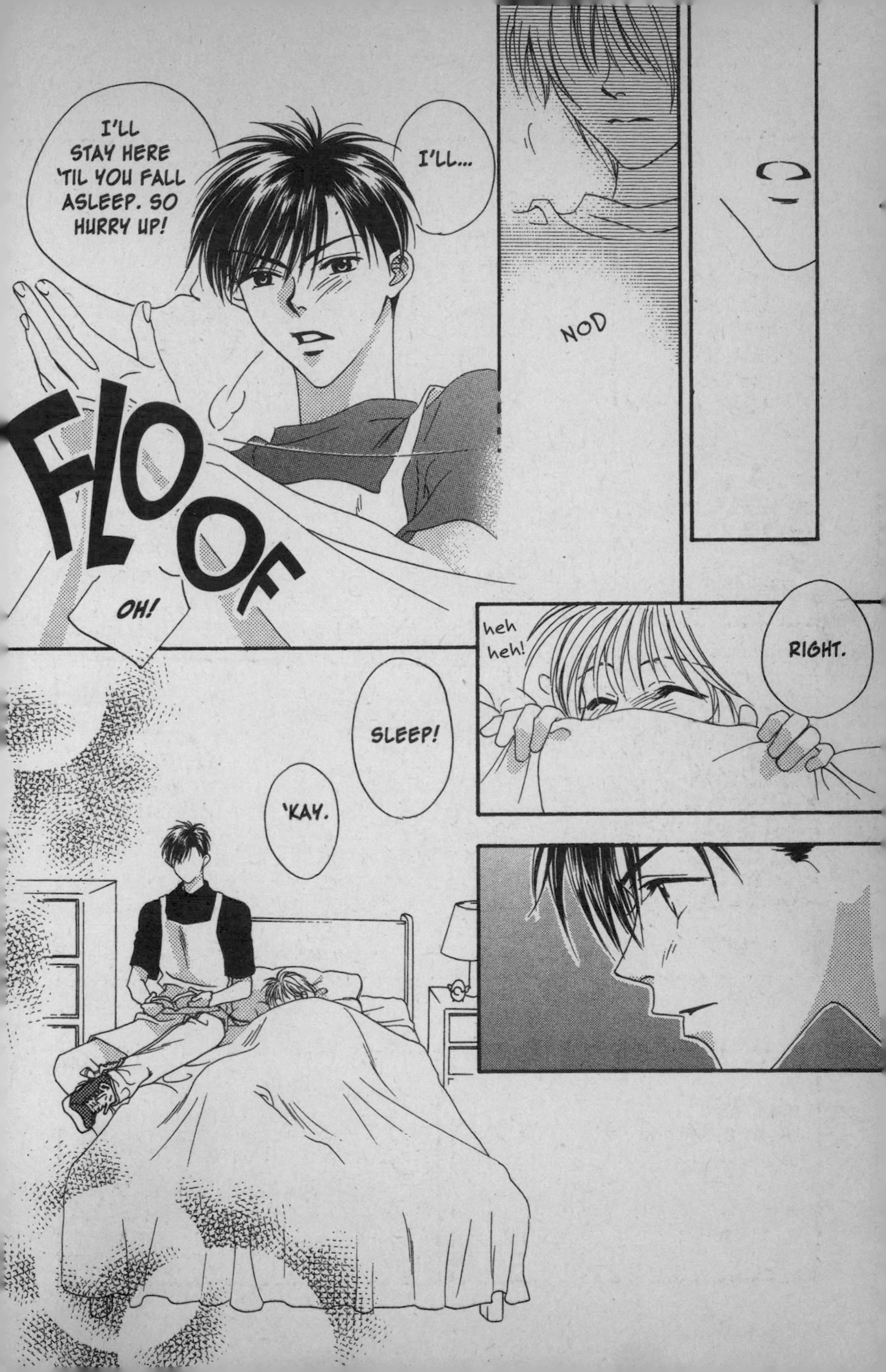
NOD
I'LL...
I'LL STAY HERE 'TIL YOU FALL ASLEEP. SO HURRY UP!
FLOOF
OH!
RIGHT.
heh heh!
SLEEP!
'KAY.

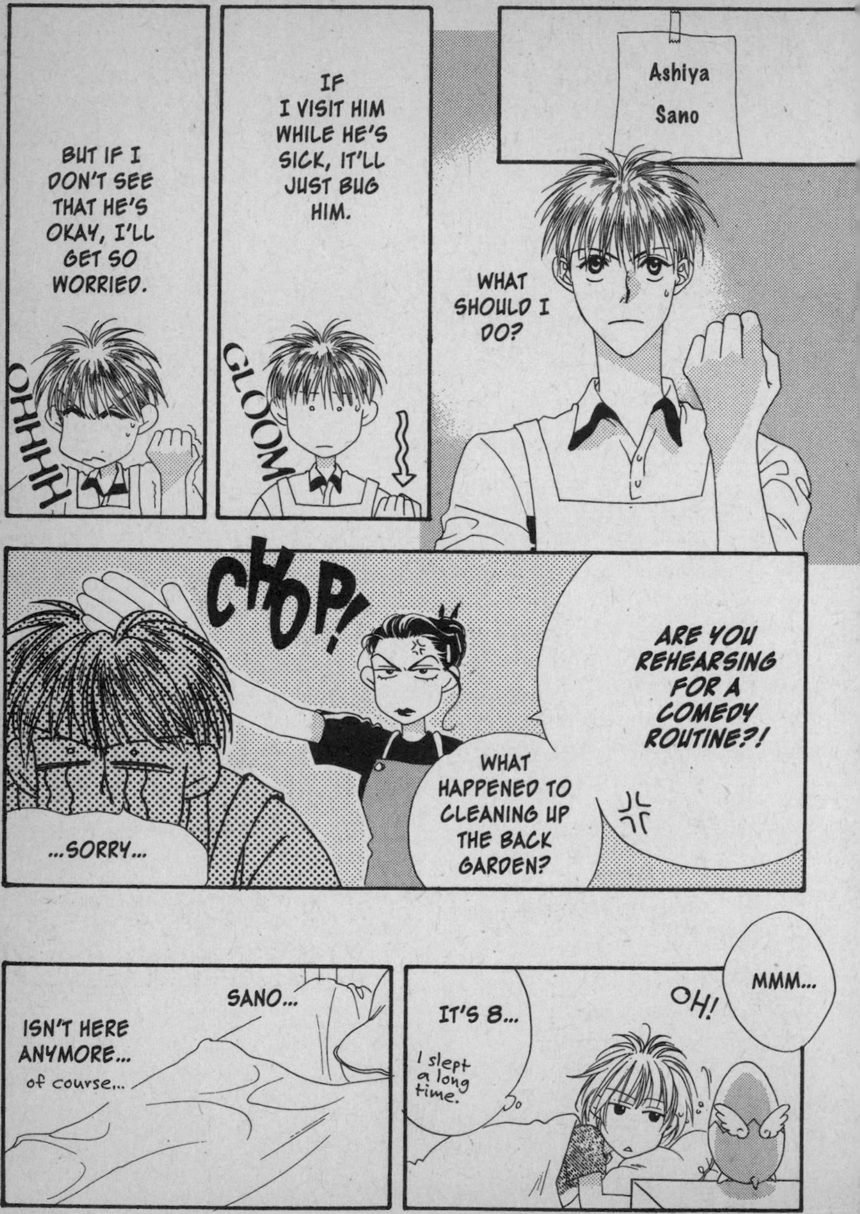
Ashiya
Sano
WHAT SHOULD I DO?
IF I VISIT HIM WHILE HE'S SICK, IT'LL JUST BUG HIM.
GLOOM
BUT IF I DON'T SEE THAT HE'S OKAY, I'LL GET SO WORRIED.
OHHHHH
CHOP!
ARE YOU REHEARSING FOR A COMEDY ROUTINE?!
WHAT HAPPENED TO CLEANING UP THE BACK GARDEN?
...SORRY...
MMM...
OH!
IT'S 8...
I slept a long time.
SANO...
ISN'T HERE ANYMORE...
of course...

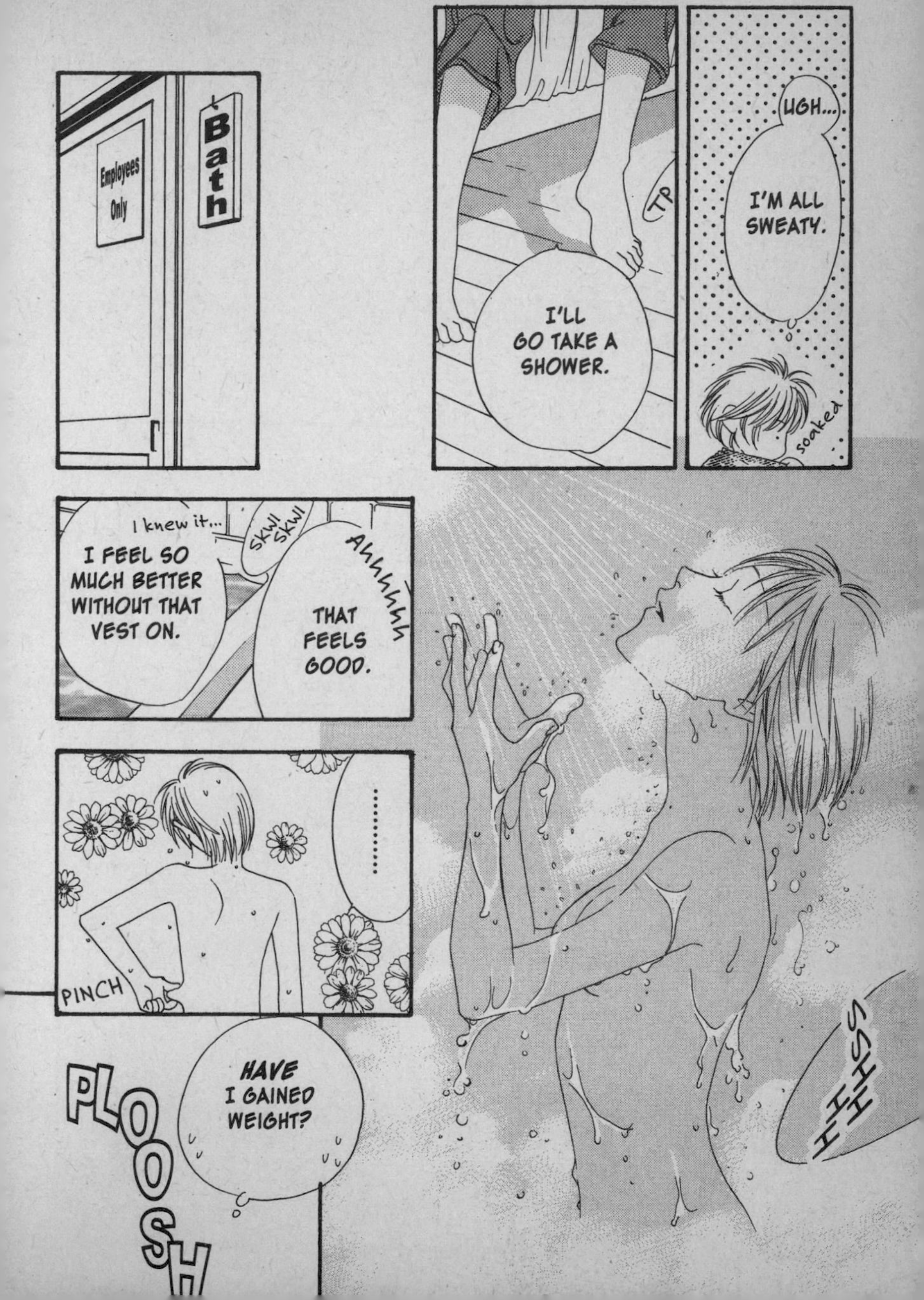
UGH...
I'M ALL SWEATY.
soaked
TP
I'LL GO TAKE A SHOWER.
Bath
Employees Only
SSHHH
AHHHHHH
THAT FEELS GOOD.
SKWI SKWI
I knew it...
I FEEL SO MUCH BETTER WITHOUT THAT VEST ON.
....
PINCH
HAVE I GAINED WEIGHT?
PLOOSH

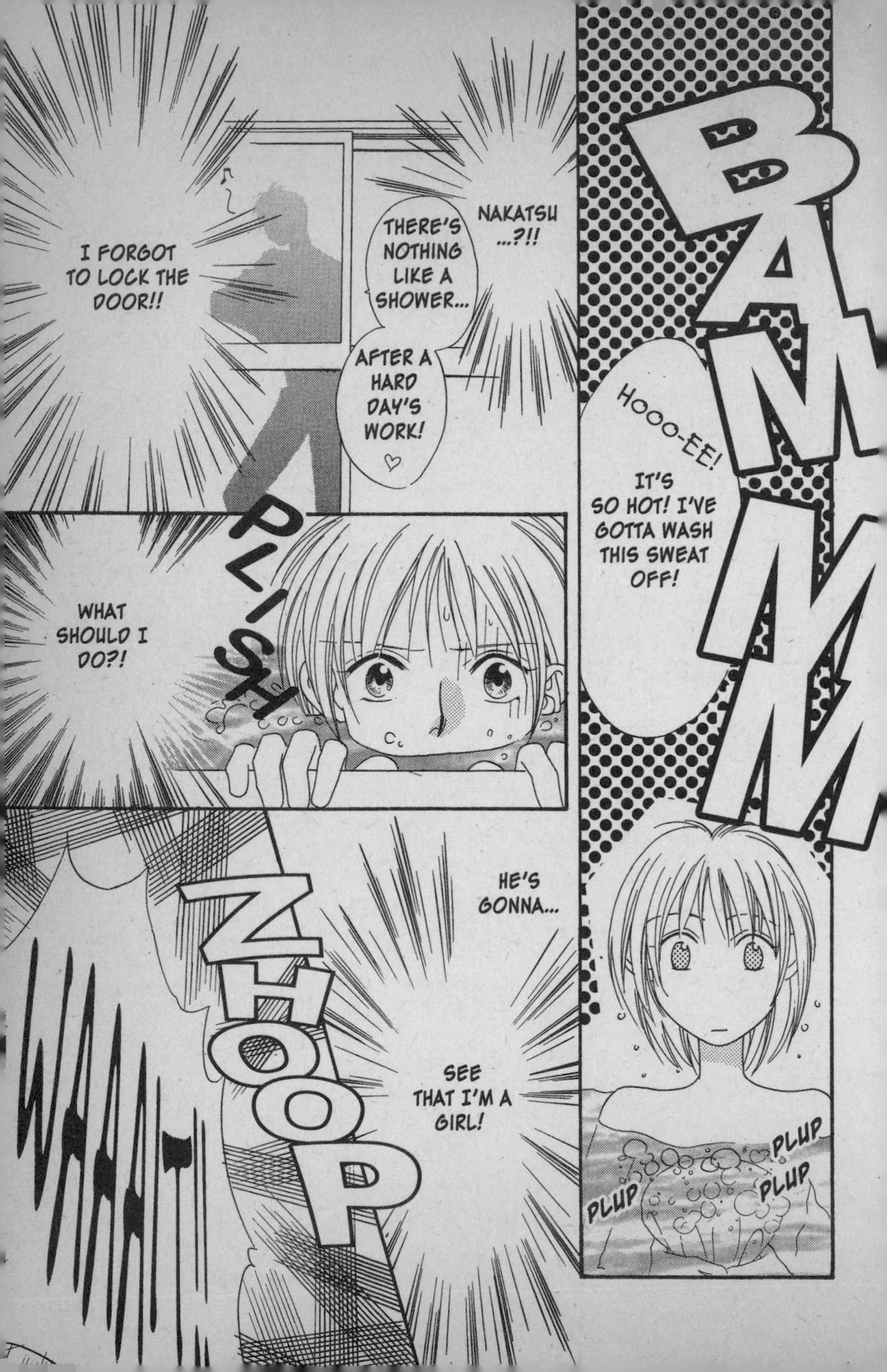
BAMMM
HOOO-EE!
IT'S SO HOT! I'VE GOTTA WASH THIS SWEAT OFF!
PLUP PLUP PLUP PLUP
NAKATSU ...?!!
THERE'S NOTHING LIKE A SHOWER...
AFTER A HARD DAY'S WORK! ♡
I FORGOT TO LOCK THE DOOR!!
PLISH
WHAT SHOULD I DO?!
HE'S GONNA...
SEE THAT I'M A GIRL!
ZHOOP
WAAAIT!

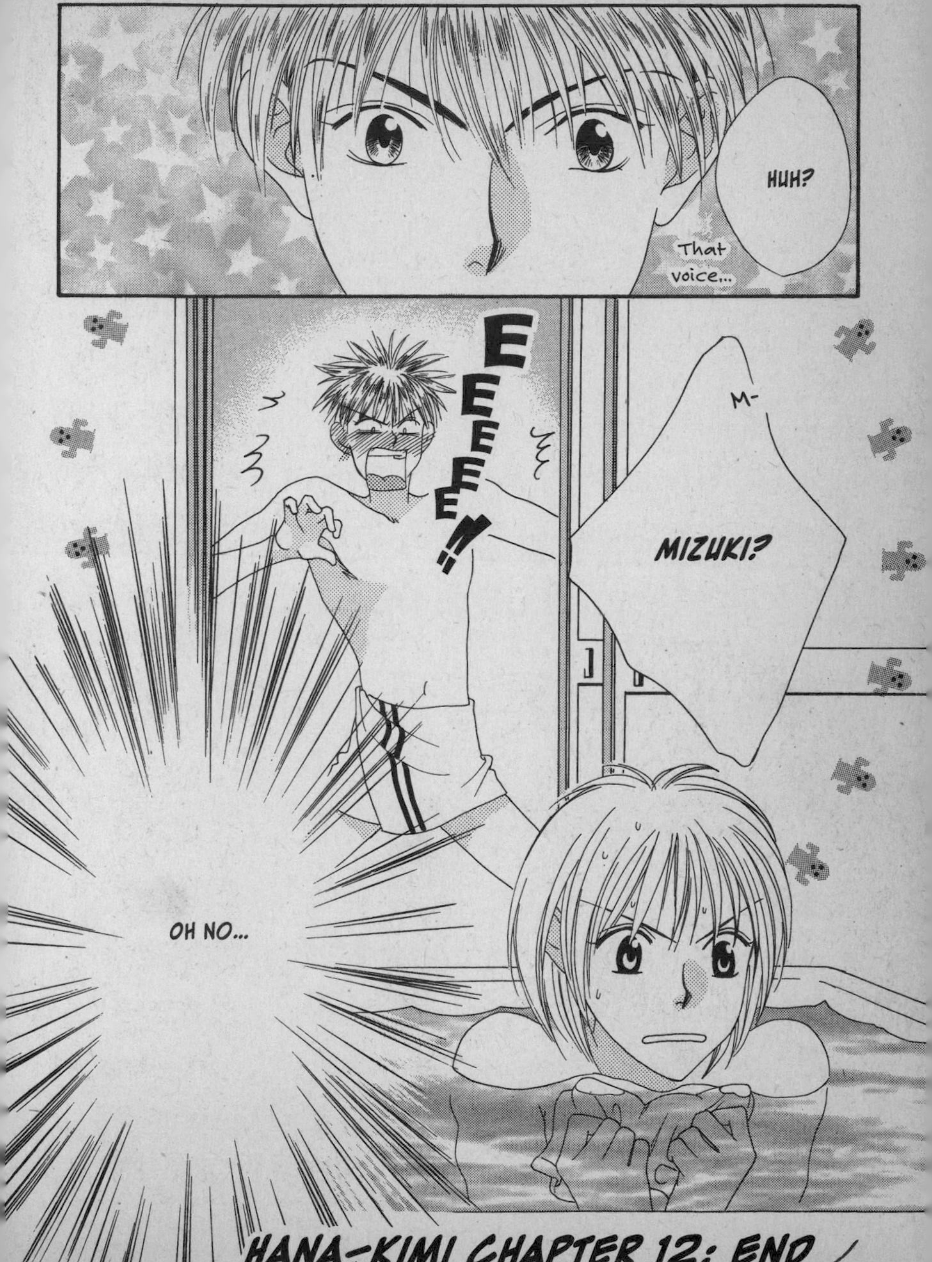
HUH?
That voice...
M- MIZUKI?
EEEEE!!
OH NO...

HANA-KIMI CHAPTER 12: END

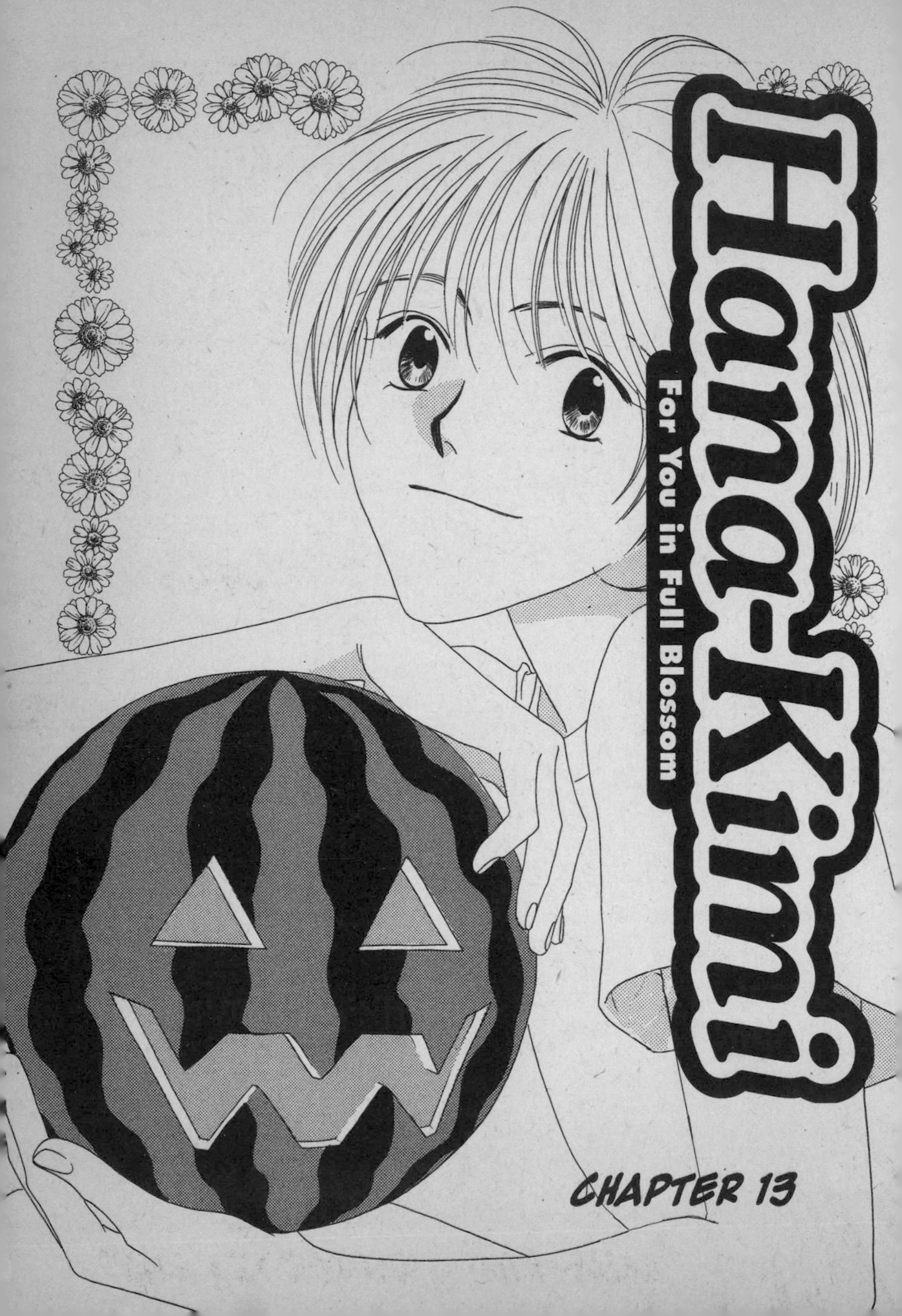
Hana-Kimi
For You in Full Blossom
CHAPTER 13

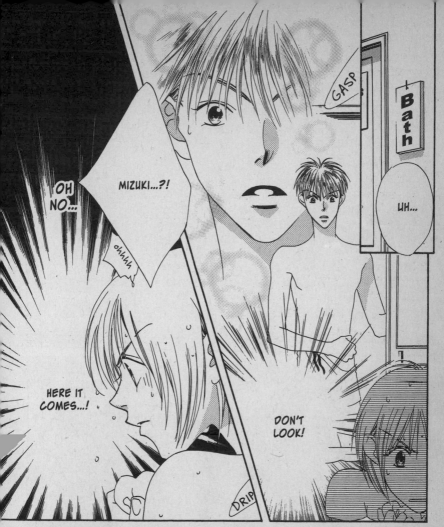

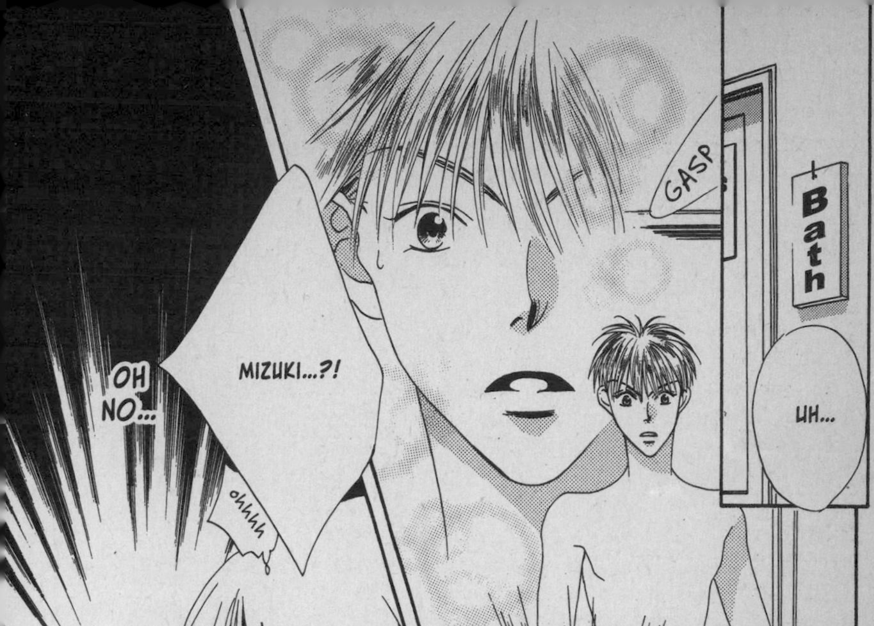
GASP
Bath
UH...
MIZUKI...?!
DON'T LOOK!
OH NO...
ohhhh
HERE IT COMES...!
DRIP

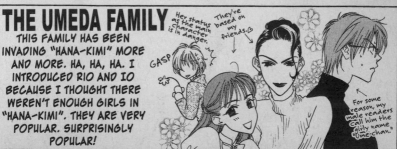

THE UMEDA FAMILY

THIS FAMILY HAS BEEN INVADING "HANA-KIMI" MORE AND MORE. HA, HA, HA. I INTRODUCED RIO AND IO BECAUSE I THOUGHT THERE WEREN'T ENOUGH GIRLS IN "HANA-KIMI". THEY ARE VERY POPULAR. SURPRISINGLY POPULAR!

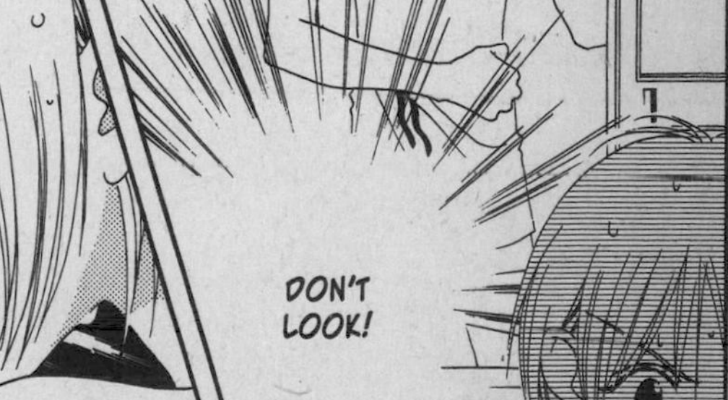
Her status as the main character is in danger.
They're based on my friends.♡
GASP
For some reason, my male readers call him the girly name "Ume-chan."

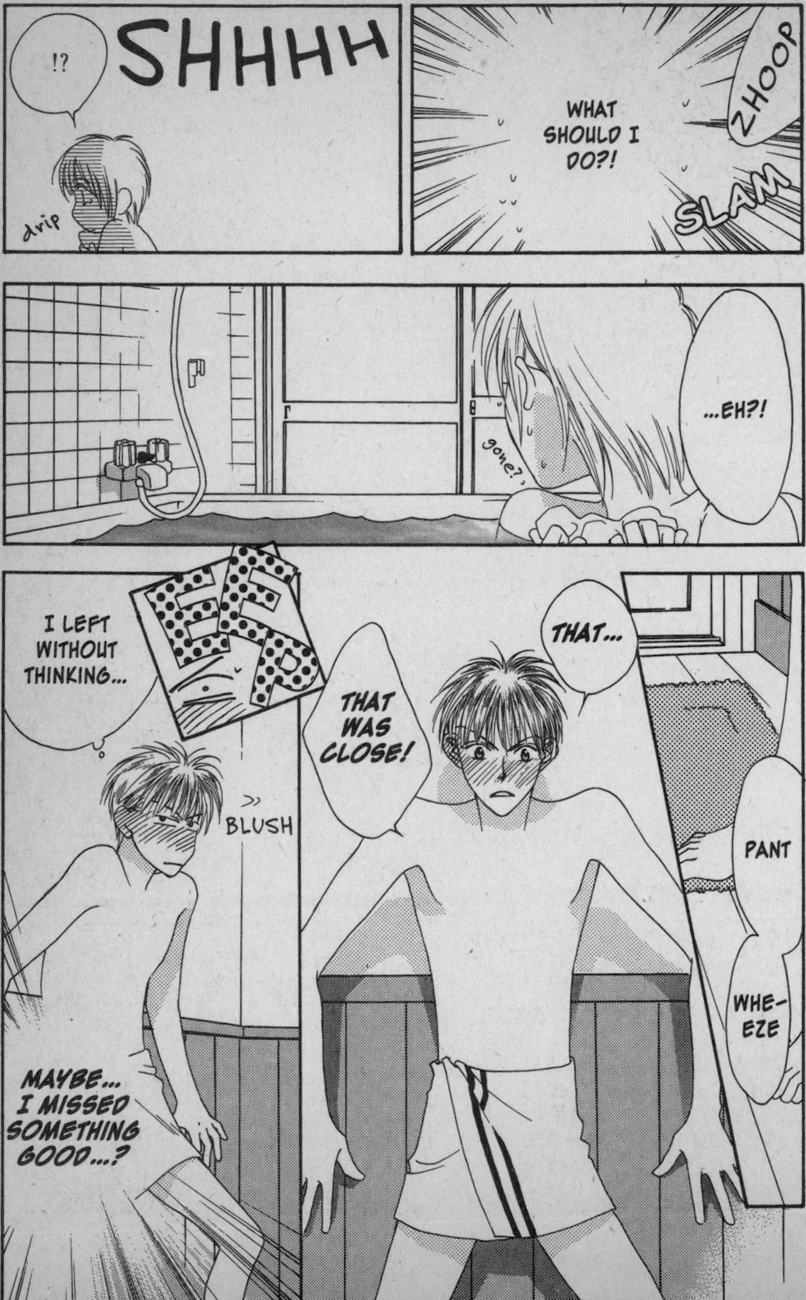
WHAT SHOULD I DO?!
ZHOOP
SLAM
SHHHH
!?
drip
...EH?!
gone?
PANT
WHE-EZE
THAT...
THAT WAS CLOSE!
EEP
I LEFT WITHOUT THINKING...
BLUSH
MAYBE... I MISSED SOMETHING GOOD...?

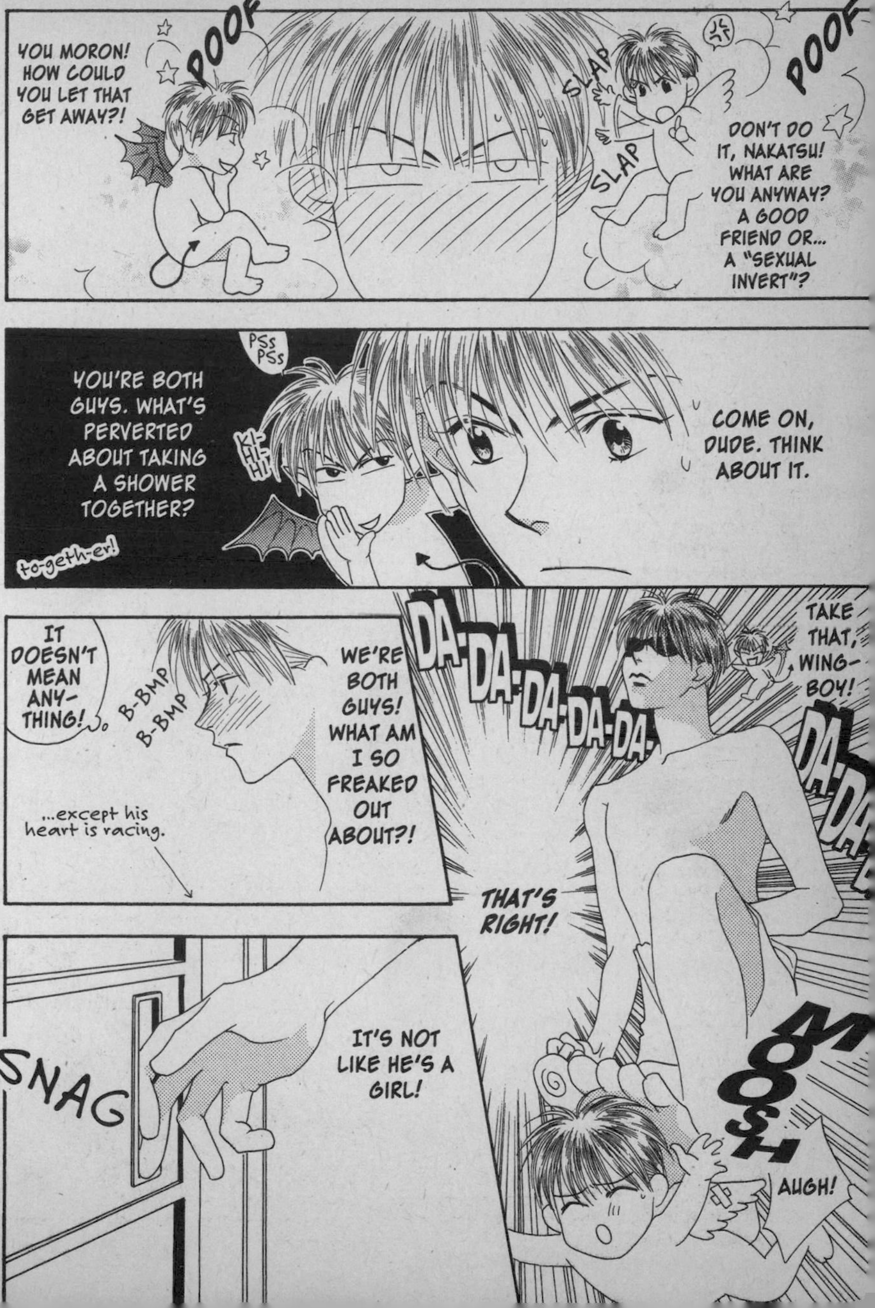
POOF
DON'T DO IT, NAKATSU! WHAT ARE YOU ANYWAY? A GOOD FRIEND OR... A "SEXUAL INVERT"?
SLAP
SLAP
POOF
YOU MORON! HOW COULD YOU LET THAT GET AWAY?!
COME ON, DUDE. THINK ABOUT IT.
PSS PSS
KI-HI-HI
YOU'RE BOTH GUYS. WHAT'S PERVERTED ABOUT TAKING A SHOWER TOGETHER?
to-geth-er!
TAKE THAT, WING-BOY!
DA-DA-DA-DA-DA-DA
DA-DA-DA
THAT'S RIGHT!
MOOSH
AUGH!
WE'RE BOTH GUYS! WHAT AM I SO FREAKED OUT ABOUT?!
B-BMP B-BMP
IT DOESN'T MEAN ANYTHING!
...except his heart is racing.
IT'S NOT LIKE HE'S A GIRL!
SNAG

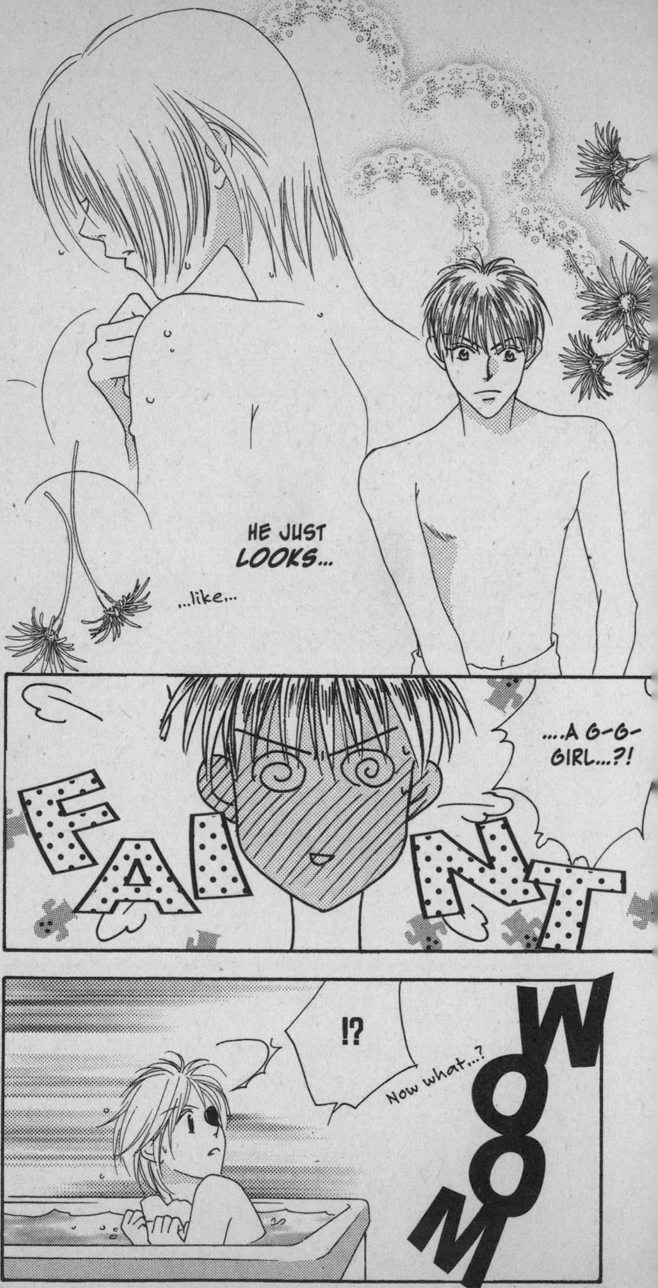
HE JUST LOOKS...
...like...
....A G-G-GIRL...?!
FAINT
WOOM
Now what...?
!?

WHISPERED SECRETS

SHUICHI NAKATSU

BIRTHDAY: AUGUST 20TH

AGE: 17

BLOOD TYPE: B

SIGN: LEO

HEIGHT: 180.CM

FAVORITE FOODS: OKONOMIYAKI, RICE OMELET, BBQ BEEF CURRY

FAVORITE MUSICIANS: URUFURUZU, YIEMON, ETC.

FAVORITE MOVIES: SPEED, DIE HARD, THE CURE

FAVORITE BRANDS: LEVIS, GOOD ENOUGH, ADIDAS

FAVORITE SPORT: SOCCER

FAVORITE PET: CATS (BECAUSE HE'S ALWAYS HAD ONE AT HOME)

FOOD HE HATES: NATTO, SALAD WITH JUST VEGETABLES IN IT, SASHIMI AND OTHER RAW FOOD

FLOWER: SUNFLOWER

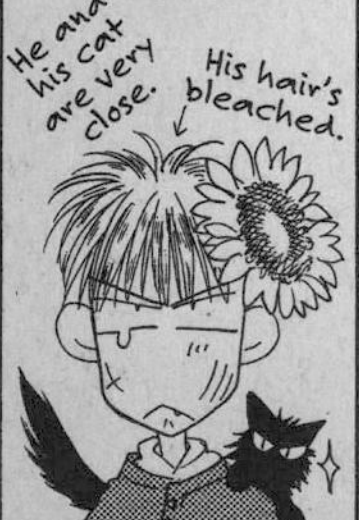
He and his cat are very close.
His hair's bleached.

Guriko (female, age 6, mix)

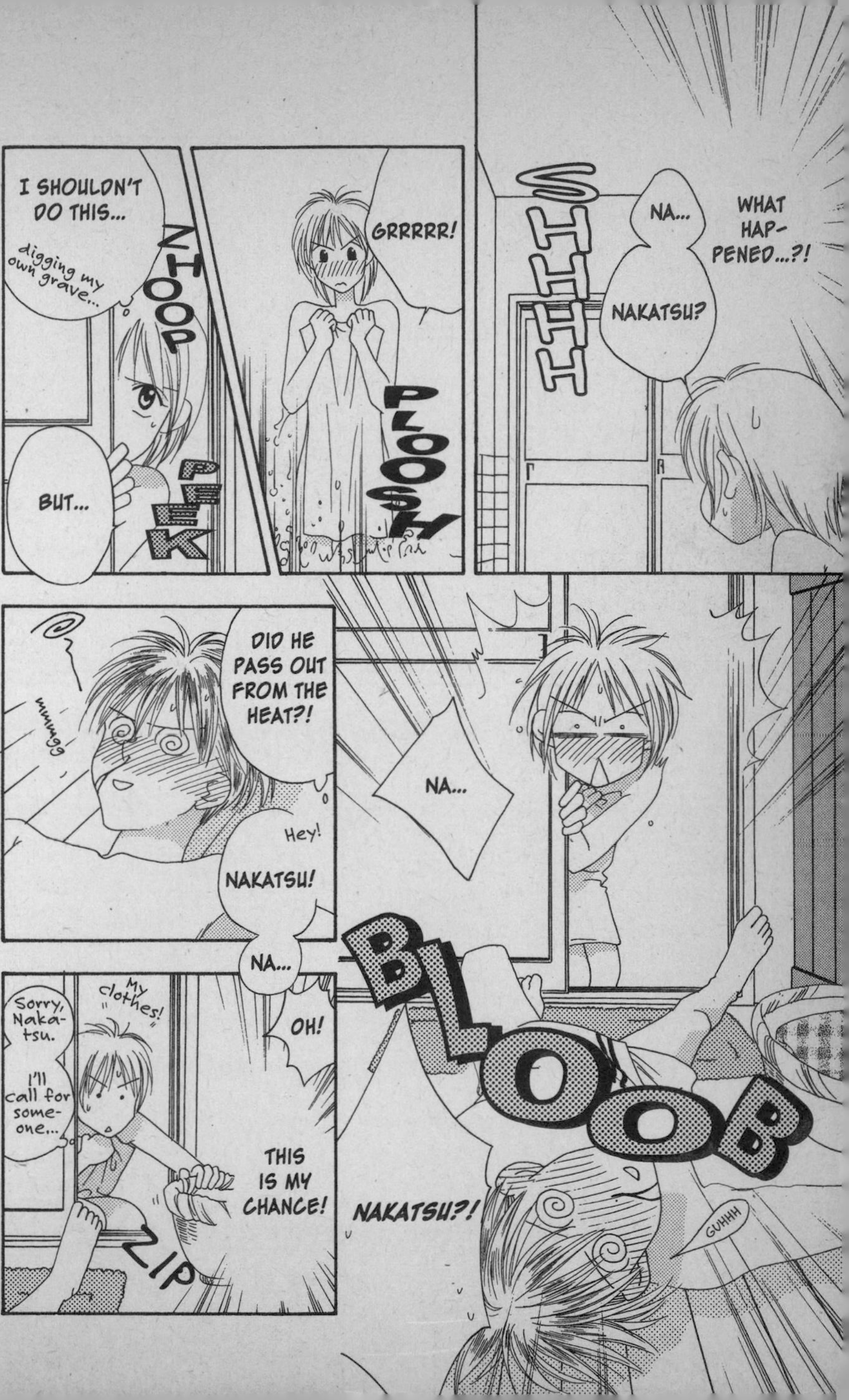
WHAT HAP-PENED...?!
NA...
NAKATSU?
SHHHH
GRRRRR!
PLOOSH
I SHOULDN'T DO THIS...
digging my own grave...
ZHOOP
BUT...
PEEK
NA...
BLOOOB
NAKATSU?!
GUHHH
DID HE PASS OUT FROM THE HEAT?!
mmmgg
Hey!
NAKATSU!
NA...
OH!
THIS IS MY CHANCE!
My clothes!
Sorry, Naka-tsu.
I'll call for some-one...
ZIP

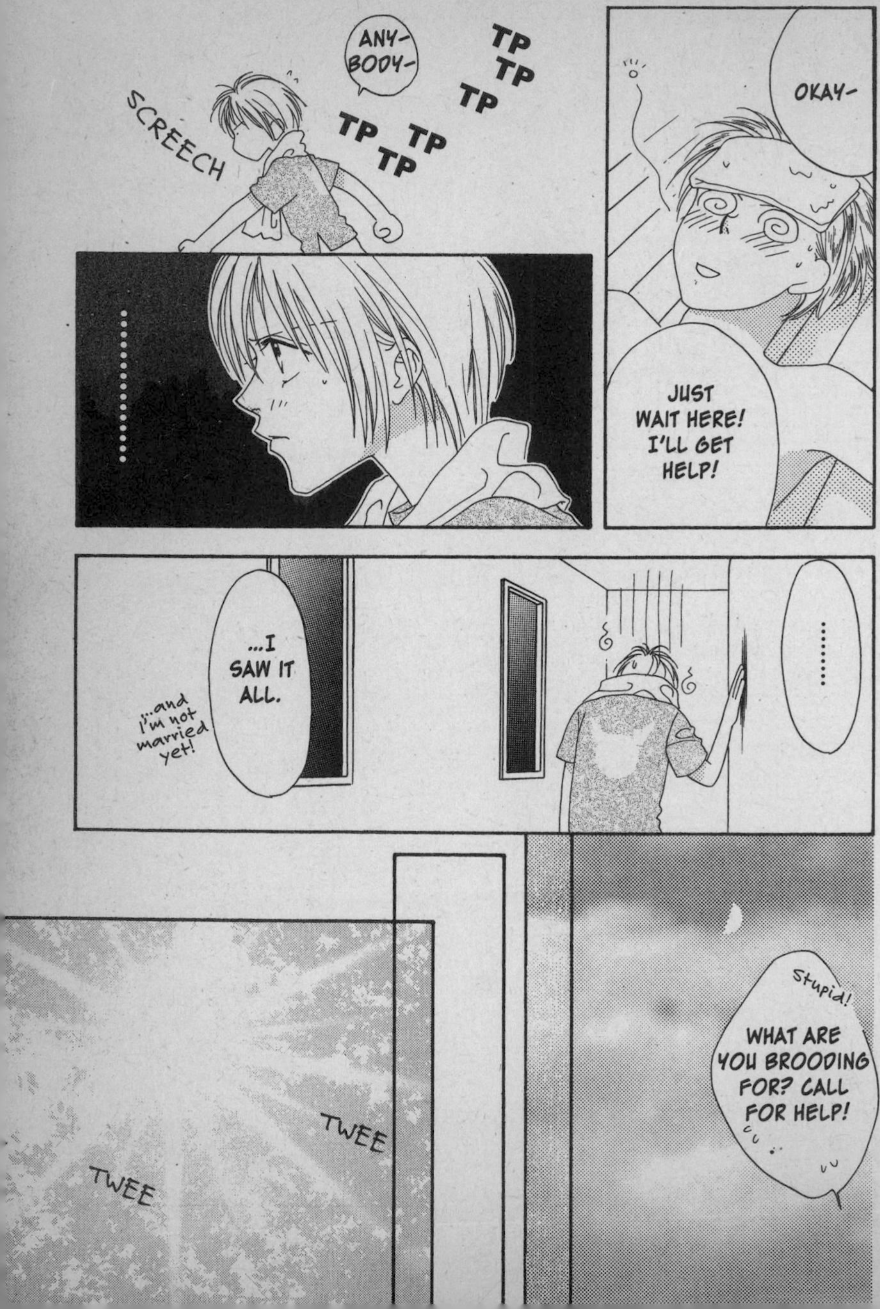
OKAY-
JUST WAIT HERE! I'LL GET HELP!
TP TP TP
ANY-BODY-
TP TP TP
SCREECH
......
......
...I SAW IT ALL.
...and I'm not married yet!
Stupid!
WHAT ARE YOU BROODING FOR? CALL FOR HELP!
TWEE
TWEE

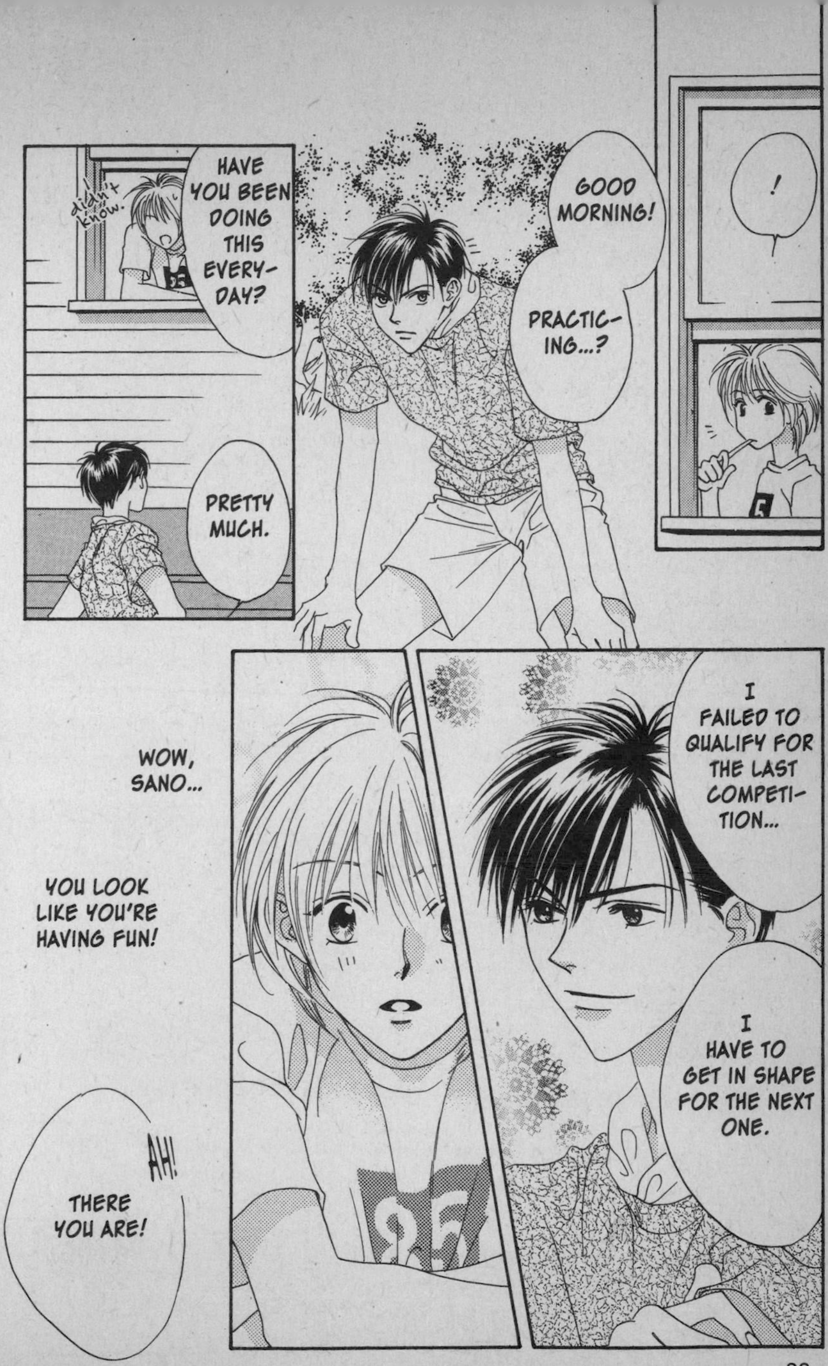
!
GOOD MORNING!
PRACTIC-ING...?
HAVE YOU BEEN DOING THIS EVERY-DAY?
I didn't know.
PRETTY MUCH.
I FAILED TO QUALIFY FOR THE LAST COMPETITI-TION...
I HAVE TO GET IN SHAPE FOR THE NEXT ONE.
WOW, SANO...
YOU LOOK LIKE YOU'RE HAVING FUN!
AH!
THERE YOU ARE!

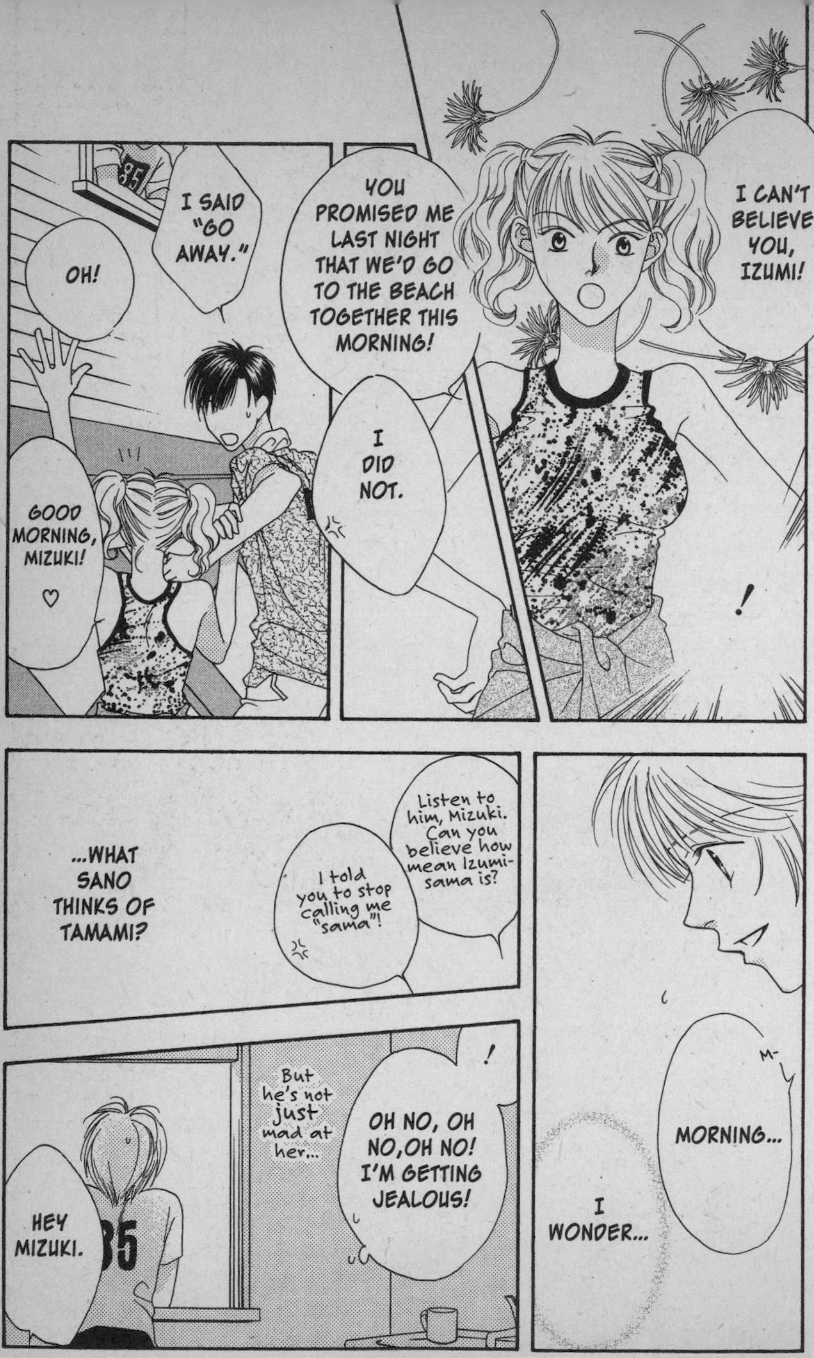
I CAN'T BELIEVE YOU, IZUMI!
!
YOU PROMISED ME LAST NIGHT THAT WE'D GO TO THE BEACH TOGETHER THIS MORNING!
I DID NOT.
I SAID "GO AWAY."
OH!
GOOD MORNING, MIZUKI! ♡
M-
MORNING...
I WONDER...
Listen to him, Mizuki. Can you believe how mean Izumi-sama is?
I told you to stop calling me "sama"!
...WHAT SANO THINKS OF TAMAMI?
!
OH NO, OH NO, OH NO! I'M GETTING JEALOUS!
But he's not just mad at her...
HEY MIZUKI.

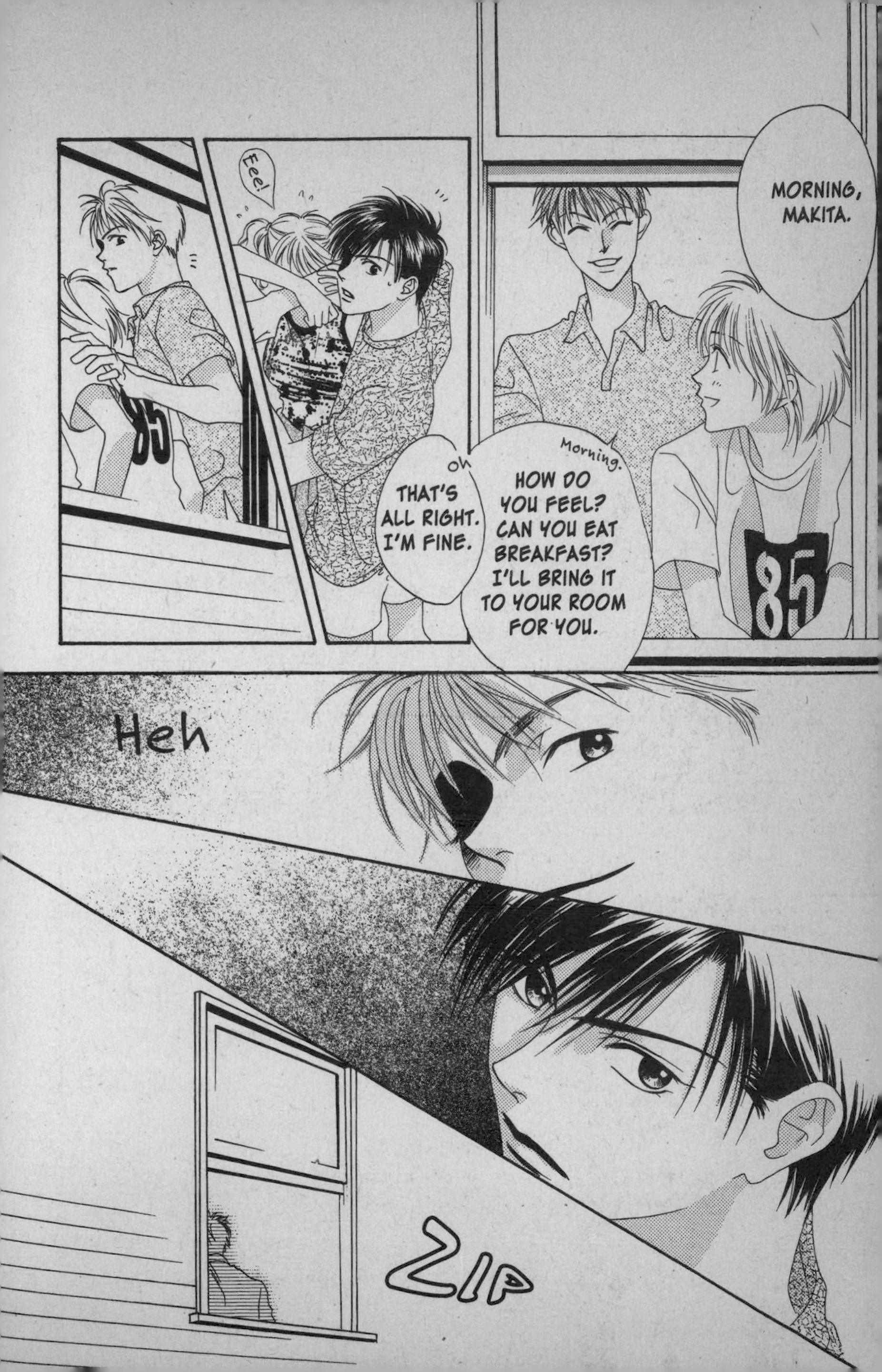
MORNING, MAKITA.
Morning.
HOW DO YOU FEEL? CAN YOU EAT BREAKFAST? I'LL BRING IT TO YOUR ROOM FOR YOU.
Oh
THAT'S ALL RIGHT. I'M FINE.
Eee!
Heh
ZIP

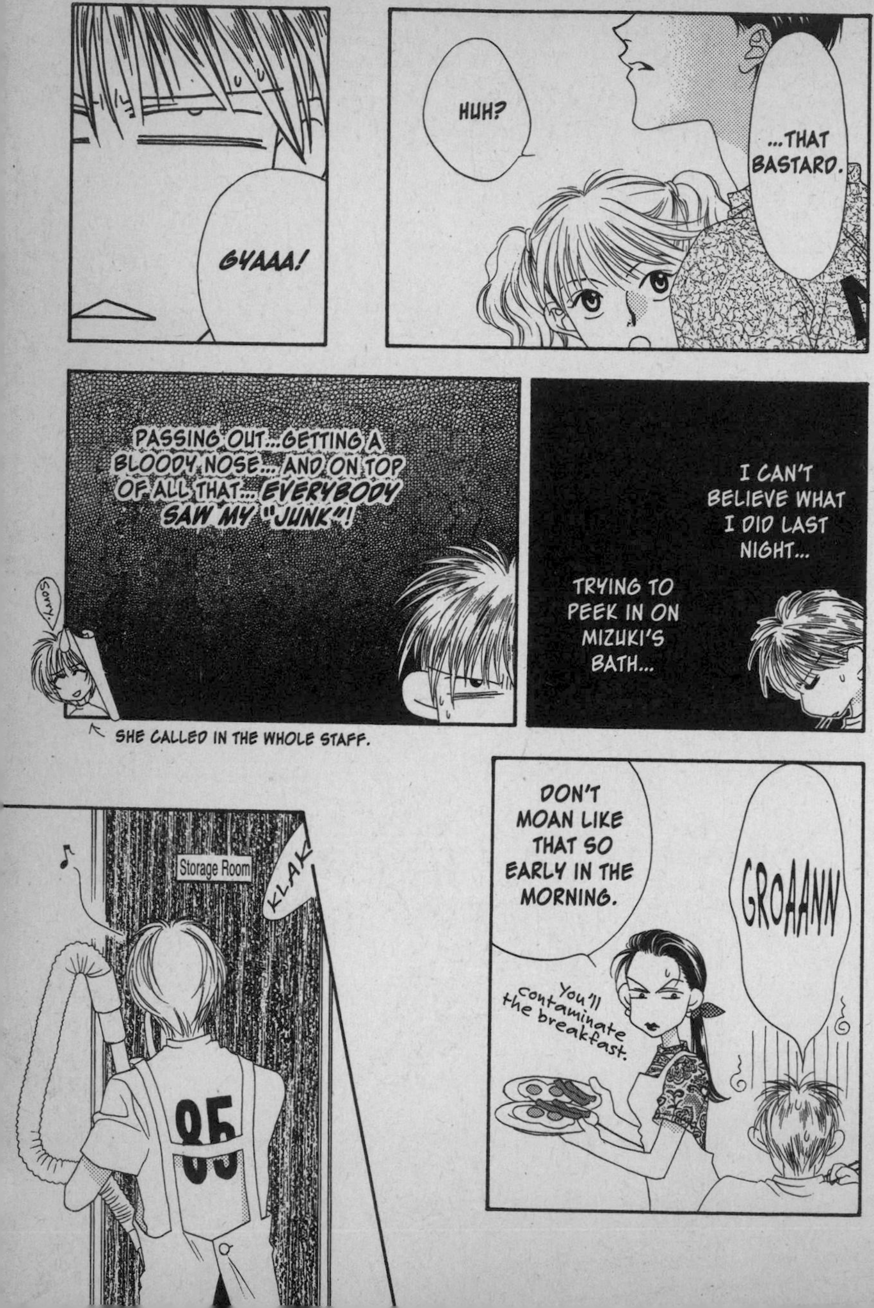
...THAT BASTARD.
HUH?
GYAAA!
I CAN'T BELIEVE WHAT I DID LAST NIGHT...
TRYING TO PEEK IN ON MIZUKI'S BATH...
PASSING OUT...GETTING A BLOODY NOSE... AND ON TOP OF ALL THAT... EVERYBODY SAW MY "JUNK"!
Sorry.
SHE CALLED IN THE WHOLE STAFF.
GROAANN
DON'T MOAN LIKE THAT SO EARLY IN THE MORNING.
You'll contaminate the breakfast.
Storage Room
KLAK

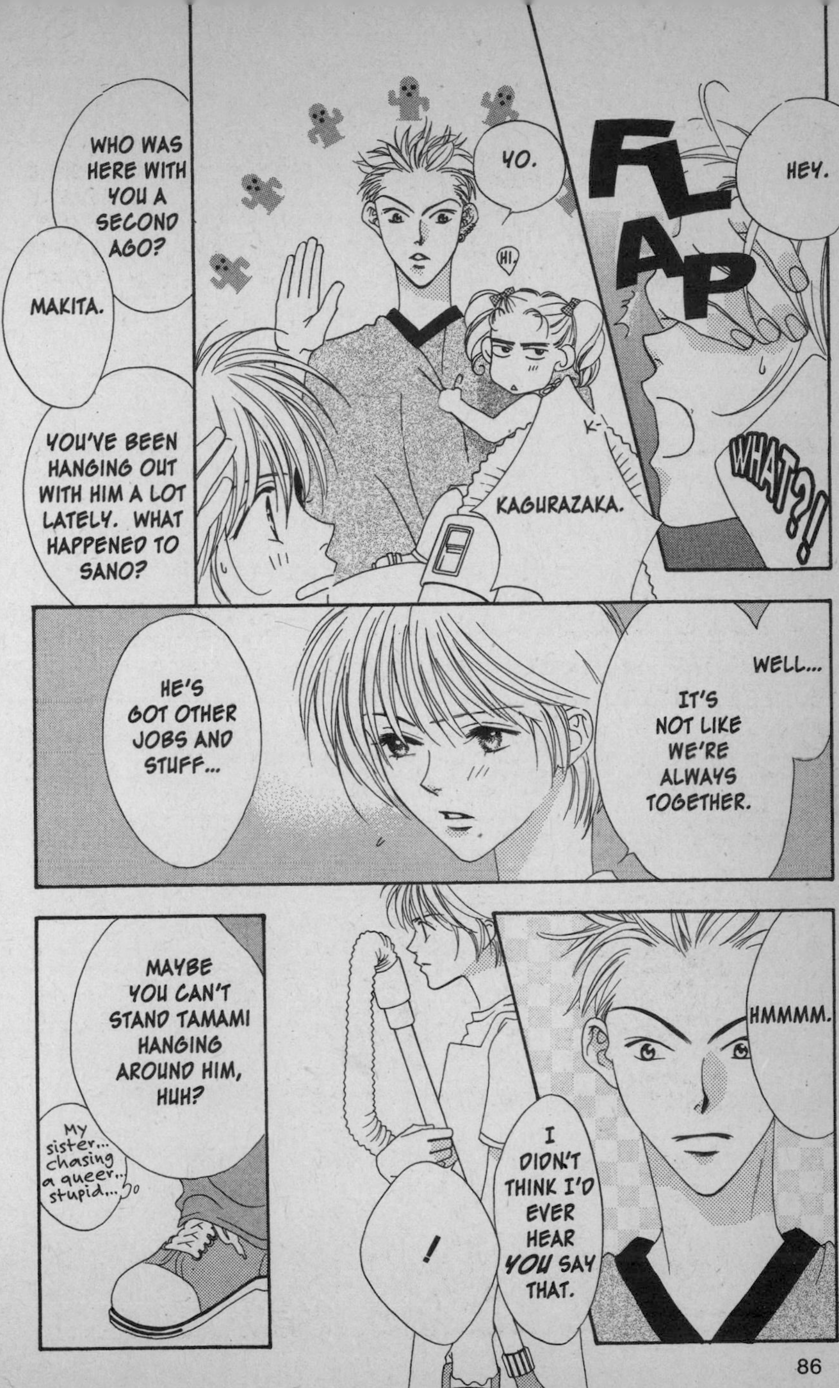
HEY.
FLAP
WHAT?!
YO.
HI.
K-
KAGURAZAKA.
WHO WAS HERE WITH YOU A SECOND AGO?
MAKITA.
YOU'VE BEEN HANGING OUT WITH HIM A LOT LATELY. WHAT HAPPENED TO SANO?
WELL...
IT'S NOT LIKE WE'RE ALWAYS TOGETHER.
HE'S GOT OTHER JOBS AND STUFF...
HMMMM.
I DIDN'T THINK I'D EVER HEAR *YOU* SAY THAT.
!
MAYBE YOU CAN'T STAND TAMAMI HANGING AROUND HIM, HUH?
My sister... chasing a queer... stupid...

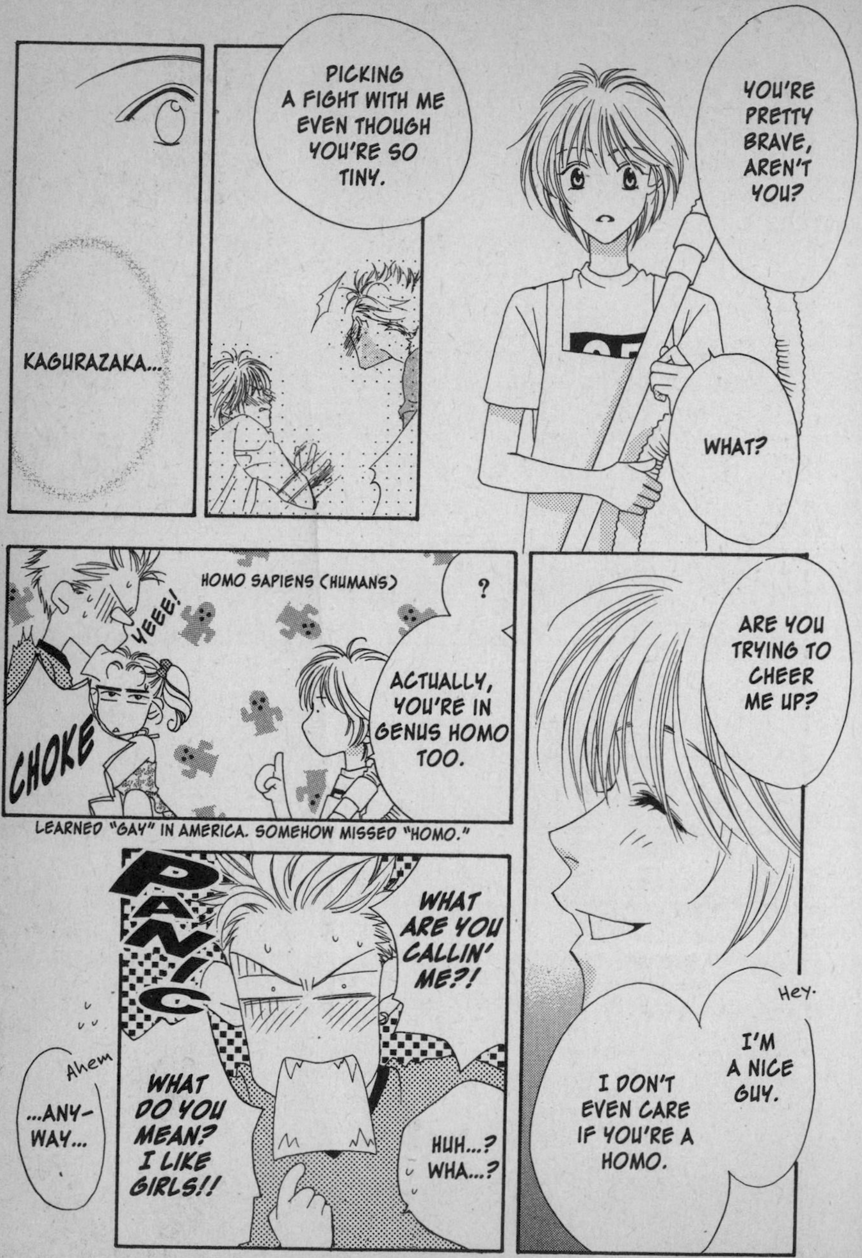
YOU'RE PRETTY BRAVE, AREN'T YOU?
WHAT?
PICKING A FIGHT WITH ME EVEN THOUGH YOU'RE SO TINY.
KAGURAZAKA...
ARE YOU TRYING TO CHEER ME UP?
Hey.
I'M A NICE GUY.
I DON'T EVEN CARE IF YOU'RE A HOMO.
?
ACTUALLY, YOU'RE IN GENUS HOMO TOO.
HOMO SAPIENS (HUMANS)
YEEE!
CHOKE
LEARNED "GAY" IN AMERICA. SOMEHOW MISSED "HOMO."
PANIC
WHAT ARE YOU CALLIN' ME?!
HUH...? WHA...?
WHAT DO YOU MEAN? I LIKE GIRLS!!
Ahem
...ANY-WAY...

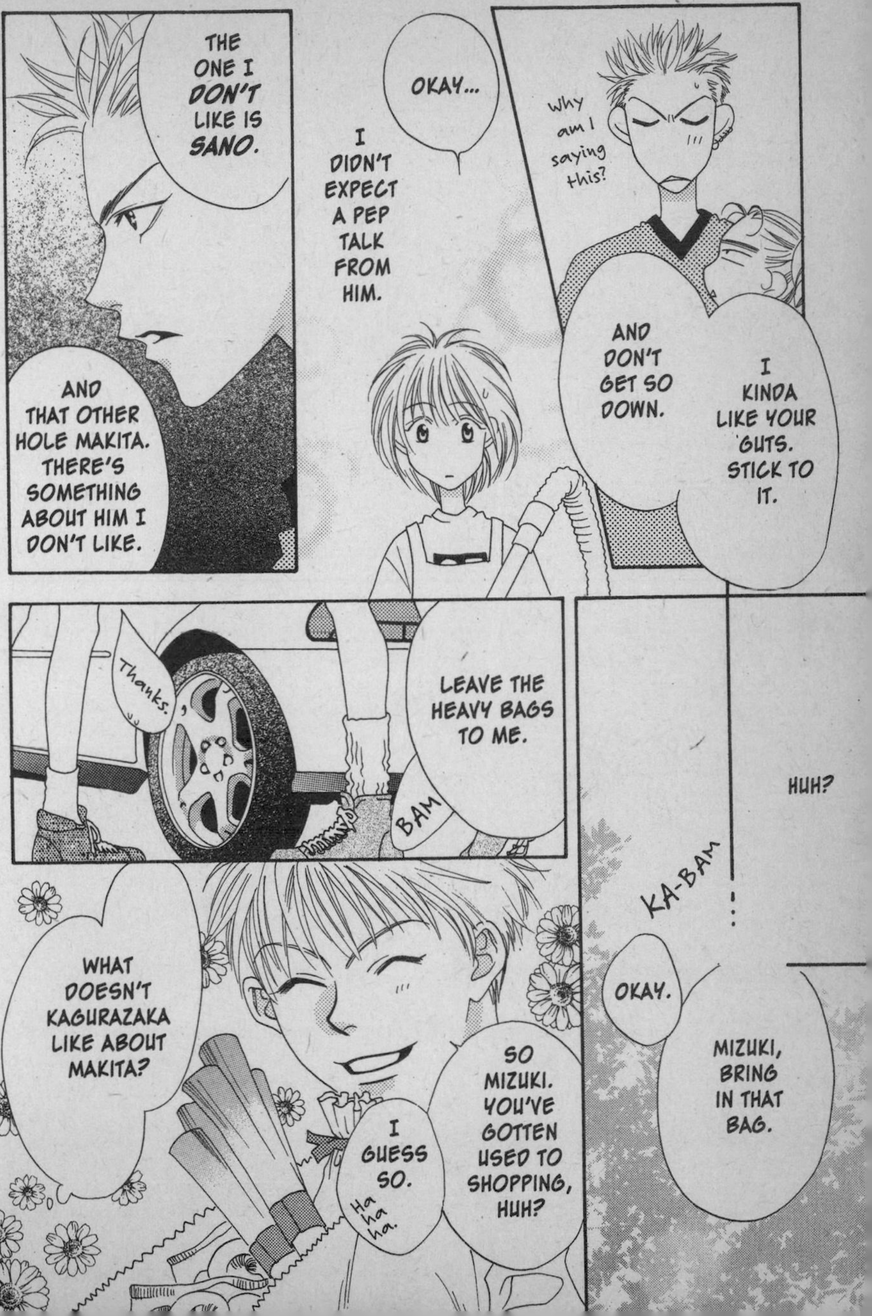
I KINDA LIKE YOUR GUTS. STICK TO IT.
AND DON'T GET SO DOWN.
Why am I saying this?
OKAY...
I DIDN'T EXPECT A PEP TALK FROM HIM.
THE ONE I DON'T LIKE IS SANO.
AND THAT OTHER HOLE MAKITA. THERE'S SOMETHING ABOUT HIM I DON'T LIKE.
HUH?
...
MIZUKI, BRING IN THAT BAG.
OKAY.
KA-BAM
LEAVE THE HEAVY BAGS TO ME.
BAM
Thanks.
SO MIZUKI. YOU'VE GOTTEN USED TO SHOPPING, HUH?
I GUESS SO.
Ha ha ha.
WHAT DOESN'T KAGURAZAKA LIKE ABOUT MAKITA?

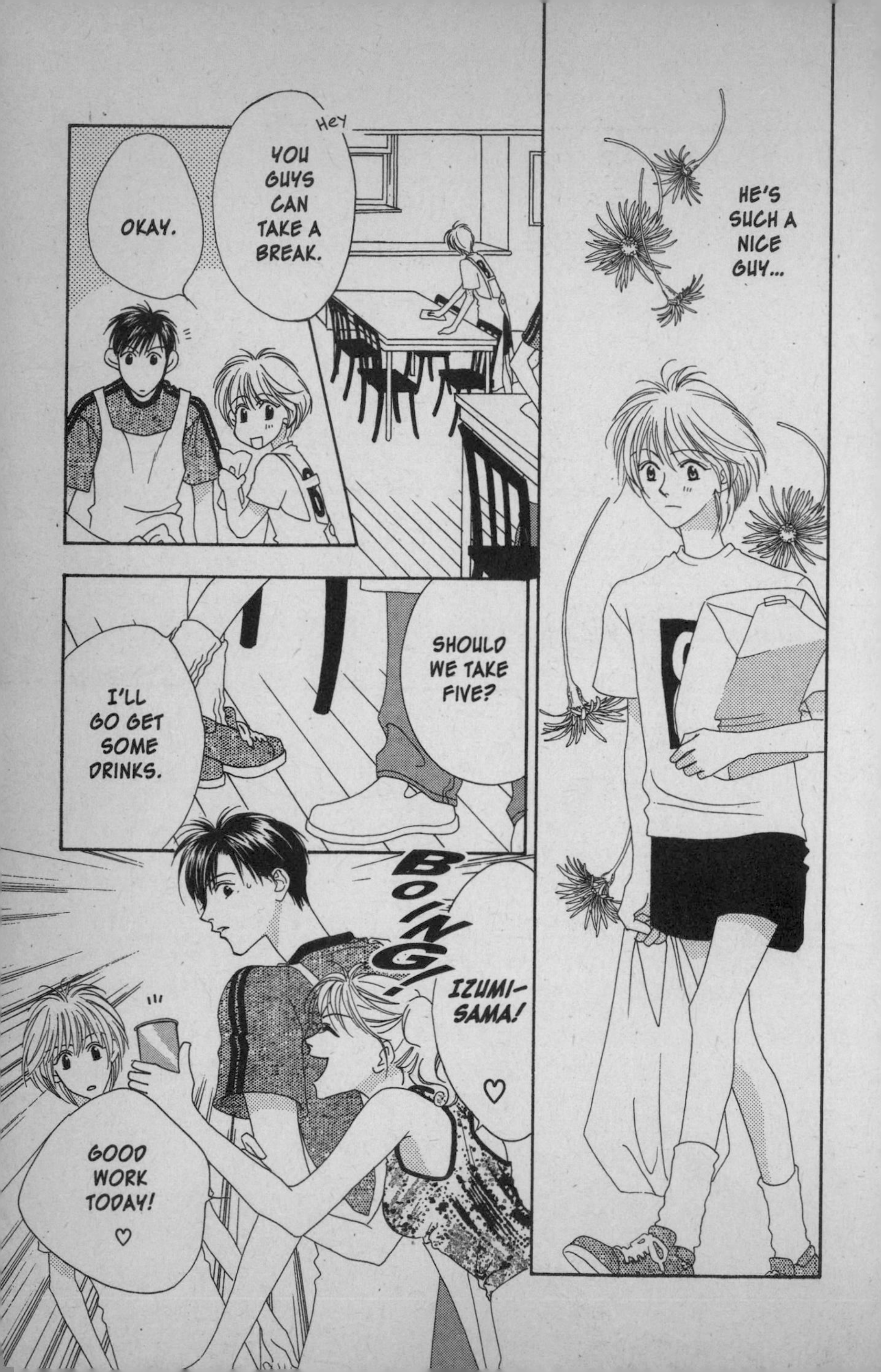
HE'S SUCH A NICE GUY...
Hey
YOU GUYS CAN TAKE A BREAK.
OKAY.
SHOULD WE TAKE FIVE?
I'LL GO GET SOME DRINKS.
BOING!!
IZUMI-SAMA! ♡
GOOD WORK TODAY! ♡

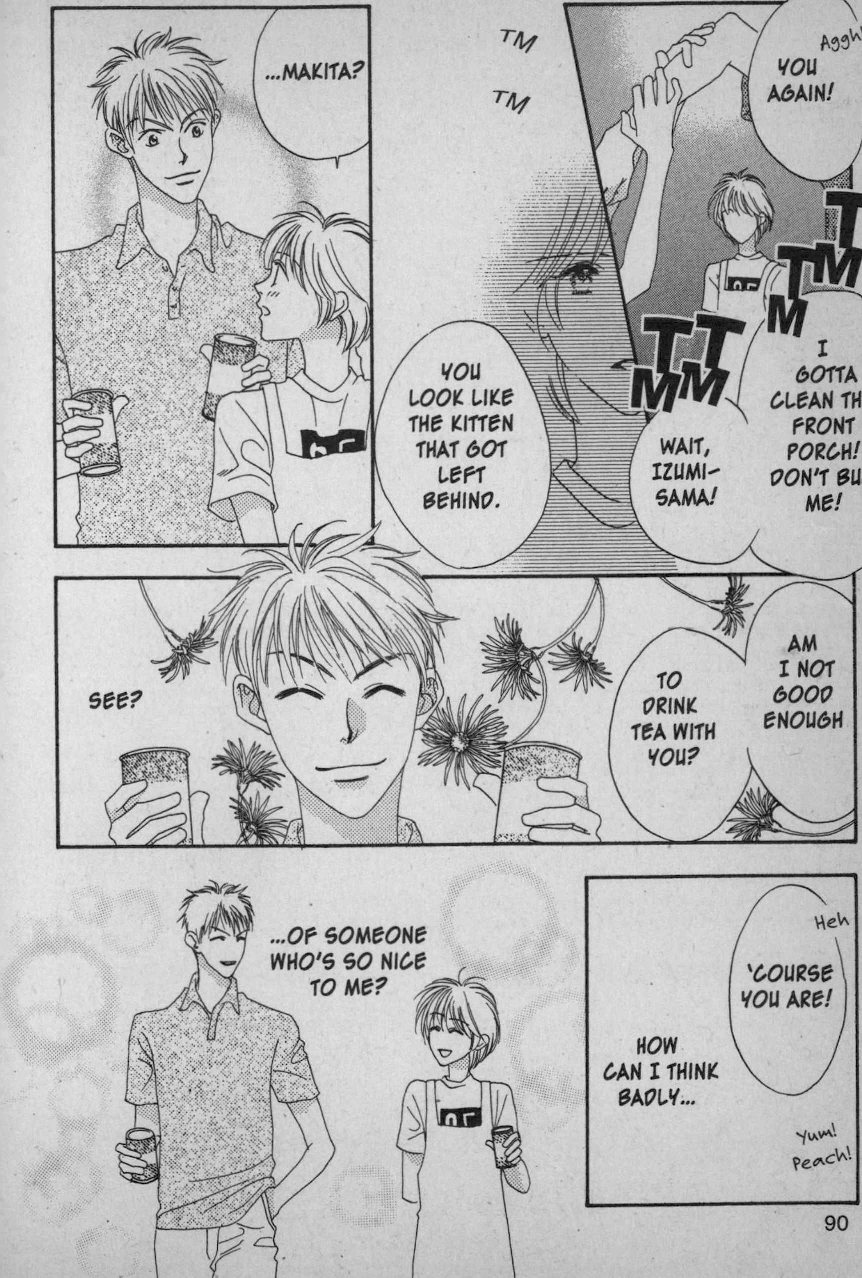
TM
TM
Aggh!
YOU AGAIN!
TTMM
I GOTTA CLEAN THE FRONT PORCH! DON'T BUG ME!
TTMM
WAIT, IZUMI-SAMA!
...MAKITA?
YOU LOOK LIKE THE KITTEN THAT GOT LEFT BEHIND.
AM I NOT GOOD ENOUGH
TO DRINK TEA WITH YOU?
SEE?
Heh
'COURSE YOU ARE!
HOW CAN I THINK BADLY...
Yum! Peach!
...OF SOMEONE WHO'S SO NICE TO ME?

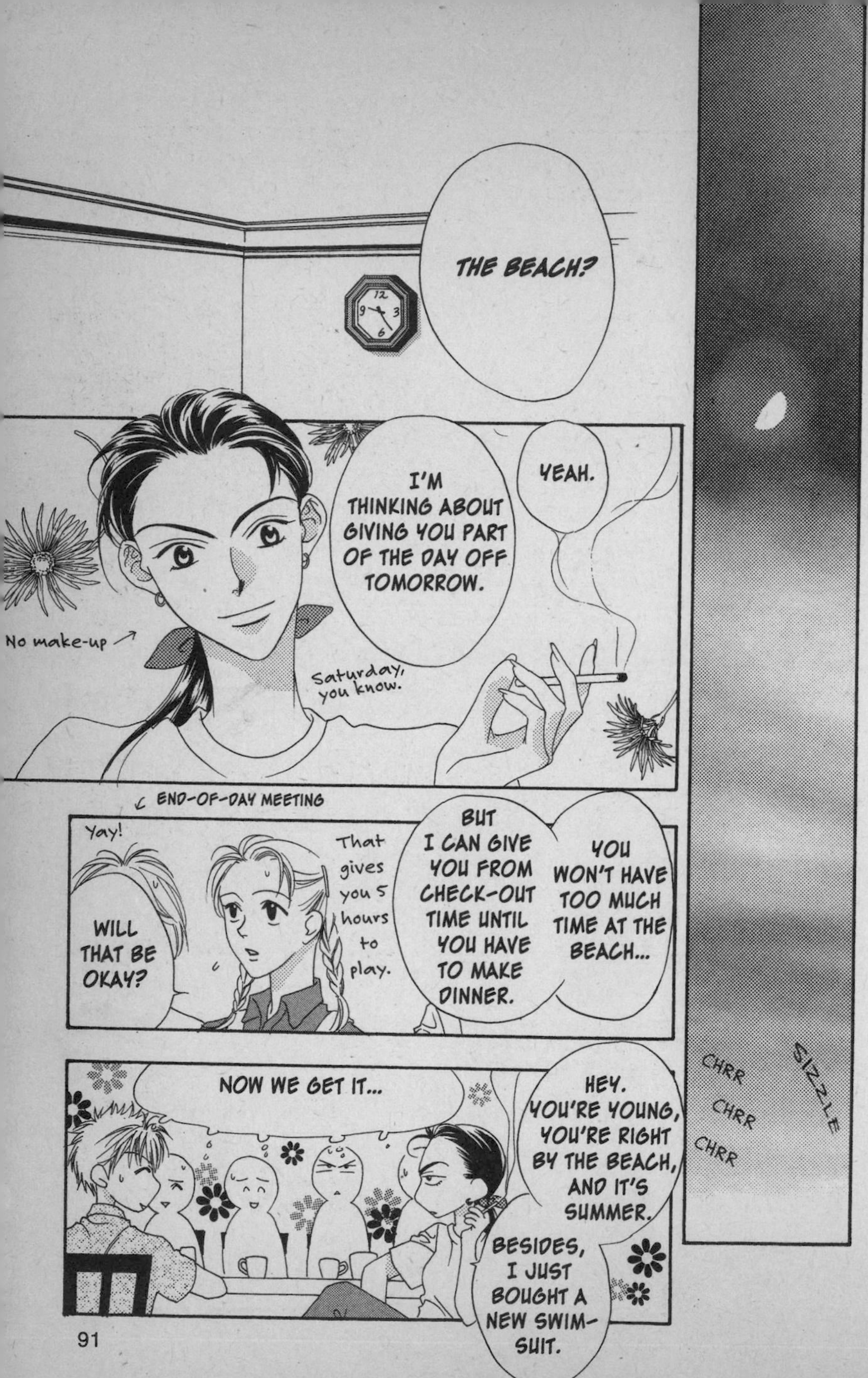
SIZZLE
CHRR
CHRR
CHRR
THE BEACH?
YEAH.
I'M THINKING ABOUT GIVING YOU PART OF THE DAY OFF TOMORROW.
Saturday, you know.
No make-up
END-OF-DAY MEETING
YOU WON'T HAVE TOO MUCH TIME AT THE BEACH...
BUT I CAN GIVE YOU FROM CHECK-OUT TIME UNTIL YOU HAVE TO MAKE DINNER.
That gives you 5 hours to play.
WILL THAT BE OKAY?
Yay!
HEY. YOU'RE YOUNG, YOU'RE RIGHT BY THE BEACH, AND IT'S SUMMER.
BESIDES, I JUST BOUGHT A NEW SWIM-SUIT.
NOW WE GET IT...

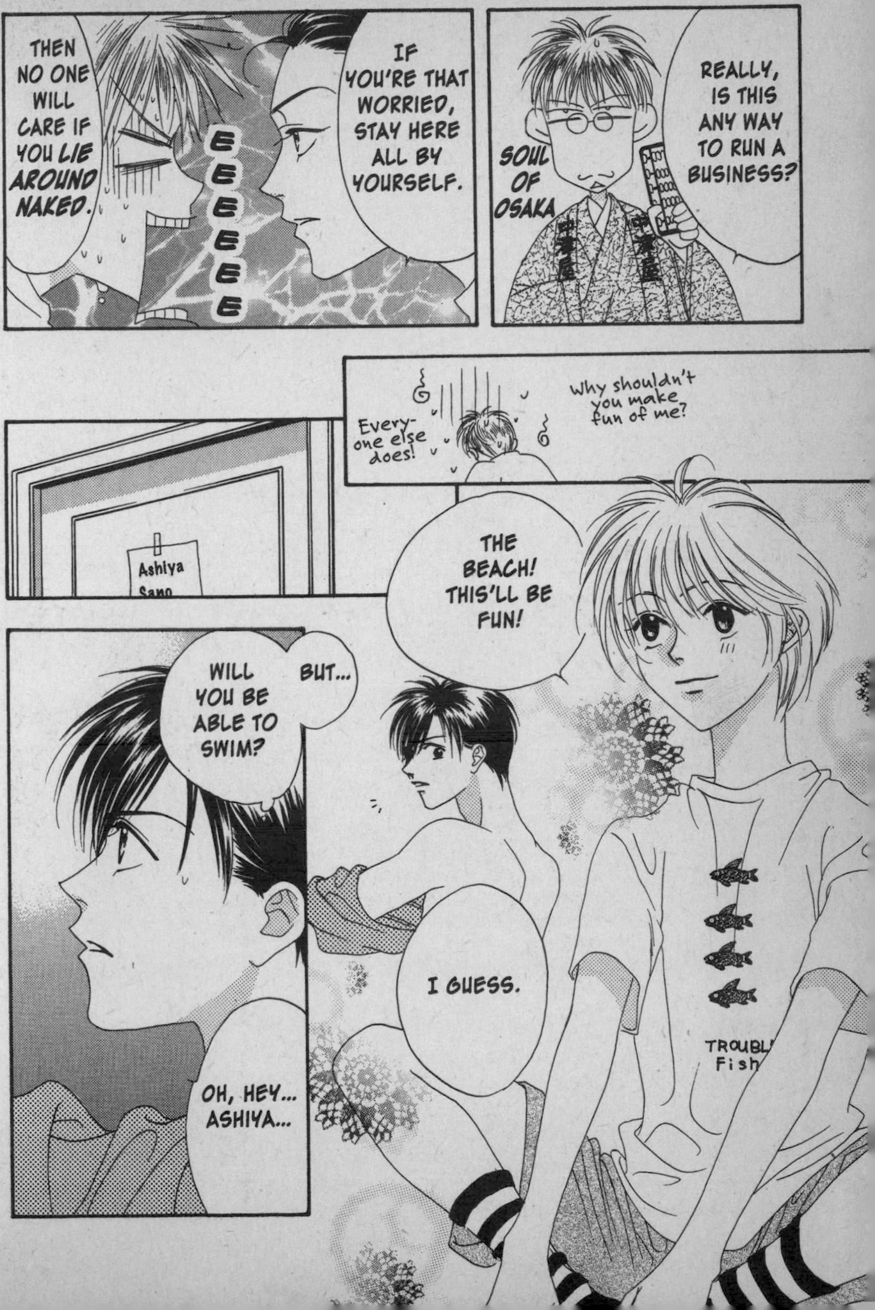
REALLY, IS THIS ANY WAY TO RUN A BUSINESS?
SOUL OF OSAKA
IF YOU'RE THAT WORRIED, STAY HERE ALL BY YOURSELF.
EEEEEE
THEN NO ONE WILL CARE IF YOU LIE AROUND NAKED.
Why shouldn't you make fun of me?
Every-one else does!
Ashiya
Sano
THE BEACH! THIS'LL BE FUN!
I GUESS.
TROUBL
Fish
BUT...
WILL YOU BE ABLE TO SWIM?
OH, HEY... ASHIYA...

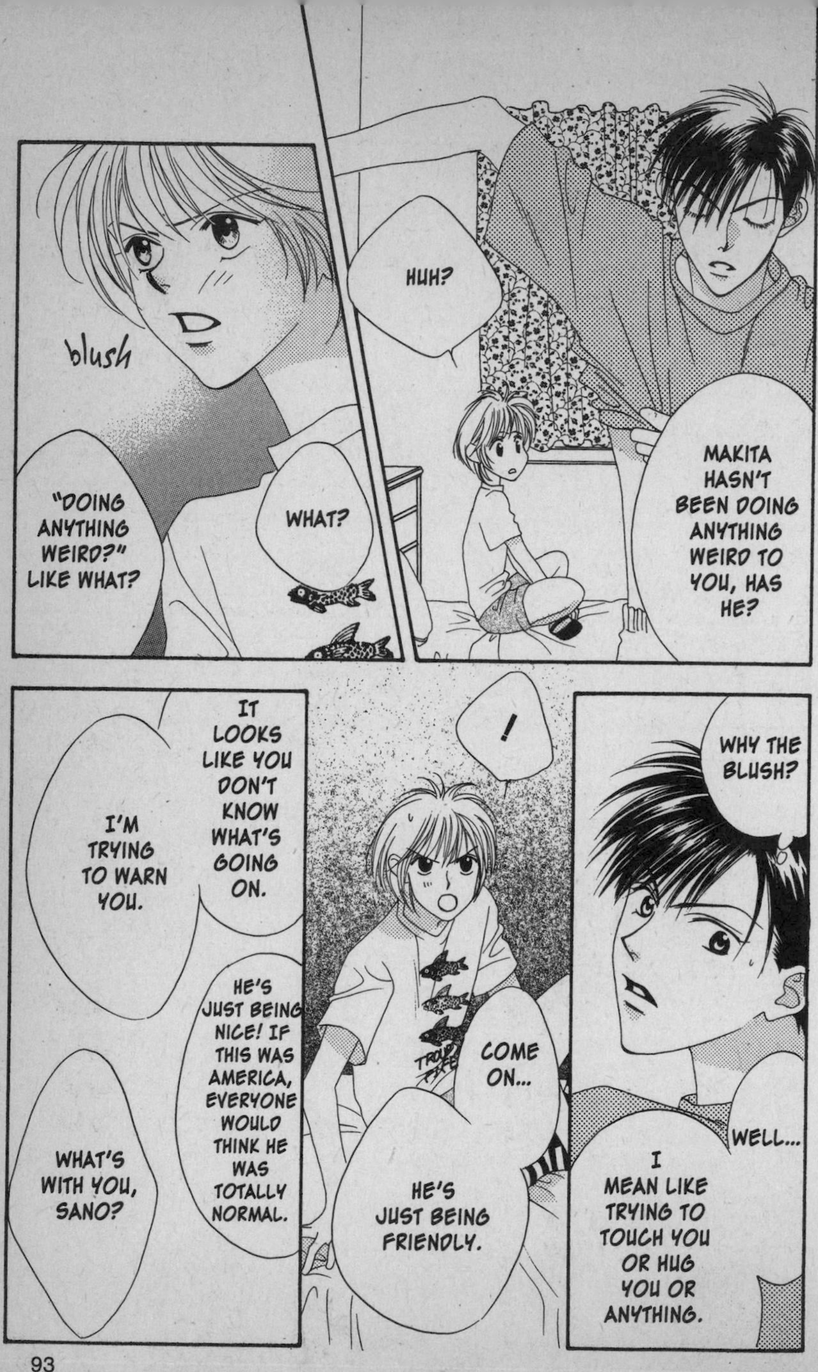
MAKITA HASN'T BEEN DOING ANYTHING WEIRD TO YOU, HAS HE?
HUH?
WHAT?
blush
"DOING ANYTHING WEIRD?" LIKE WHAT?
WHY THE BLUSH?
WELL...
I MEAN LIKE TRYING TO TOUCH YOU OR HUG YOU OR ANYTHING.
!
COME ON...
HE'S JUST BEING FRIENDLY.
IT LOOKS LIKE YOU DON'T KNOW WHAT'S GOING ON.
I'M TRYING TO WARN YOU.
HE'S JUST BEING NICE! IF THIS WAS AMERICA, EVERYONE WOULD THINK HE WAS TOTALLY NORMAL.
WHAT'S WITH YOU, SANO?

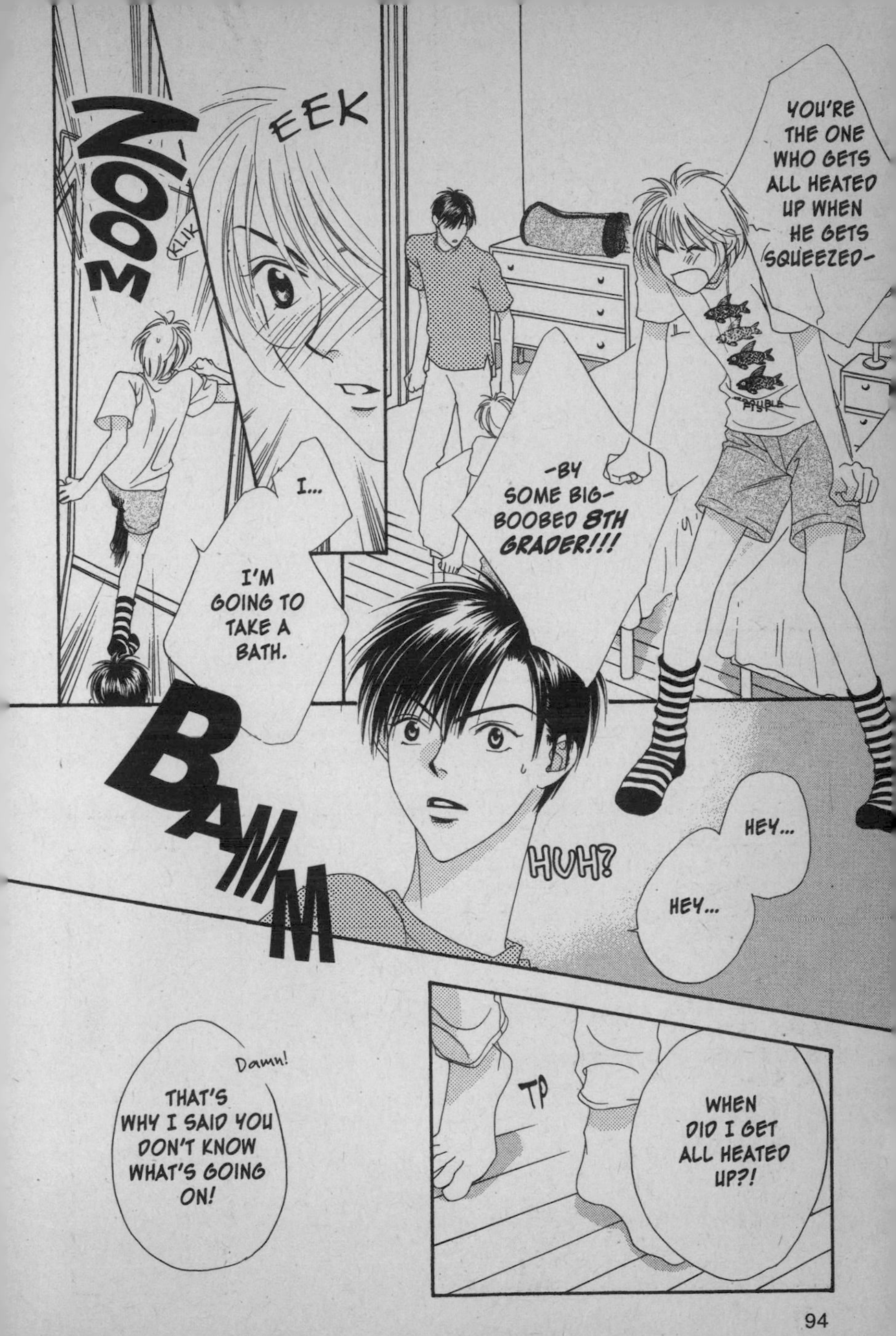
YOU'RE THE ONE WHO GETS ALL HEATED UP WHEN HE GETS SQUEEZED-
-BY SOME BIG-BOOBED 8TH GRADER!!!
EEK
I...
I'M GOING TO TAKE A BATH.
ZOOM
KLIK
BAMM
HUH?
HEY...
HEY...
TP
WHEN DID I GET ALL HEATED UP?!
Damn!
THAT'S WHY I SAID YOU DON'T KNOW WHAT'S GOING ON!

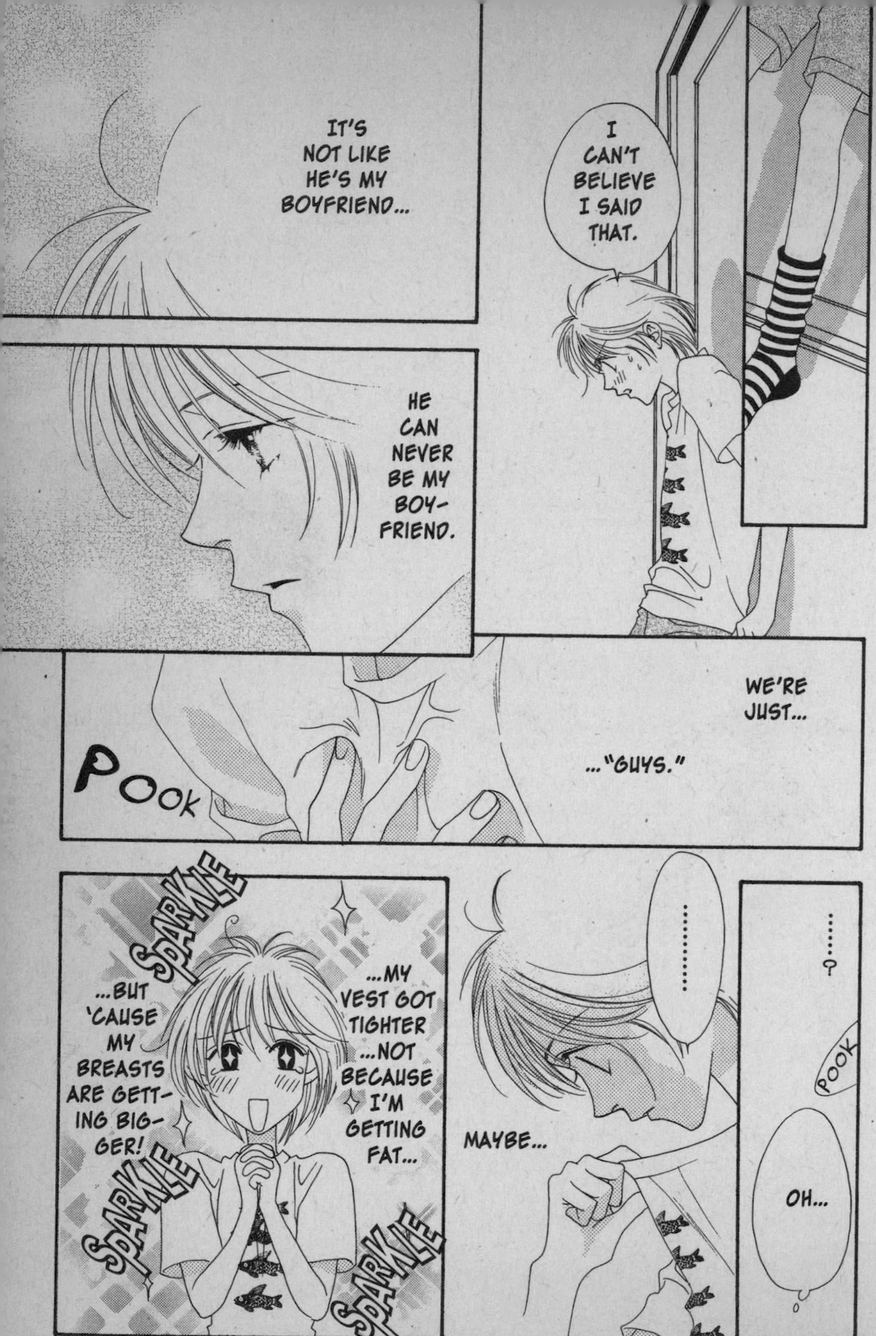
I CAN'T BELIEVE I SAID THAT.
IT'S NOT LIKE HE'S MY BOYFRIEND...
HE CAN NEVER BE MY BOY-FRIEND.
WE'RE JUST...
..."GUYS."
POOK
......?
POOK
OH...
......
MAYBE...
...MY VEST GOT TIGHTER ...NOT BECAUSE I'M GETTING FAT...
...BUT 'CAUSE MY BREASTS ARE GETT-ING BIG-GER!
SPARKLE
SPARKLE
SPARKLE
SPARKLE

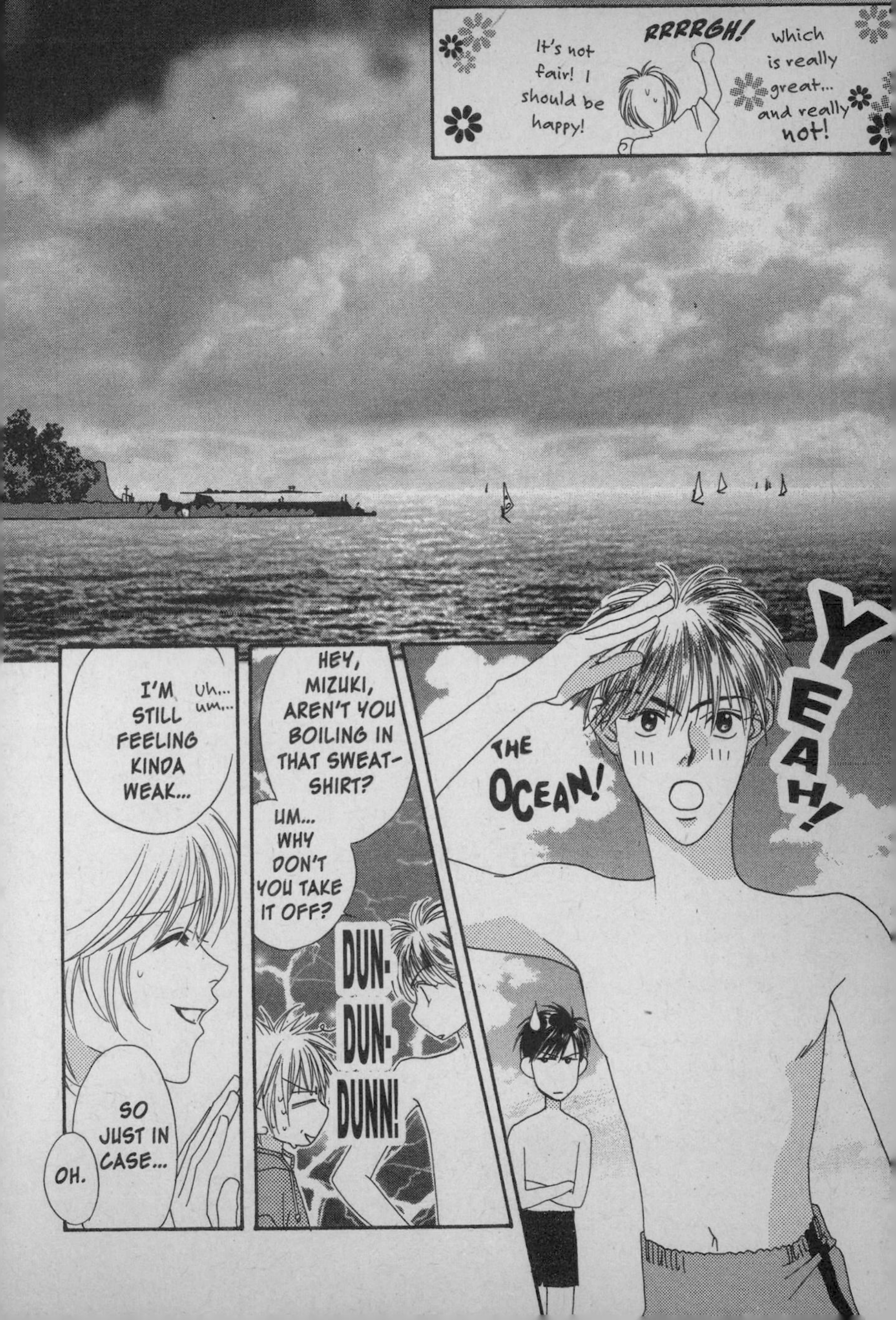
Which is really great... and really not!
RRRRGH!
It's not fair! I should be happy!
YEAH!
THE OCEAN!
HEY, MIZUKI, AREN'T YOU BOILING IN THAT SWEAT-SHIRT?
UM... WHY DON'T YOU TAKE IT OFF?
DUN-DUN-DUN-DUNN!
I'M STILL FEELING KINDA WEAK...
Uh... um...
SO JUST IN CASE...
OH.

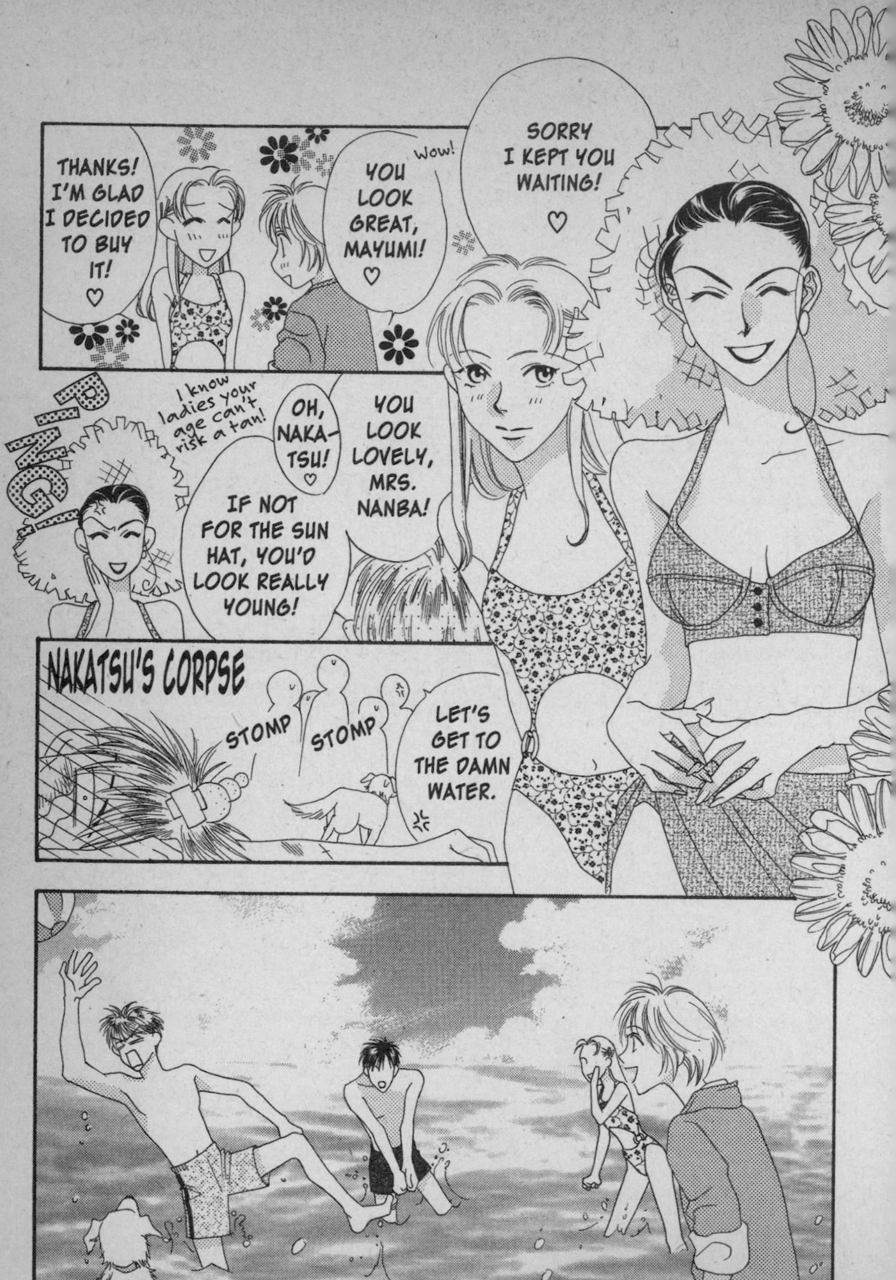
SORRY I KEPT YOU WAITING! ♡
Wow!
YOU LOOK GREAT, MAYUMI! ♡
THANKS! I'M GLAD I DECIDED TO BUY IT! ♡
YOU LOOK LOVELY, MRS. NANBA!
OH, NAKATSU! ♡
IF NOT FOR THE SUN HAT, YOU'D LOOK REALLY YOUNG!
I know ladies your age can't risk a tan!
PING!
LET'S GET TO THE DAMN WATER.
STOMP
STOMP
NAKATSU'S CORPSE

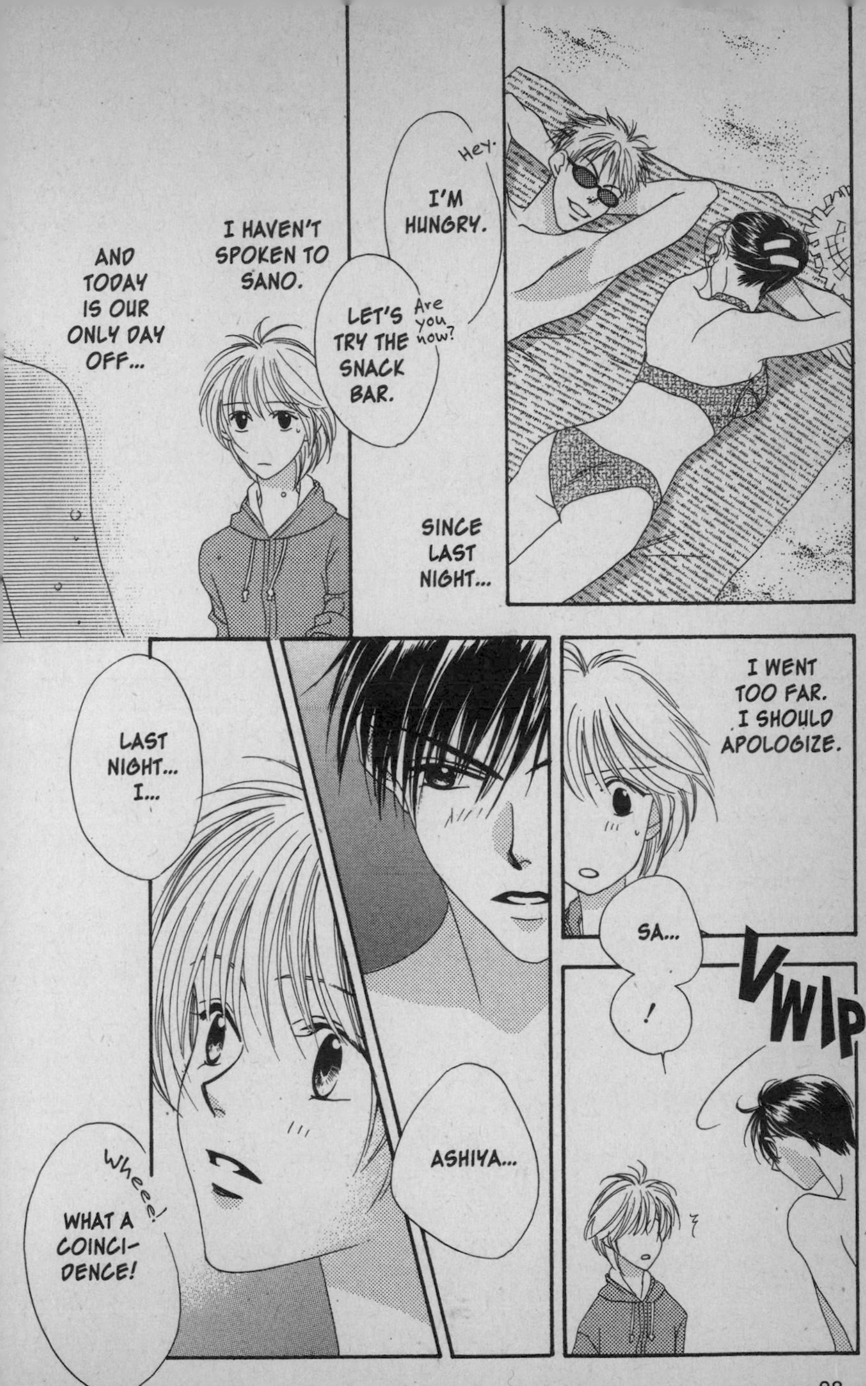
Hey.
I'M HUNGRY.
LET'S TRY THE SNACK BAR.
Are you now?
SINCE LAST NIGHT...
I HAVEN'T SPOKEN TO SANO.
AND TODAY IS OUR ONLY DAY OFF...
I WENT TOO FAR. I SHOULD APOLOGIZE.
SA...
!
VWIP
ASHIYA...
LAST NIGHT... I...
Wheee!
WHAT A COINCI-DENCE!

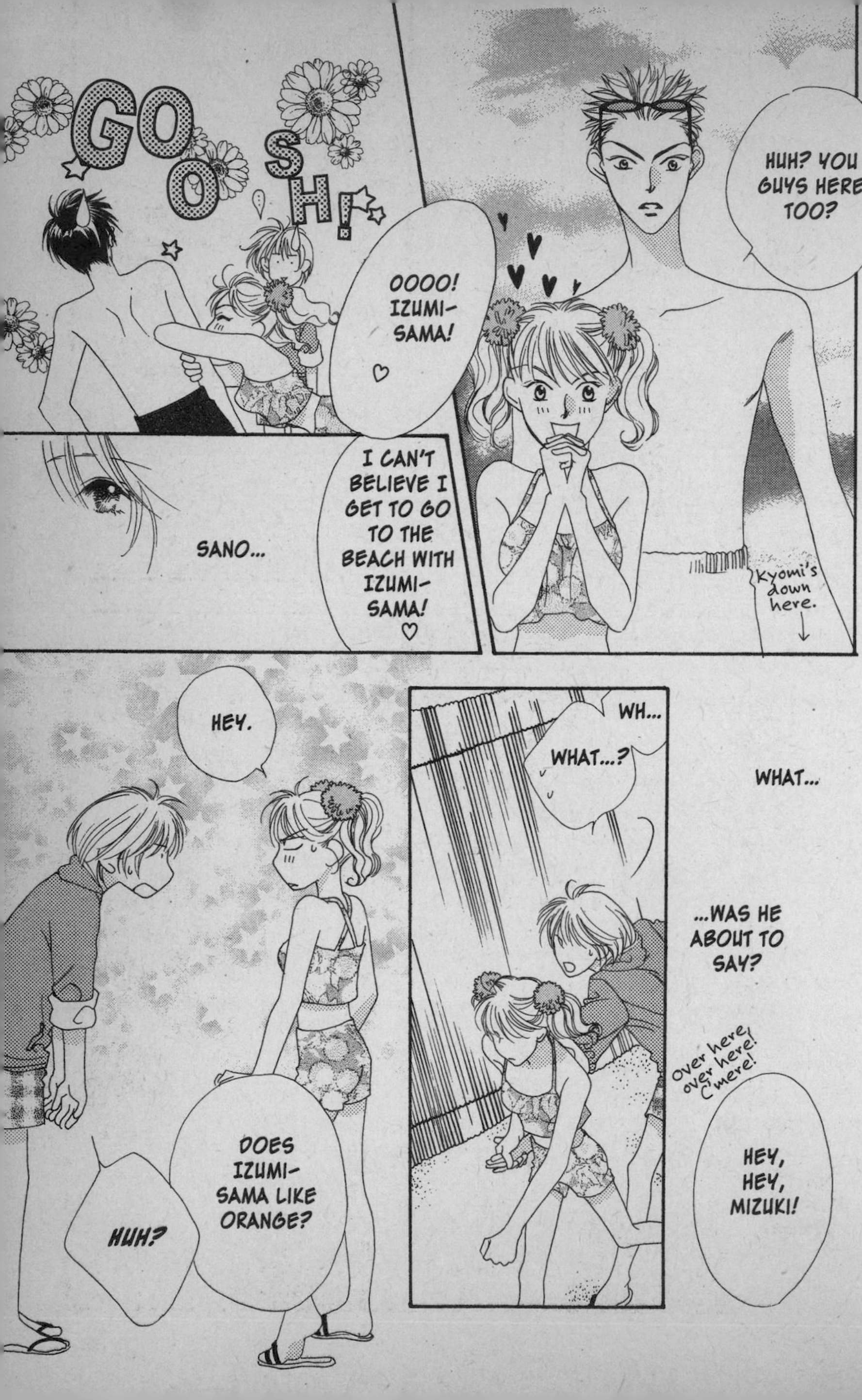
HUH? YOU GUYS HERE TOO?
Kyomi's down here.
GOOSH!
OOOO! IZUMI-SAMA! ♡
I CAN'T BELIEVE I GET TO GO TO THE BEACH WITH IZUMI-SAMA! ♡
SANO...
WHAT...
...WAS HE ABOUT TO SAY?
Over here, over here! C'mere!
HEY, HEY, MIZUKI!
WH...
WHAT...?
HEY.
DOES IZUMI-SAMA LIKE ORANGE?
HUH?

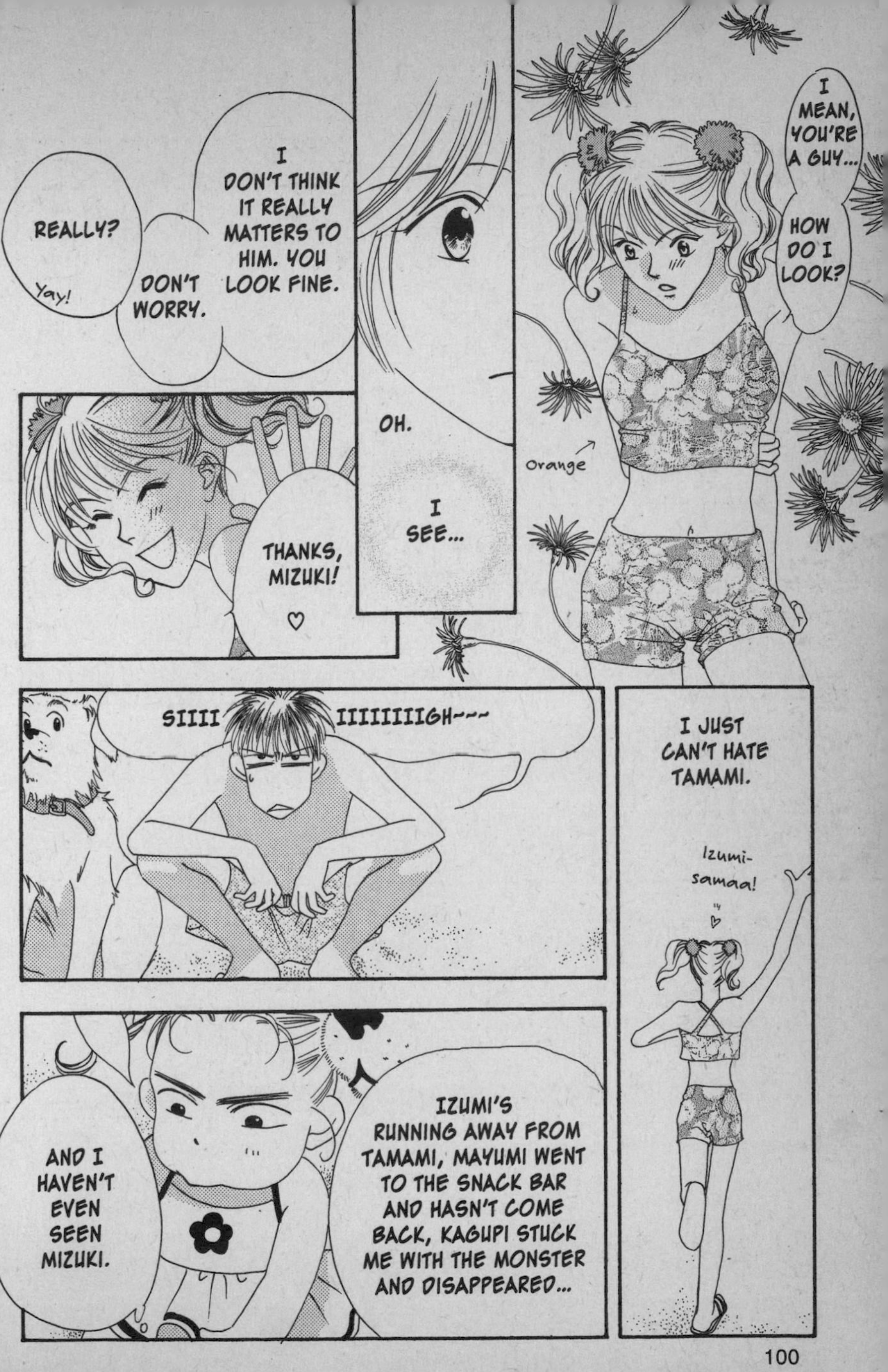
I MEAN, YOU'RE A GUY...
HOW DO I LOOK?
Orange
OH.
I SEE...
I DON'T THINK IT REALLY MATTERS TO HIM. YOU LOOK FINE.
DON'T WORRY.
REALLY?
Yay!
THANKS, MIZUKI! ♡
I JUST CAN'T HATE TAMAMI.
Izumi-samaa! ♡
SIIII IIIIIIIIGH---
IZUMI'S RUNNING AWAY FROM TAMAMI, MAYUMI WENT TO THE SNACK BAR AND HASN'T COME BACK, KAGUPI STUCK ME WITH THE MONSTER AND DISAPPEARED...
AND I HAVEN'T EVEN SEEN MIZUKI.

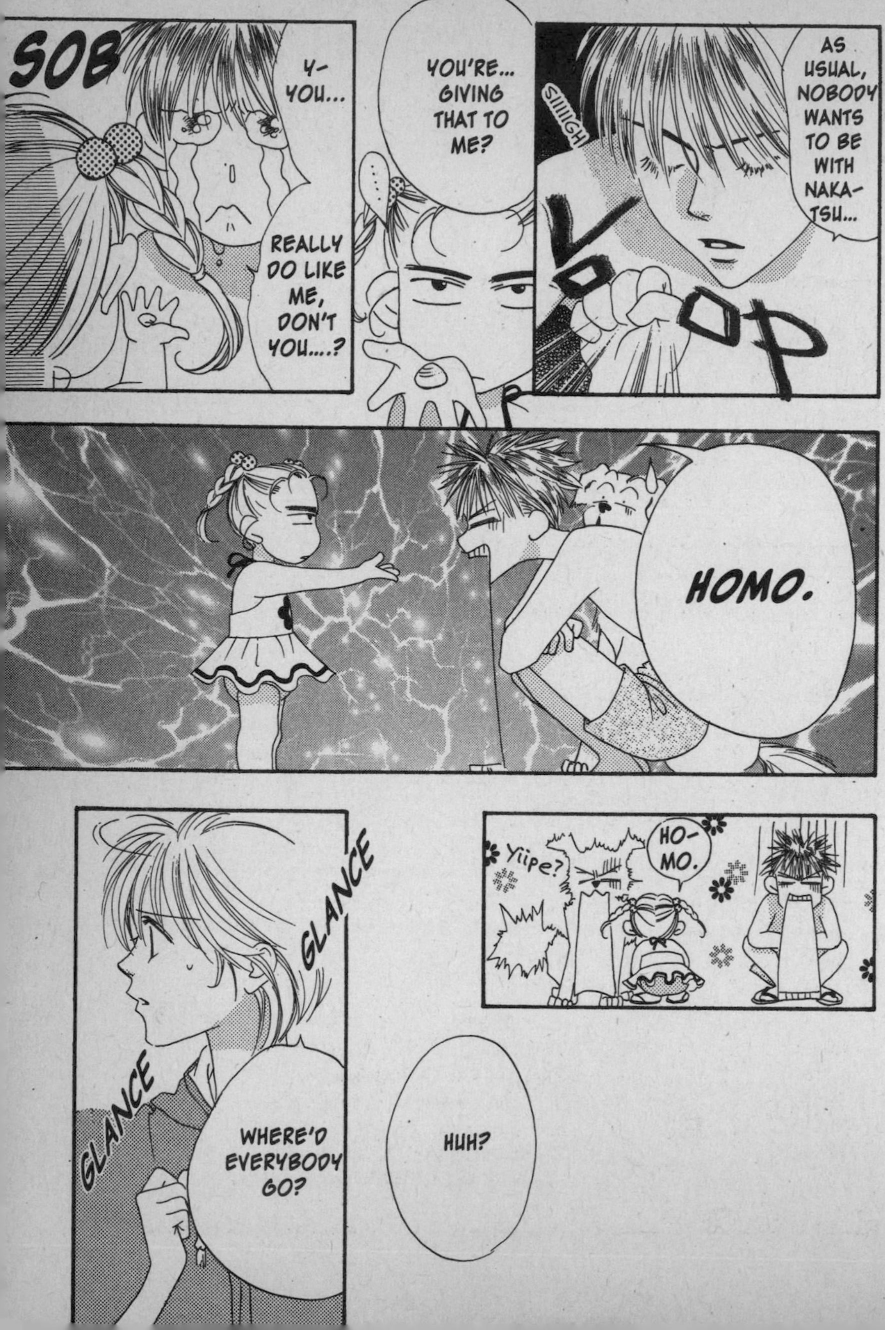
SIIIIGH
AS USUAL, NOBODY WANTS TO BE WITH NAKATSU...
VOOP
YOU'RE... GIVING THAT TO ME?
...
SOB
Y-YOU...
REALLY DO LIKE ME, DON'T YOU....?
HOMO.
HO-MO.
Yiipe?
GLANCE
GLANCE
HUH?
WHERE'D EVERYBODY GO?

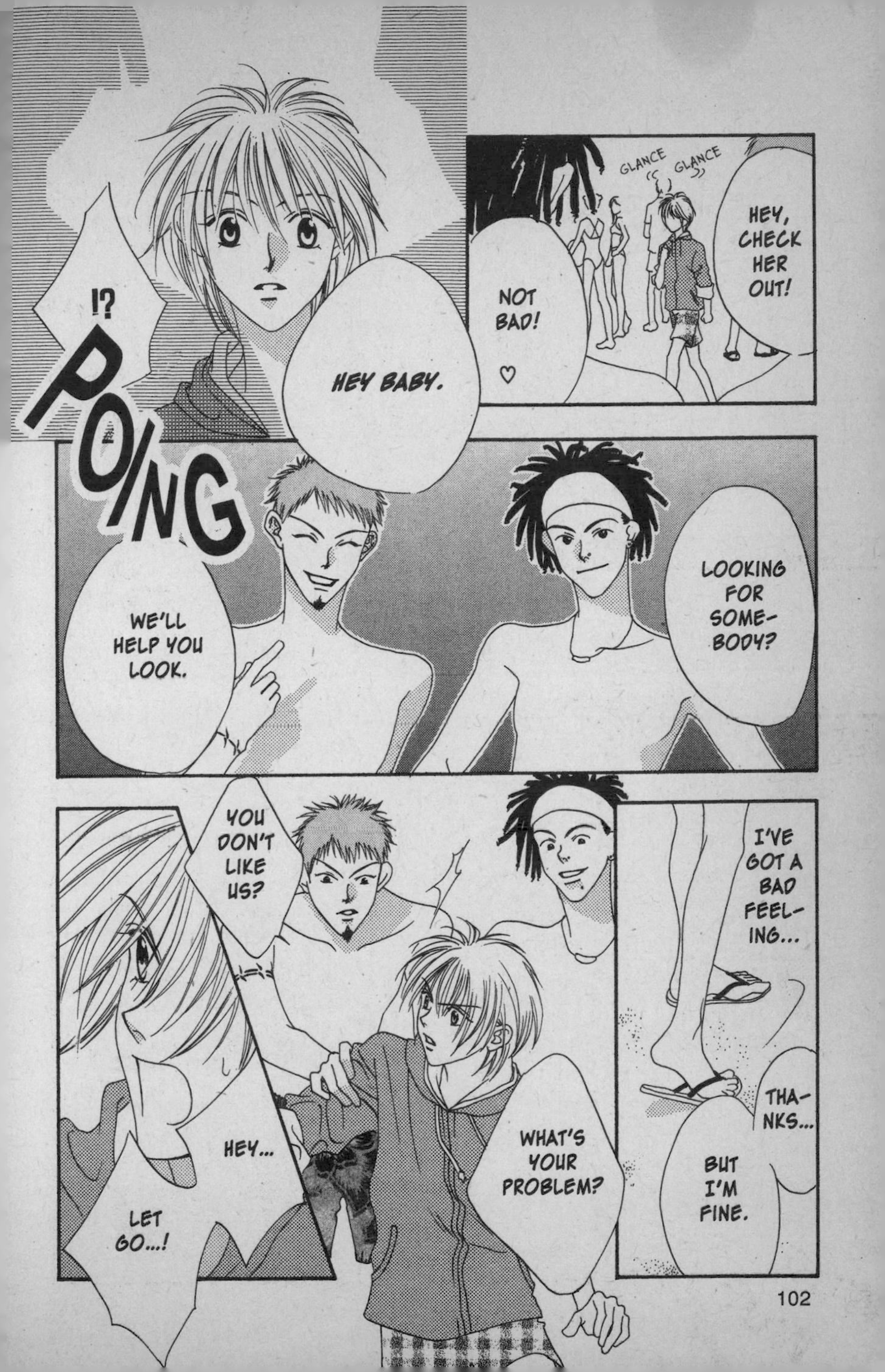
GLANCE
GLANCE
HEY, CHECK HER OUT!
NOT BAD! ♡
HEY BABY.
!?
POING
LOOKING FOR SOME-BODY?
WE'LL HELP YOU LOOK.
I'VE GOT A BAD FEEL-ING...
THA-NKS...
BUT I'M FINE.
YOU DON'T LIKE US?
WHAT'S YOUR PROBLEM?
HEY...
LET GO...!

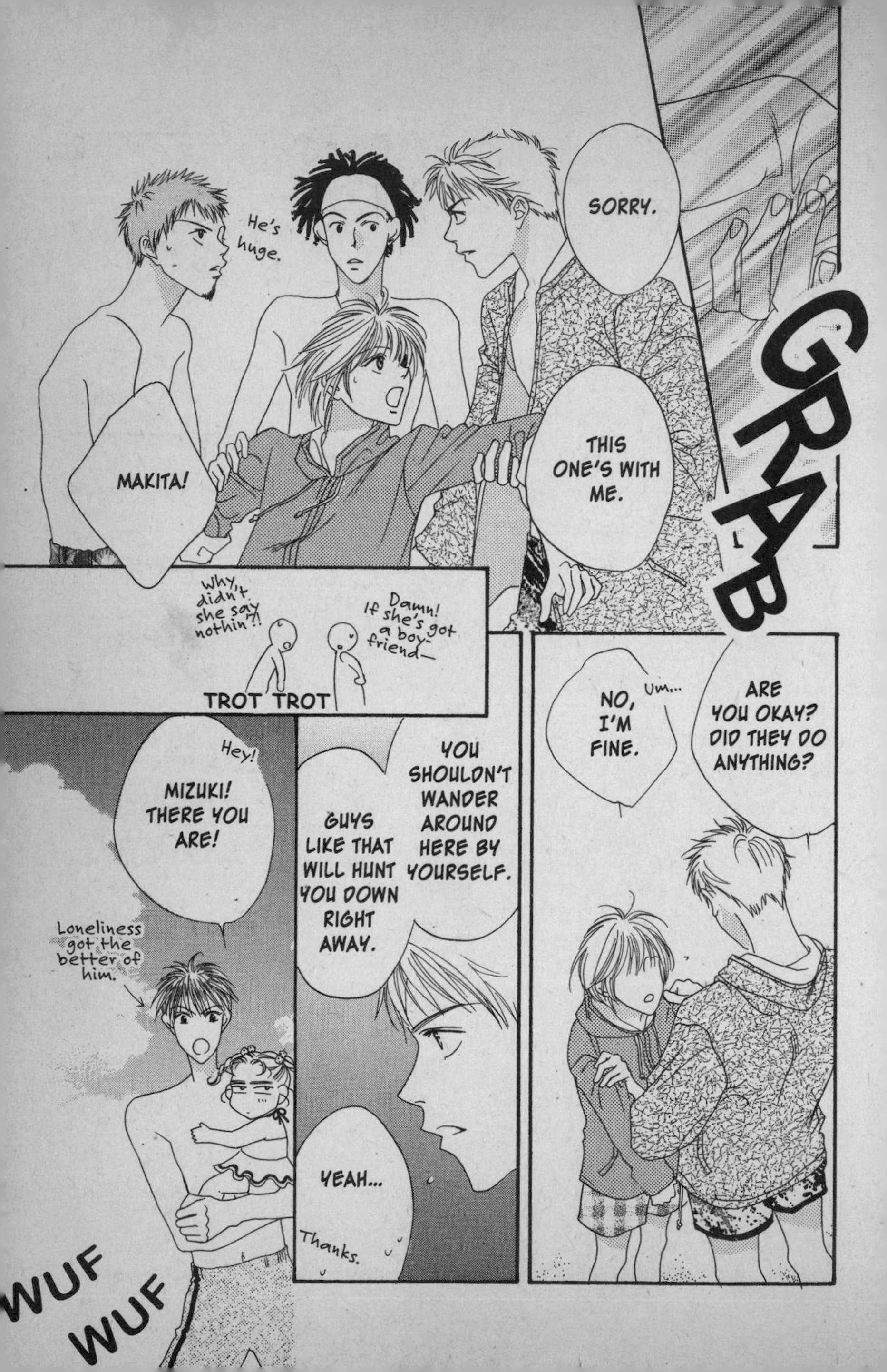
GRAB
SORRY.
THIS ONE'S WITH ME.
He's huge.
MAKITA!
Damn! If she's got a boy-friend—
Why didn't she say nothin'?!
TROT TROT
ARE YOU OKAY? DID THEY DO ANYTHING?
Um...
NO, I'M FINE.
YOU SHOULDN'T WANDER AROUND HERE BY YOURSELF.
GUYS LIKE THAT WILL HUNT YOU DOWN RIGHT AWAY.
YEAH...
Thanks.
Hey!
MIZUKI! THERE YOU ARE!
Loneliness got the better of him.
WUF WUF

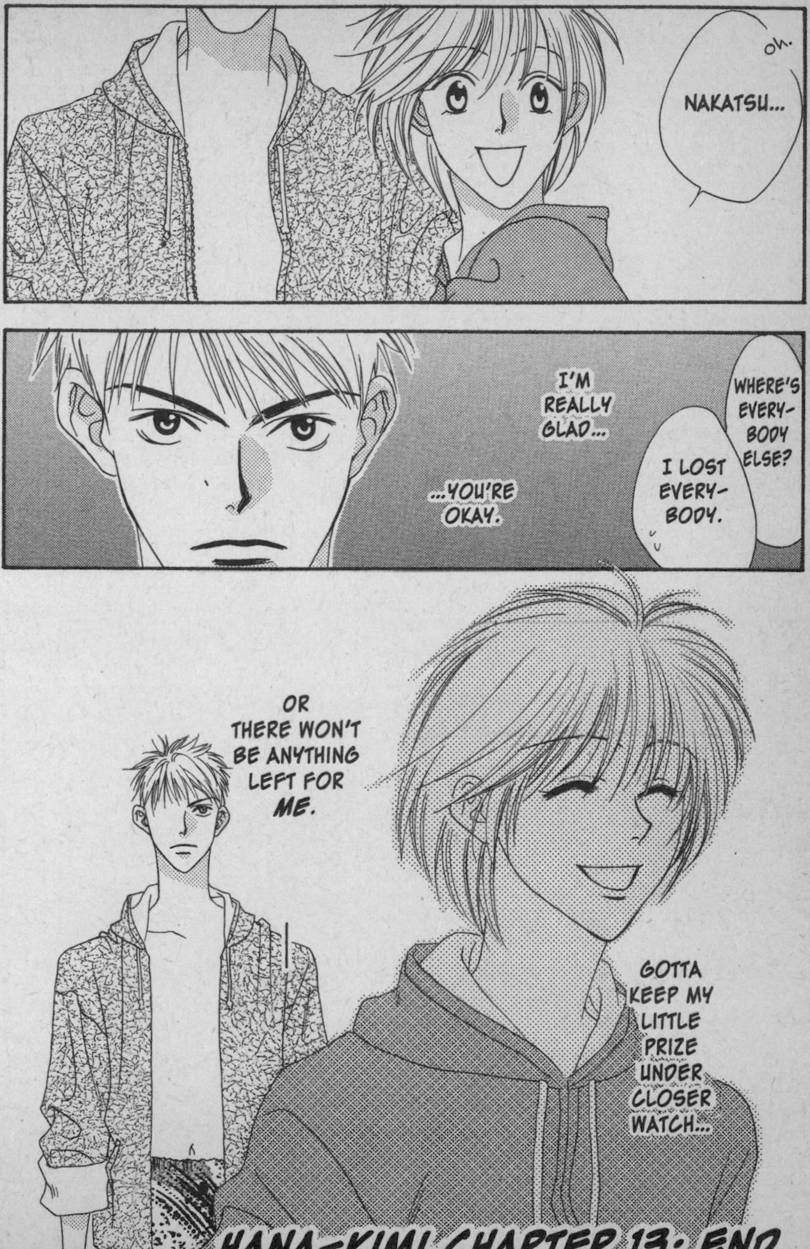
Oh.
NAKATSU...
WHERE'S EVERY-BODY ELSE?
I LOST EVERY-BODY.
I'M REALLY GLAD...
...YOU'RE OKAY.
GOTTA KEEP MY LITTLE PRIZE UNDER CLOSER WATCH...
OR THERE WON'T BE ANYTHING LEFT FOR ME.
HANA-KIMI CHAPTER 13: END

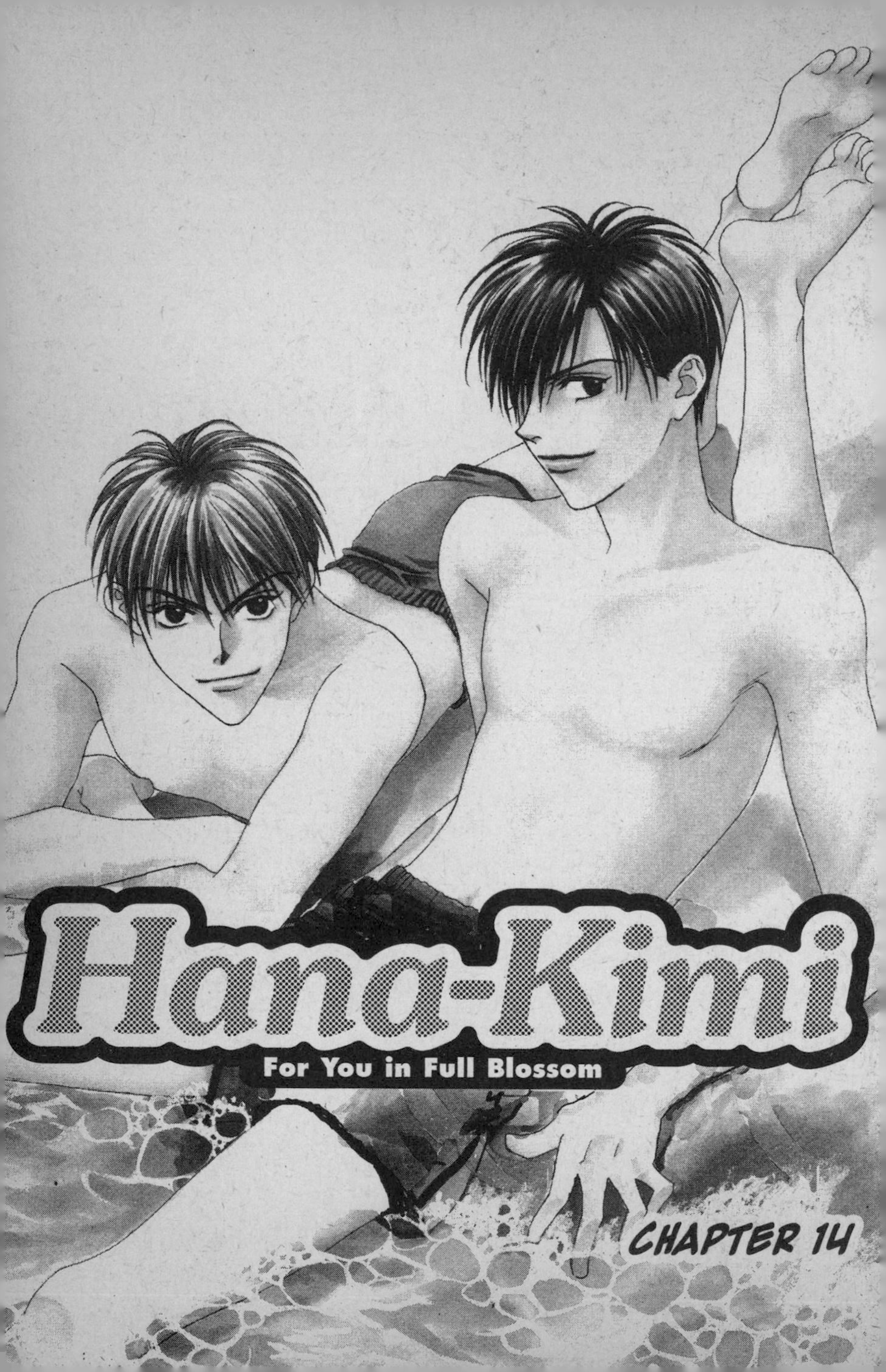
Hana-Kimi
For You in Full Blossom
CHAPTER 14

Ugh!
ARE YOU GONNA FOLLOW ME EVERY-WHERE?
BUT IZUMI-SAMA...
JUST LET GO OF ME!
No.
ASHIYA...
HEY...

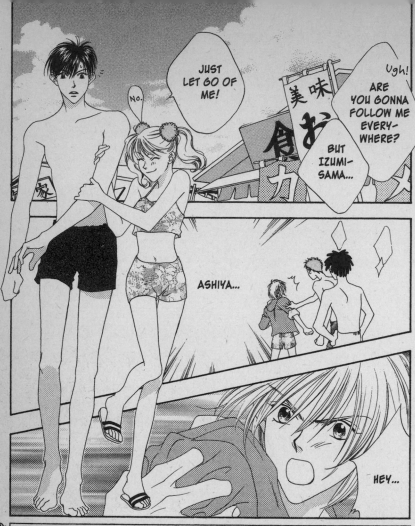

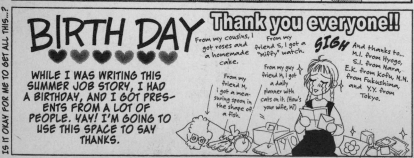

BIRTH DAY

Thank you everyone!!

WHILE I WAS WRITING THIS SUMMER JOB STORY, I HAD A BIRTHDAY, AND I GOT PRESENTS FROM A LOT OF PEOPLE. YAY! I'M GOING TO USE THIS SPACE TO SAY THANKS.

From my cousins, I got roses and a homemade cake.

From my friend S, I got a "Miffy" watch.

From my friend M, i got a measuring spoon in the shape of a fish.

From my guy friend M, I got a daily planner with cats on it. (How's your wife, M?)

SIGH

And thanks to... M.I. from Hyogo, S.I. from Nara, E.K. from Kofu, N.N. from Fukushima, and Y.Y. from Tokyo.

IS IT OKAY FOR ME TO GET ALL THIS...?

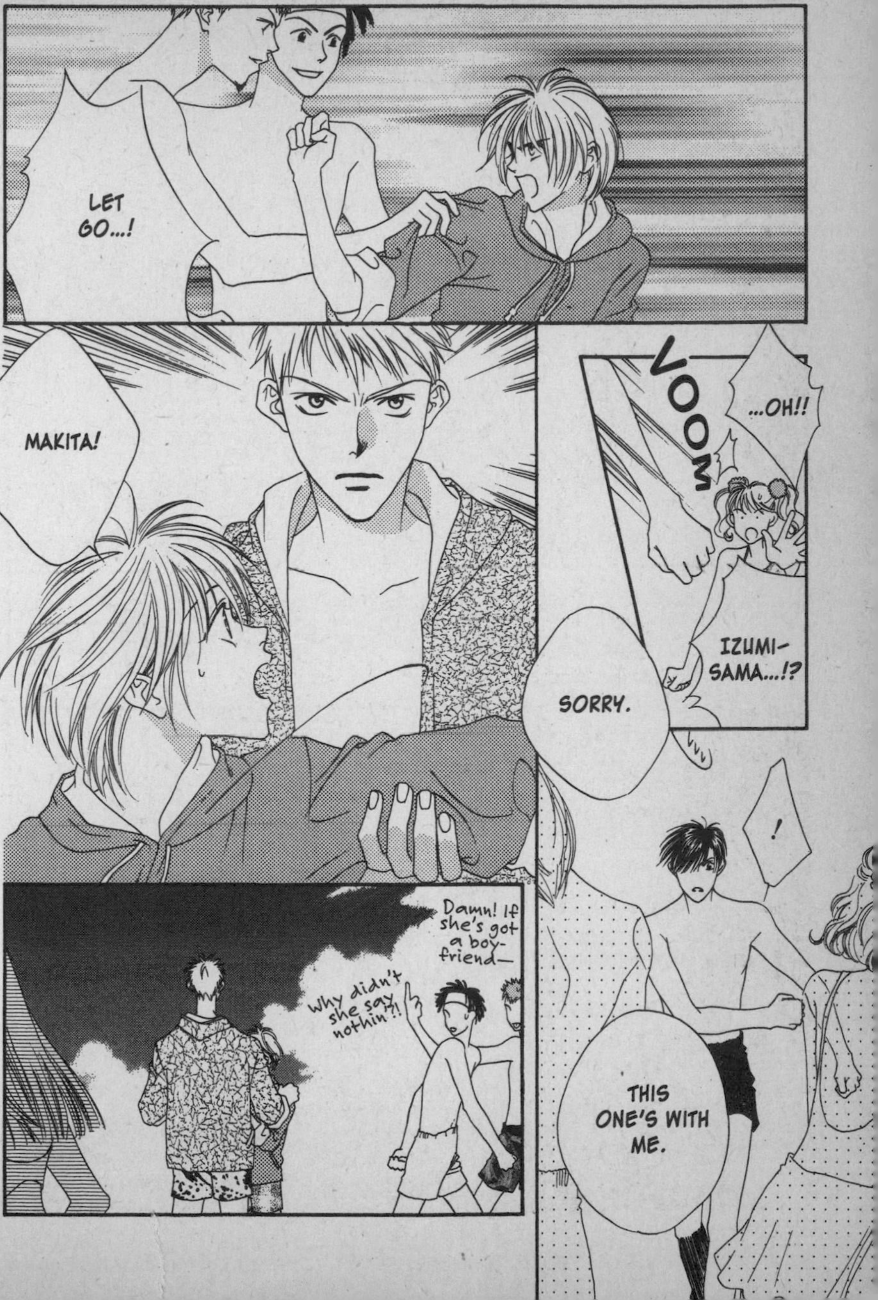
LET GO...!
VOOM
...OH!!
IZUMI-SAMA...!?
MAKITA!
SORRY.
!
THIS ONE'S WITH ME.
Damn! If she's got a boy-friend—
why didn't she say nothin'?!

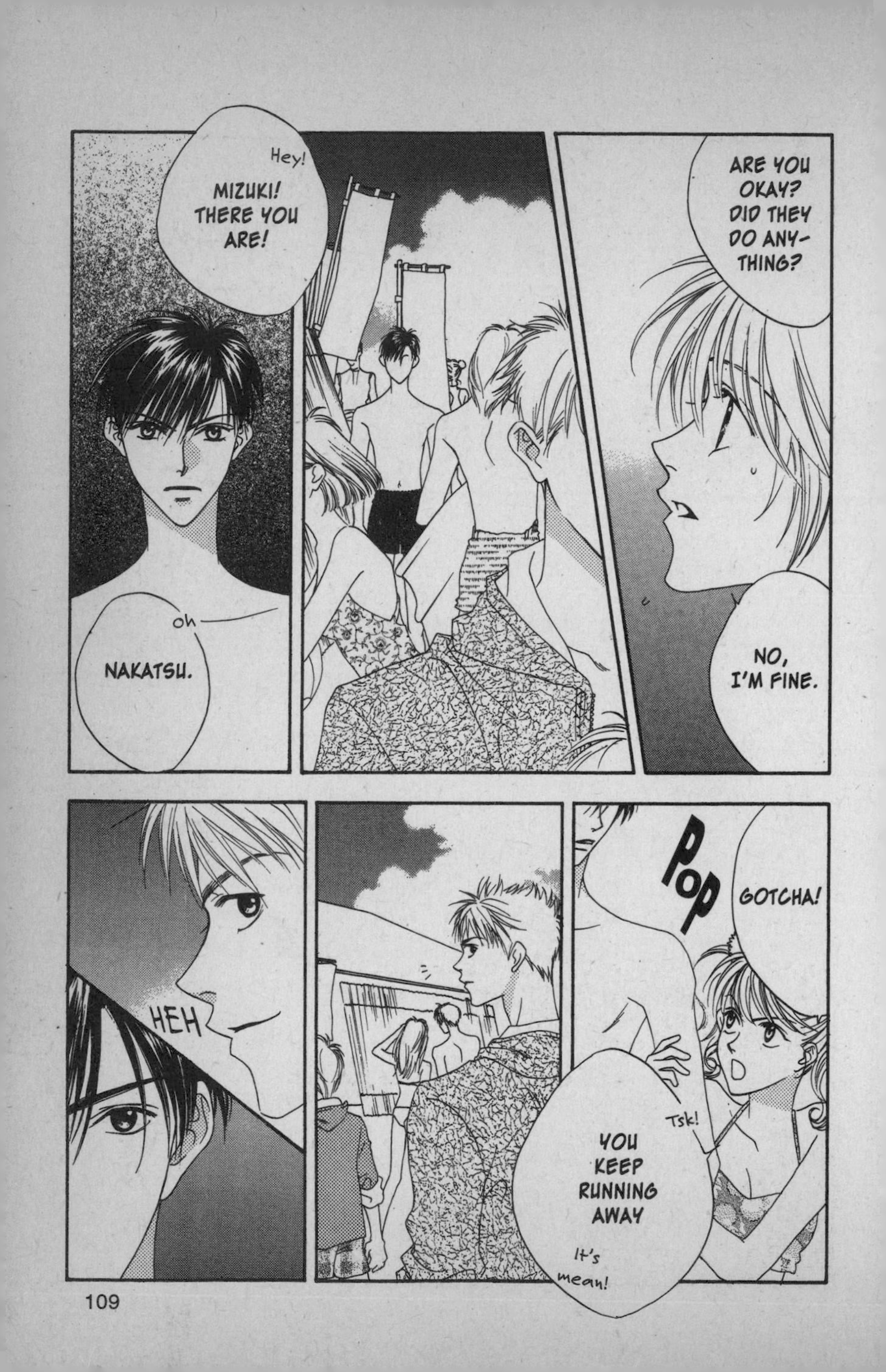
ARE YOU OKAY? DID THEY DO ANY-THING?
NO, I'M FINE.
Hey!
MIZUKI! THERE YOU ARE!
oh
NAKATSU.
POP
GOTCHA!
Tsk!
YOU KEEP RUNNING AWAY
It's mean!
HEH

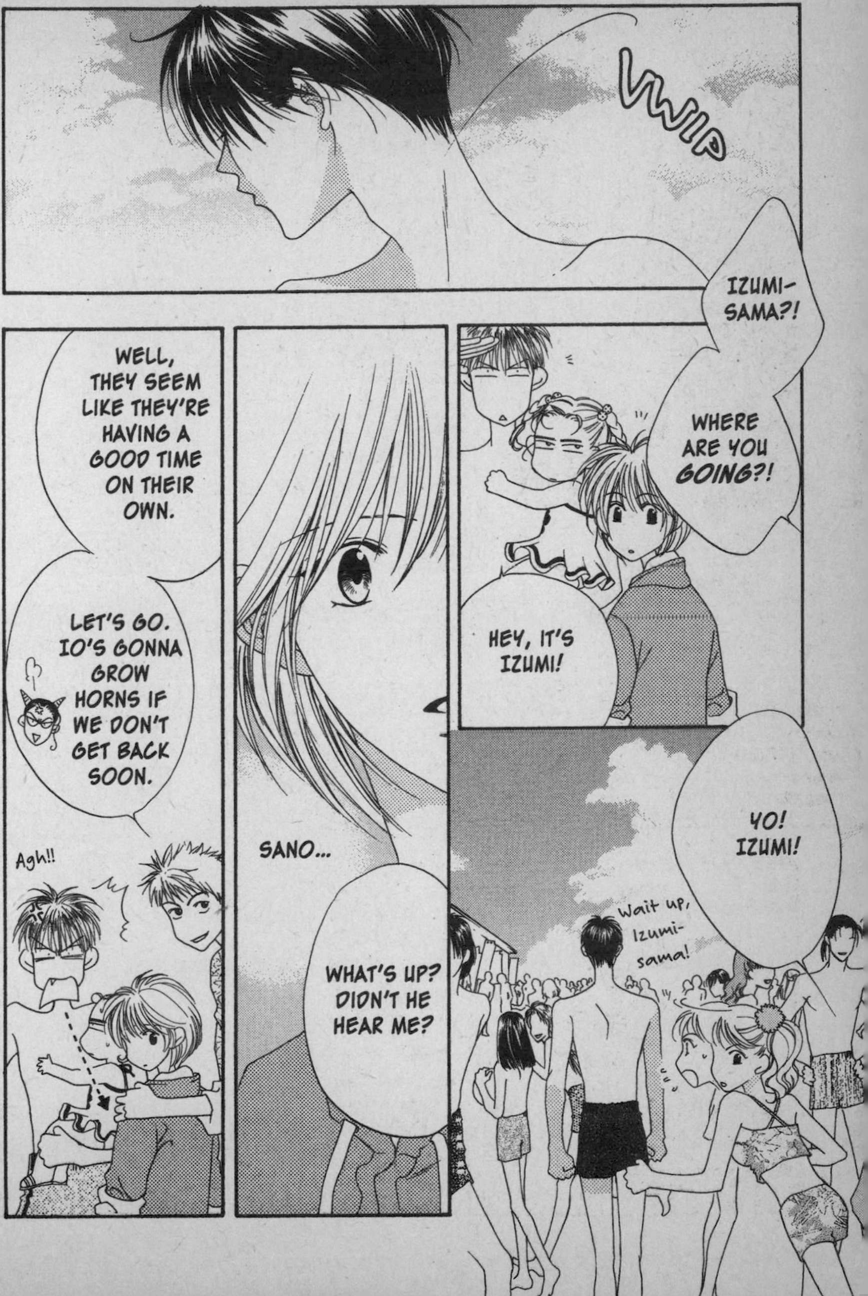
VWIP
IZUMI-SAMA?!
WHERE ARE YOU GOING?!
HEY, IT'S IZUMI!
YO! IZUMI!
Wait up, Izumi-sama!
SANO...
WHAT'S UP? DIDN'T HE HEAR ME?
WELL, THEY SEEM LIKE THEY'RE HAVING A GOOD TIME ON THEIR OWN.
LET'S GO. IO'S GONNA GROW HORNS IF WE DON'T GET BACK SOON.
Agh!!

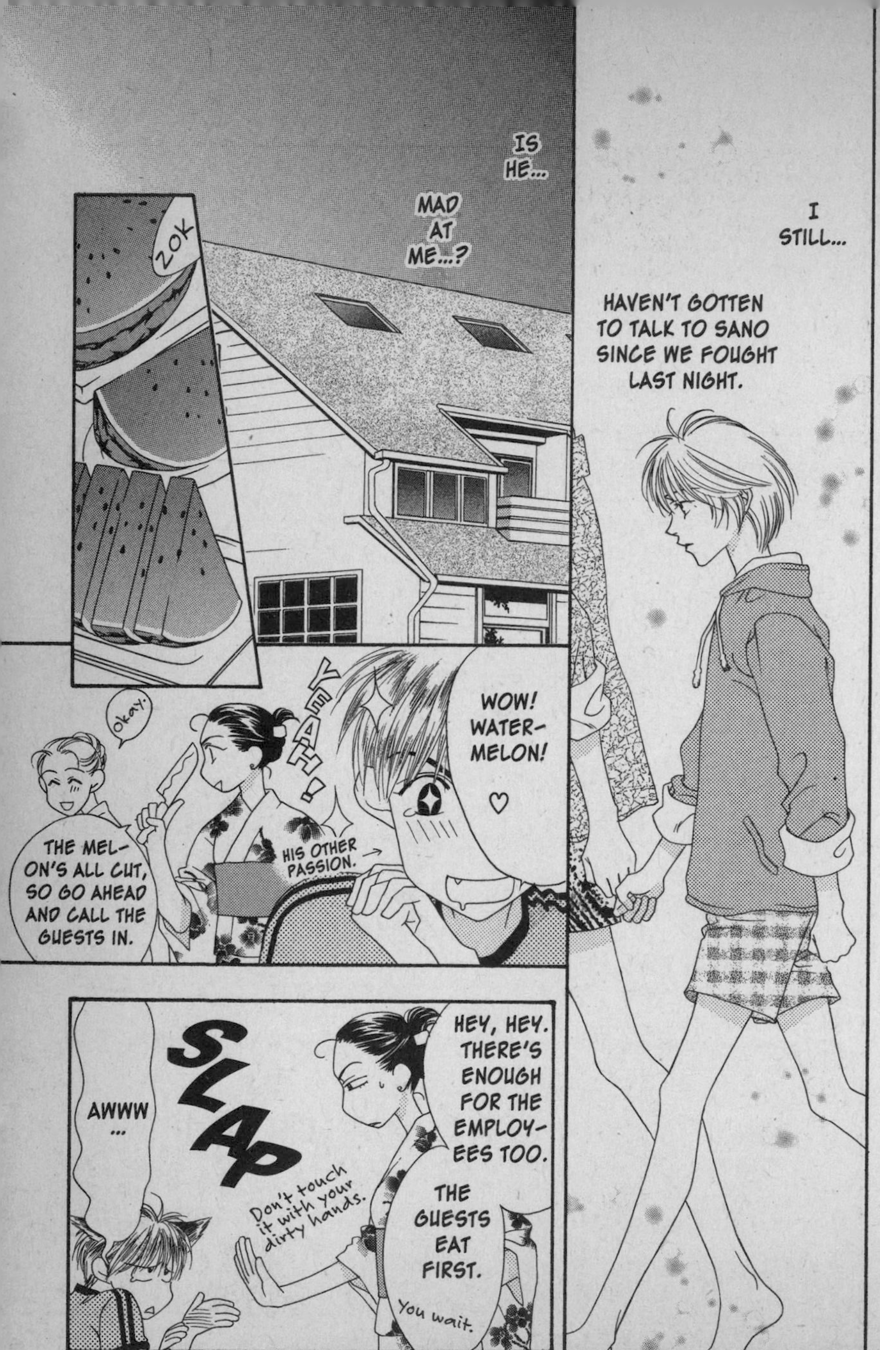

I STILL...
HAVEN'T GOTTEN TO TALK TO SANO SINCE WE FOUGHT LAST NIGHT.
IS HE...
MAD AT ME...?
ZOK
WOW! WATER-MELON! ♡
YEAH!
HIS OTHER PASSION.
Okay.
THE MEL-ON'S ALL CUT, SO GO AHEAD AND CALL THE GUESTS IN.
HEY, HEY. THERE'S ENOUGH FOR THE EMPLOY-EES TOO.
THE GUESTS EAT FIRST.
You wait.
SLAP
Don't touch it with your dirty hands.
AWWW...

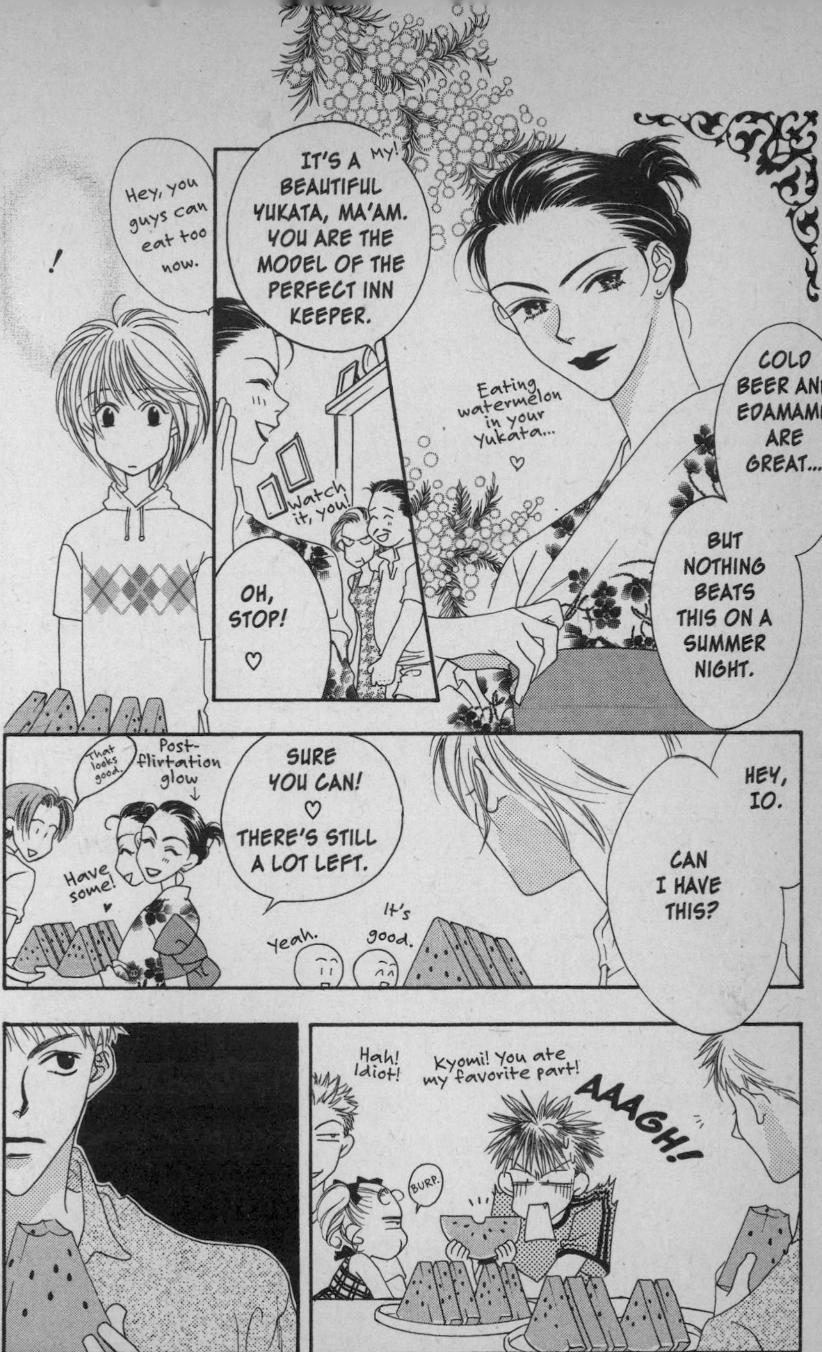
Eating watermelon in your Yukata...
COLD BEER AND EDAMAME ARE GREAT...
BUT NOTHING BEATS THIS ON A SUMMER NIGHT.
IT'S A BEAUTIFUL YUKATA, MA'AM. YOU ARE THE MODEL OF THE PERFECT INN KEEPER.
My!
Watch it, you!
OH, STOP! ♡
!
Hey, you guys can eat too now.
HEY, IO.
CAN I HAVE THIS?
SURE YOU CAN! ♡ THERE'S STILL A LOT LEFT.
Post-flirtation glow
That looks good.
Have some!
It's good.
Yeah.
AAAGH!
Kyomi! You ate my favorite part!
Hah! Idiot!
BURP.

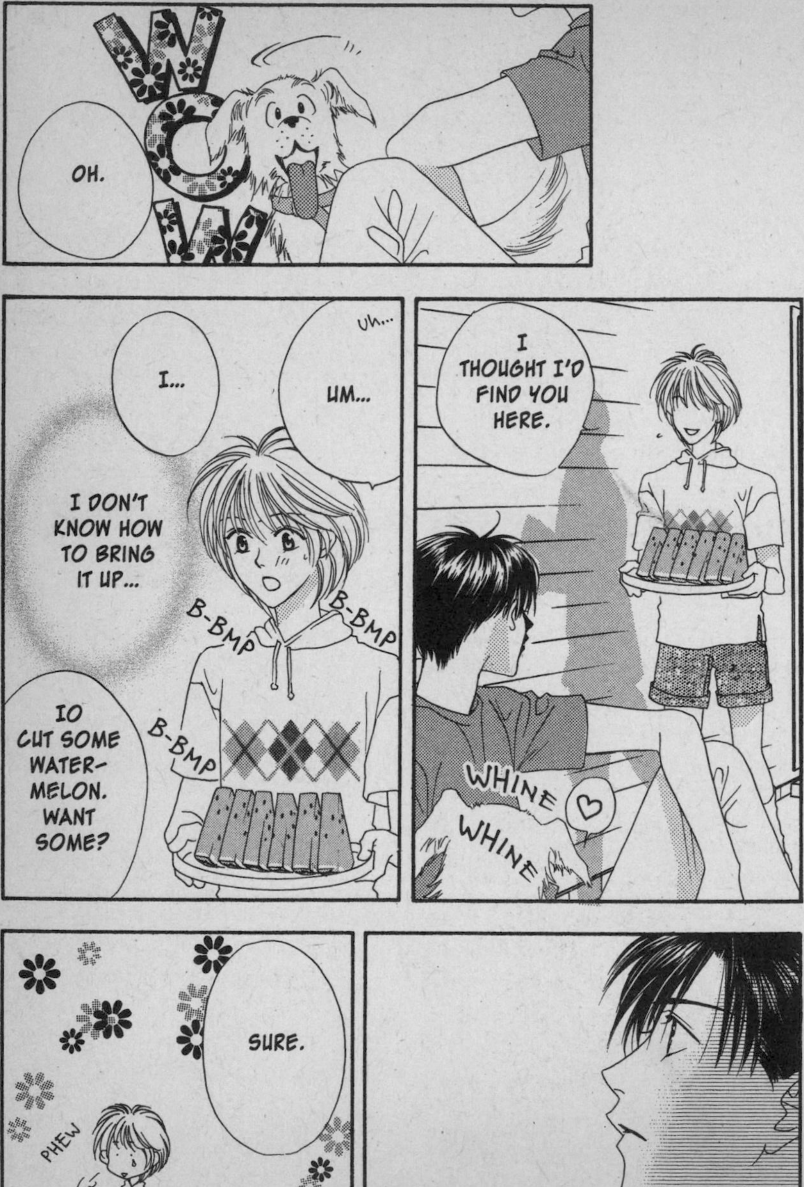
WOW
OH.
I THOUGHT I'D FIND YOU HERE.
WHINE
WHINE
Uh...
UM...
I...
I DON'T KNOW HOW TO BRING IT UP...
B-BMP
B-BMP
B-BMP
IO CUT SOME WATER-MELON. WANT SOME?
SURE.
PHEW

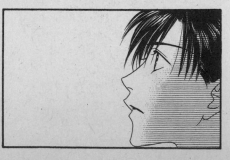

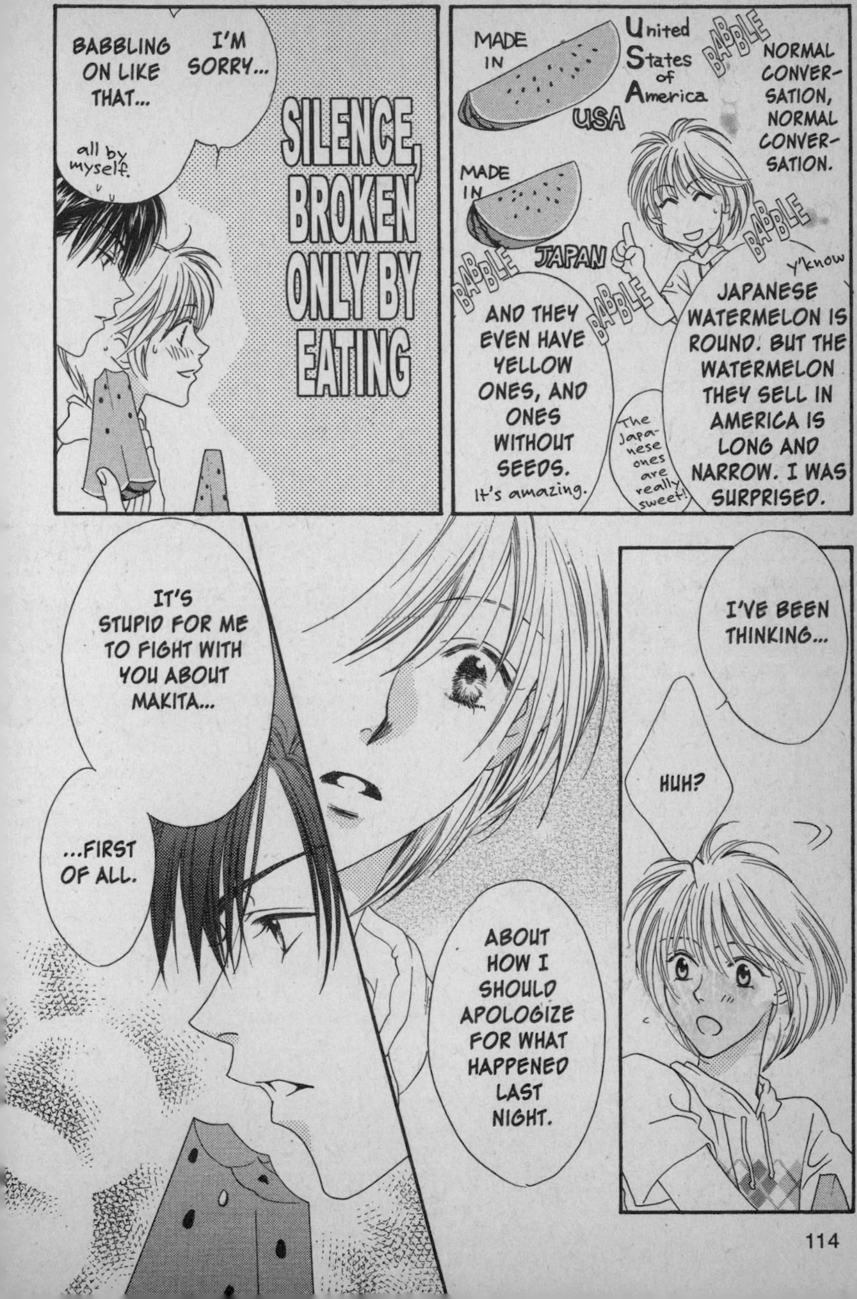
NORMAL CONVERSATION, NORMAL CONVERSATION.
BABBLE
United States of America
MADE IN USA
MADE IN JAPAN
BABBLE
y'know
JAPANESE WATERMELON IS ROUND. BUT THE WATERMELON THEY SELL IN AMERICA IS LONG AND NARROW. I WAS SURPRISED.
The Japanese ones are really sweet!
BABBLE
BABBLE
AND THEY EVEN HAVE YELLOW ONES, AND ONES WITHOUT SEEDS.
It's amazing.
I'M SORRY...
BABBLING ON LIKE THAT...
all by myself.
SILENCE, BROKEN ONLY BY EATING
I'VE BEEN THINKING...
HUH?
ABOUT HOW I SHOULD APOLOGIZE FOR WHAT HAPPENED LAST NIGHT.
IT'S STUPID FOR ME TO FIGHT WITH YOU ABOUT MAKITA...
...FIRST OF ALL.

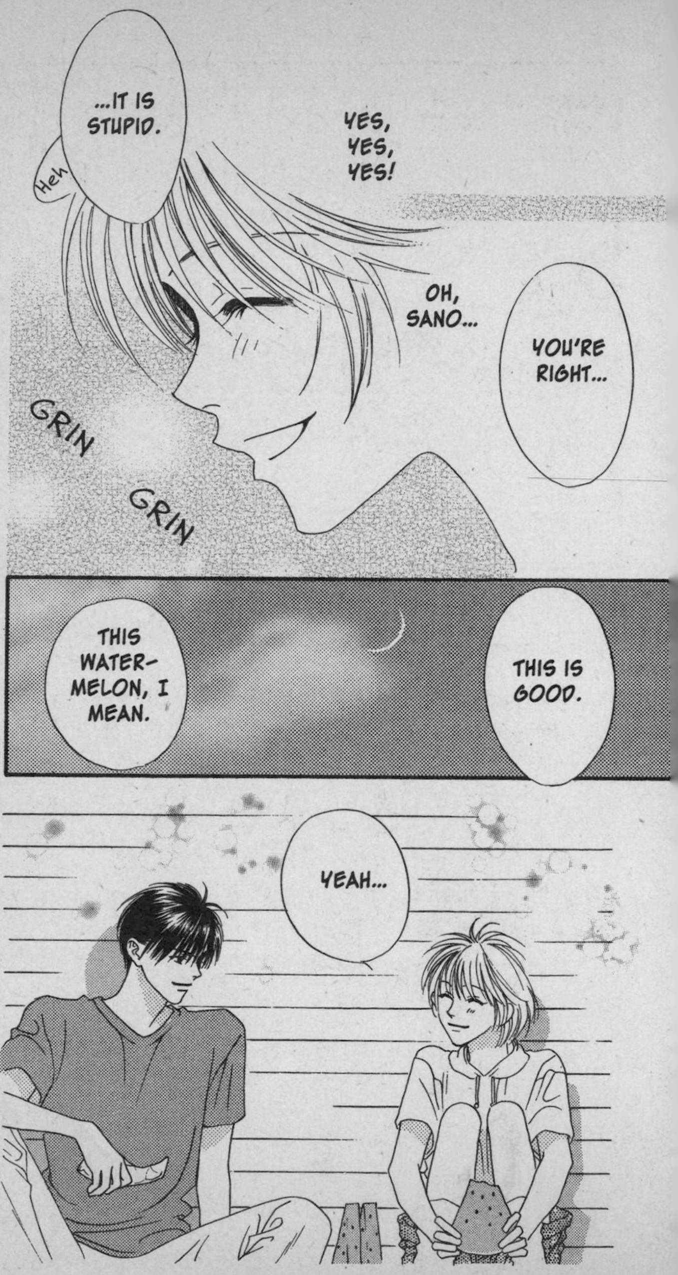
YOU'RE RIGHT...
OH, SANO...
YES, YES, YES!
...IT IS STUPID.
Heh
GRIN
GRIN
THIS IS GOOD.
THIS WATER-MELON, I MEAN.
YEAH...

Whispered Secrets

MINAMI NANBA

BIRTHDAY: JUNE 5TH
AGE: 18
BLOOD TYPE: A
SIGN: GEMINI
HEIGHT: 182CM
FAVORITE FOOD: ITALIAN AND FRENCH
FAVORITE MUSICIANS: MARIAH CAREY, WHITNEY HOUSTON
FAVORITE MOVIES: EVITA, PIANO LESSON, LA FEMME NIKITA
FAVORITE BRANDS: CHROME HEARTS, GALSON, BEAUTY AND BEAST.
FAVORITE SPORT: BASKETBALL (HIS FAVORITE NBA TEAM IS THE BULLS.)
FAVORITE PET: HIS FAMILY'S IRISH SETTER
FOODS HE HATES: DRIED FOODS, SMALL FISH, PRE-PACKAGED READY-MADE MEALS.
FLOWER: ORCHID

He's gotten really popular lately.

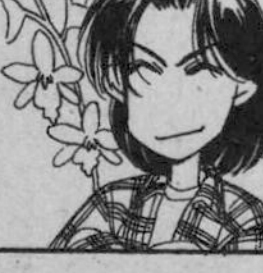

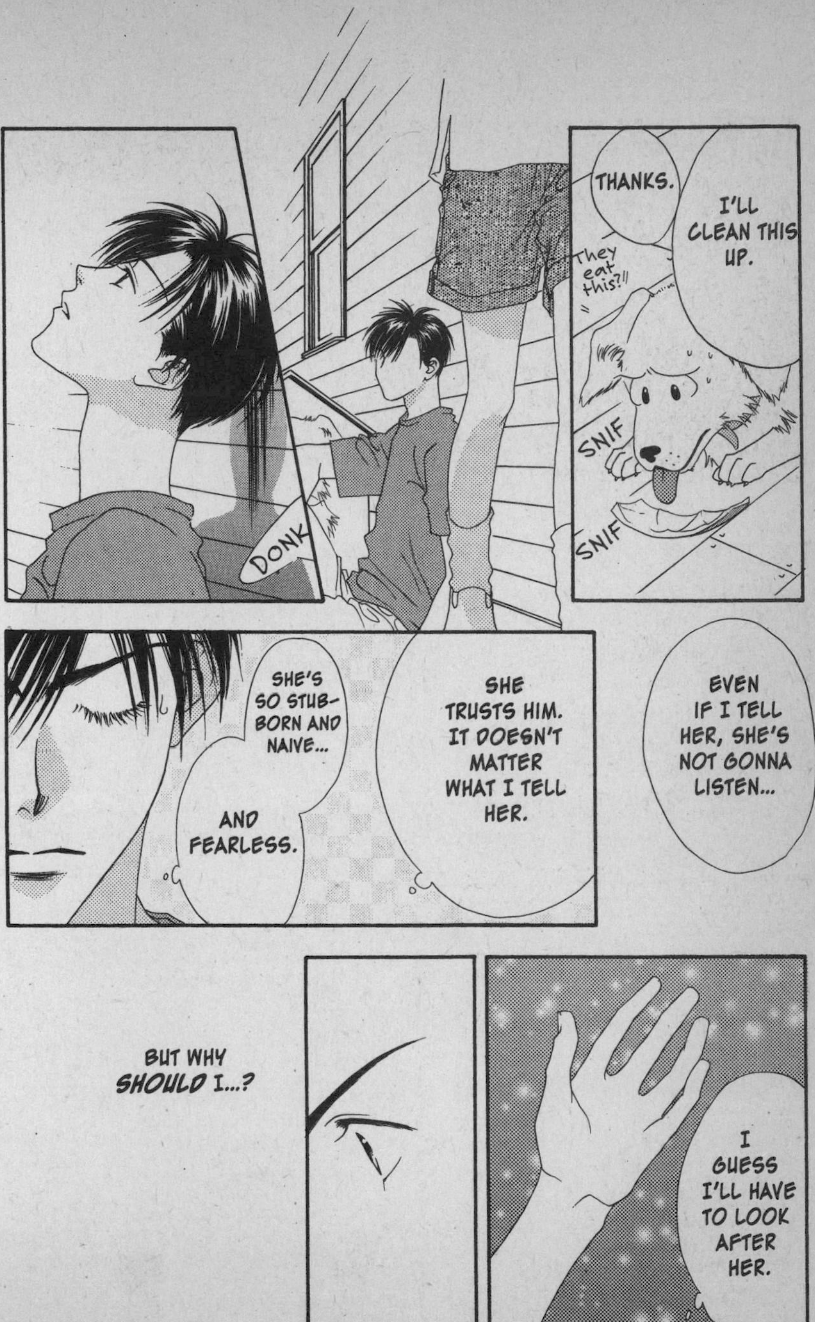

I'LL CLEAN THIS UP.
THANKS.
They eat this?!
SNIF
SNIF
DONK
EVEN IF I TELL HER, SHE'S NOT GONNA LISTEN...
SHE TRUSTS HIM. IT DOESN'T MATTER WHAT I TELL HER.
SHE'S SO STUBBORN AND NAIVE...
AND FEARLESS.
I GUESS I'LL HAVE TO LOOK AFTER HER.
BUT WHY SHOULD I...?

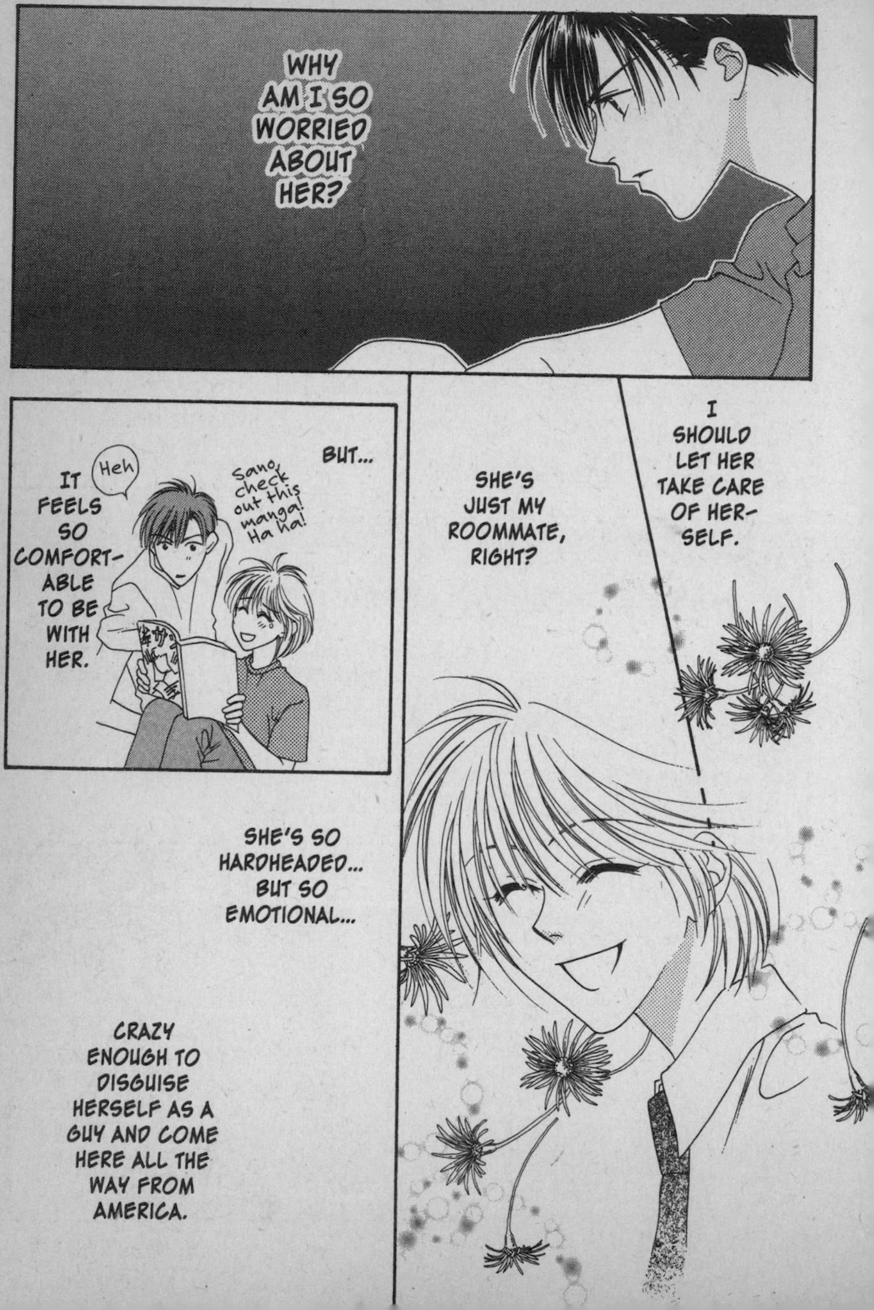
WHY AM I SO WORRIED ABOUT HER?
I SHOULD LET HER TAKE CARE OF HER-SELF.
SHE'S JUST MY ROOMMATE, RIGHT?
BUT...
Sano, check out this manga! Ha ha!
Heh
IT FEELS SO COMFORT-ABLE TO BE WITH HER.
SHE'S SO HARDHEADED... BUT SO EMOTIONAL...
CRAZY ENOUGH TO DISGUISE HERSELF AS A GUY AND COME HERE ALL THE WAY FROM AMERICA.

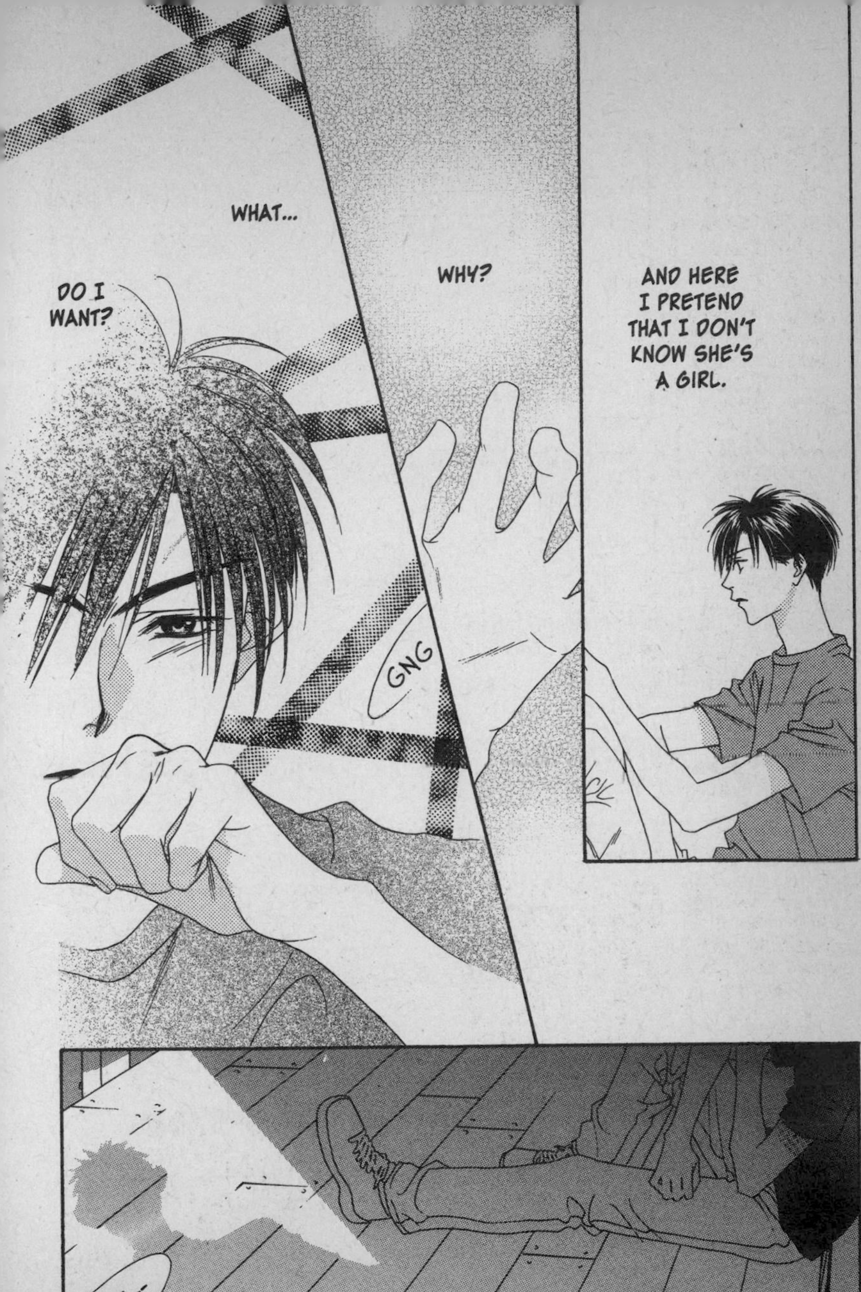
AND HERE I PRETEND THAT I DON'T KNOW SHE'S A GIRL.
WHY?
GNG
WHAT...
DO I WANT?
KCH-

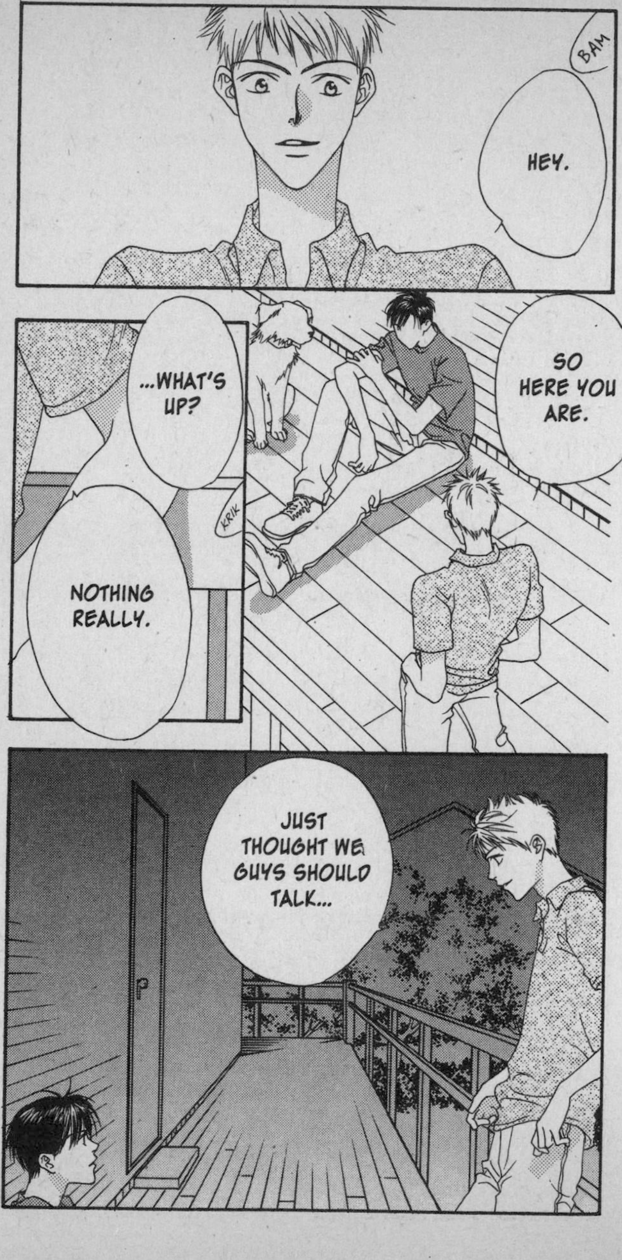
BAM
HEY.
SO HERE YOU ARE.
KRIK
...WHAT'S UP?
NOTHING REALLY.
JUST THOUGHT WE GUYS SHOULD TALK...

Whispered Secrets

HOKUTO UMEDA
BIRTHDAY: OCTOBER 31ST
AGE: 26
BLOOD TYPE: O
SIGN: SCORPIO
HEIGHT: 183CM
FAVORITE FOOD: COFFEE, ALCOHOL, JAPANESE FOOD
FAVORITE MUSICIANS: PRODIGY, T99, DOA ETC.
FAVORITE MOVIES: SALOME, BLADE RUNNER, YUSEI KARA NO BUTTAI X ("X, THE THING FROM OUTER SPACE"), ETC.
FAVORITE BRANDS: HELMUT LANG, DIRK BICKENBERG
FAVORITE SPORTS: HATES SPORTS. HE GOES TO A BOXING GYM ONCE A WHILE.
FAVORITE PET: NONE IN PARTICULAR (BUT HE DOESN'T HATE THEM)
FOODS HE HATES: SWEET DESSERTS
FLOWER: ANTHURIUM

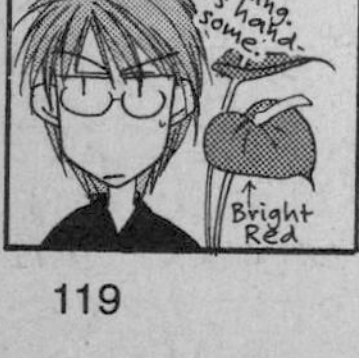
I try to draw him so he's good looking. He's handsome.
Bright Red

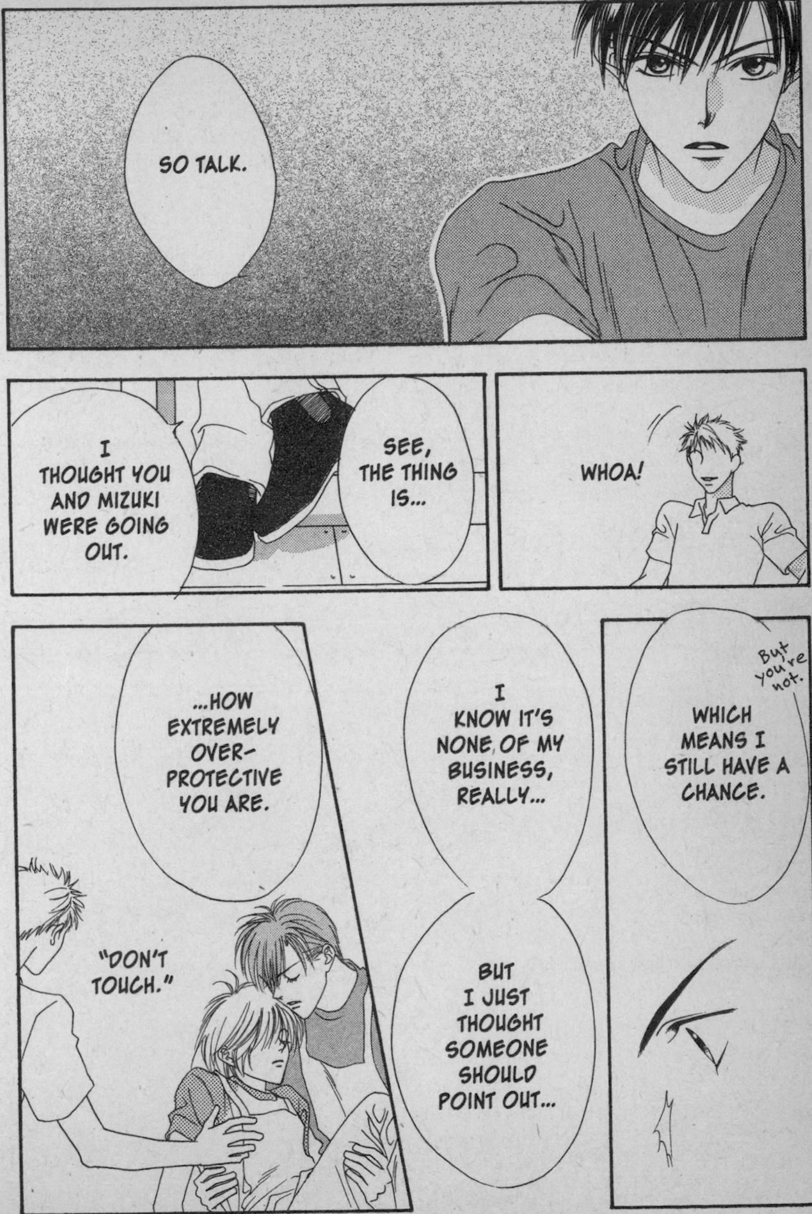
SO TALK.
WHOA!
SEE, THE THING IS...
I THOUGHT YOU AND MIZUKI WERE GOING OUT.
But you're not.
WHICH MEANS I STILL HAVE A CHANCE.
I KNOW IT'S NONE OF MY BUSINESS, REALLY...
BUT I JUST THOUGHT SOMEONE SHOULD POINT OUT...
...HOW EXTREMELY OVER-PROTECTIVE YOU ARE.
"DON'T TOUCH."

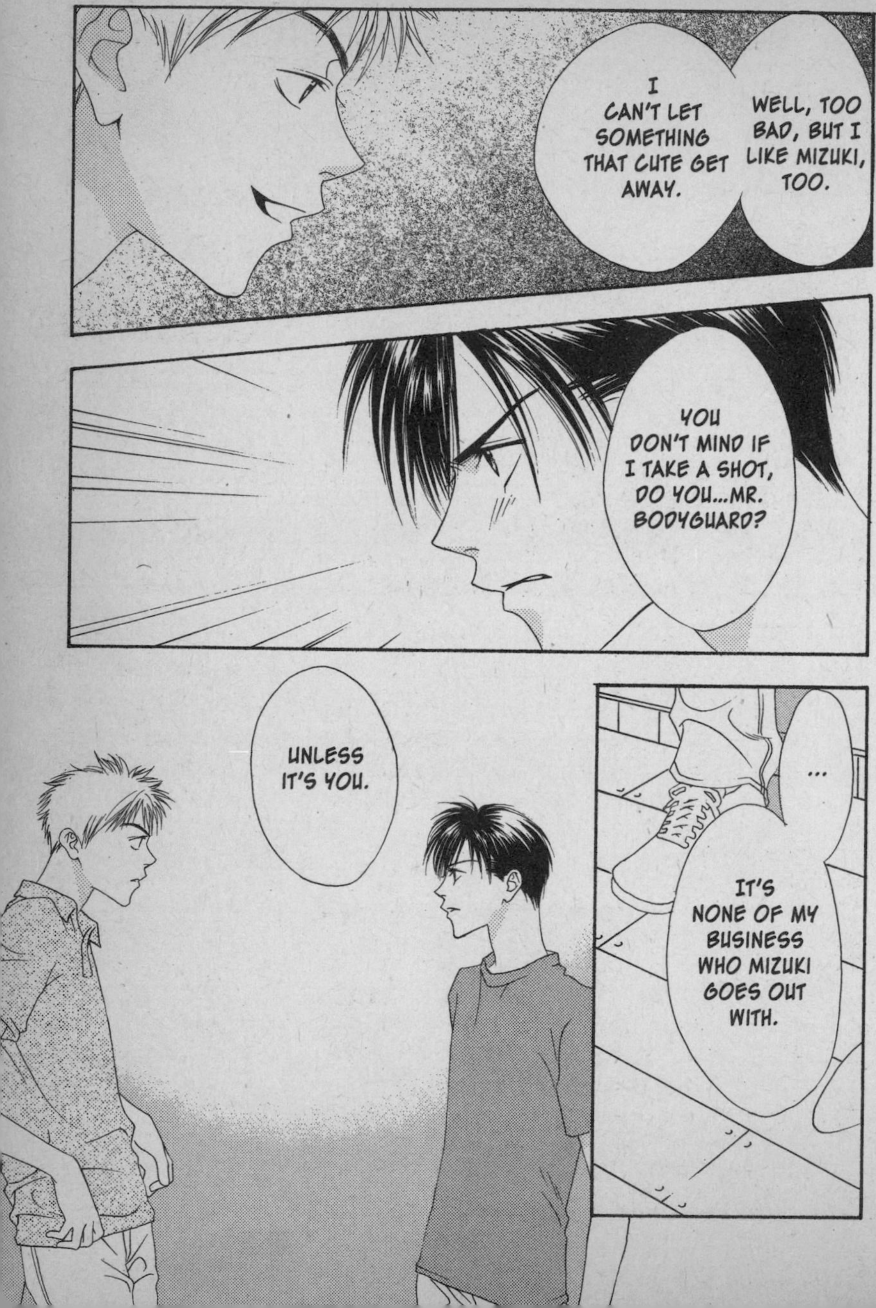
WELL, TOO BAD, BUT I LIKE MIZUKI, TOO.
I CAN'T LET SOMETHING THAT CUTE GET AWAY.
YOU DON'T MIND IF I TAKE A SHOT, DO YOU...MR. BODYGUARD?
...
IT'S NONE OF MY BUSINESS WHO MIZUKI GOES OUT WITH.
UNLESS IT'S YOU.

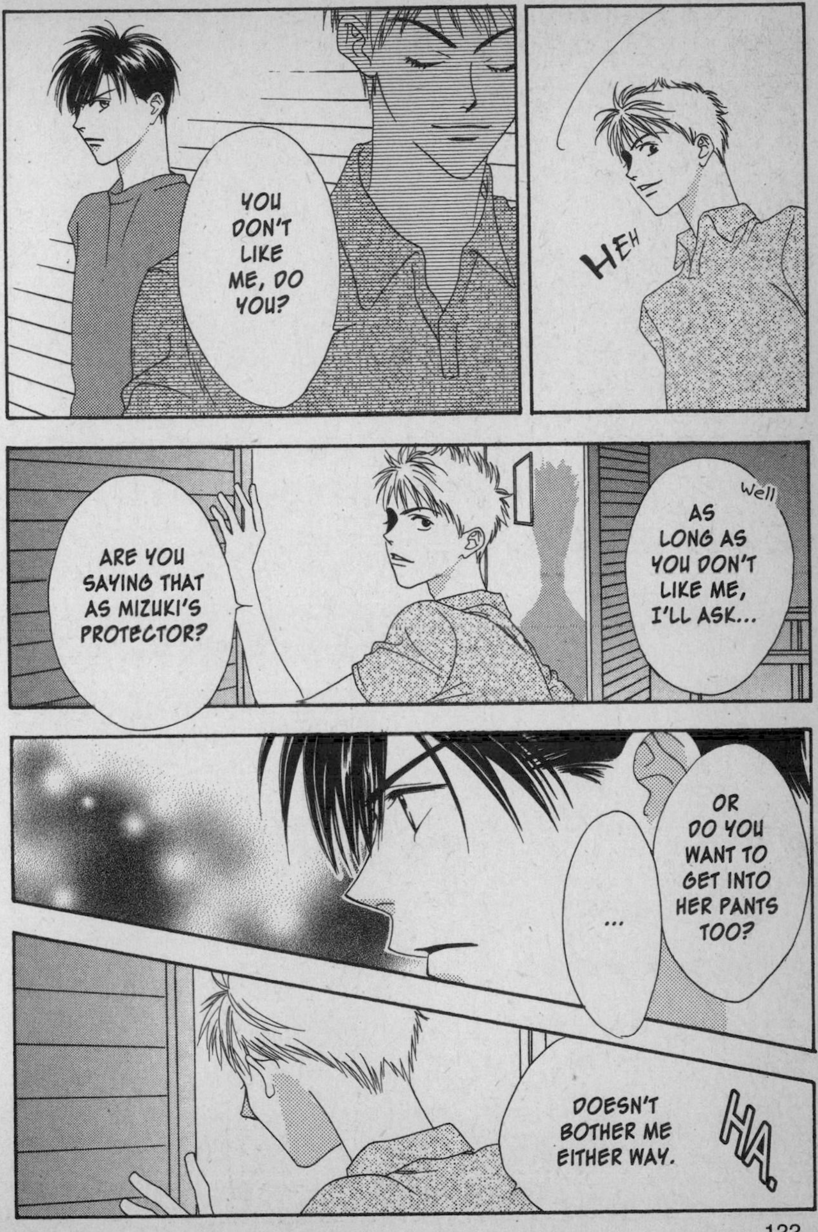
HEH
YOU DON'T LIKE ME, DO YOU?
Well
AS LONG AS YOU DON'T LIKE ME, I'LL ASK...
ARE YOU SAYING THAT AS MIZUKI'S PROTECTOR?
OR DO YOU WANT TO GET INTO HER PANTS TOO?
...
HA.
DOESN'T BOTHER ME EITHER WAY.

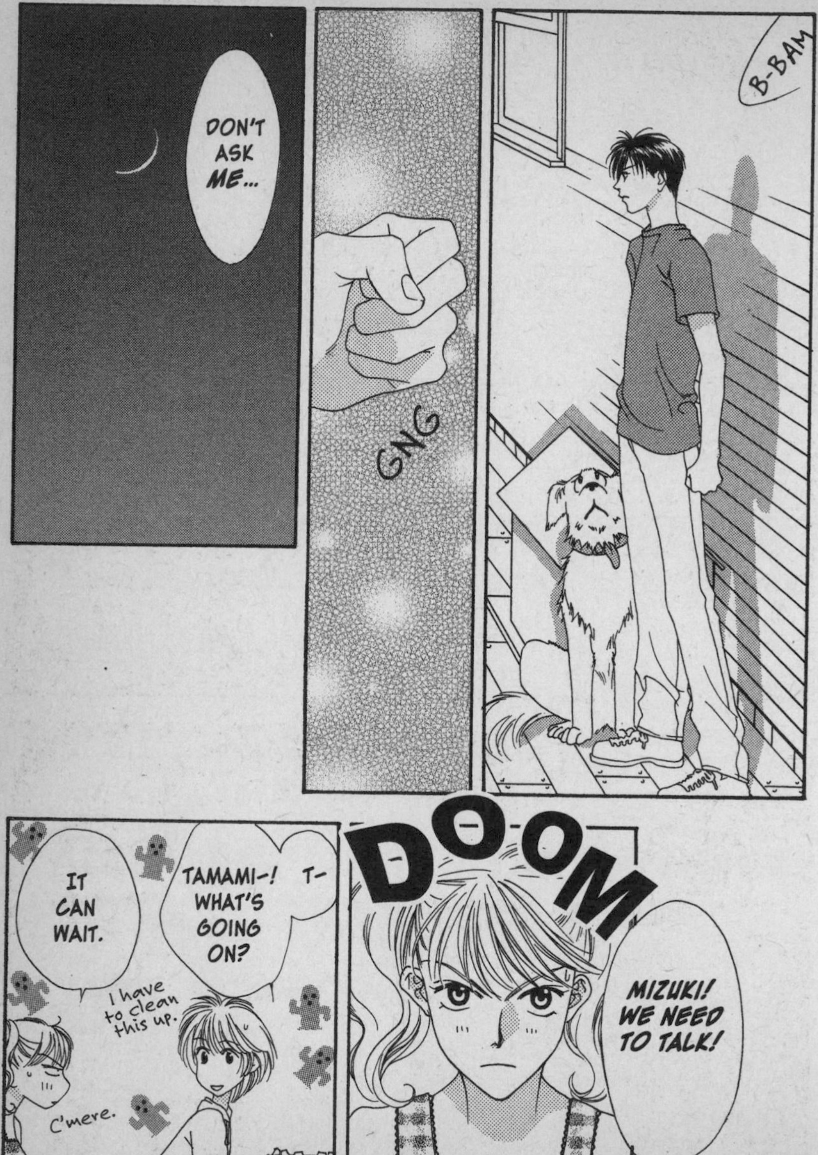
B-BAM
GNG
DON'T ASK ME...
DOOM
MIZUKI! WE NEED TO TALK!
T-
TAMAMI-! WHAT'S GOING ON?
IT CAN WAIT.
I have to clean this up.
C'mere.

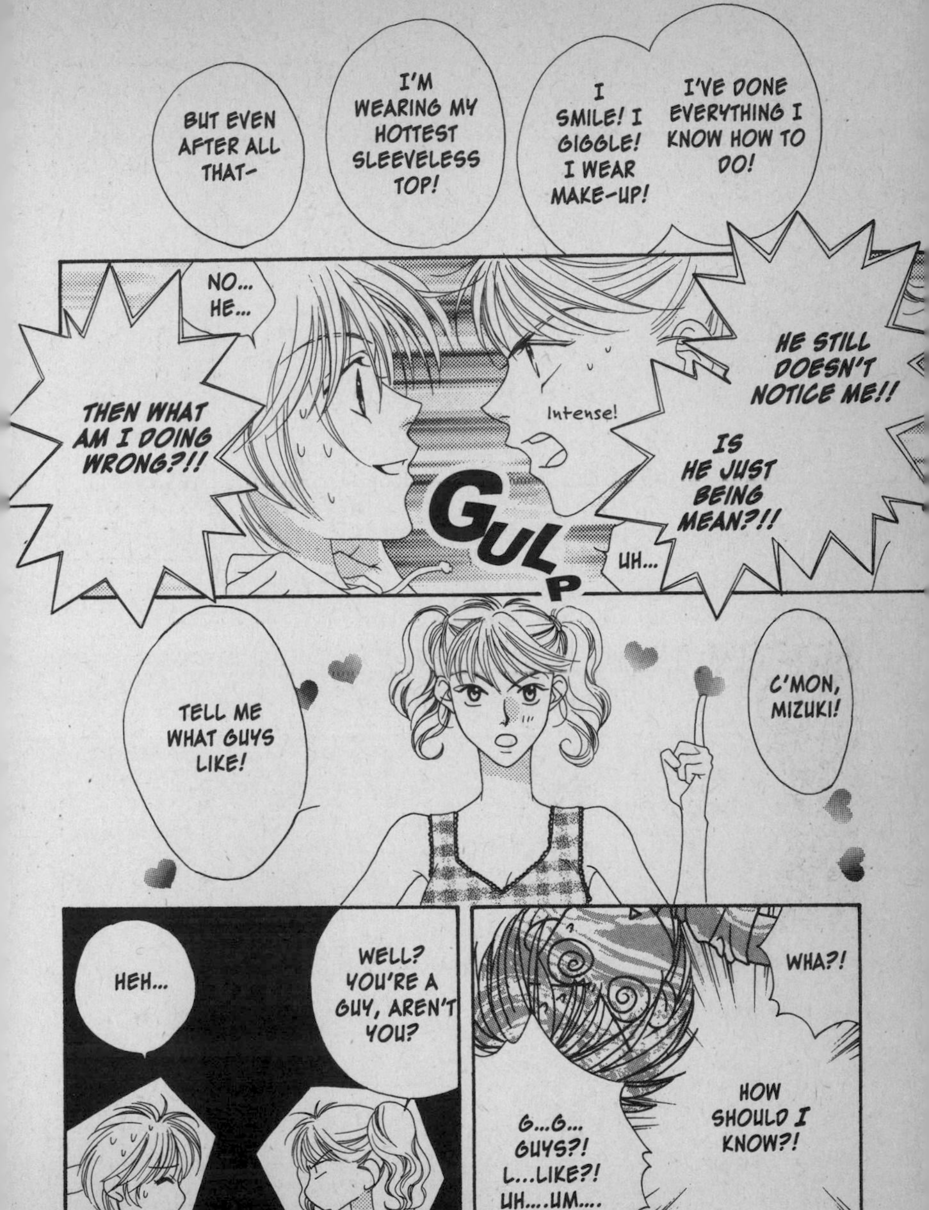
I'VE DONE EVERYTHING I KNOW HOW TO DO!
I SMILE! I GIGGLE! I WEAR MAKE-UP!
I'M WEARING MY HOTTEST SLEEVELESS TOP!
BUT EVEN AFTER ALL THAT-
HE STILL DOESN'T NOTICE ME!!
IS HE JUST BEING MEAN?!!
Intense!
UH...
GULP
NO... HE...
THEN WHAT AM I DOING WRONG?!!
C'MON, MIZUKI!
TELL ME WHAT GUYS LIKE!
WHA?!
HOW SHOULD I KNOW?!
G...G... GUYS?! L...LIKE?! UH....UM....
WELL? YOU'RE A GUY, AREN'T YOU?
HEH...

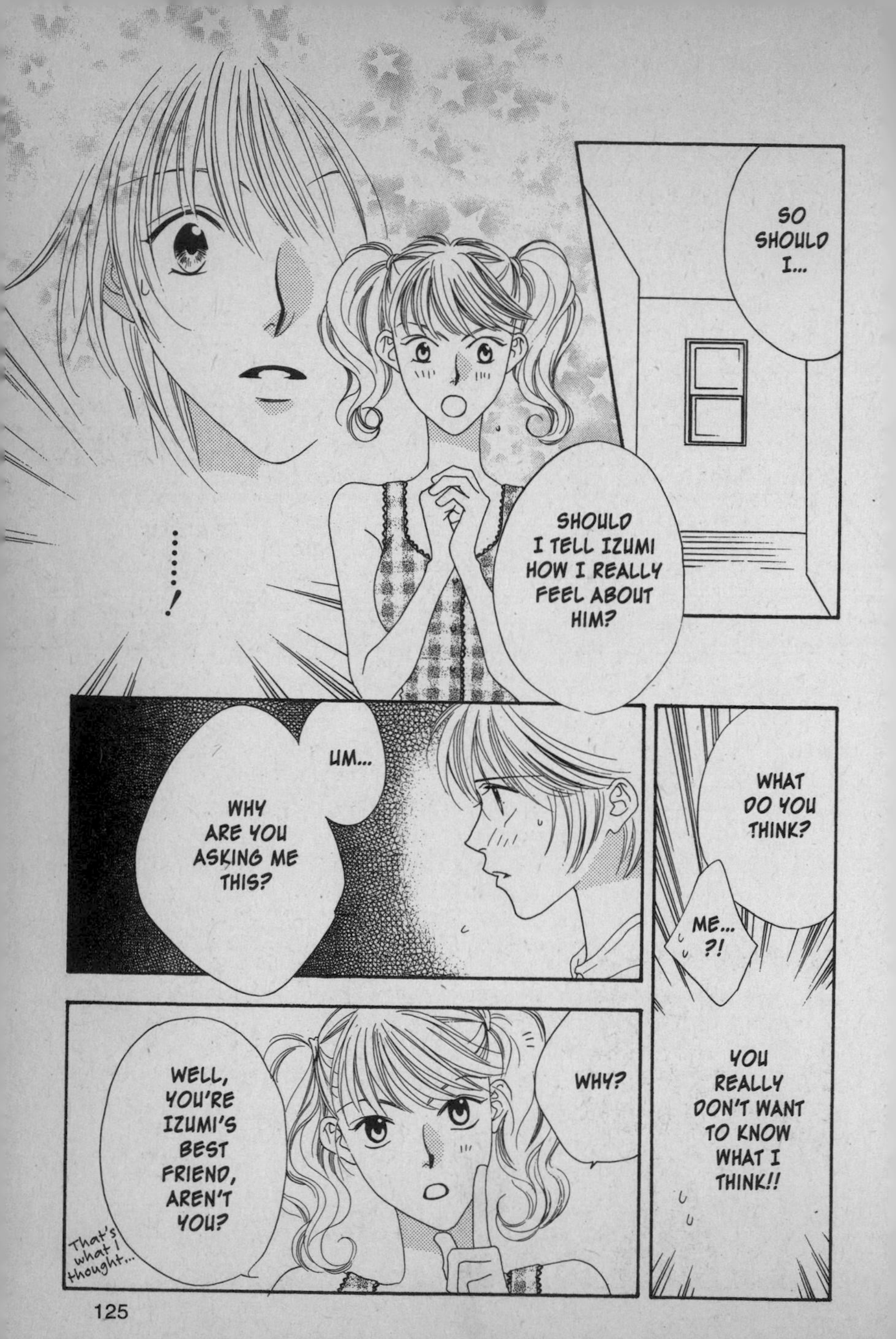
SO SHOULD I...
SHOULD I TELL IZUMI HOW I REALLY FEEL ABOUT HIM?
......!
WHAT DO YOU THINK?
ME... ?!
YOU REALLY DON'T WANT TO KNOW WHAT I THINK!!
UM...
WHY ARE YOU ASKING ME THIS?
WHY?
WELL, YOU'RE IZUMI'S BEST FRIEND, AREN'T YOU?
That's what I thought...

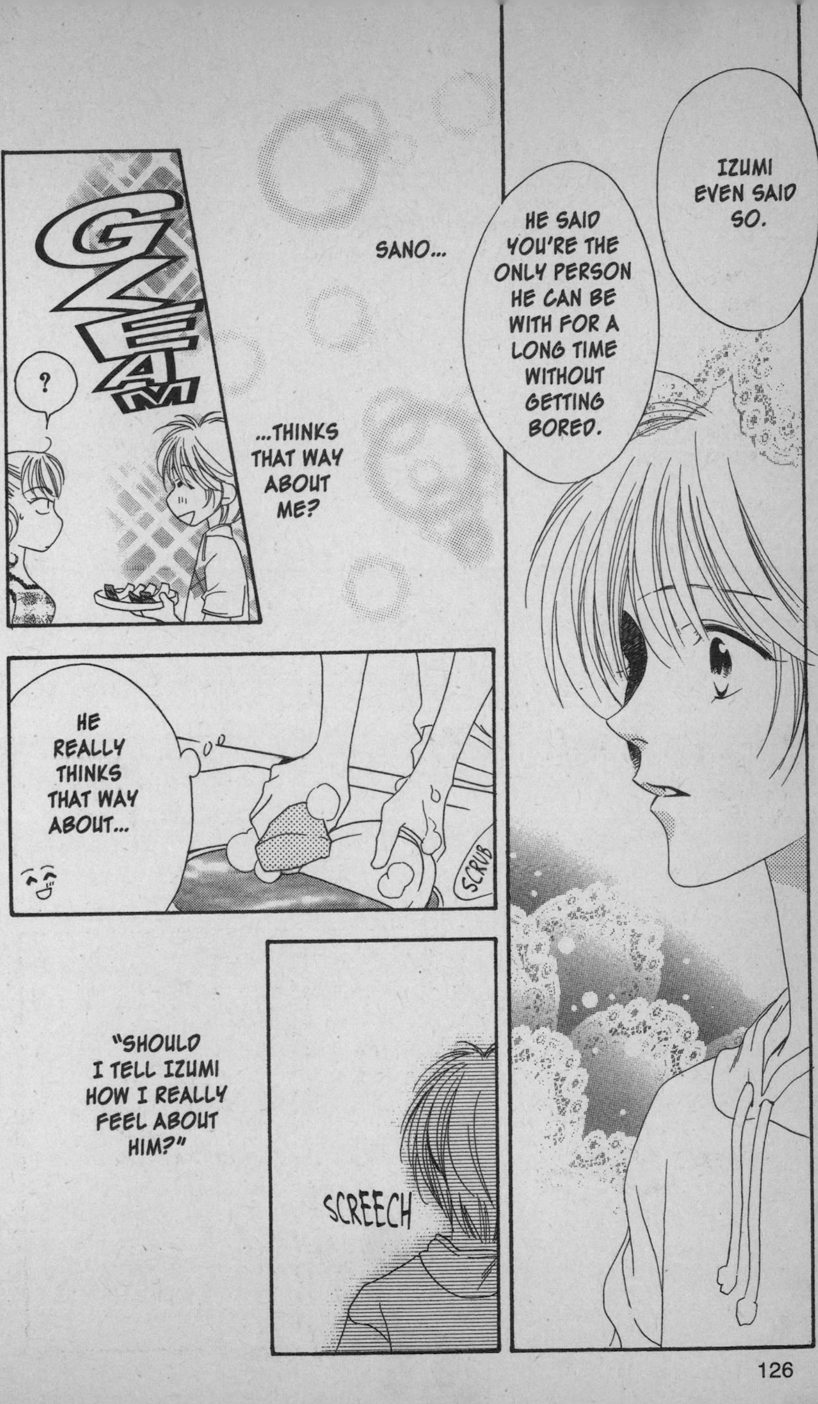
IZUMI EVEN SAID SO.
HE SAID YOU'RE THE ONLY PERSON HE CAN BE WITH FOR A LONG TIME WITHOUT GETTING BORED.
SANO...
...THINKS THAT WAY ABOUT ME?
GLEAM
?
SCRUB
HE REALLY THINKS THAT WAY ABOUT...
SCREECH
"SHOULD I TELL IZUMI HOW I REALLY FEEL ABOUT HIM?"

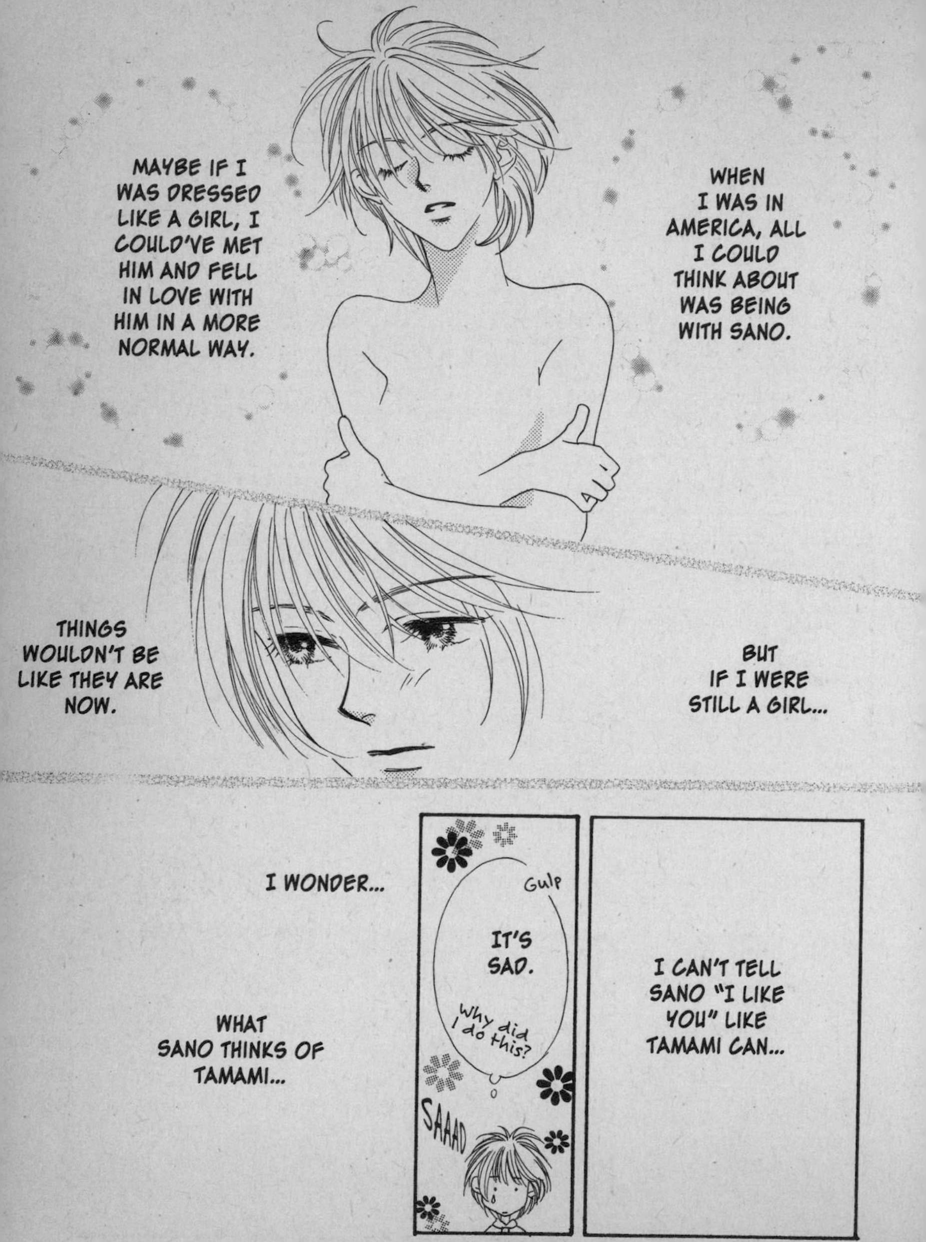
WHEN I WAS IN AMERICA, ALL I COULD THINK ABOUT WAS BEING WITH SANO.
MAYBE IF I WAS DRESSED LIKE A GIRL, I COULD'VE MET HIM AND FELL IN LOVE WITH HIM IN A MORE NORMAL WAY.
BUT IF I WERE STILL A GIRL...
THINGS WOULDN'T BE LIKE THEY ARE NOW.
I CAN'T TELL SANO "I LIKE YOU" LIKE TAMAMI CAN...
Gulp
IT'S SAD.
Why did I do this?
SAAAD
I WONDER...
WHAT SANO THINKS OF TAMAMI...

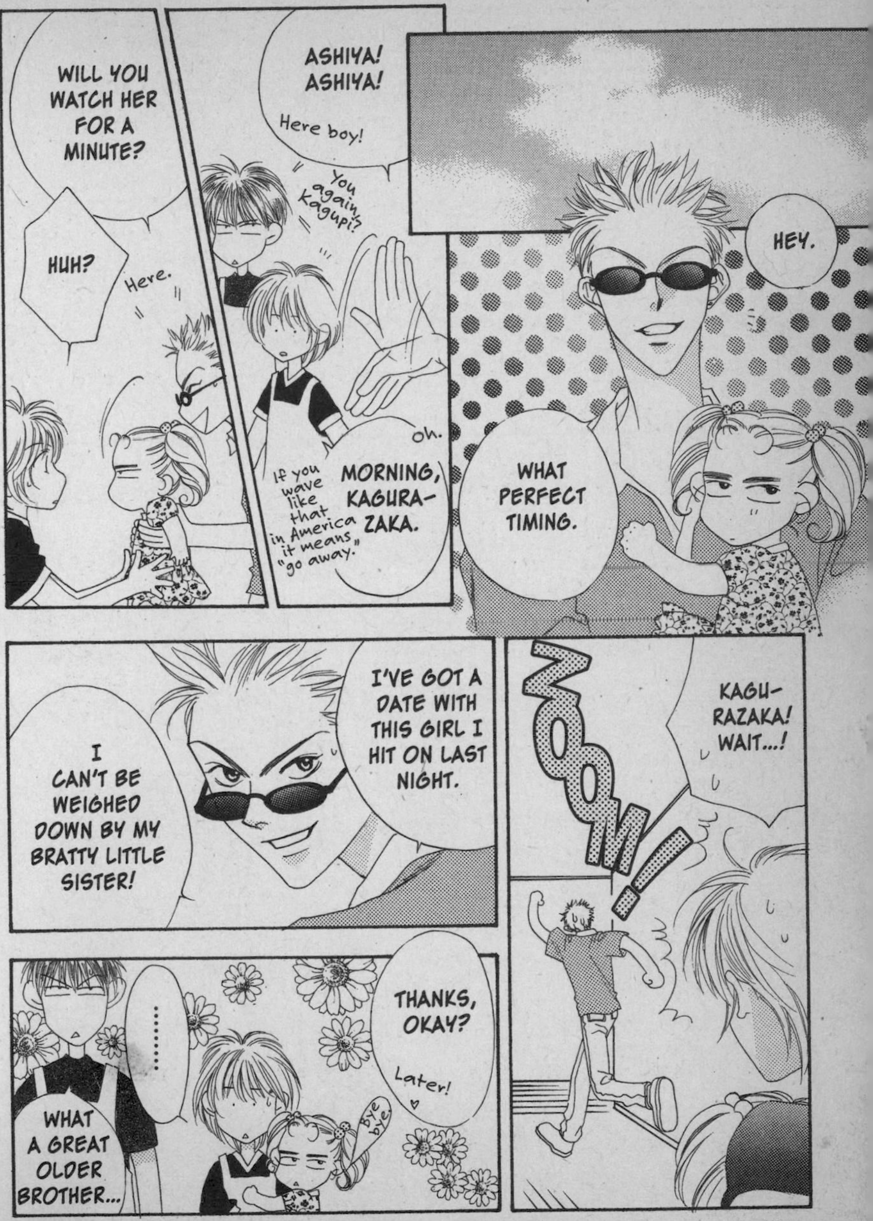
HEY.
WHAT PERFECT TIMING.
ASHIYA! ASHIYA!
Here boy!
You again, Kagupi!?
Oh.
MORNING, KAGURA-ZAKA.
If you wave like that in America it means "go away."
WILL YOU WATCH HER FOR A MINUTE?
HUH?
Here.
KAGU-RAZAKA! WAIT...!
ZOOM!!
I'VE GOT A DATE WITH THIS GIRL I HIT ON LAST NIGHT.
I CAN'T BE WEIGHED DOWN BY MY BRATTY LITTLE SISTER!
THANKS, OKAY?
Later!
Bye bye
......
WHAT A GREAT OLDER BROTHER...

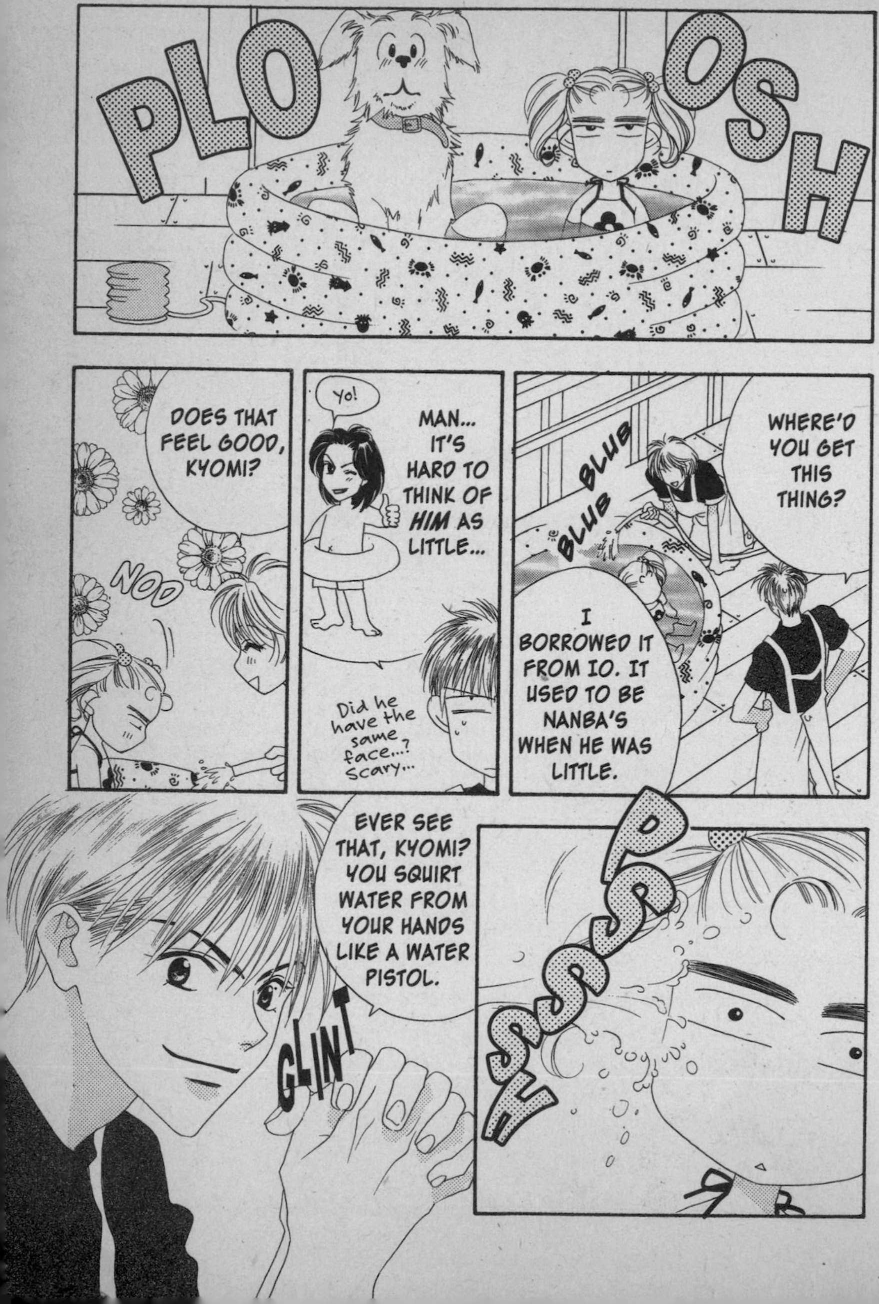
PLOOSH
WHERE'D YOU GET THIS THING?
BLUB BLUB
I BORROWED IT FROM IO. IT USED TO BE NANBA'S WHEN HE WAS LITTLE.
MAN... IT'S HARD TO THINK OF *HIM* AS LITTLE...
Yo!
Did he have the same face...? Scary...
DOES THAT FEEL GOOD, KYOMI?
NOD
EVER SEE THAT, KYOMI? YOU SQUIRT WATER FROM YOUR HANDS LIKE A WATER PISTOL.
GLINT

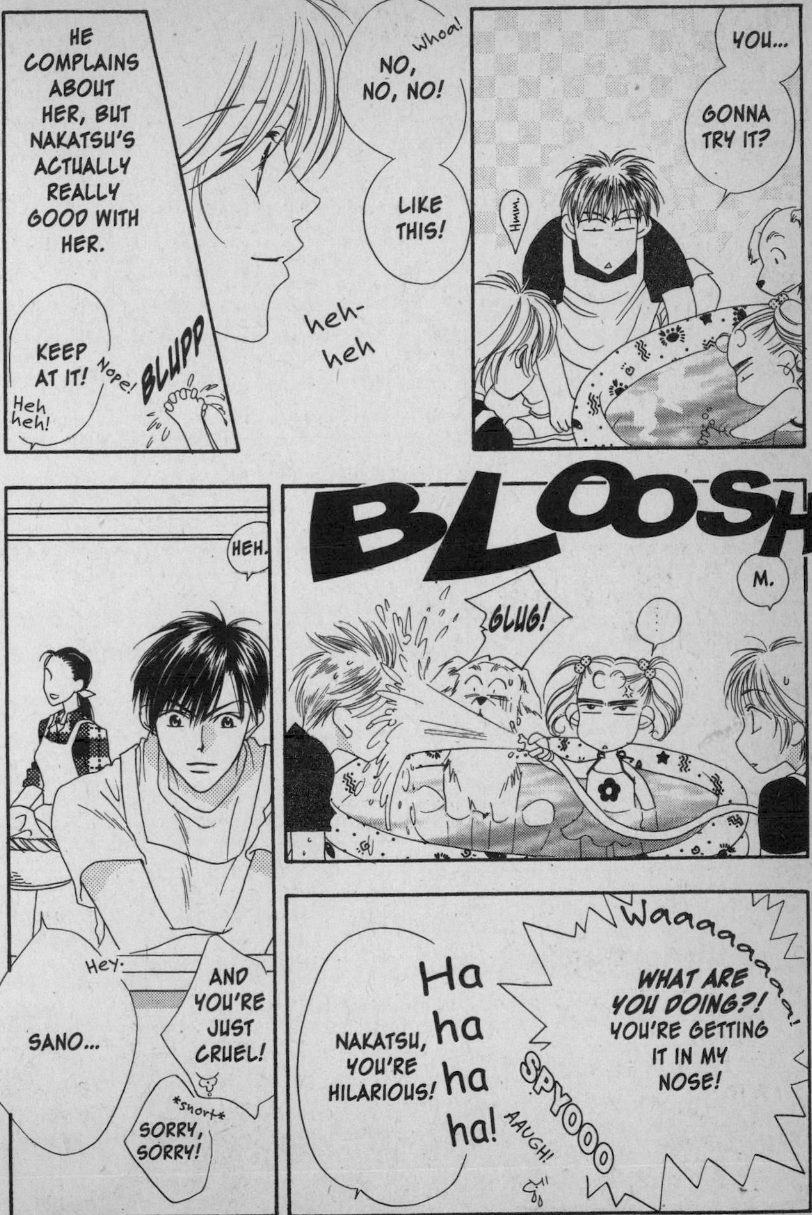
YOU...
GONNA TRY IT?
Hmm.
Whoa!
NO, NO, NO!
LIKE THIS!
heh-heh
HE COMPLAINS ABOUT HER, BUT NAKATSU'S ACTUALLY REALLY GOOD WITH HER.
KEEP AT IT!
Nope!
BLUPP
Heh heh!
BLOOSH
M.
GLUG!
...
Waaaaaaaa!
WHAT ARE YOU DOING?! YOU'RE GETTING IT IN MY NOSE!
SPYOOO
AAUGH!
Ha ha ha ha!
NAKATSU, YOU'RE HILARIOUS!
HEH.
Hey.
AND YOU'RE JUST CRUEL!
SANO...
snort
SORRY, SORRY!

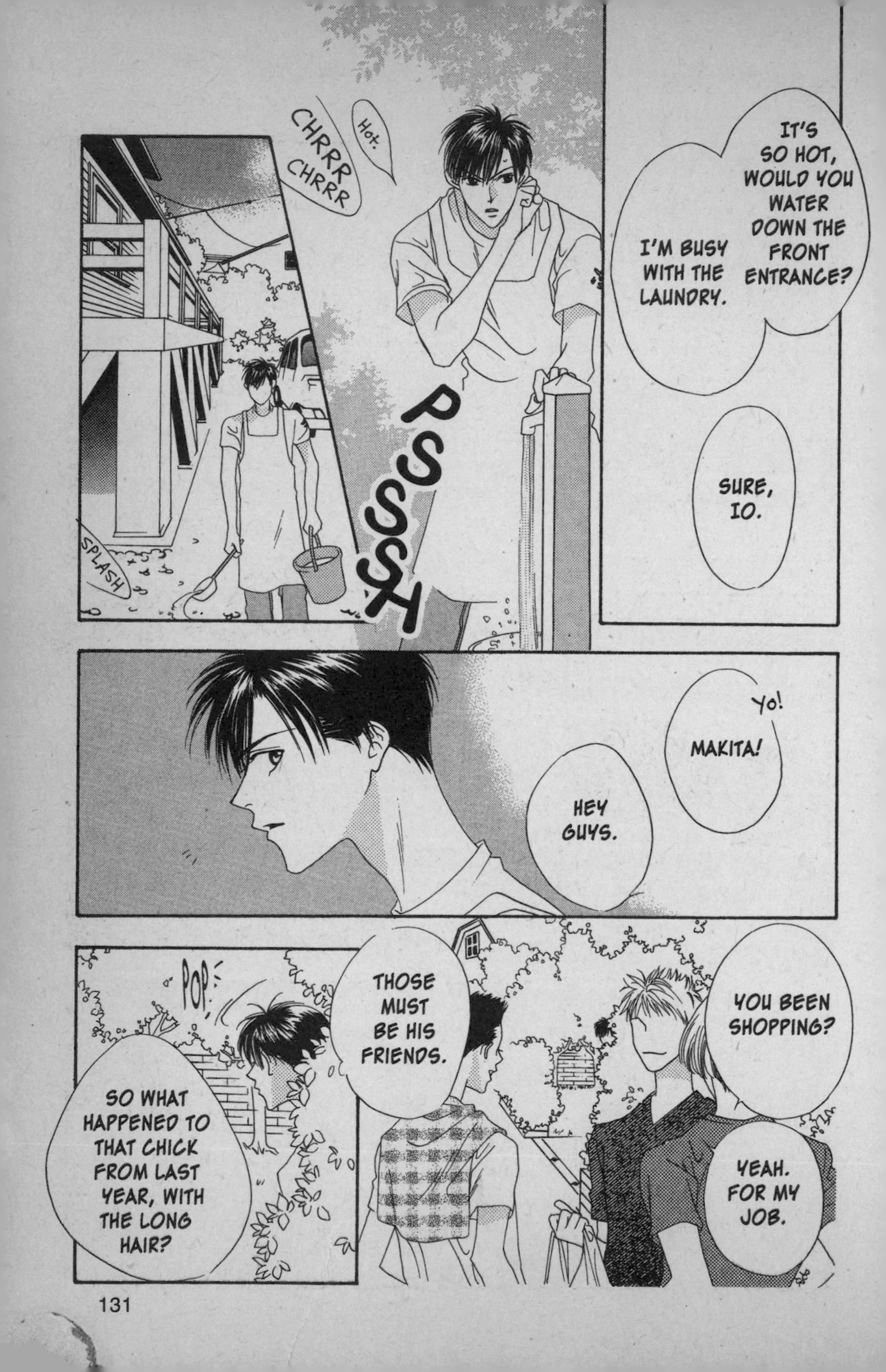
IT'S SO HOT, WOULD YOU WATER DOWN THE FRONT ENTRANCE?
I'M BUSY WITH THE LAUNDRY.
SURE, IO.
Hot.
CHRRR CHRRR
PSSSH
SPLASH
YO! MAKITA!
HEY GUYS.
YOU BEEN SHOPPING?
YEAH. FOR MY JOB.
THOSE MUST BE HIS FRIENDS.
POP
SO WHAT HAPPENED TO THAT CHICK FROM LAST YEAR, WITH THE LONG HAIR?

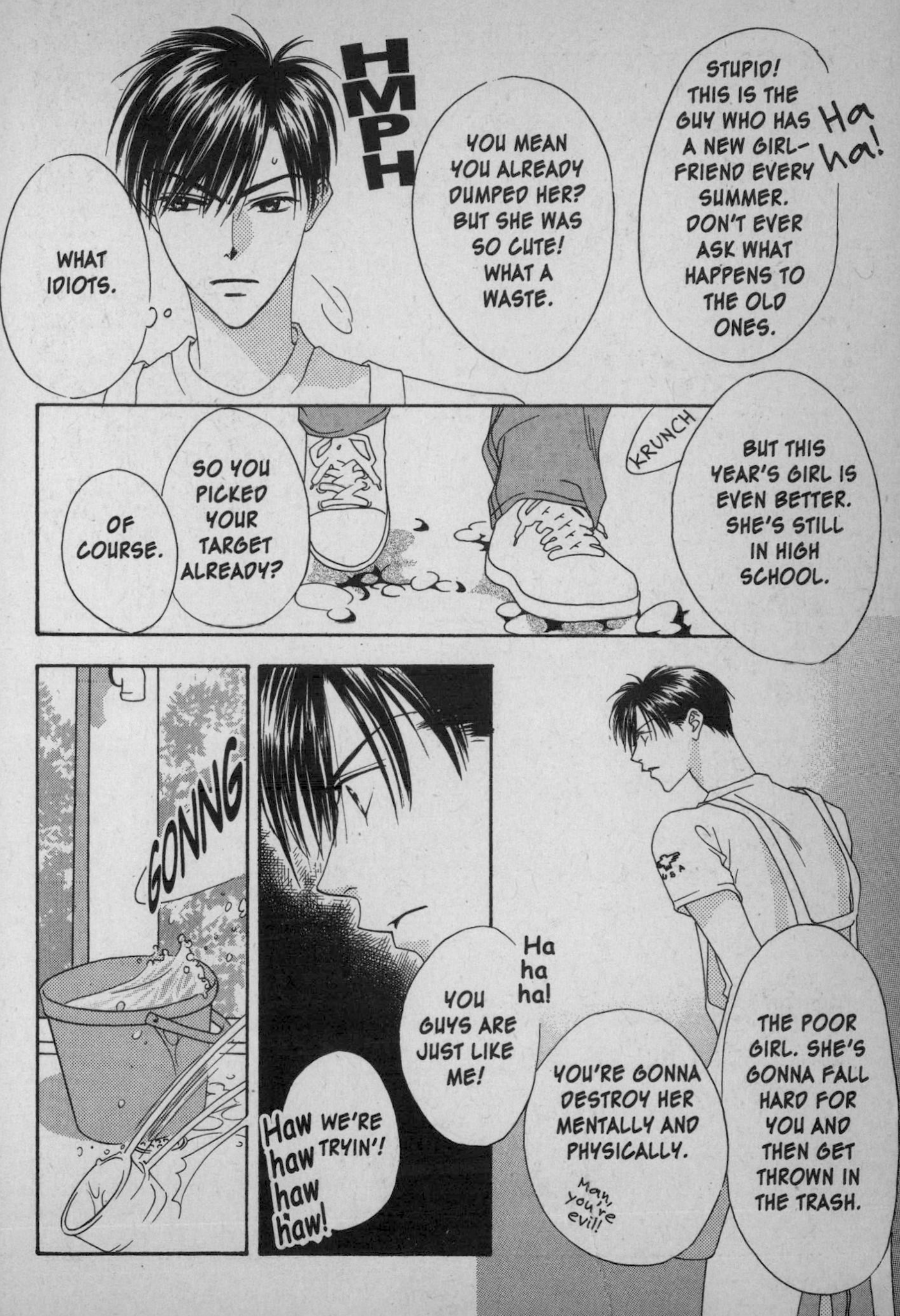
STUPID! THIS IS THE GUY WHO HAS A NEW GIRL-FRIEND EVERY SUMMER. DON'T EVER ASK WHAT HAPPENS TO THE OLD ONES.
Ha ha!
YOU MEAN YOU ALREADY DUMPED HER? BUT SHE WAS SO CUTE! WHAT A WASTE.
HMPH
WHAT IDIOTS.
BUT THIS YEAR'S GIRL IS EVEN BETTER. SHE'S STILL IN HIGH SCHOOL.
KRUNCH
SO YOU PICKED YOUR TARGET ALREADY?
OF COURSE.
THE POOR GIRL. SHE'S GONNA FALL HARD FOR YOU AND THEN GET THROWN IN THE TRASH.
YOU'RE GONNA DESTROY HER MENTALLY AND PHYSICALLY.
Man, you're evil!!
Ha ha ha!
YOU GUYS ARE JUST LIKE ME!
WE'RE TRYIN'!
Haw haw haw haw!
GONNG

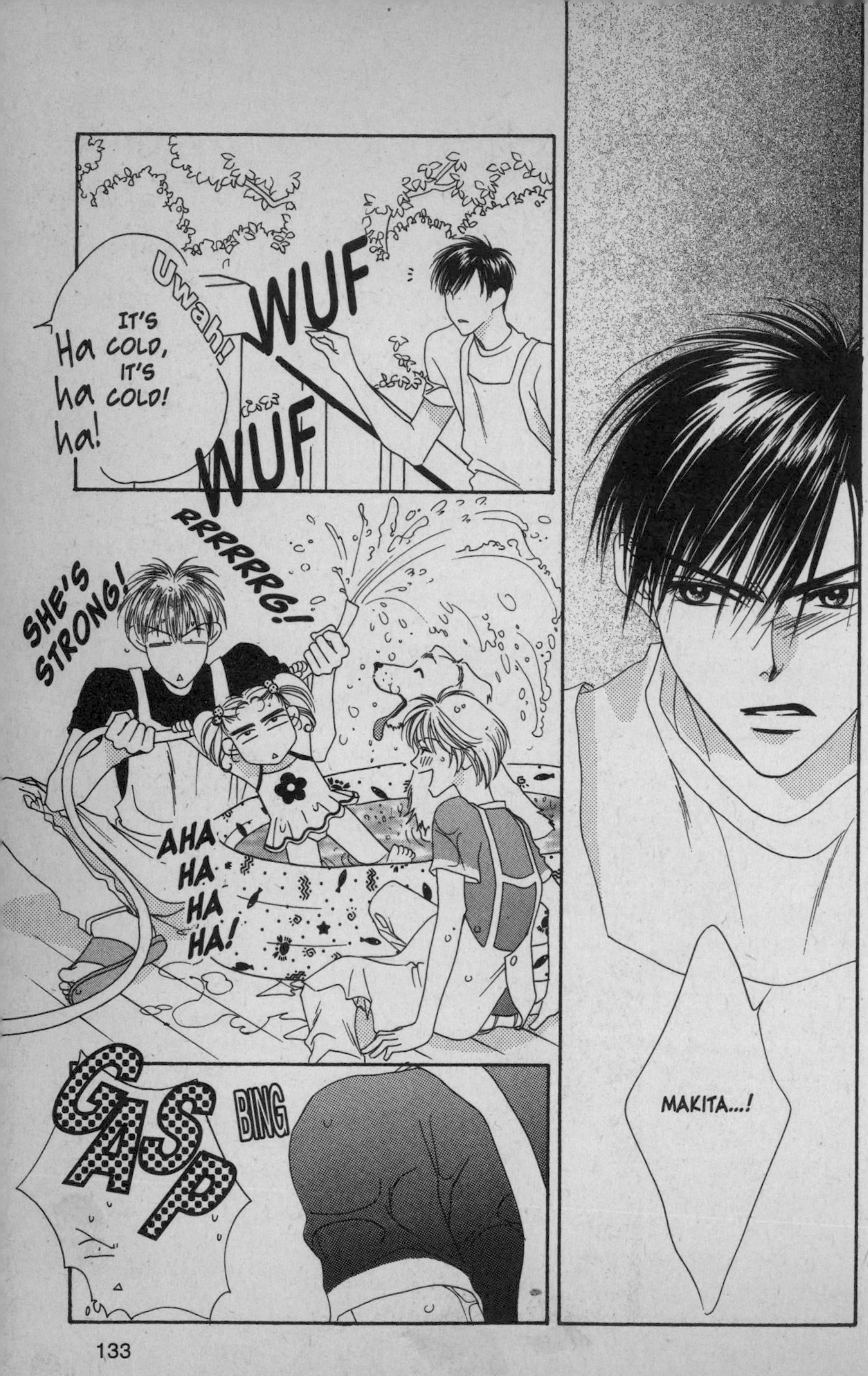
MAKITA...!
WUF
WUF
Uwah!
IT'S COLD, IT'S COLD!
Ha ha ha!
RRRRRRG!
SHE'S STRONG!
AHA HA HA HA!
BING
GASP

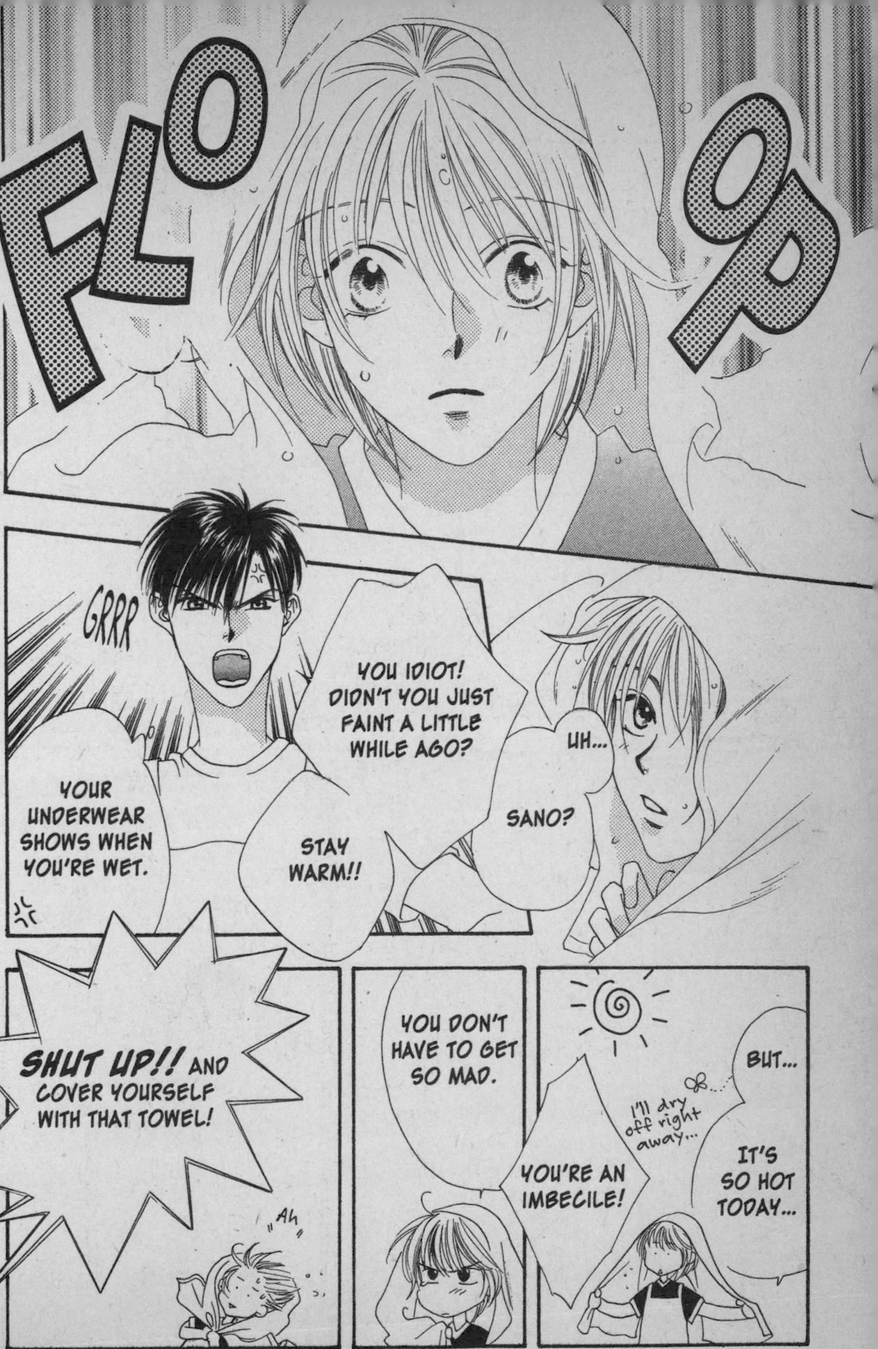
FLOOP
UH...
SANO?
GRRR
YOU IDIOT! DIDN'T YOU JUST FAINT A LITTLE WHILE AGO?
STAY WARM!!
YOUR UNDERWEAR SHOWS WHEN YOU'RE WET.
BUT...
IT'S SO HOT TODAY...
I'll dry off right away...
YOU'RE AN IMBECILE!
YOU DON'T HAVE TO GET SO MAD.
SHUT UP!! AND COVER YOURSELF WITH THAT TOWEL!
Ah

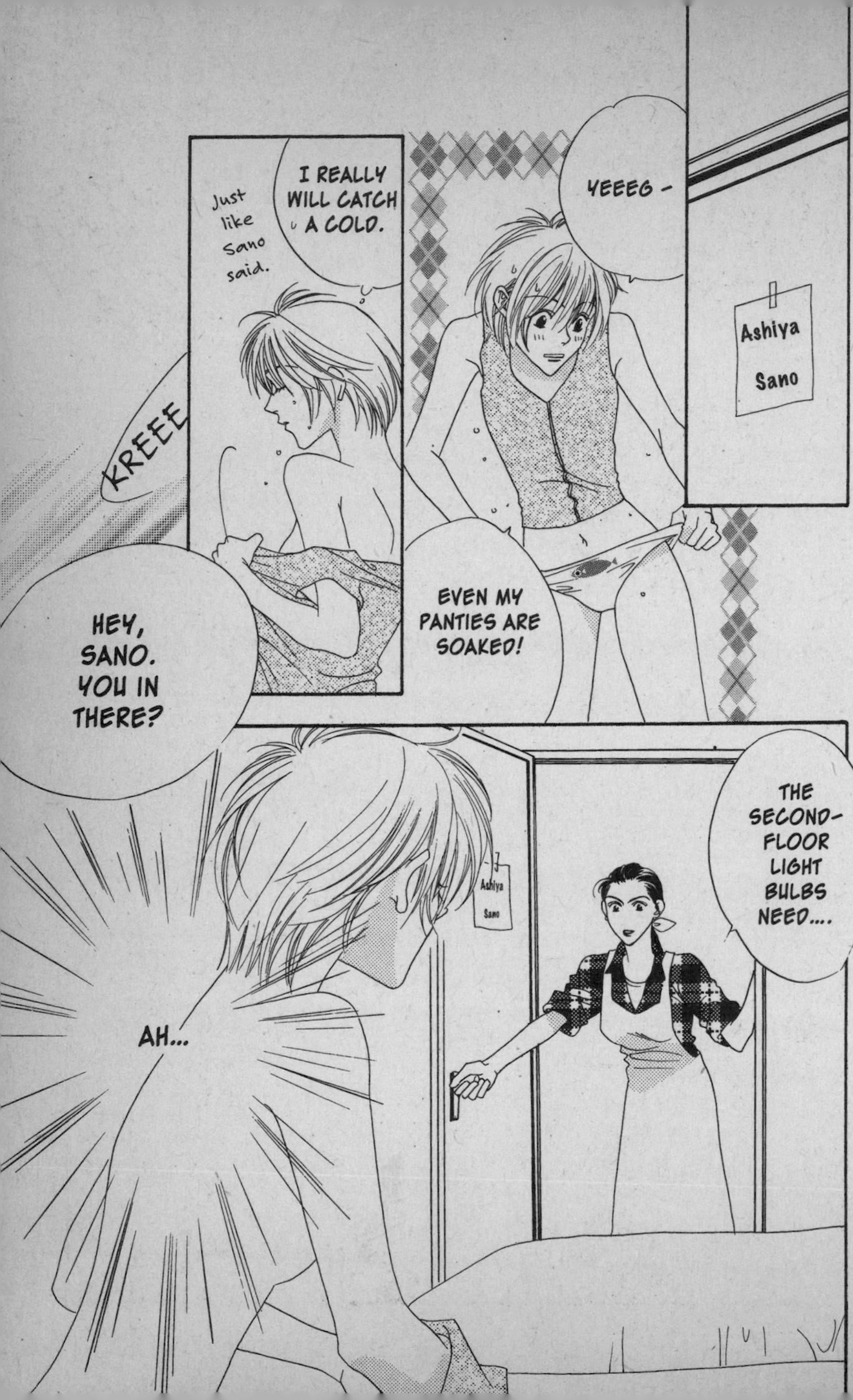
YEEEG -
Ashiya
Sano
EVEN MY PANTIES ARE SOAKED!
I REALLY WILL CATCH A COLD.
Just like Sano said.
KREEE
HEY, SANO. YOU IN THERE?
Ashiya
Sano
THE SECOND-FLOOR LIGHT BULBS NEED....
AH...

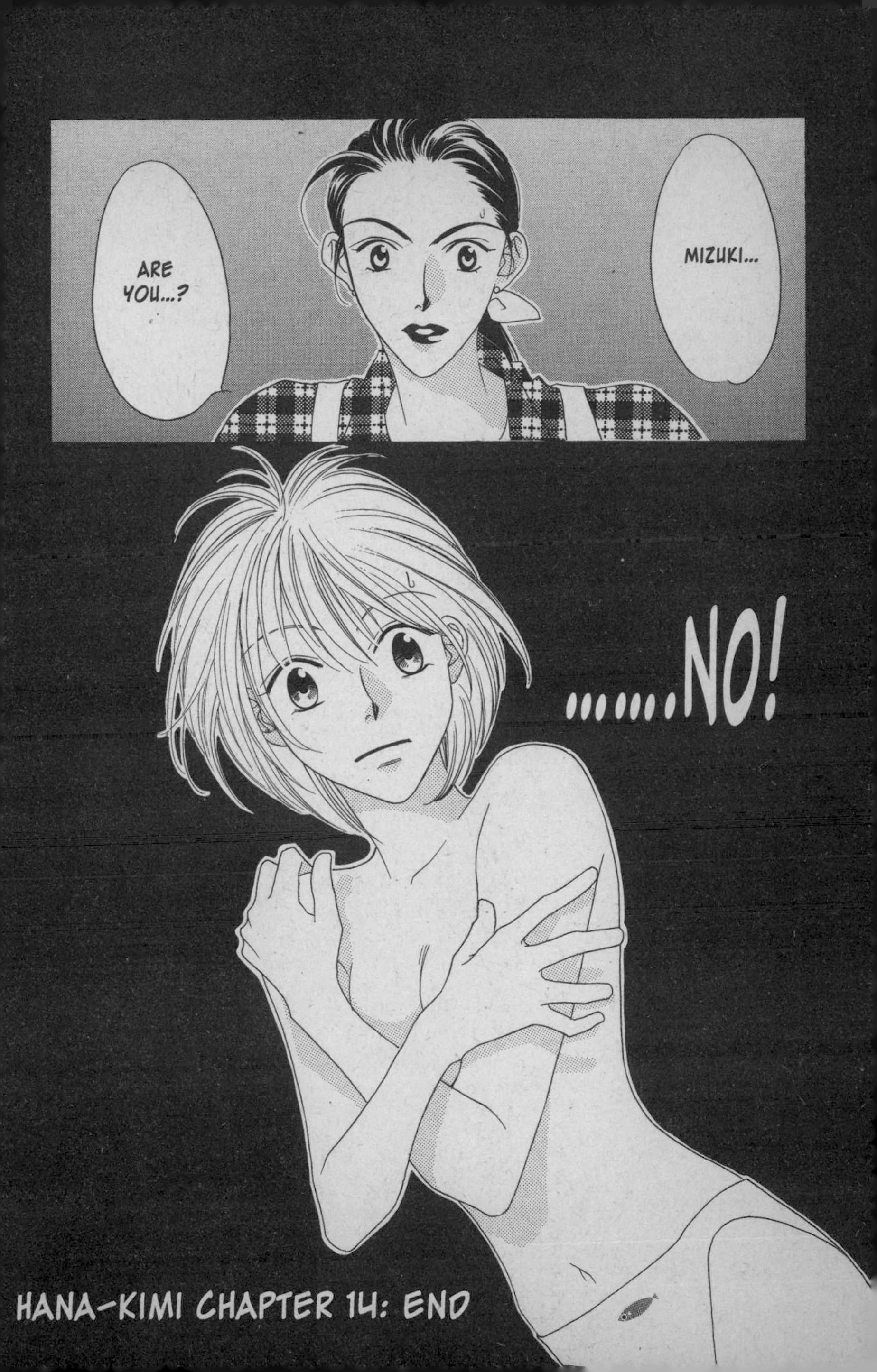
MIZUKI...
ARE YOU...?
......NO!
HANA-KIMI CHAPTER 14: END

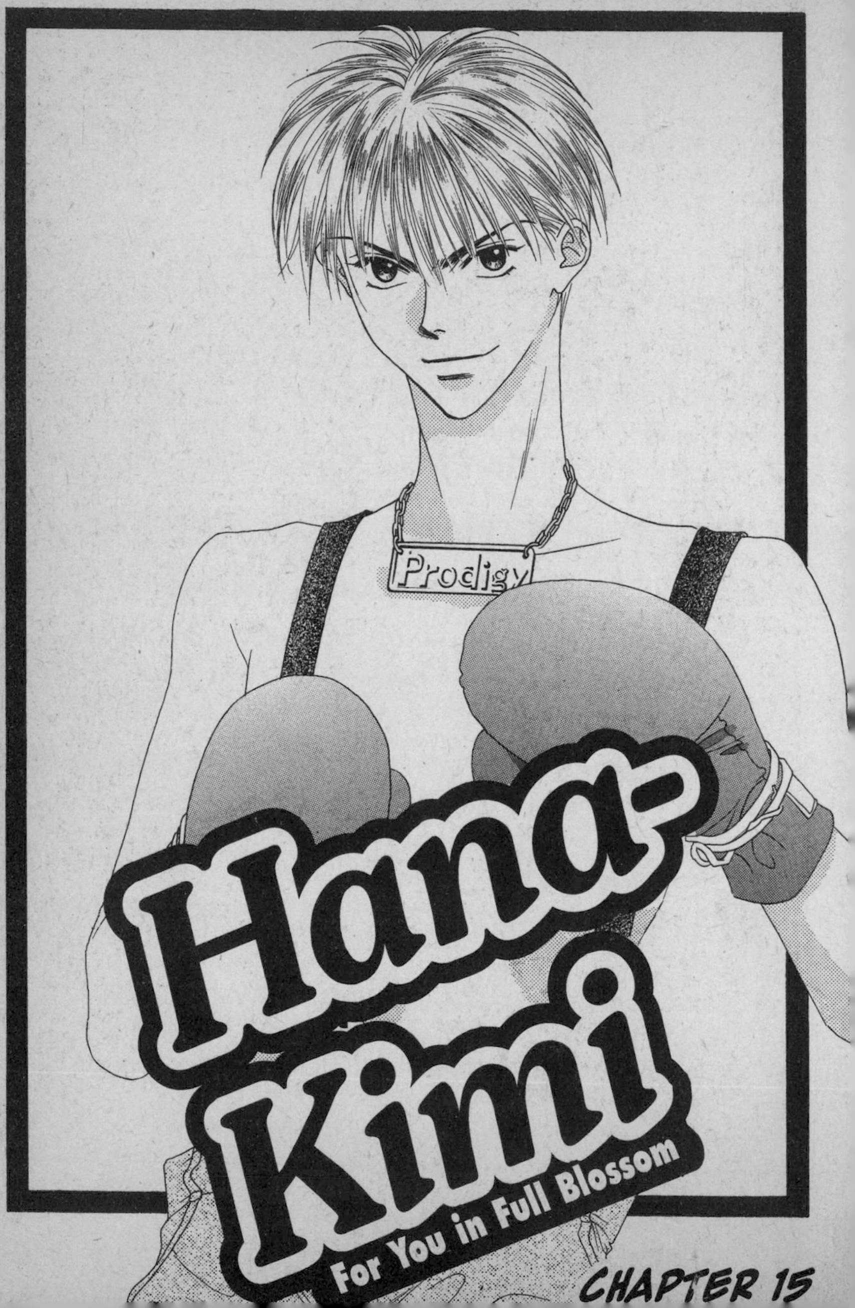
Prodigy
Hana-Kimi
For You in Full Blossom
CHAPTER 15

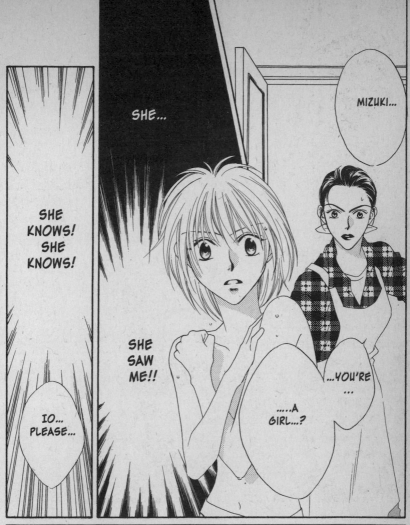

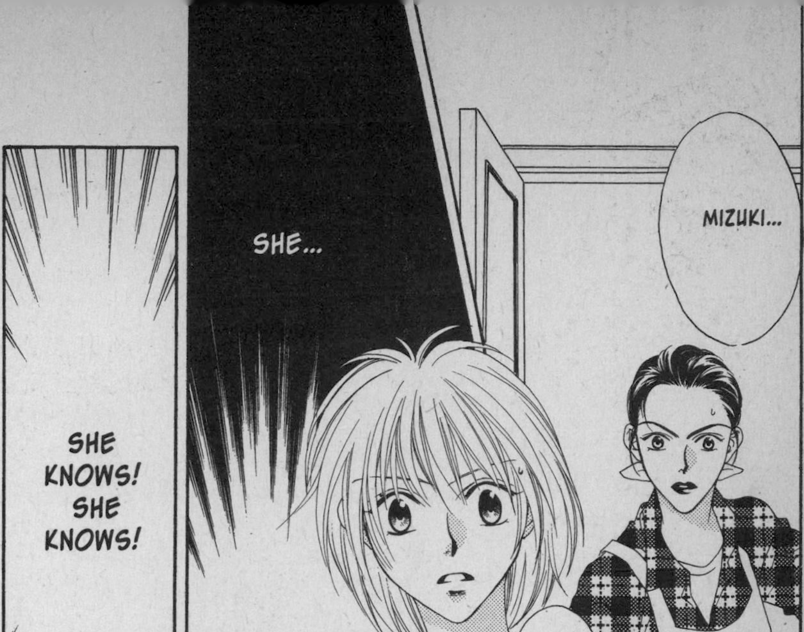
MIZUKI...
SHE...
...YOU'RE ...
SHE SAW ME!!
.....A GIRL...?
SHE KNOWS! SHE KNOWS!
IO... PLEASE...

Alcohol

IT'S NOT THAT I HAVE HIGH TOLERANCE OR THAT I'M A HEAVY DRINKER OR ANYTHING BUT I CAN'T GET DRUNK! (HA-HA!) NO MATTER HOW MANY COCKTAILS I HAVE, I CAN STILL WALK STRAIGHT. I EVEN STARTED TO DRINK SAKE AFTER MY EDITOR INTRODUCED ME TO IT. (I LIKE "TAKE NO KANBAI.") I DON'T REALLY DRINK BEER, BUT I DO LIKE IT WHEN IT'S POURED WELL. I NEVER DRINK SO MUCH THAT I BLACK OUT. (I DON'T WANNA THROW UP ON THE STREET.) BUT AT A CERTAIN BAR, I ONCE GOT DRUNK JUST FROM HAVING 2 SIPS OF CHU-HI. I ALWAYS GO THERE WITH THE SAME PEOPLE, SO I FEEL RELAXED AND COMFORTABLE.

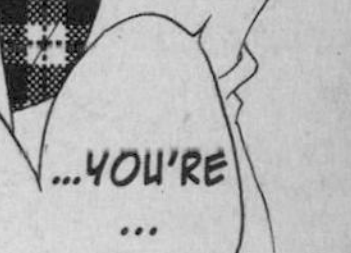
When I drink I get red, though.
Even my scalp gets red. I get sleepy right away.
MMMMM

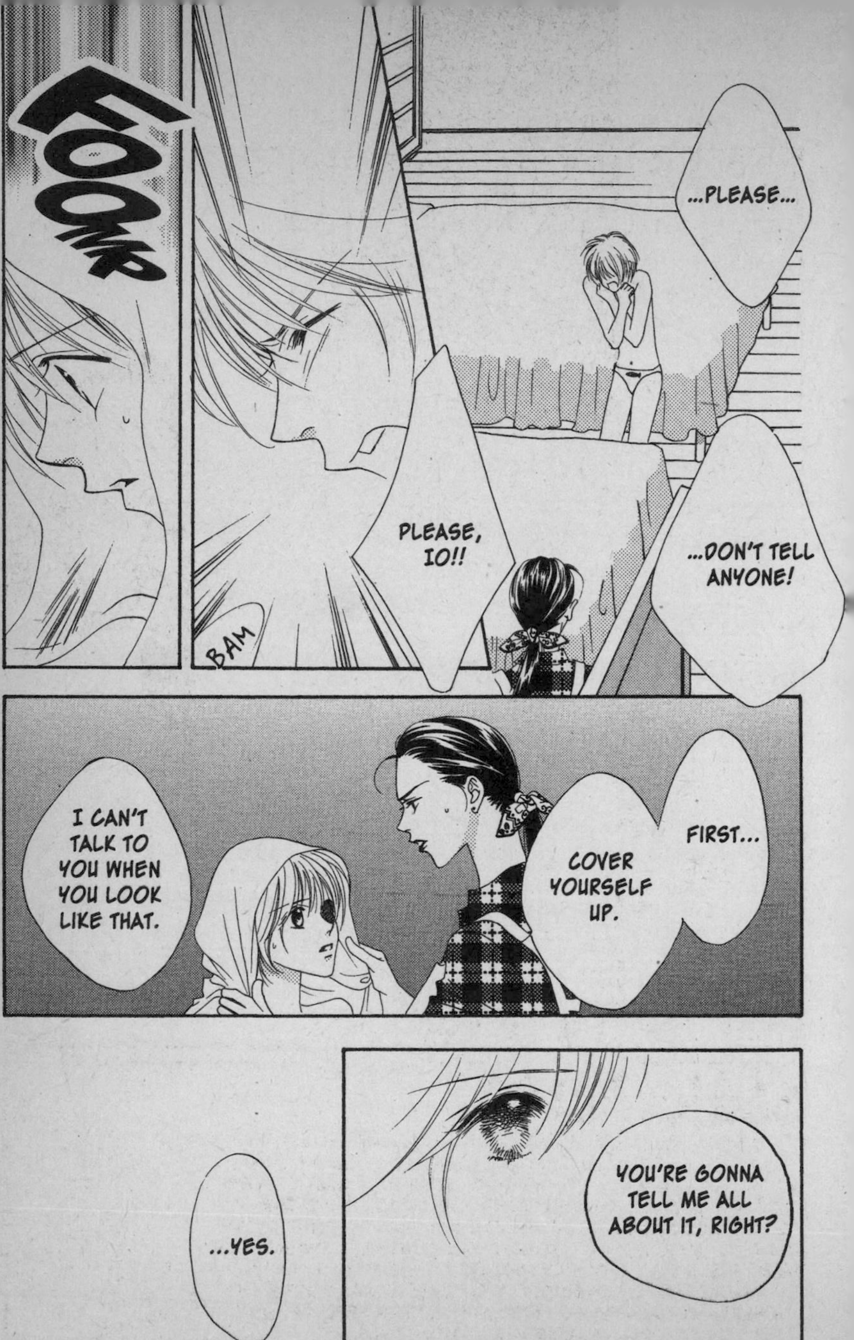
...PLEASE...
...DON'T TELL ANYONE!
PLEASE, IO!!
BAM
FOOMP
FIRST...
COVER YOURSELF UP.
I CAN'T TALK TO YOU WHEN YOU LOOK LIKE THAT.
YOU'RE GONNA TELL ME ALL ABOUT IT, RIGHT?
...YES.

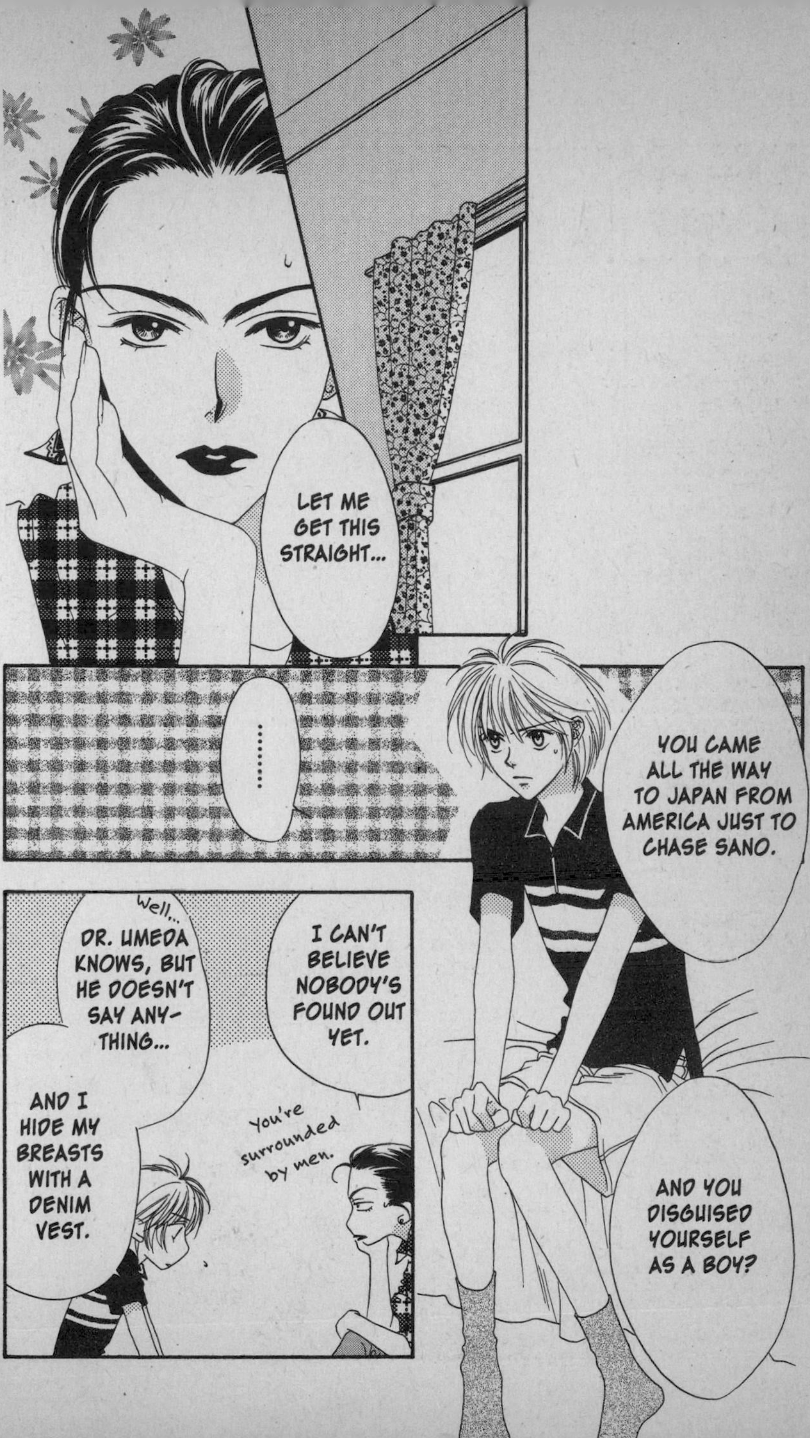
LET ME GET THIS STRAIGHT...
YOU CAME ALL THE WAY TO JAPAN FROM AMERICA JUST TO CHASE SANO.
AND YOU DISGUISED YOURSELF AS A BOY?
......
I CAN'T BELIEVE NOBODY'S FOUND OUT YET.
Well... DR. UMEDA KNOWS, BUT HE DOESN'T SAY ANY-THING...
AND I HIDE MY BREASTS WITH A DENIM VEST.
You're surrounded by men.

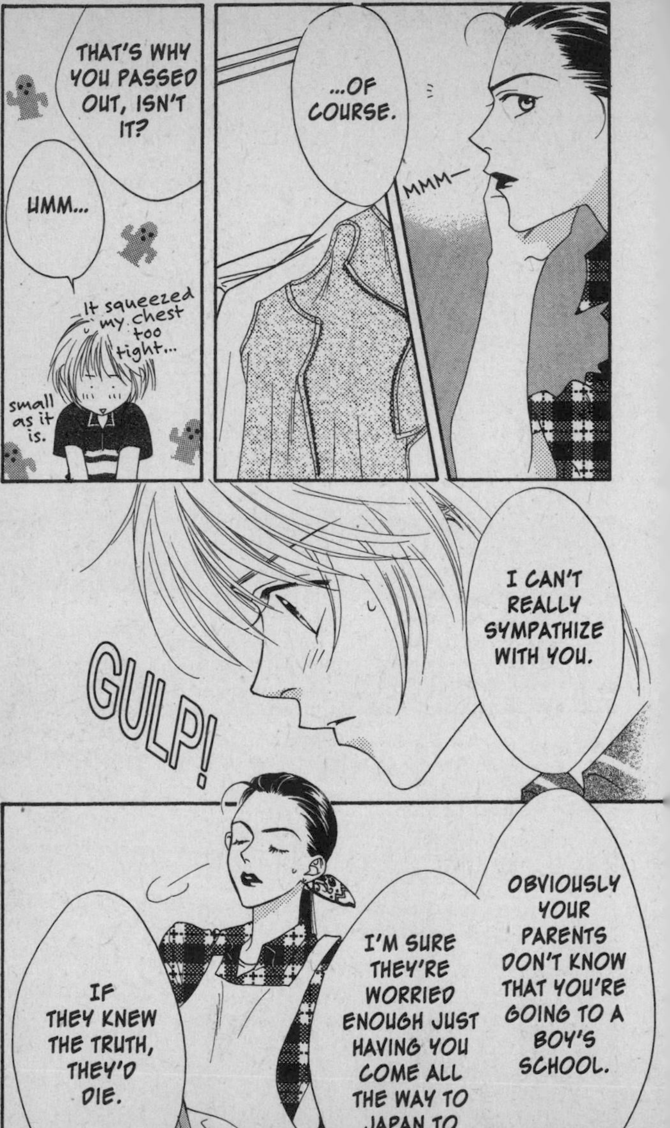
...OF COURSE.
MMM—
THAT'S WHY YOU PASSED OUT, ISN'T IT?
UMM...
It squeezed my chest too tight...
small as it is.
I CAN'T REALLY SYMPATHIZE WITH YOU.
GULP!
OBVIOUSLY YOUR PARENTS DON'T KNOW THAT YOU'RE GOING TO A BOY'S SCHOOL.
I'M SURE THEY'RE WORRIED ENOUGH JUST HAVING YOU COME ALL THE WAY TO JAPAN TO STUDY.
IF THEY KNEW THE TRUTH, THEY'D DIE.

Whispered Secrets

Things I Like

AHHHH, I'M TIRED! I SHOULDN'T JUST TRY AND WHIP OUT A PROFILE SO QUICKLY... UH... I REALLY LOVE THE MOVIE "BLADE RUNNER," THAT BOTH SANO AND UMEDA SAID THAT THEY LIKED. THE ORIGINAL BOOK WAS GOOD, TOO. THE THEME MUSIC, SET DESIGN, AND EVEN THE MADE-UP WORD "REPLICANT" WERE COOL. DARYL HANNAH WAS COOL, TOO. I HAVE NO COMPLAINTS. I LIKE IT SO MUCH I'D EVEN SAY THAT IT'S THE BEST OF ALL THE FUTURISTIC SCI-FI MOVIES. PEOPLE SAY THAT I JUST LIKE RIDLEY SCOTT MOVIES, AND I GUESS IT'S TRUE.

That's right. I love the first Alien movie. Yeah, but it doesn't really matter who makes them, I just like movies like that.

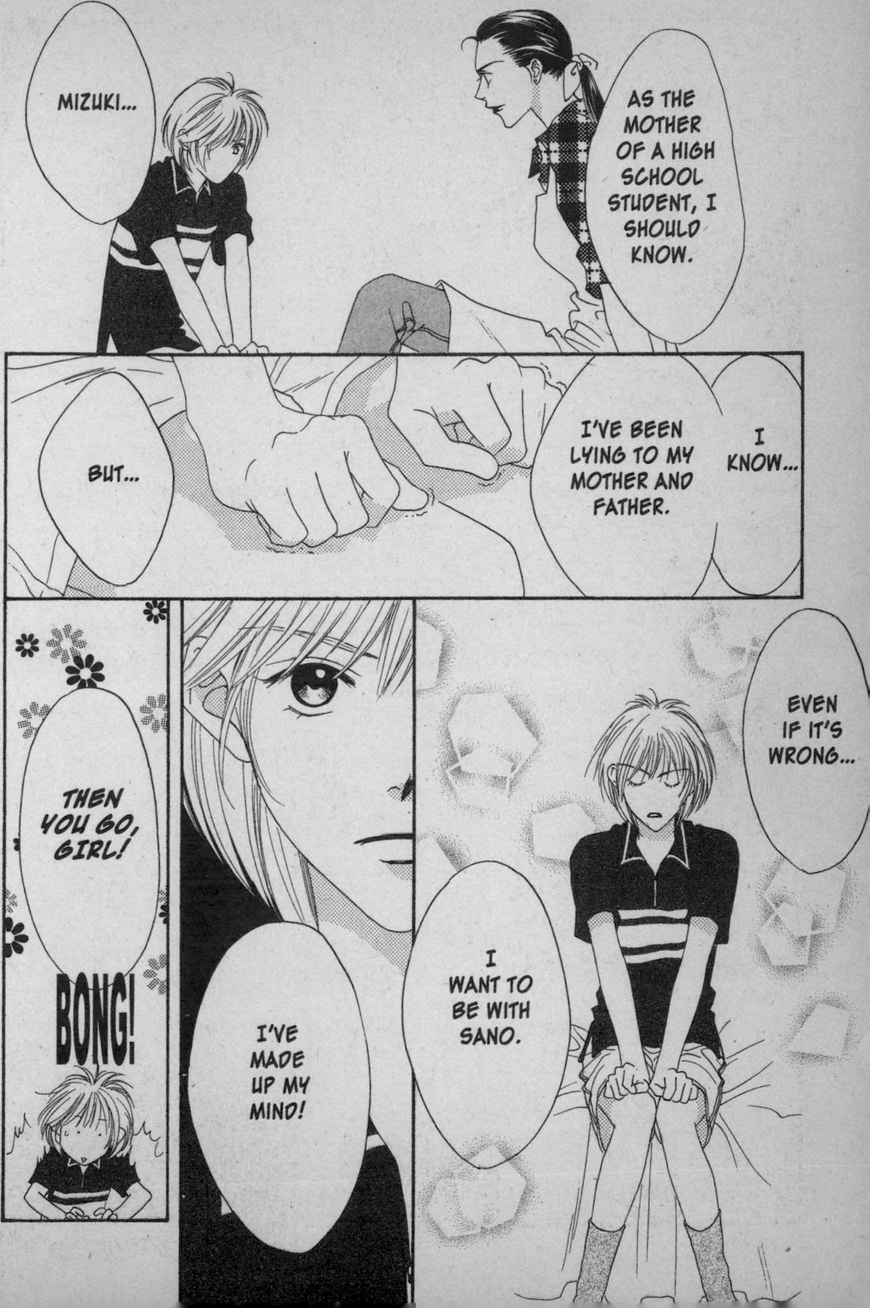
AS THE MOTHER OF A HIGH SCHOOL STUDENT, I SHOULD KNOW.
MIZUKI...
I KNOW...
I'VE BEEN LYING TO MY MOTHER AND FATHER.
BUT...
EVEN IF IT'S WRONG...
I WANT TO BE WITH SANO.
I'VE MADE UP MY MIND!
THEN YOU GO, GIRL!
BONG!

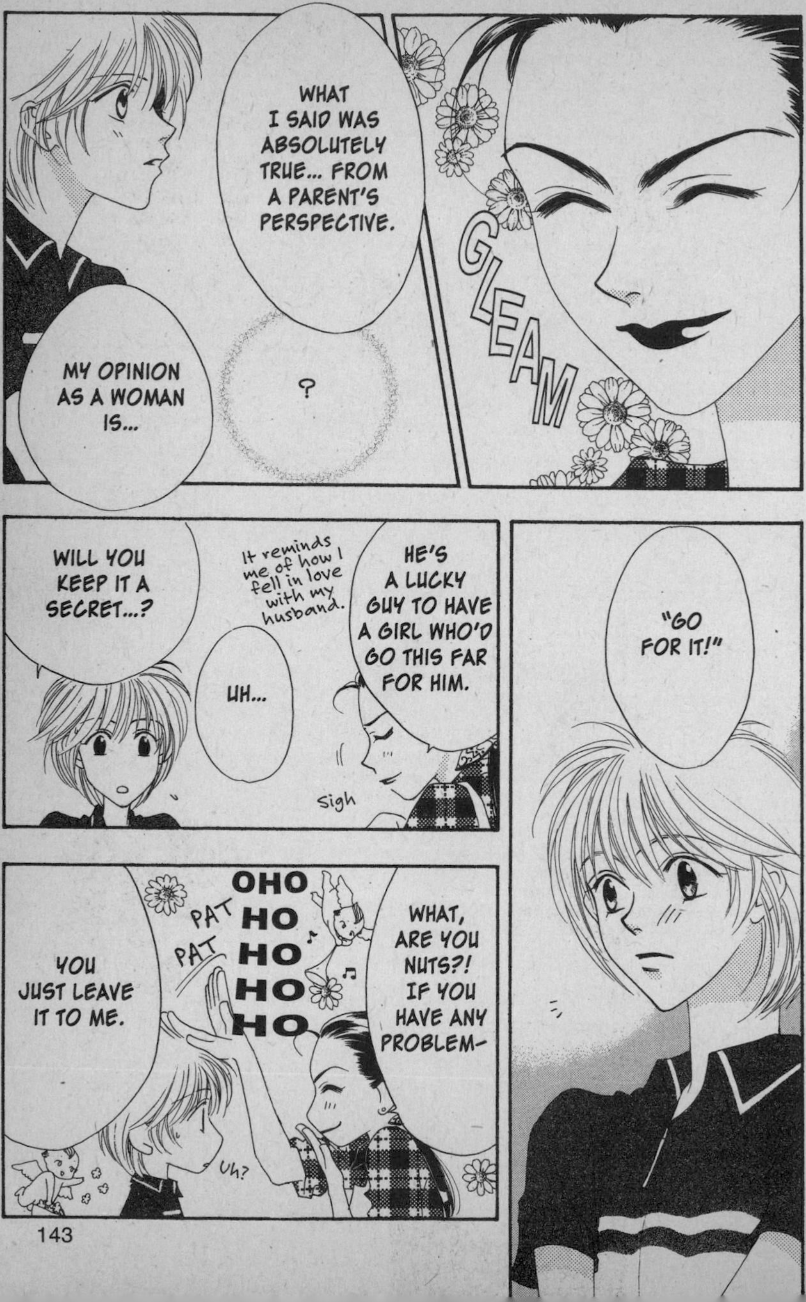
GLEAM
WHAT I SAID WAS ABSOLUTELY TRUE... FROM A PARENT'S PERSPECTIVE.
?
MY OPINION AS A WOMAN IS...
"GO FOR IT!"
HE'S A LUCKY GUY TO HAVE A GIRL WHO'D GO THIS FAR FOR HIM.
It reminds me of how I fell in love with my husband.
Sigh
UH...
WILL YOU KEEP IT A SECRET...?
WHAT, ARE YOU NUTS?! IF YOU HAVE ANY PROBLEM-
OHO HO HO HO HO
PAT PAT
YOU JUST LEAVE IT TO ME.
Uh?

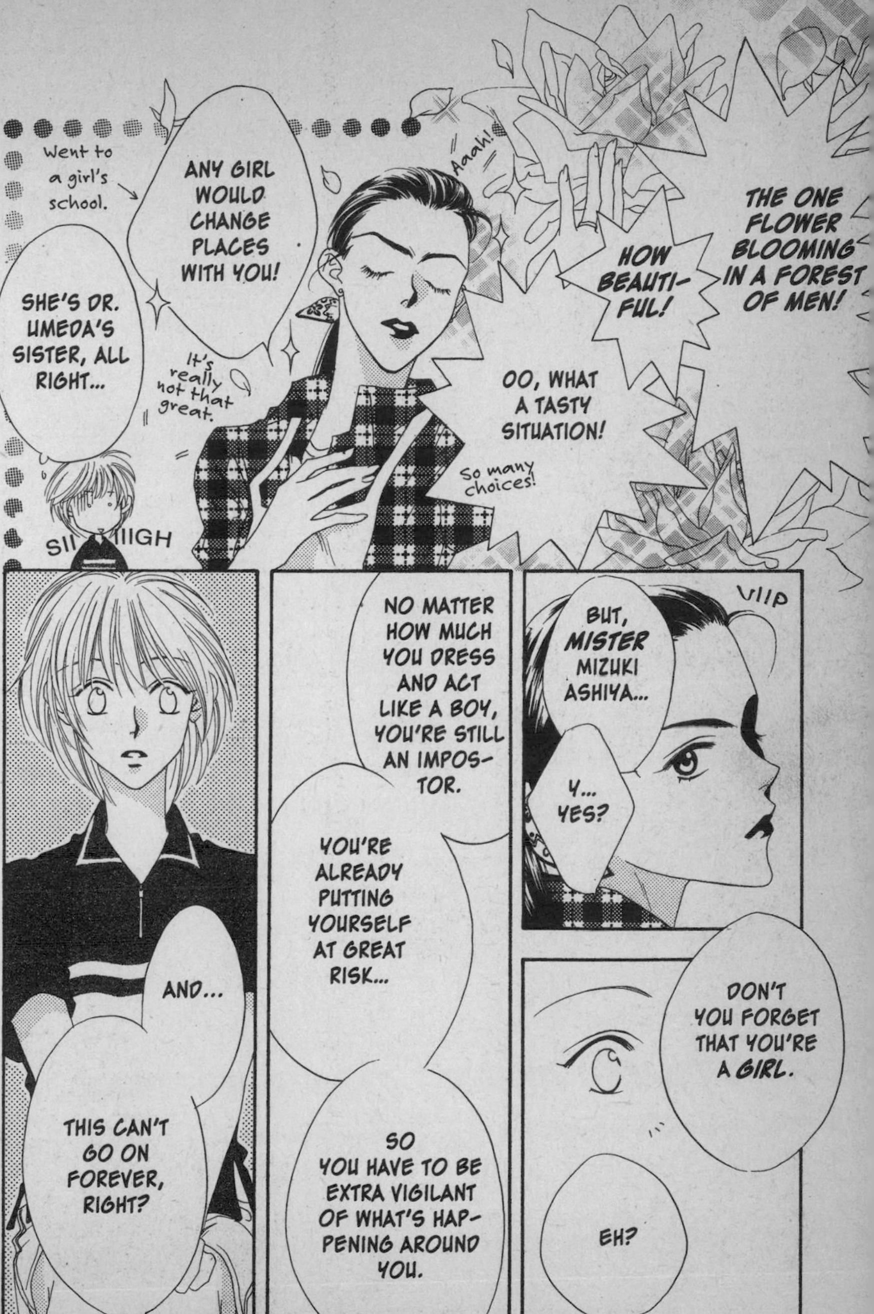
THE ONE FLOWER BLOOMING IN A FOREST OF MEN!
HOW BEAUTIFUL!
Aaah!
OO, WHAT A TASTY SITUATION!
So many choices!
ANY GIRL WOULD CHANGE PLACES WITH YOU!
Went to a girl's school.
It's really not that great.
SHE'S DR. UMEDA'S SISTER, ALL RIGHT...
SII IIIGH
VIIP
BUT, **MISTER** MIZUKI ASHIYA...
Y... YES?
DON'T YOU FORGET THAT YOU'RE A **GIRL**.
EH?
NO MATTER HOW MUCH YOU DRESS AND ACT LIKE A BOY, YOU'RE STILL AN IMPOSTOR.
YOU'RE ALREADY PUTTING YOURSELF AT GREAT RISK...
SO YOU HAVE TO BE EXTRA VIGILANT OF WHAT'S HAPPENING AROUND YOU.
AND...
THIS CAN'T GO ON FOREVER, RIGHT?

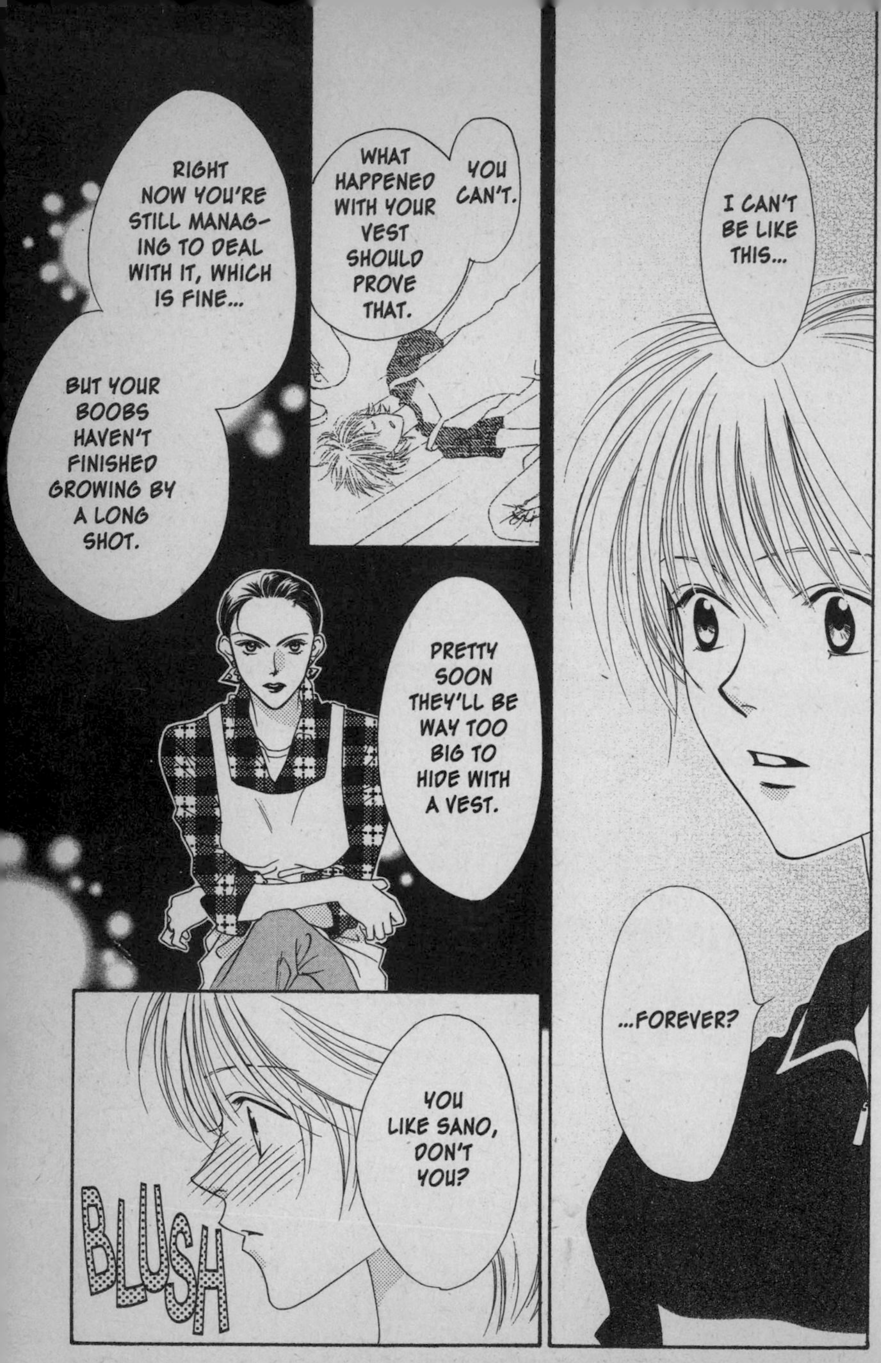
I CAN'T BE LIKE THIS...
...FOREVER?
YOU CAN'T.
WHAT HAPPENED WITH YOUR VEST SHOULD PROVE THAT.
RIGHT NOW YOU'RE STILL MANAG-ING TO DEAL WITH IT, WHICH IS FINE...
BUT YOUR BOOBS HAVEN'T FINISHED GROWING BY A LONG SHOT.
PRETTY SOON THEY'LL BE WAY TOO BIG TO HIDE WITH A VEST.
YOU LIKE SANO, DON'T YOU?
BLUSH

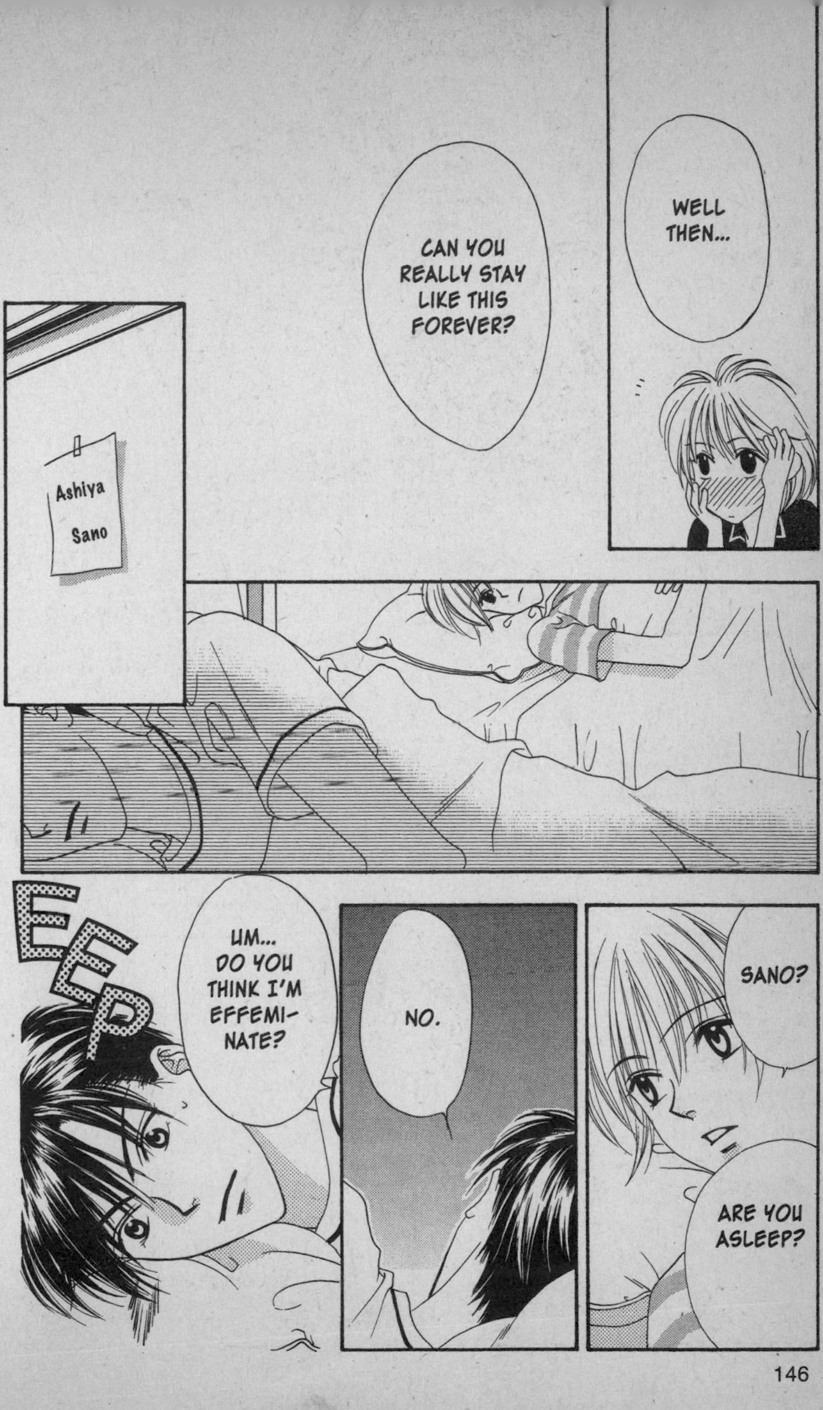
WELL THEN...
CAN YOU REALLY STAY LIKE THIS FOREVER?
Ashiya
Sano
SANO?
ARE YOU ASLEEP?
NO.
UM... DO YOU THINK I'M EFFEMINATE?
EEP

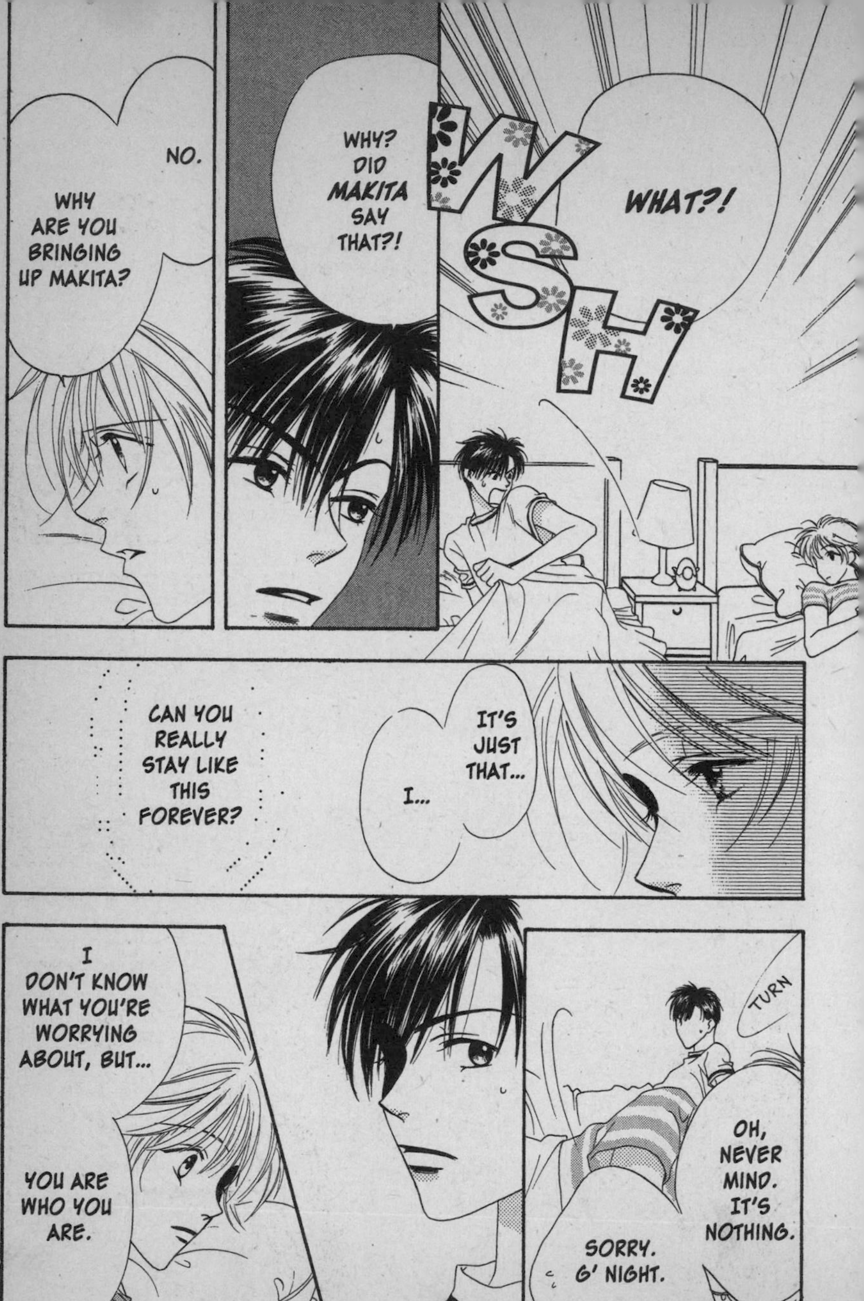
WHAT?!
WSH
WHY? DID MAKITA SAY THAT?!
NO.
WHY ARE YOU BRINGING UP MAKITA?
IT'S JUST THAT...
I...
CAN YOU REALLY STAY LIKE THIS FOREVER?
TURN
OH, NEVER MIND. IT'S NOTHING.
SORRY. G' NIGHT.
I DON'T KNOW WHAT YOU'RE WORRYING ABOUT, BUT...
YOU ARE WHO YOU ARE.

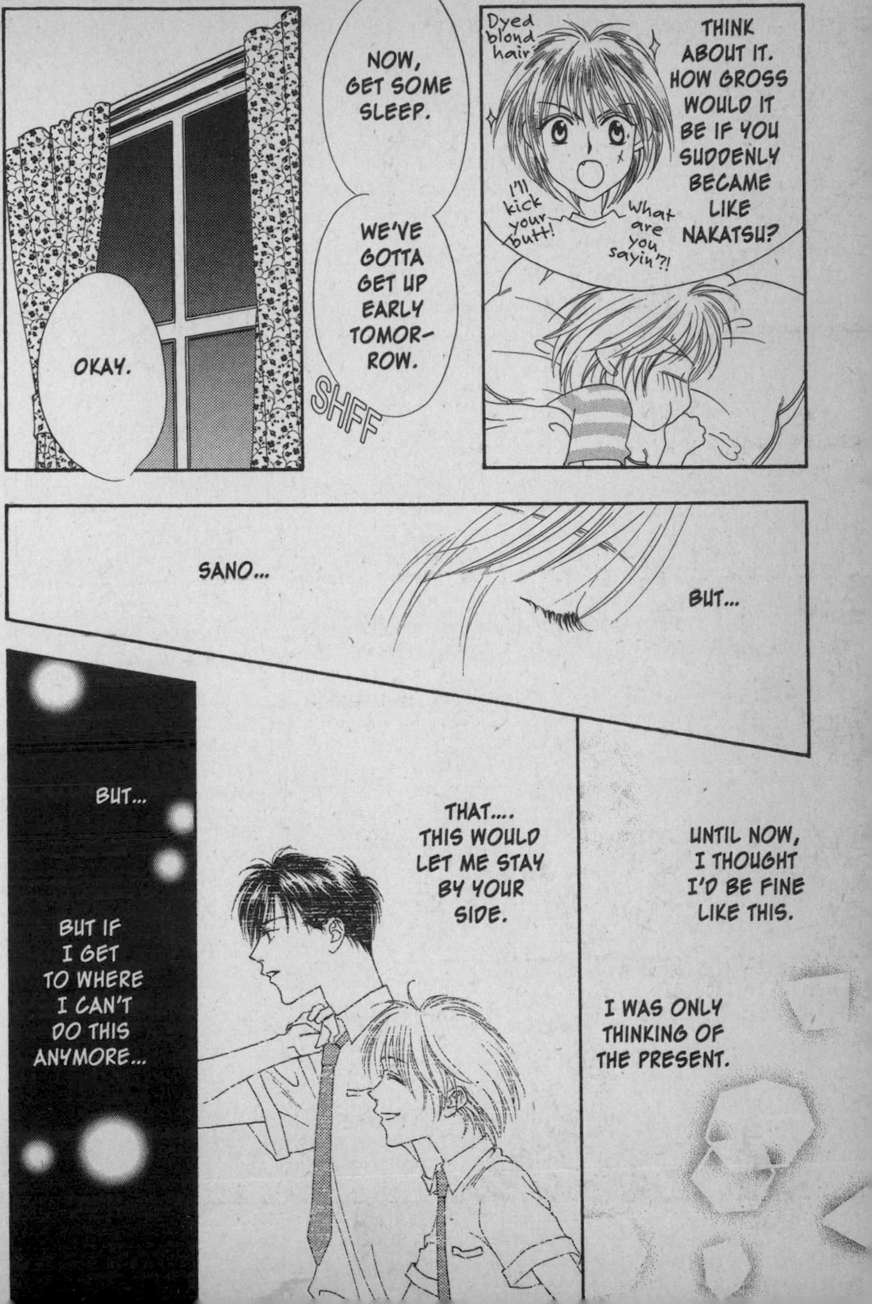
THINK ABOUT IT. HOW GROSS WOULD IT BE IF YOU SUDDENLY BECAME LIKE NAKATSU?
Dyed blond hair
What are you sayin'?!
I'll kick your butt!
NOW, GET SOME SLEEP.
WE'VE GOTTA GET UP EARLY TOMORROW.
SHFF
OKAY.
SANO...
BUT...
UNTIL NOW, I THOUGHT I'D BE FINE LIKE THIS.
I WAS ONLY THINKING OF THE PRESENT.
THAT.... THIS WOULD LET ME STAY BY YOUR SIDE.
BUT...
BUT IF I GET TO WHERE I CAN'T DO THIS ANYMORE...

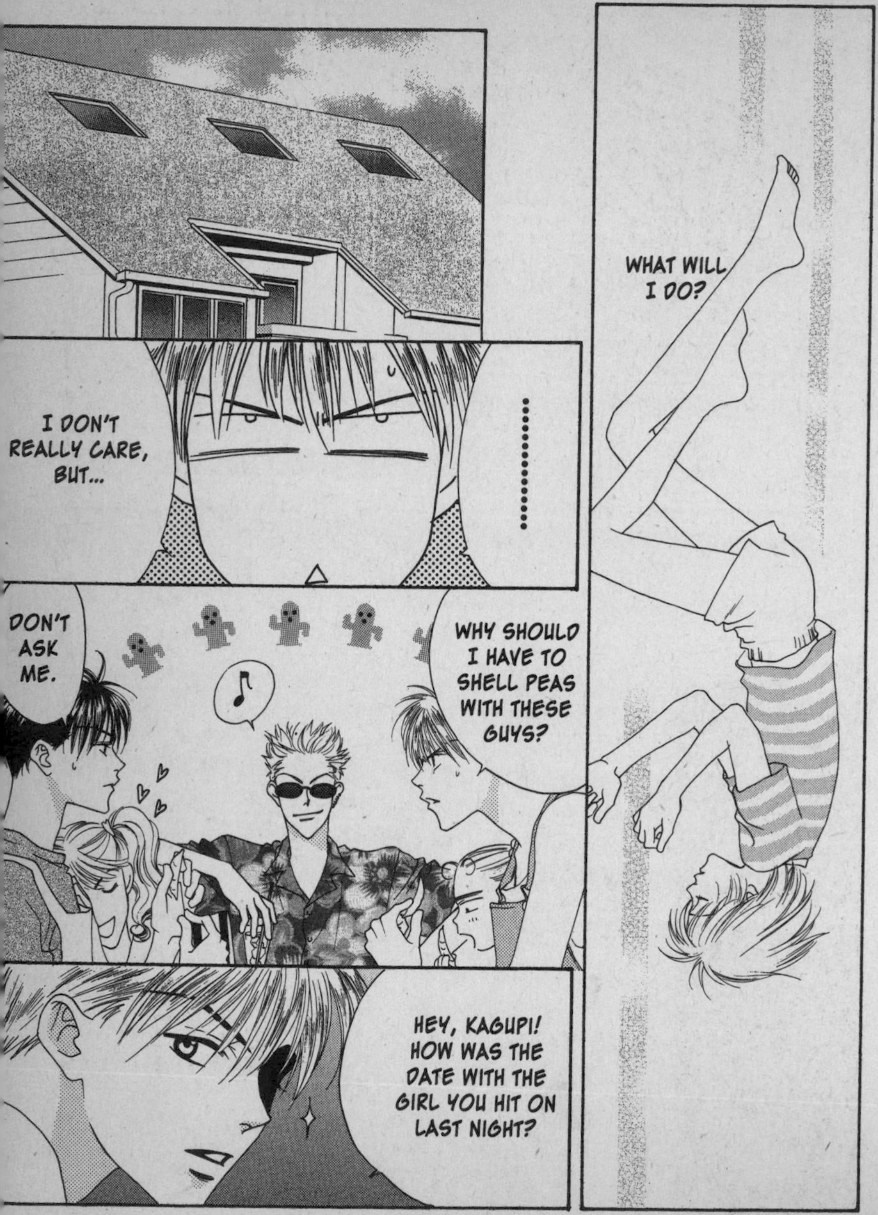
WHAT WILL I DO?
....
I DON'T REALLY CARE, BUT...
WHY SHOULD I HAVE TO SHELL PEAS WITH THESE GUYS?
DON'T ASK ME.
HEY, KAGUPI! HOW WAS THE DATE WITH THE GIRL YOU HIT ON LAST NIGHT?

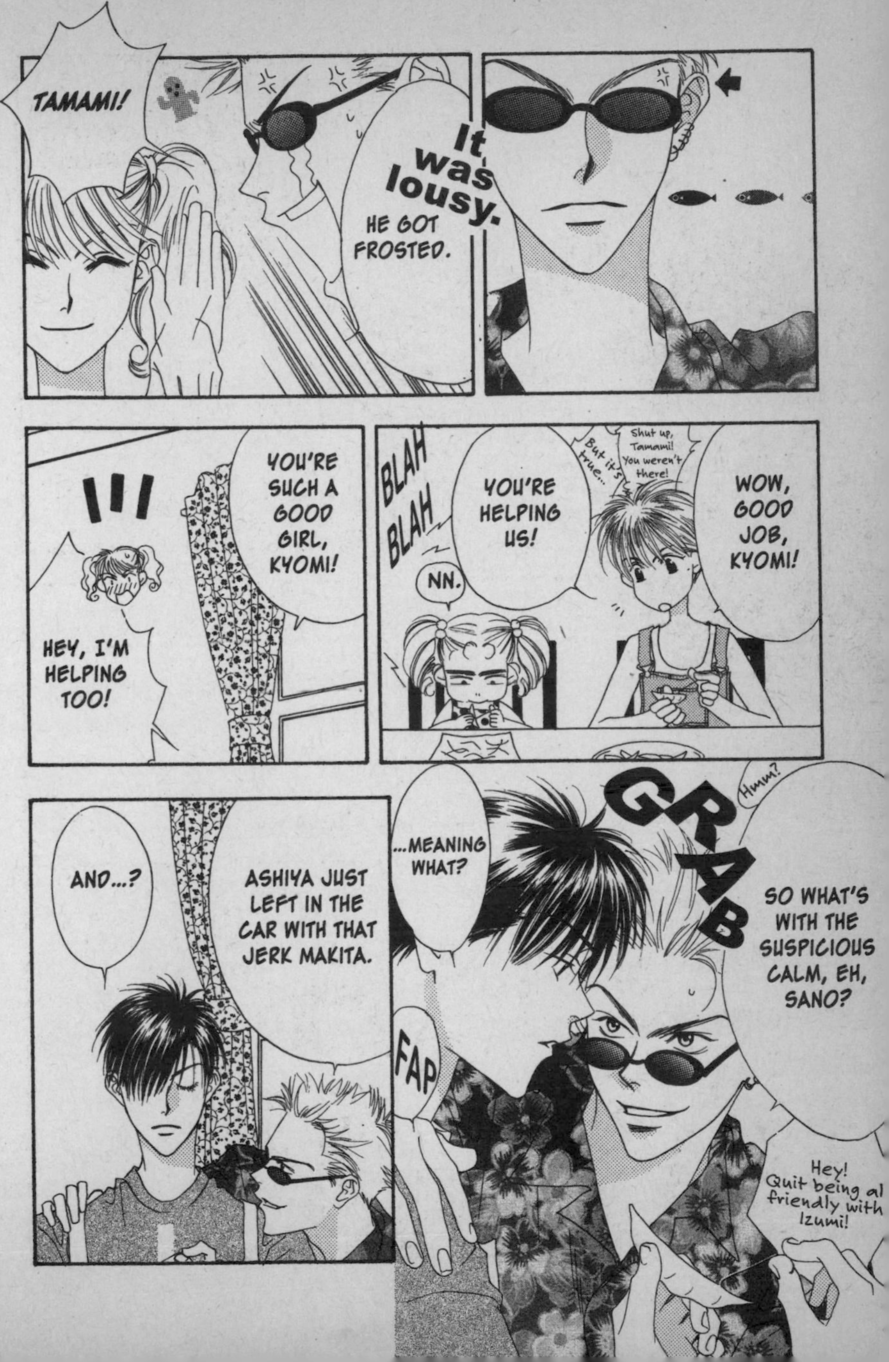
It was lousy.
HE GOT FROSTED.
TAMAMI!
WOW, GOOD JOB, KYOMI!
Shut up, Tamami! You weren't there!
But it's true...
YOU'RE HELPING US!
BLAH BLAH
NN.
YOU'RE SUCH A GOOD GIRL, KYOMI!
!!!
HEY, I'M HELPING TOO!
Hmm?
GRAB
SO WHAT'S WITH THE SUSPICIOUS CALM, EH, SANO?
...MEANING WHAT?
FAP
Hey! Quit being al friendly with Izumi!
ASHIYA JUST LEFT IN THE CAR WITH THAT JERK MAKITA.
AND...?

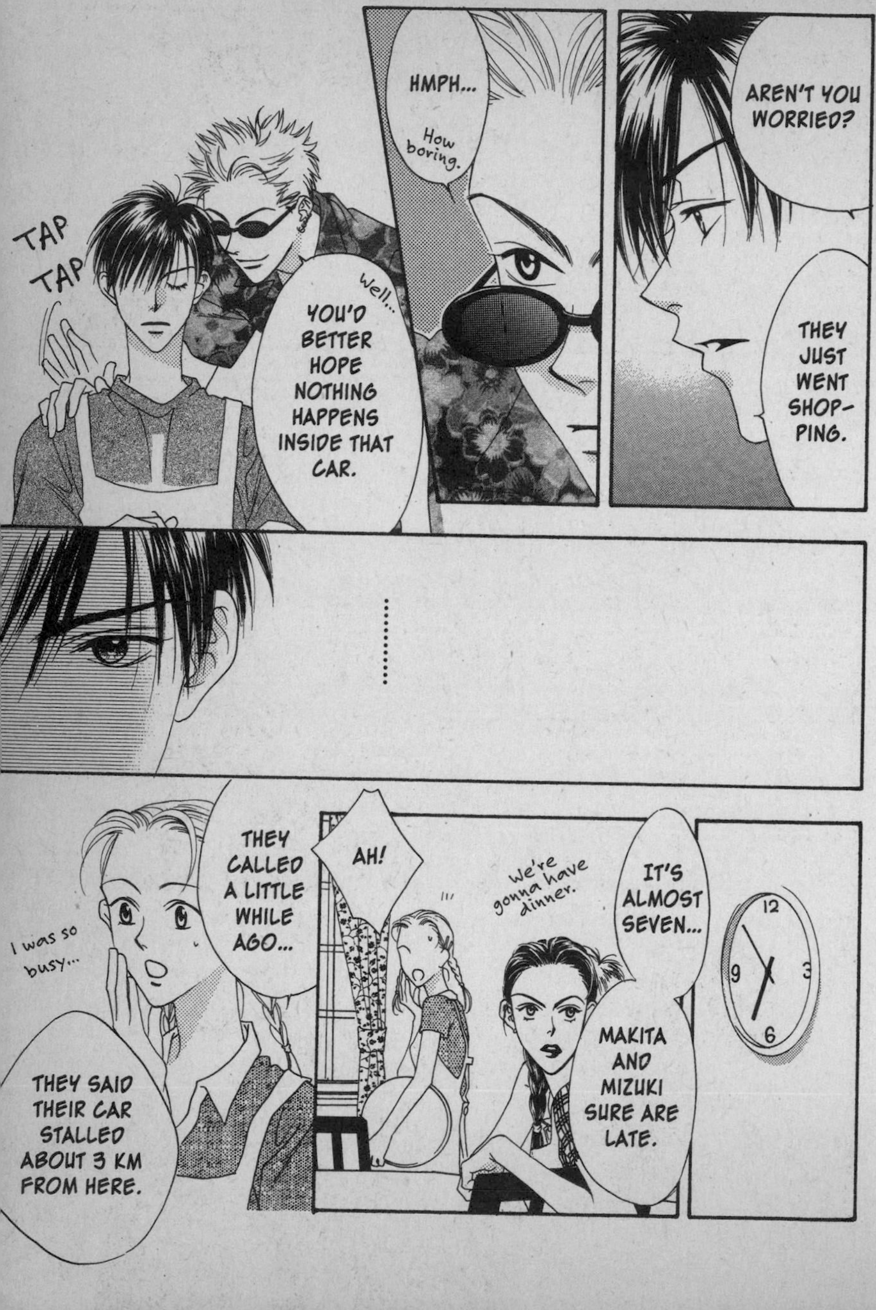
AREN'T YOU WORRIED?
THEY JUST WENT SHOP-PING.
HMPH...
How boring.
TAP TAP
Well...
YOU'D BETTER HOPE NOTHING HAPPENS INSIDE THAT CAR.
....
IT'S ALMOST SEVEN...
We're gonna have dinner.
MAKITA AND MIZUKI SURE ARE LATE.
AH!
THEY CALLED A LITTLE WHILE AGO...
I was so busy...
THEY SAID THEIR CAR STALLED ABOUT 3 KM FROM HERE.

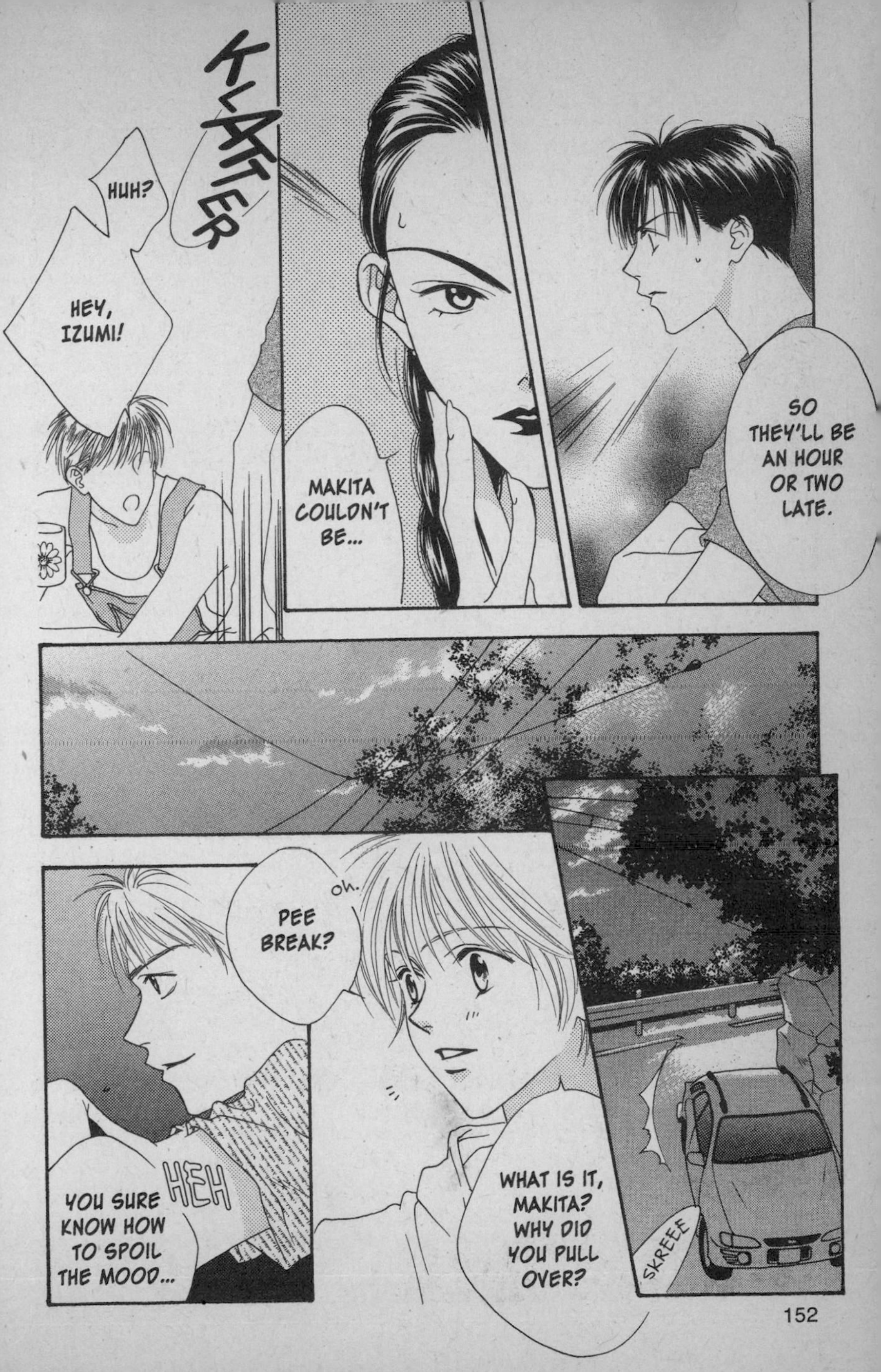
SO THEY'LL BE AN HOUR OR TWO LATE.
MAKITA COULDN'T BE...
KLATTER
HUH?
HEY, IZUMI!
SKREEE
WHAT IS IT, MAKITA? WHY DID YOU PULL OVER?
oh.
PEE BREAK?
HEH
YOU SURE KNOW HOW TO SPOIL THE MOOD...

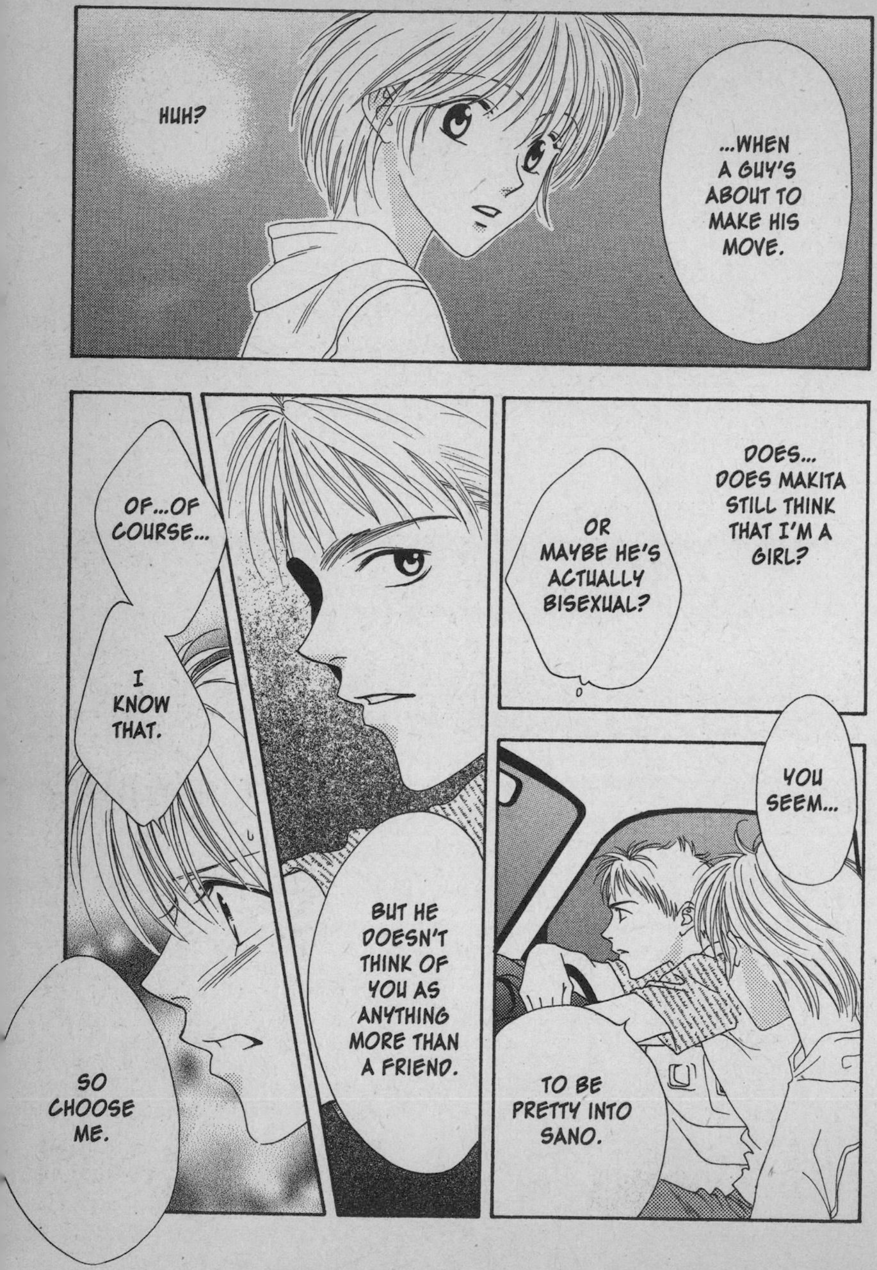
...WHEN A GUY'S ABOUT TO MAKE HIS MOVE.
HUH?
DOES... DOES MAKITA STILL THINK THAT I'M A GIRL?
OR MAYBE HE'S ACTUALLY BISEXUAL?
YOU SEEM...
TO BE PRETTY INTO SANO.
BUT HE DOESN'T THINK OF YOU AS ANYTHING MORE THAN A FRIEND.
OF...OF COURSE...
I KNOW THAT.
SO CHOOSE ME.

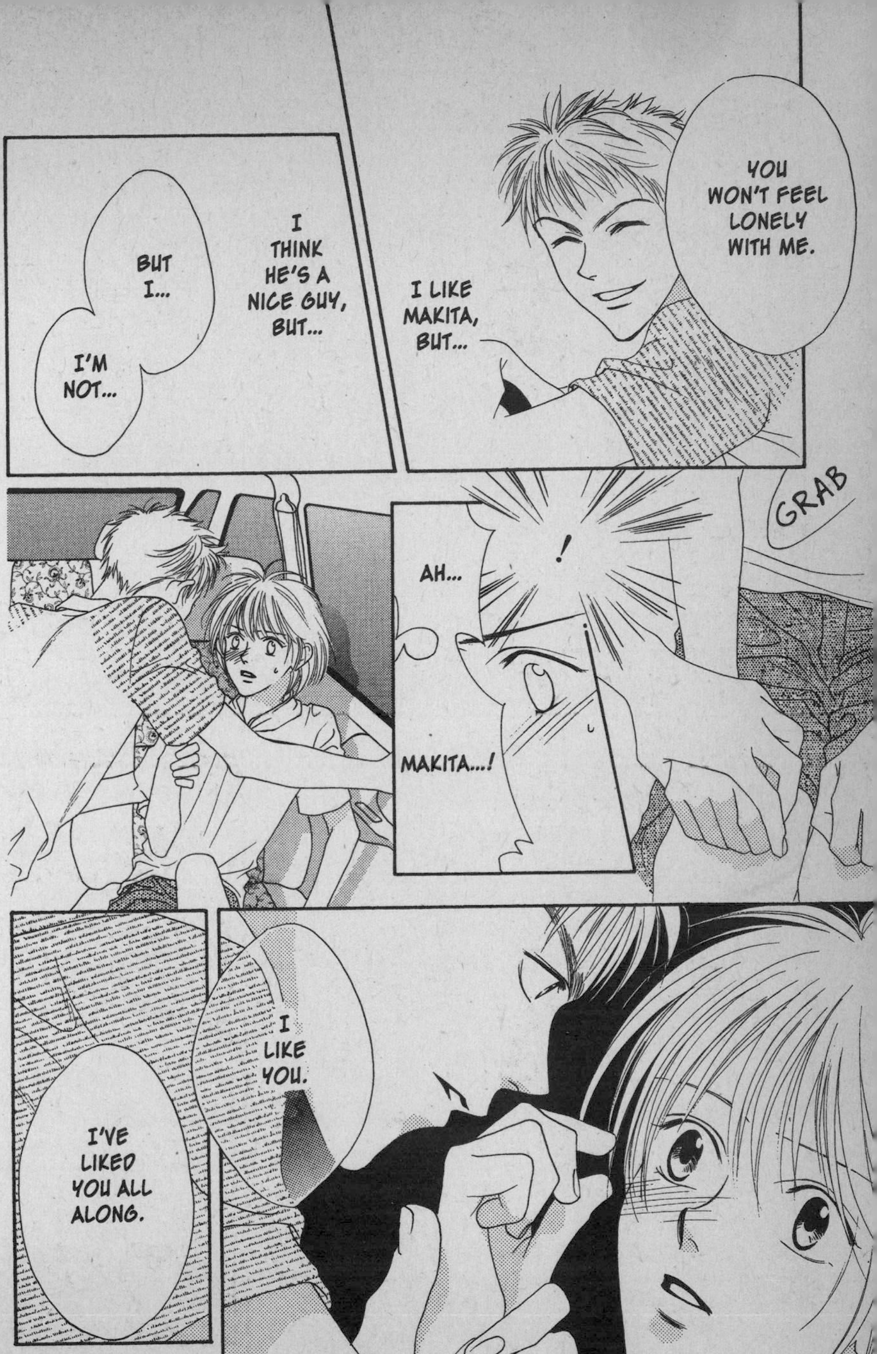
YOU WON'T FEEL LONELY WITH ME.
I LIKE MAKITA, BUT...
I THINK HE'S A NICE GUY, BUT...
BUT I...
I'M NOT...
GRAB
!
AH...
MAKITA...!
I LIKE YOU.
I'VE LIKED YOU ALL ALONG.

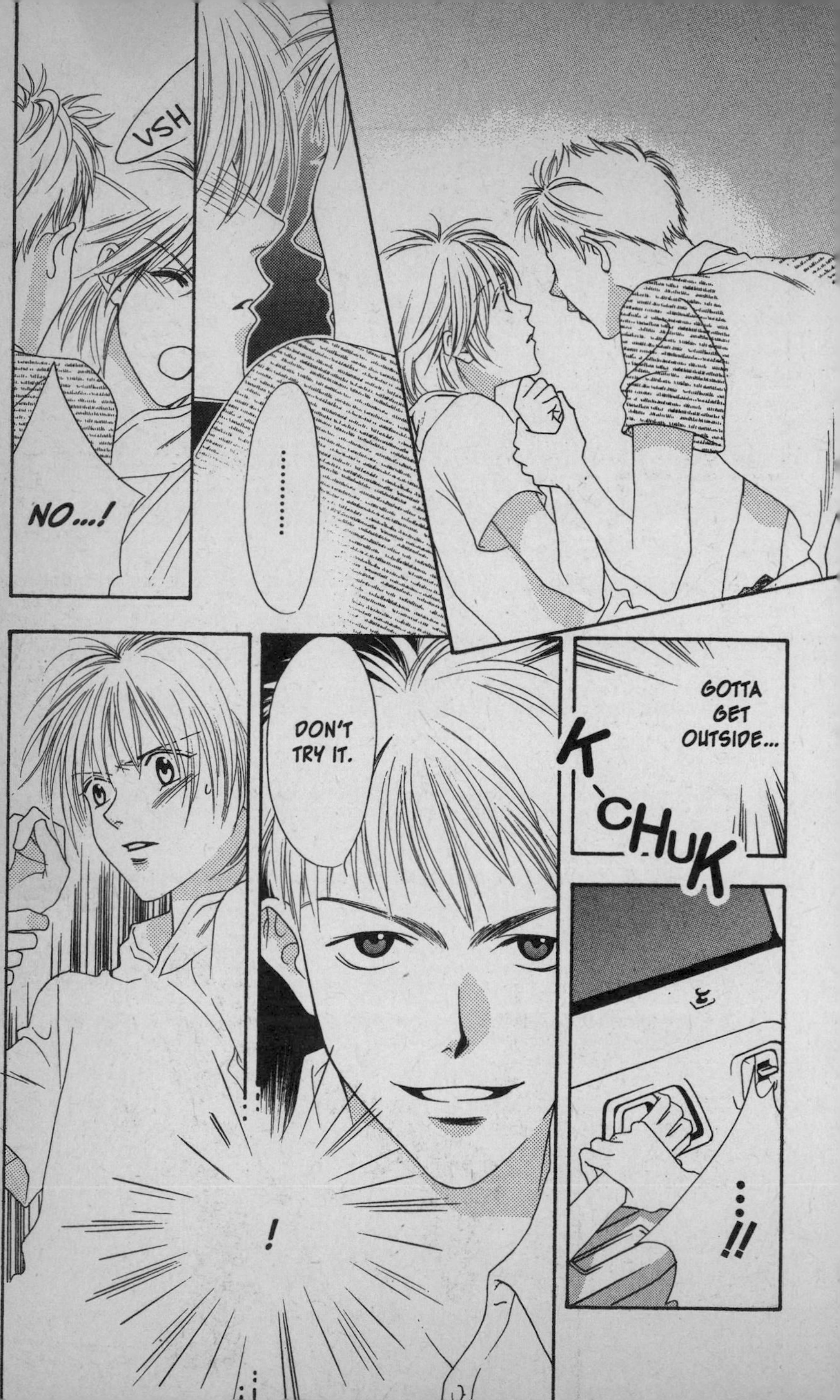
......
VSH
NO...!
GOTTA GET OUTSIDE...
K-CHUK
...!!
DON'T TRY IT.
!

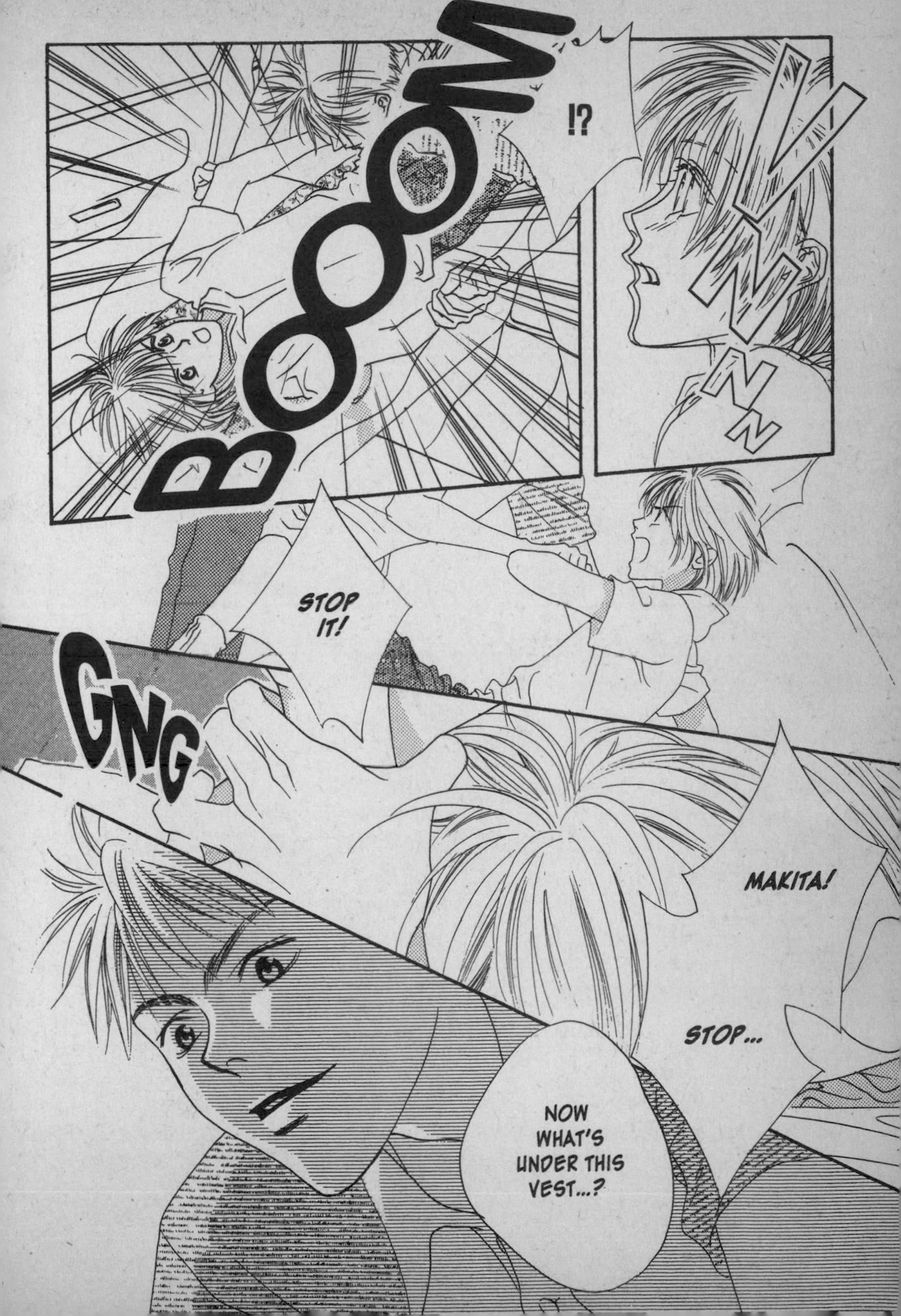
VWNNN
!?
BOOOM
STOP IT!
GNG
MAKITA!
STOP...
NOW WHAT'S UNDER THIS VEST...?

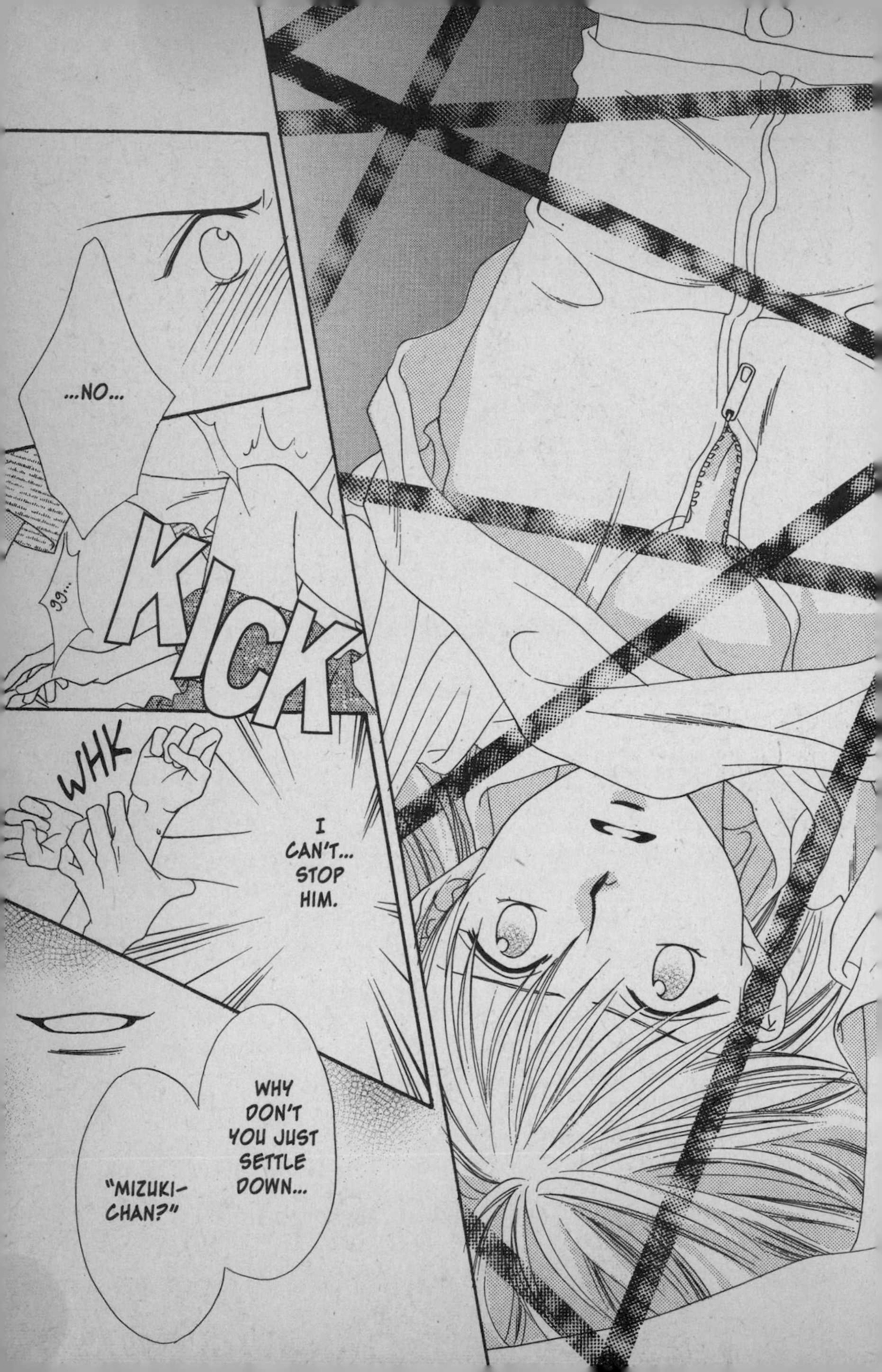
...NO...
gg...
KICK
WHK
I CAN'T... STOP HIM.
WHY DON'T YOU JUST SETTLE DOWN...
"MIZUKI-CHAN?"

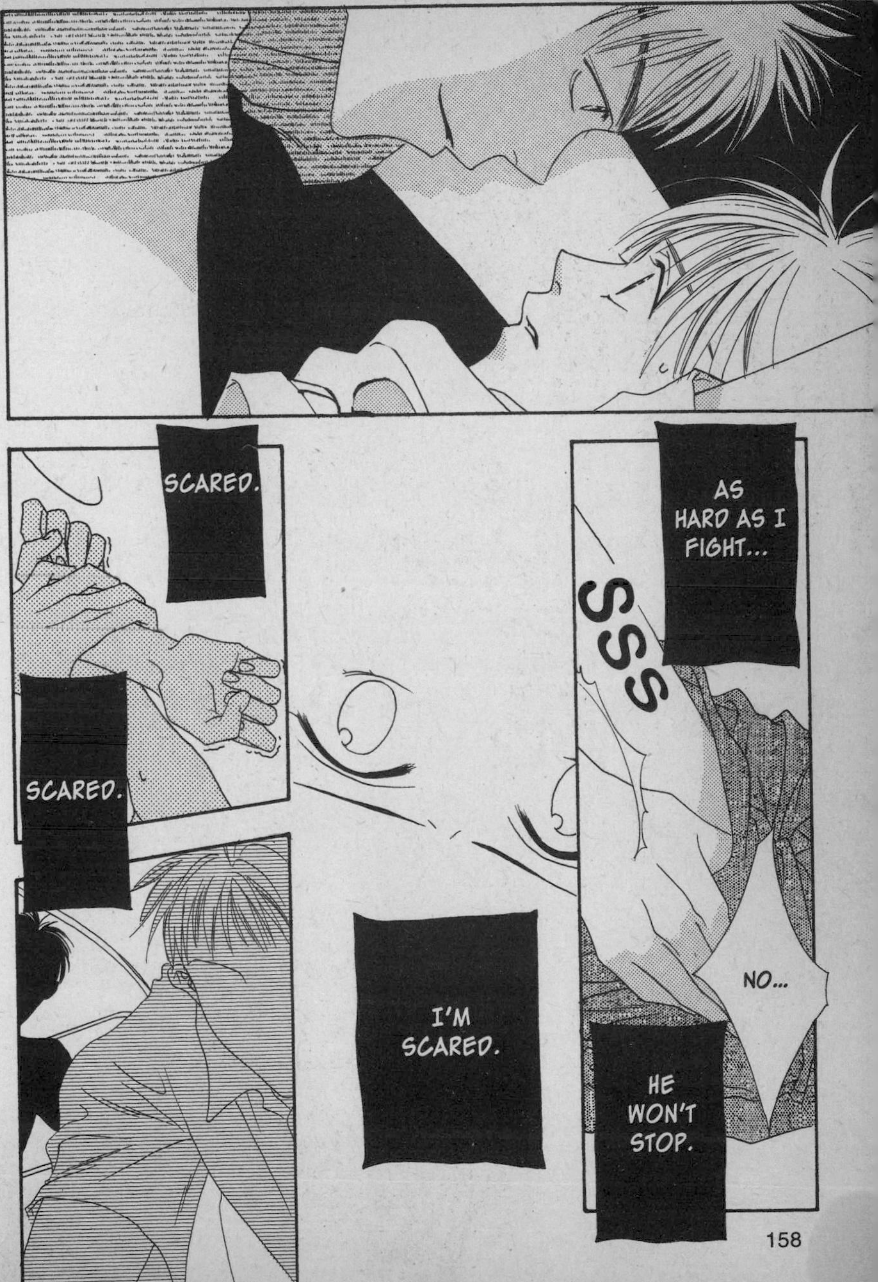
AS HARD AS I FIGHT...
SSS
NO...
HE WON'T STOP.
SCARED.
SCARED.
I'M SCARED.

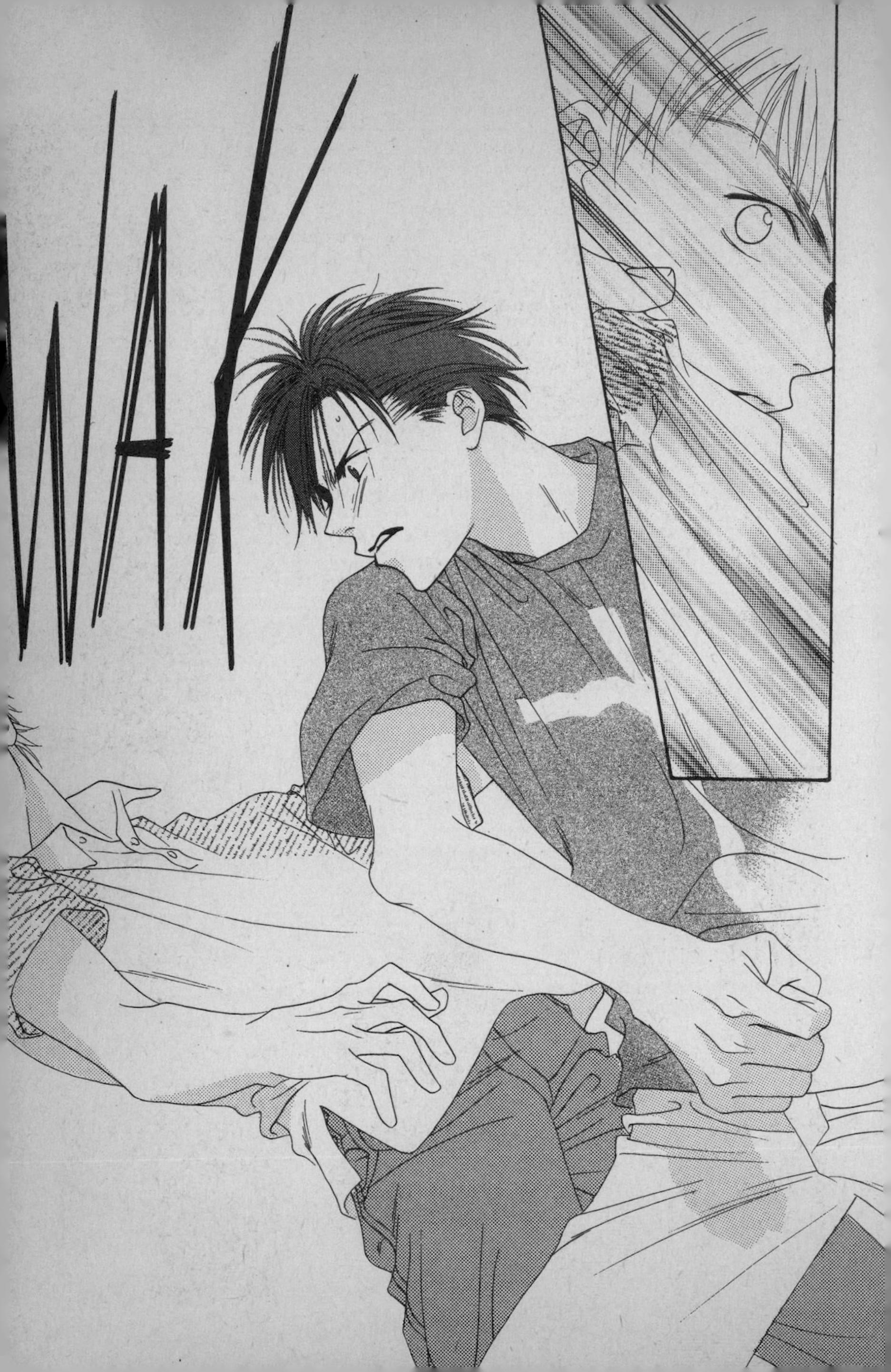
WAK

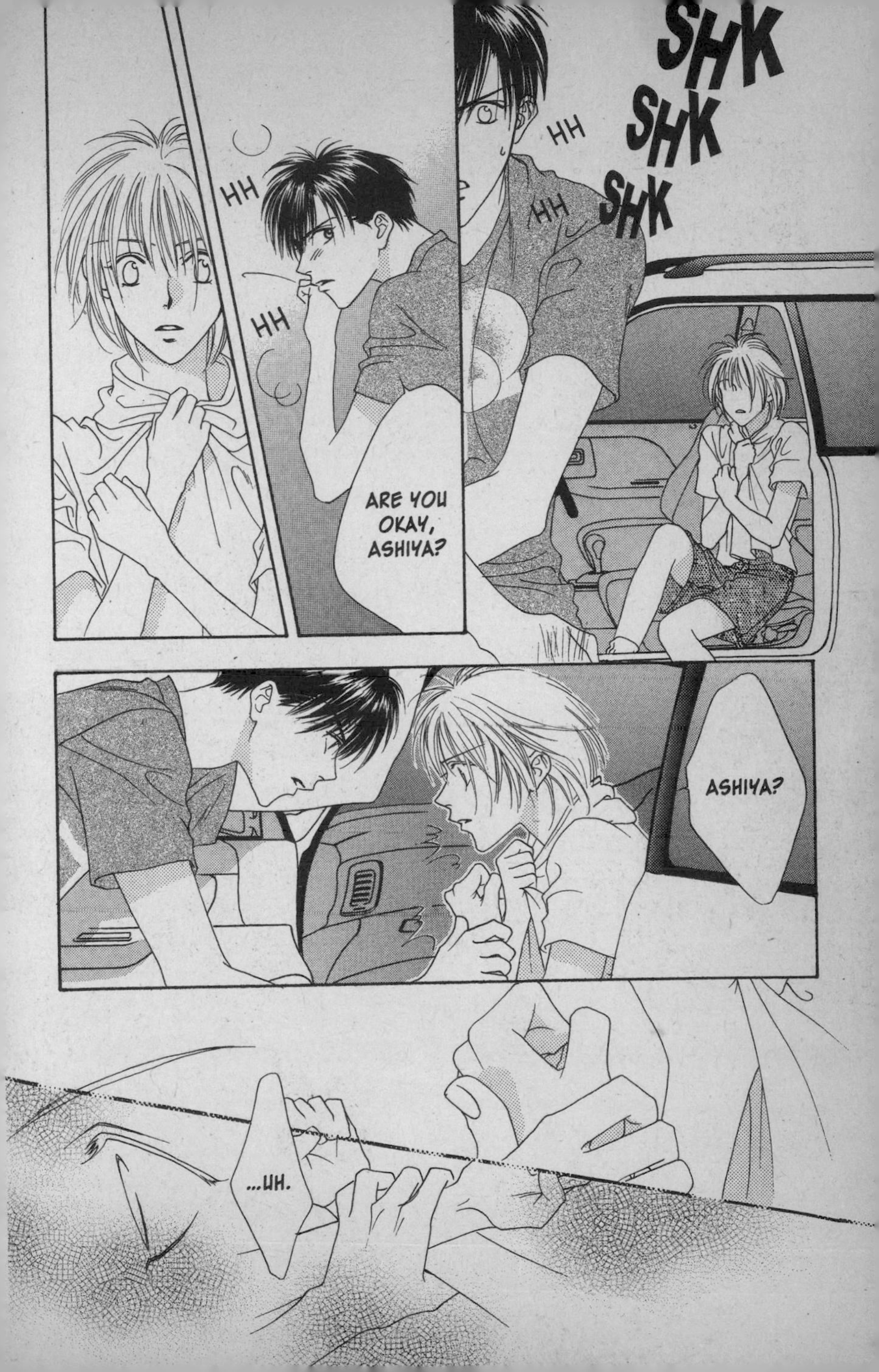
SHK
SHK
SHK
HH
HH
HH
HH
ARE YOU OKAY, ASHIYA?
ASHIYA?
...UH.

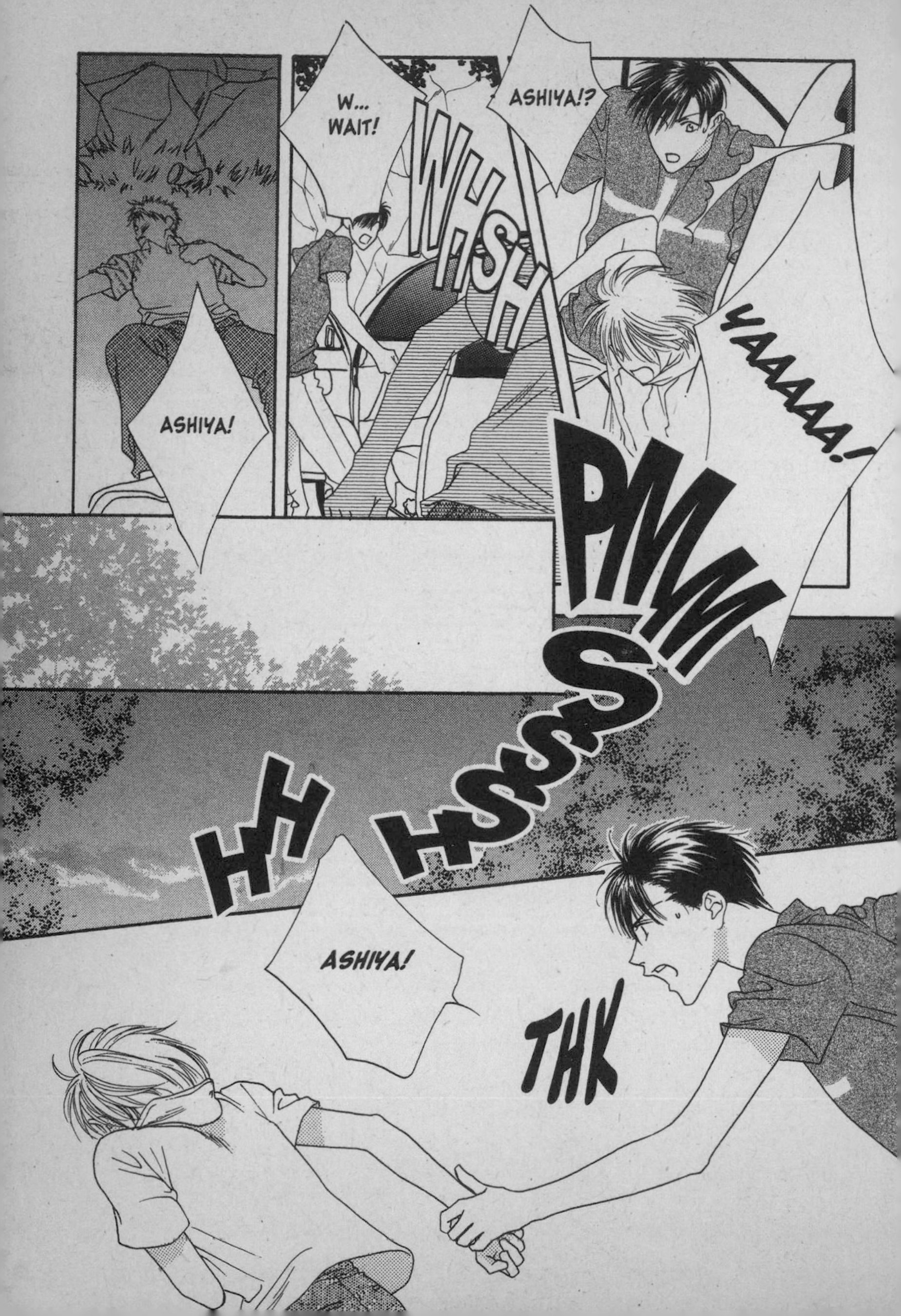
ASHIYA!?
YAAAAAA!
W... WAIT!
WHSH
ASHIYA!
PMMSSSSHHH
ASHIYA!
THK

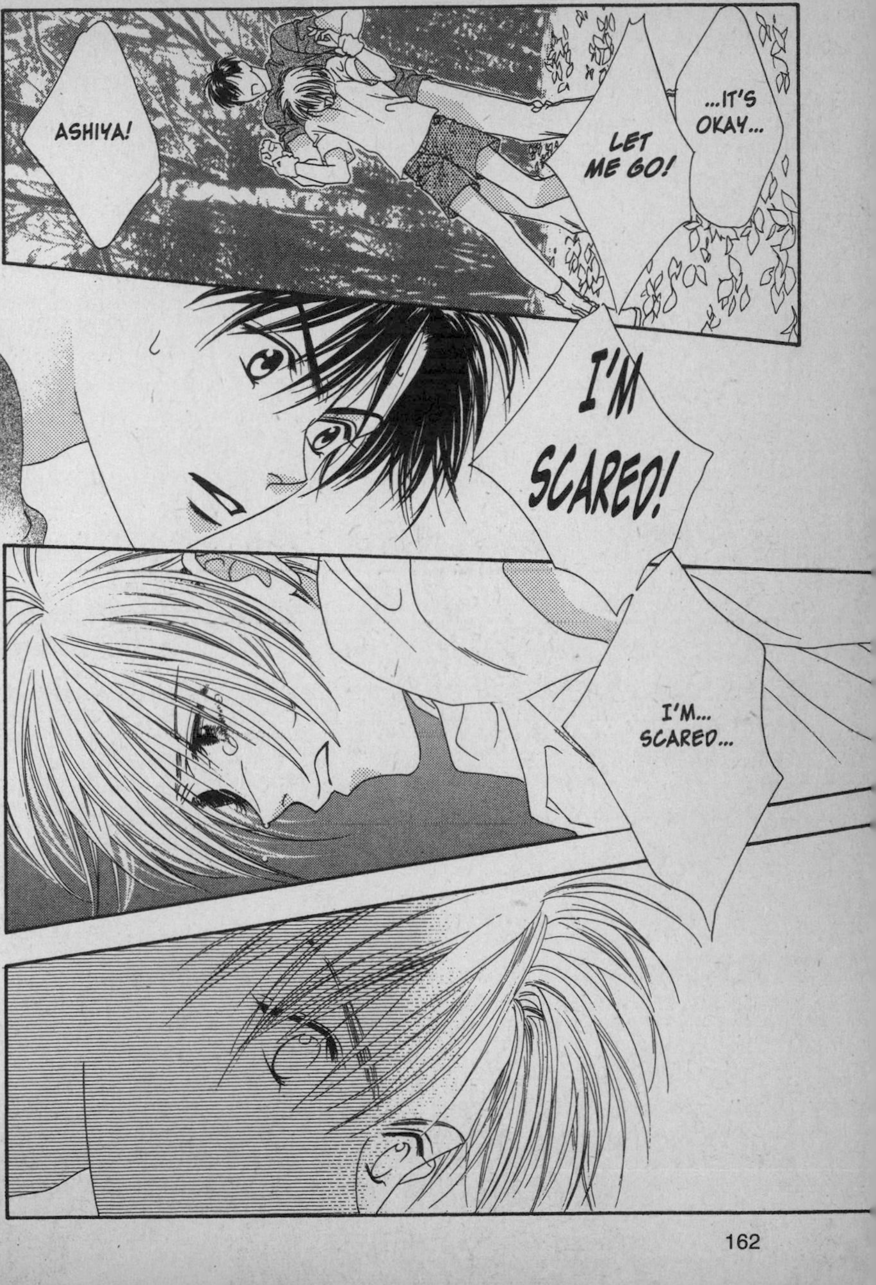
...IT'S OKAY...
LET ME GO!
ASHIYA!
I'M SCARED!
I'M... SCARED...

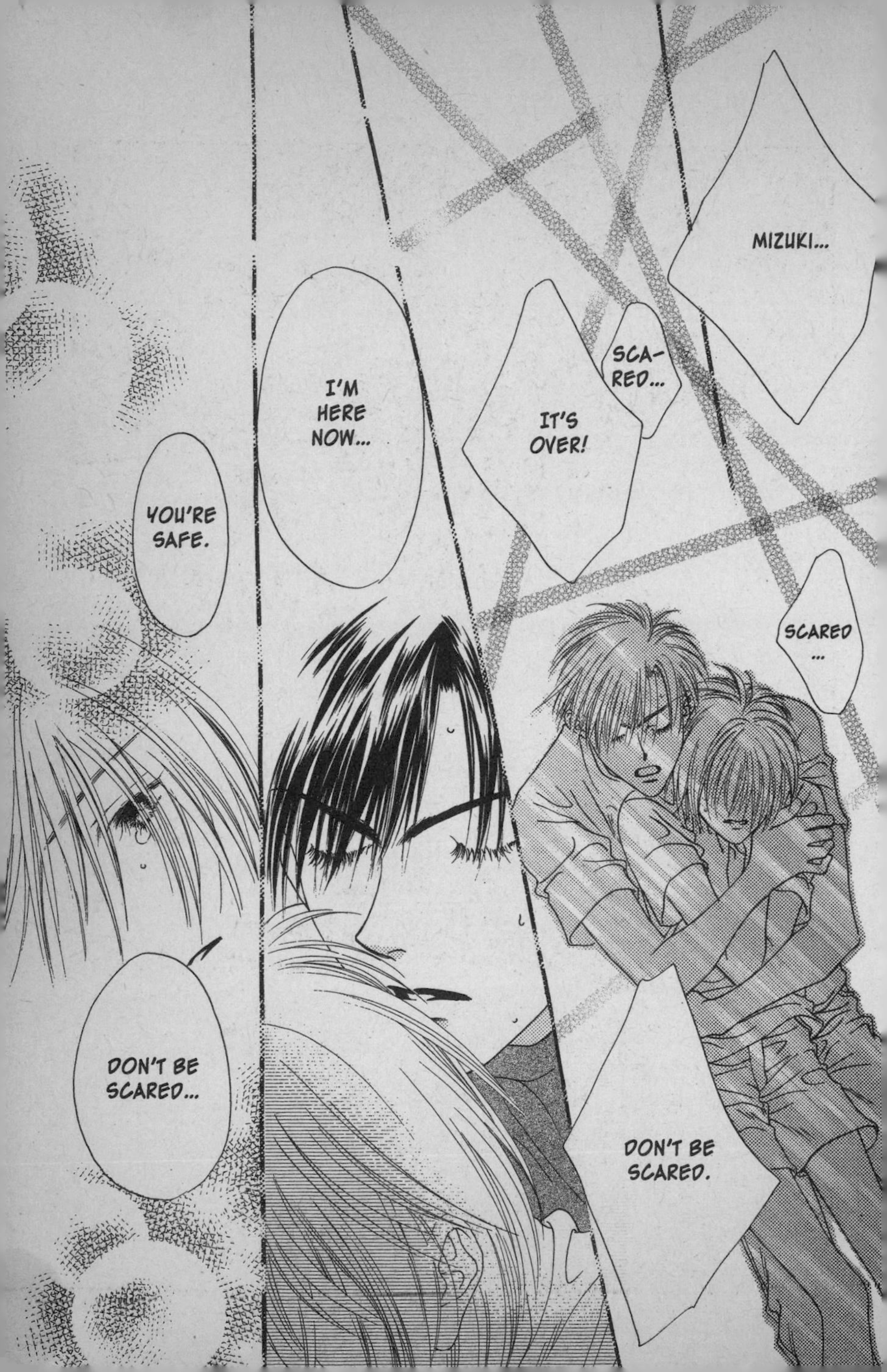
MIZUKI...
SCA-RED...
IT'S OVER!
SCARED ...
DON'T BE SCARED.
I'M HERE NOW...
YOU'RE SAFE.
DON'T BE SCARED...

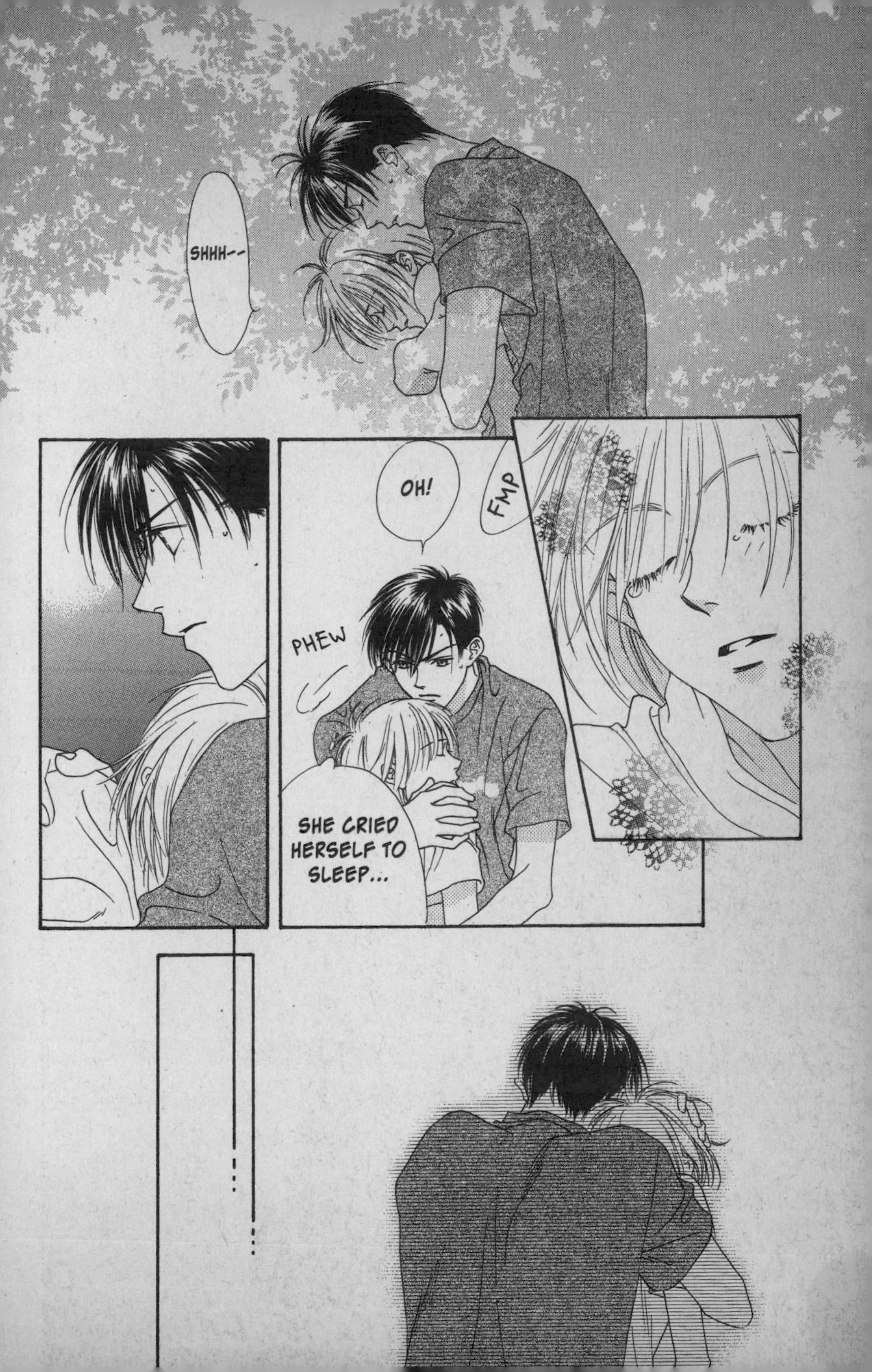
SHHH--
FMP
OH!
PHEW
SHE CRIED HERSELF TO SLEEP...
...
...

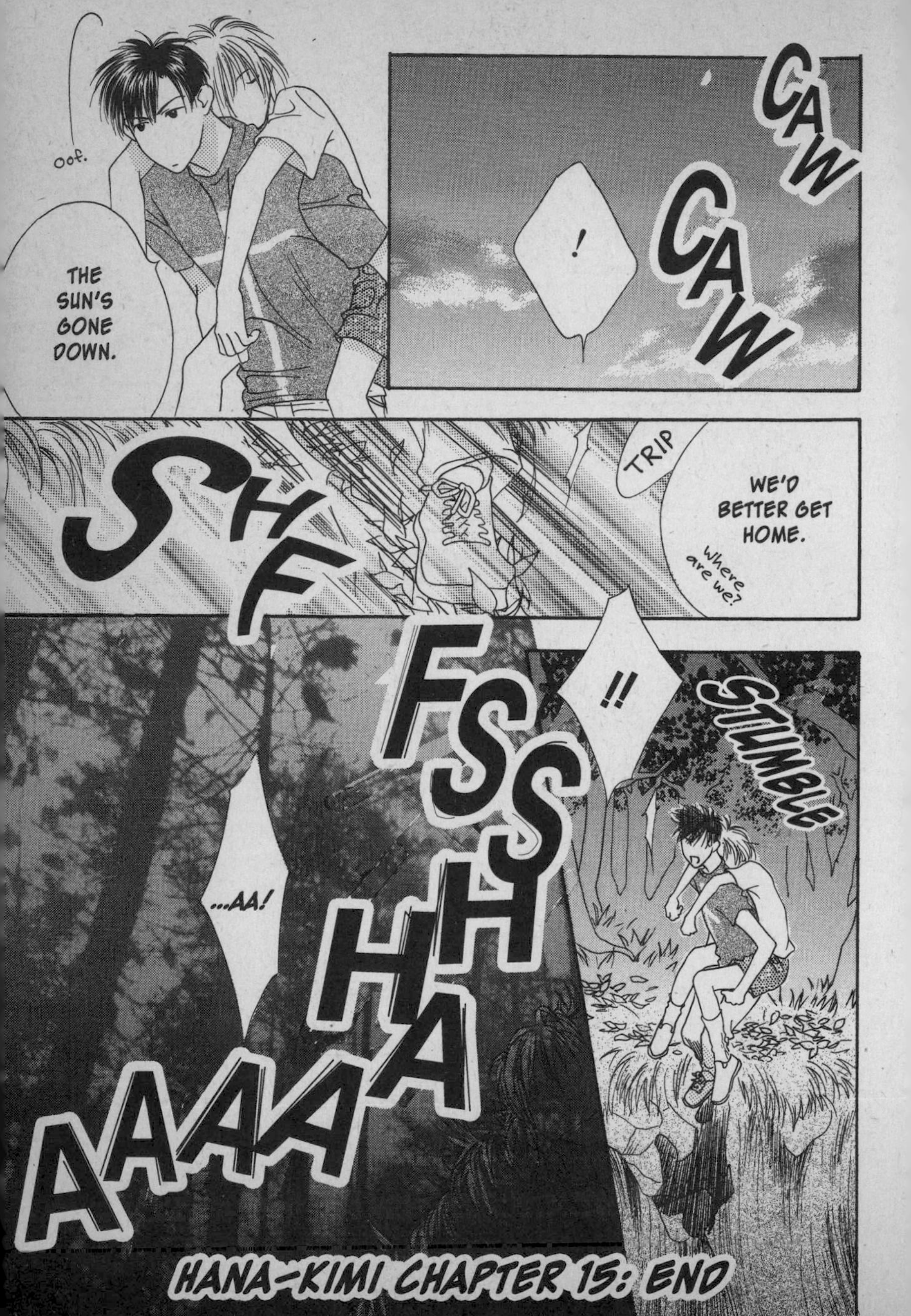
CAW
CAW
!
oof.
THE SUN'S GONE DOWN.
TRIP
WE'D BETTER GET HOME.
where are we?
SHFF
!!
STUMBLE
...AA!
FSSHHHAAAAA
HANA-KIMI CHAPTER 15: END

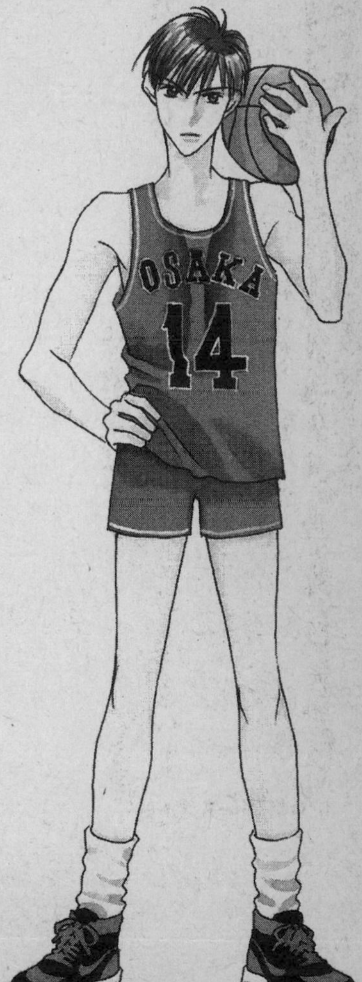
OSAKA
14

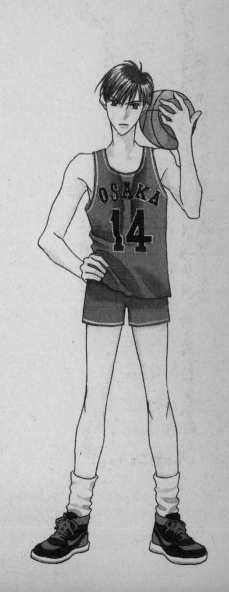

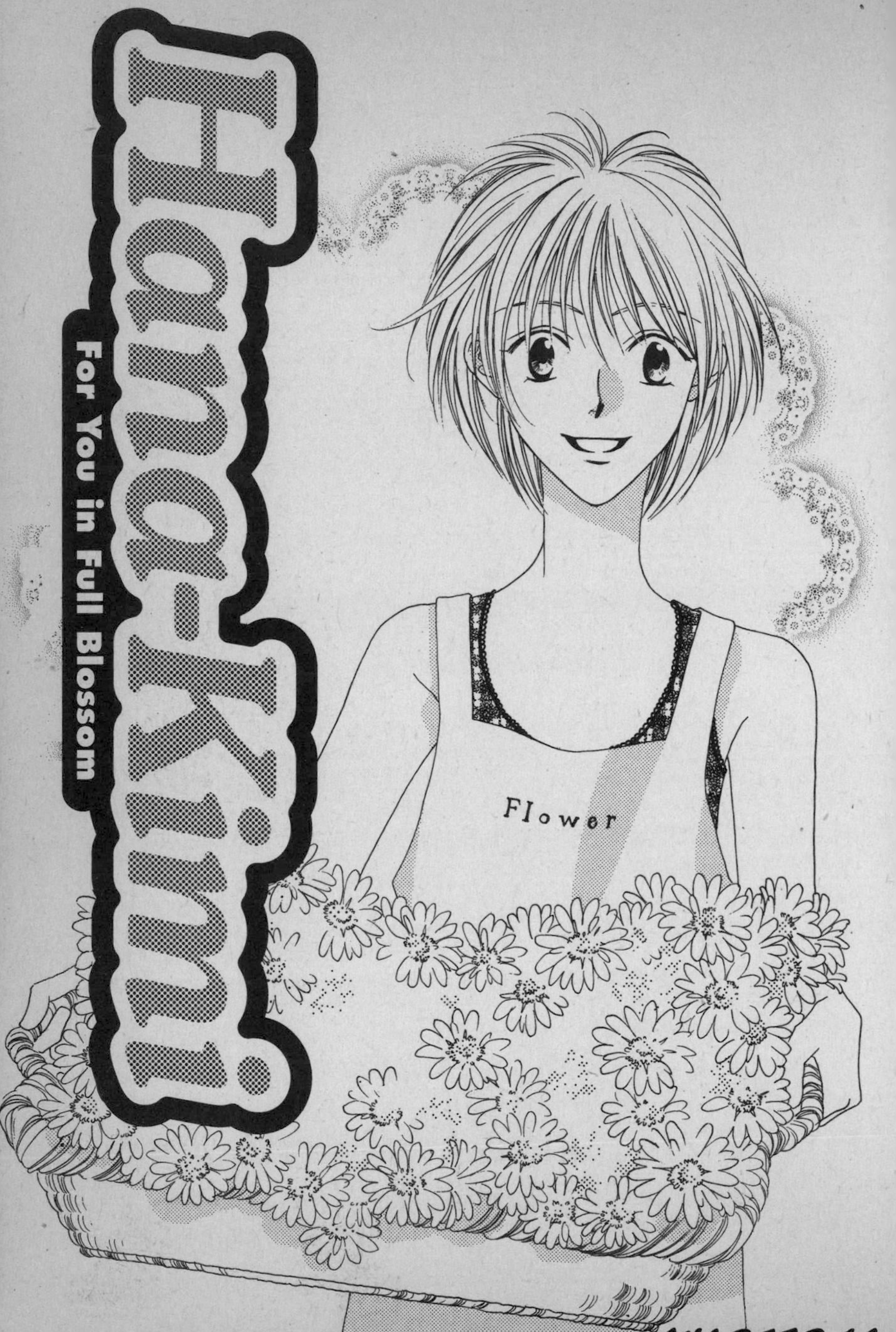
Hana-Kimi
For You in Full Blossom
Flower

CHAPTER 16

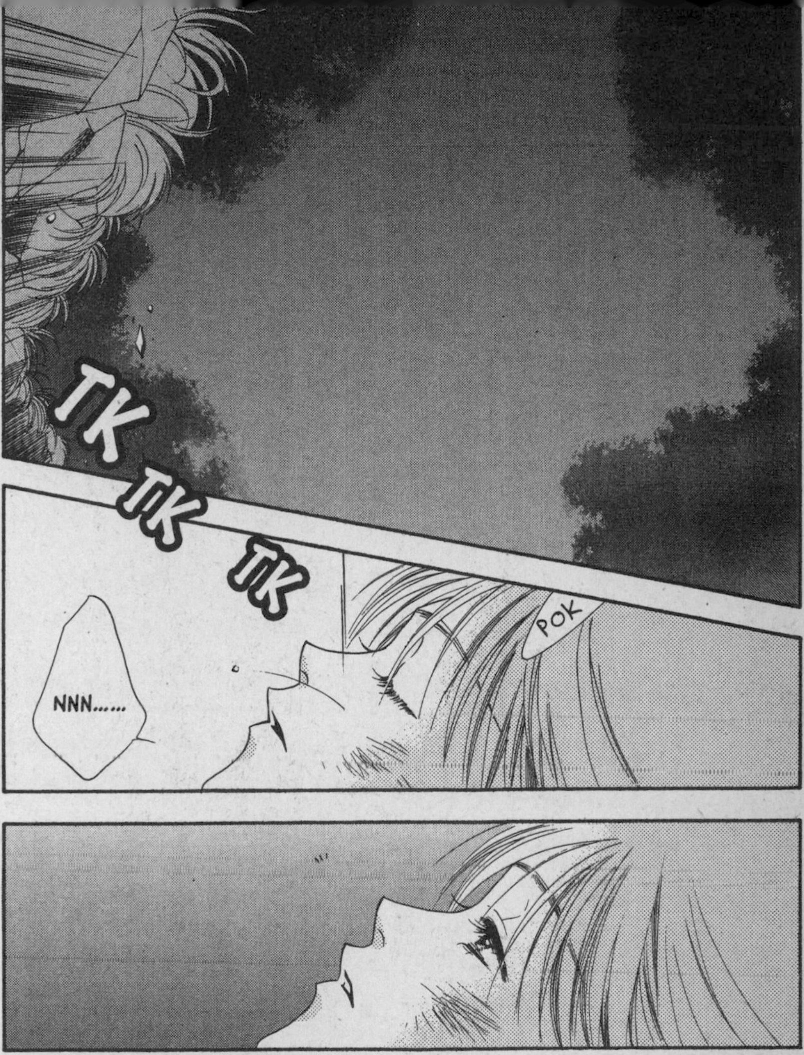
TK
TK
TK
POK
NNN......

The Bad Guys

DEFINITELY MAKITA (HA)! SOME READERS EVEN WROTE IN SAYING "HE SHOULD DIE!" I GUESS HE DESERVES IT. I HAVE A HARD TIME DRAWING HIS FACE. BUT BY HIS FOURTH CHAPTER, I WAS USED TO IT. EVEN THOUGH KAGURAZAKA IS A TROUBLE MAKER TOO, THERE ARE STILL SOME READERS WHO SAY THAT THEY LIKE HIM.

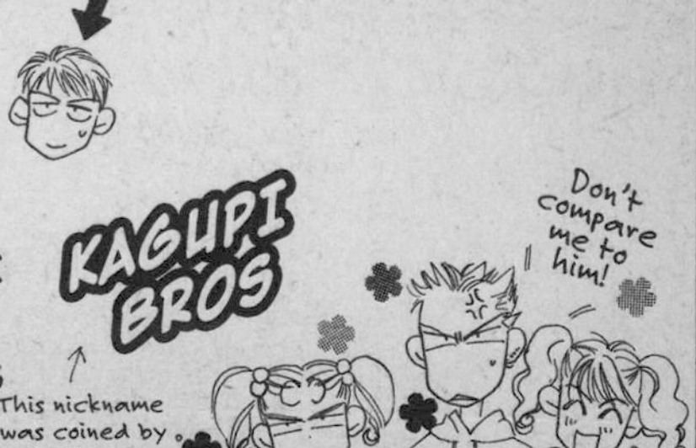
KAGUPI BROS
This nickname was coined by Nanpei Yamada.
Don't compare me to him!

P.S. YAMADA GAVE ME SOME REFERENCE PHOTOS OF THE MORITO BEACH AREA, WHERE THIS TAKES PLACE. IT HELPED. THANKS!

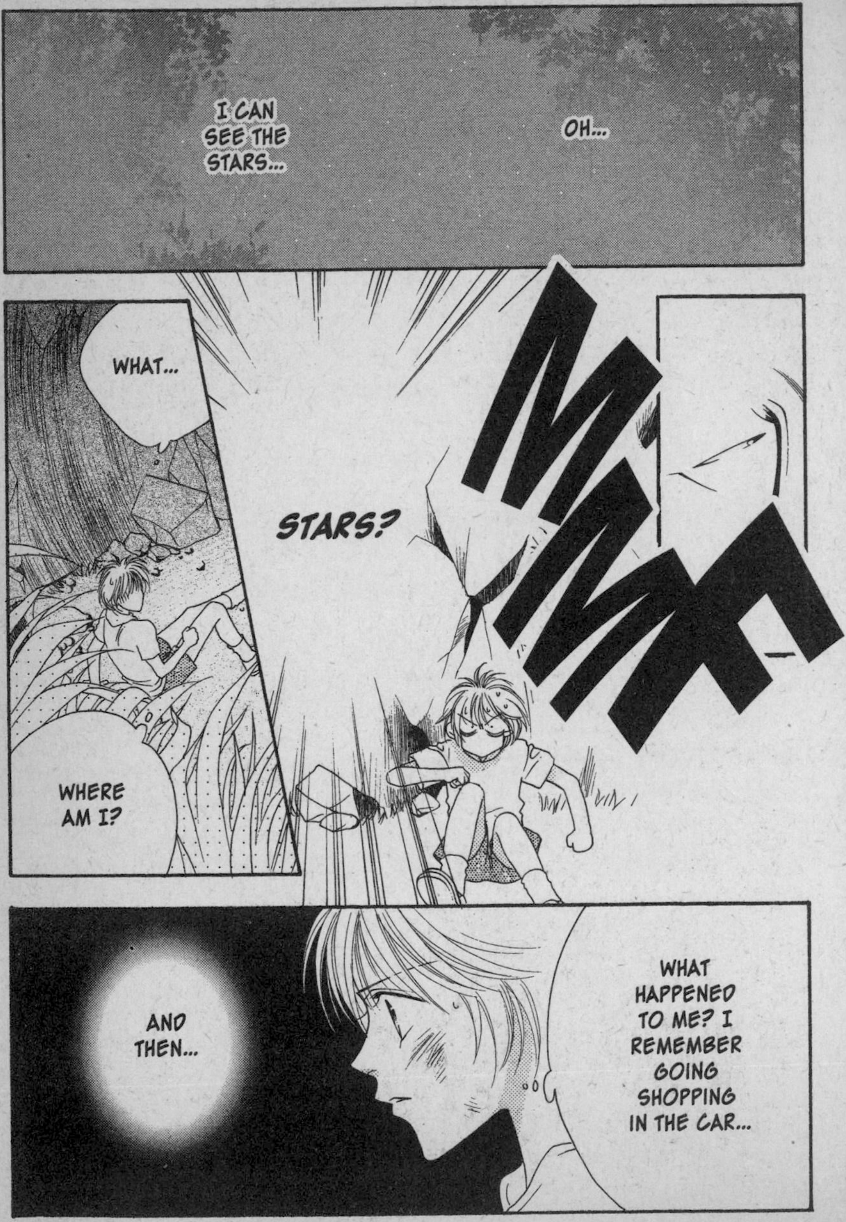
OH...
I CAN SEE THE STARS...
MMF
STARS?
WHAT...
WHERE AM I?
WHAT HAPPENED TO ME? I REMEMBER GOING SHOPPING IN THE CAR...
AND THEN...

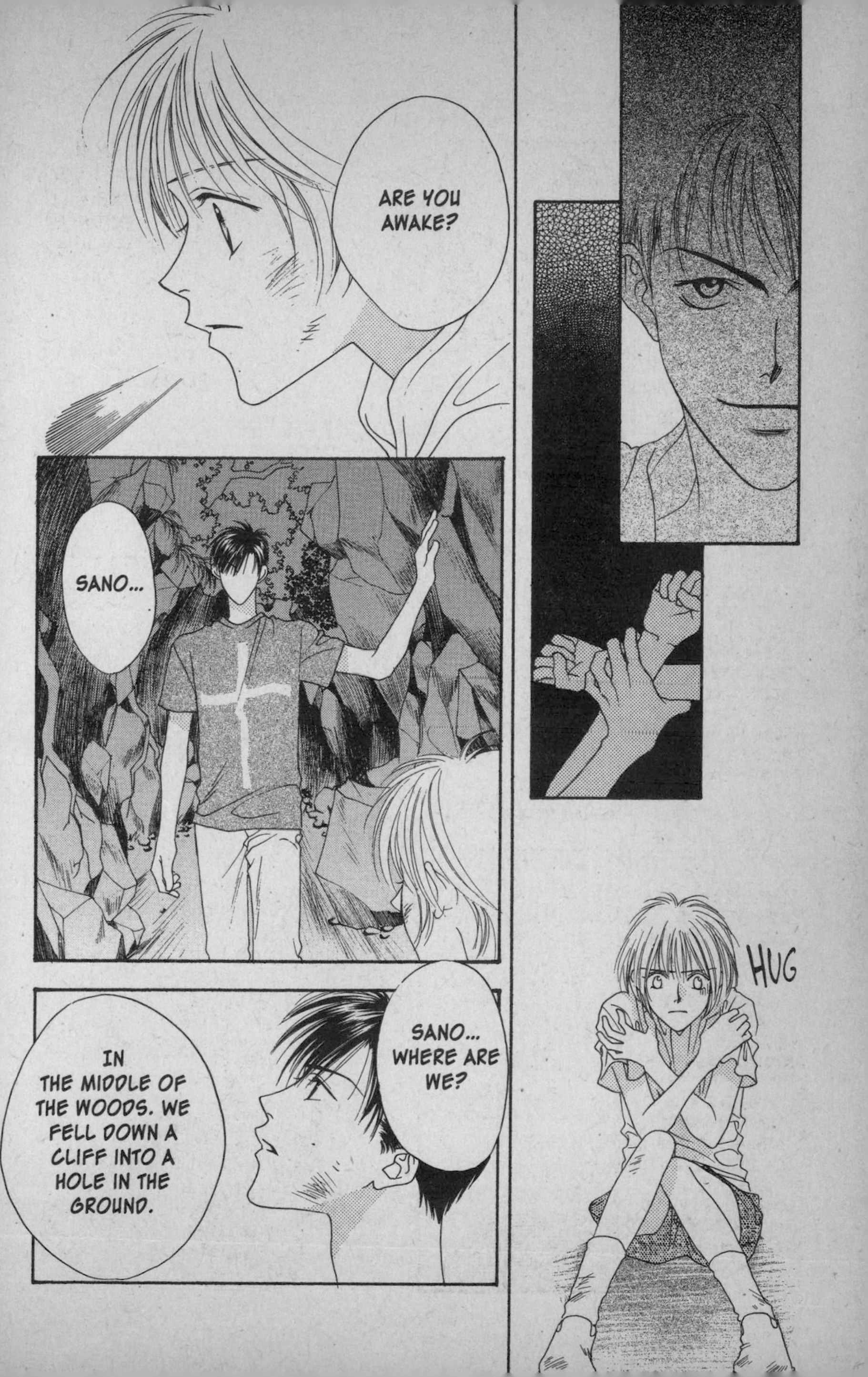
HUG
ARE YOU AWAKE?
SANO...
SANO... WHERE ARE WE?
IN THE MIDDLE OF THE WOODS. WE FELL DOWN A CLIFF INTO A HOLE IN THE GROUND.

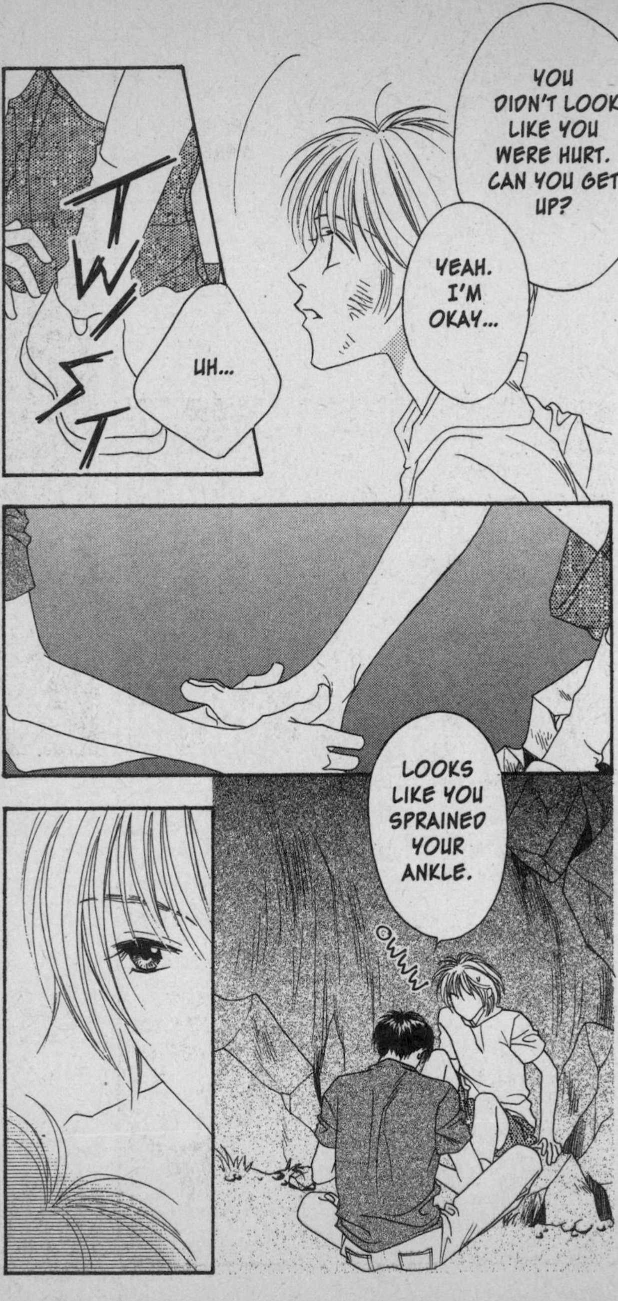
YOU DIDN'T LOOK LIKE YOU WERE HURT. CAN YOU GET UP?
YEAH. I'M OKAY...
TWIST
UH...
LOOKS LIKE YOU SPRAINED YOUR ANKLE.
OWWW

Fan Letters

THANK YOU, EVERYBODY! I READ ALL MY LETTERS, SO PLEASE DON'T WORRY! ♥ BUT IT TAKES A WHILE FOR THE LETTERS TO GET TO ME. THEY SEND ME 2 OR 3 MONTHS' WORTH OF LETTERS AT A TIME. I CAN'T ANSWER ALL THE QUESTIONS THAT YOU ASK. BUT I'D LIKE TO ANSWER A FEW OF THEM IN THE BOOKS. SOMETIMES, PEOPLE WRITE "PLEASE REPLY TO THIS LETTER" AND THEN DON'T LEAVE THEIR ADDRESS. WILL THE MANGA ARTIST WHO WROTE PLEASE SEND ME YOUR PEN NAME? (HA-HA) I'VE BEEN GETTING MORE LETTERS FROM BOYS LATELY! ♥ THEY DON'T MAKE UP EVEN 10% OF THE READERSHIP, BUT I GET LETTERS SAYING "MY OLDER BROTHER LOVES HANA-KIMI." (OLDER BROTHERS, PLEASE SEND IN YOUR OPINIONS!) I KNOW THAT I'VE MADE A MESS OF THIS COLUMN, BUT ANYWAY, I'M ALWAYS HAPPY TO GET YOUR LETTERS. ♥I'LL SEE YOU IN BOOK 4!

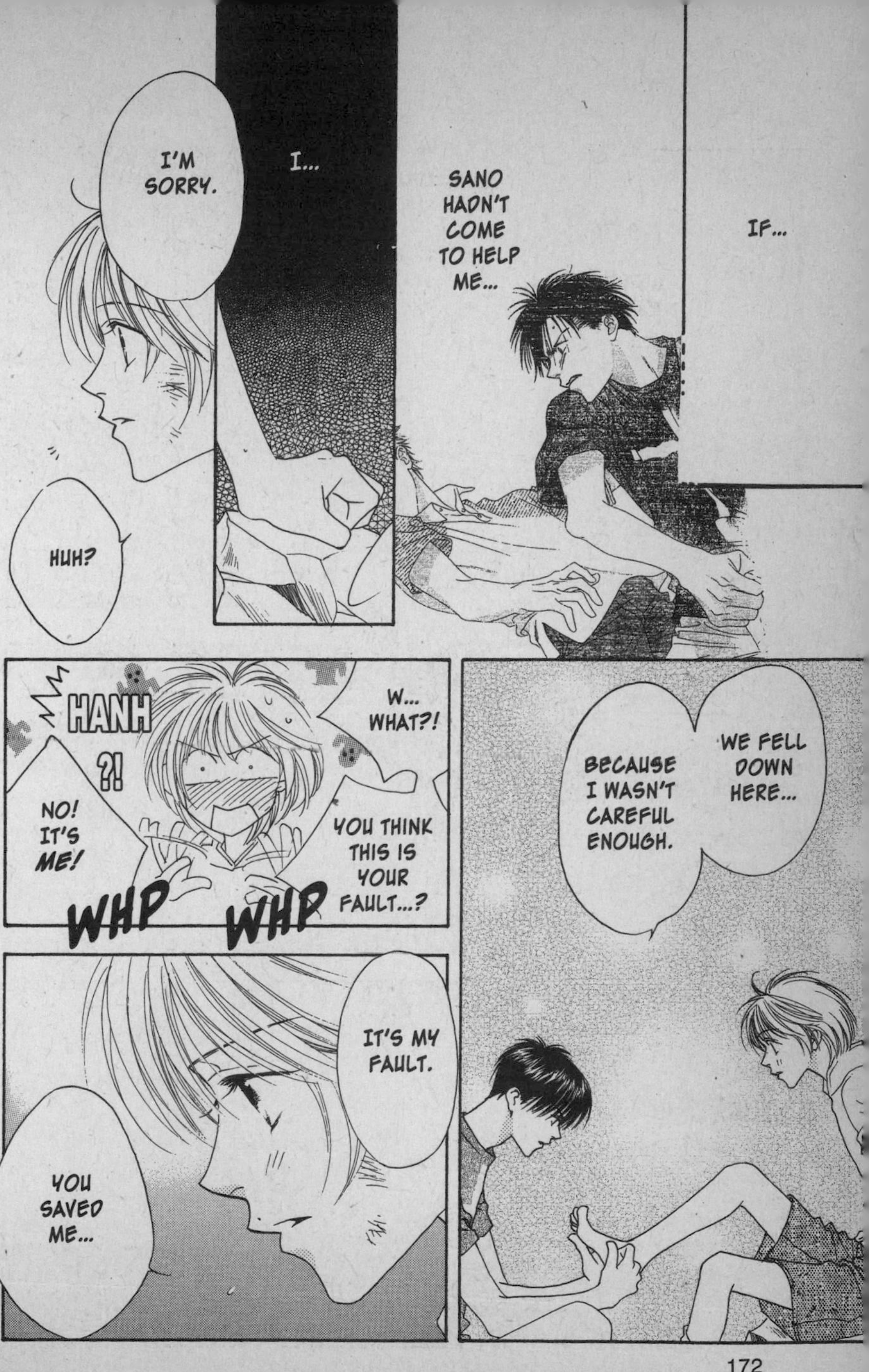
IF...
SANO HADN'T COME TO HELP ME...
I...
I'M SORRY.
HUH?
WE FELL DOWN HERE...
BECAUSE I WASN'T CAREFUL ENOUGH.
W... WHAT?!
HANH?!
YOU THINK THIS IS YOUR FAULT...?
NO! IT'S ME!
WHP
WHP
IT'S MY FAULT.
YOU SAVED ME...

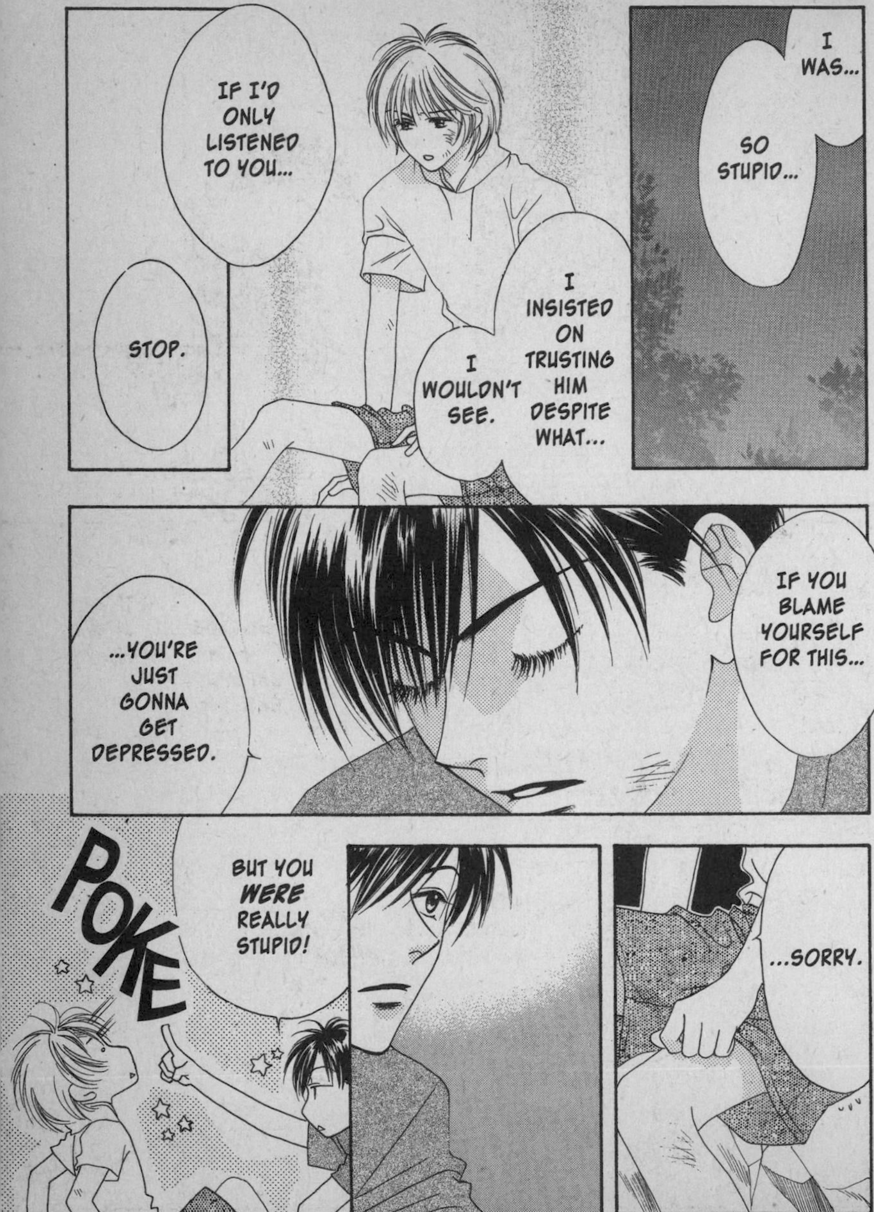
I WAS...
SO STUPID...
I INSISTED ON TRUSTING HIM DESPITE WHAT...
I WOULDN'T SEE.
IF I'D ONLY LISTENED TO YOU...
STOP.
IF YOU BLAME YOURSELF FOR THIS...
...YOU'RE JUST GONNA GET DEPRESSED.
...SORRY.
BUT YOU *WERE* REALLY STUPID!
POKE

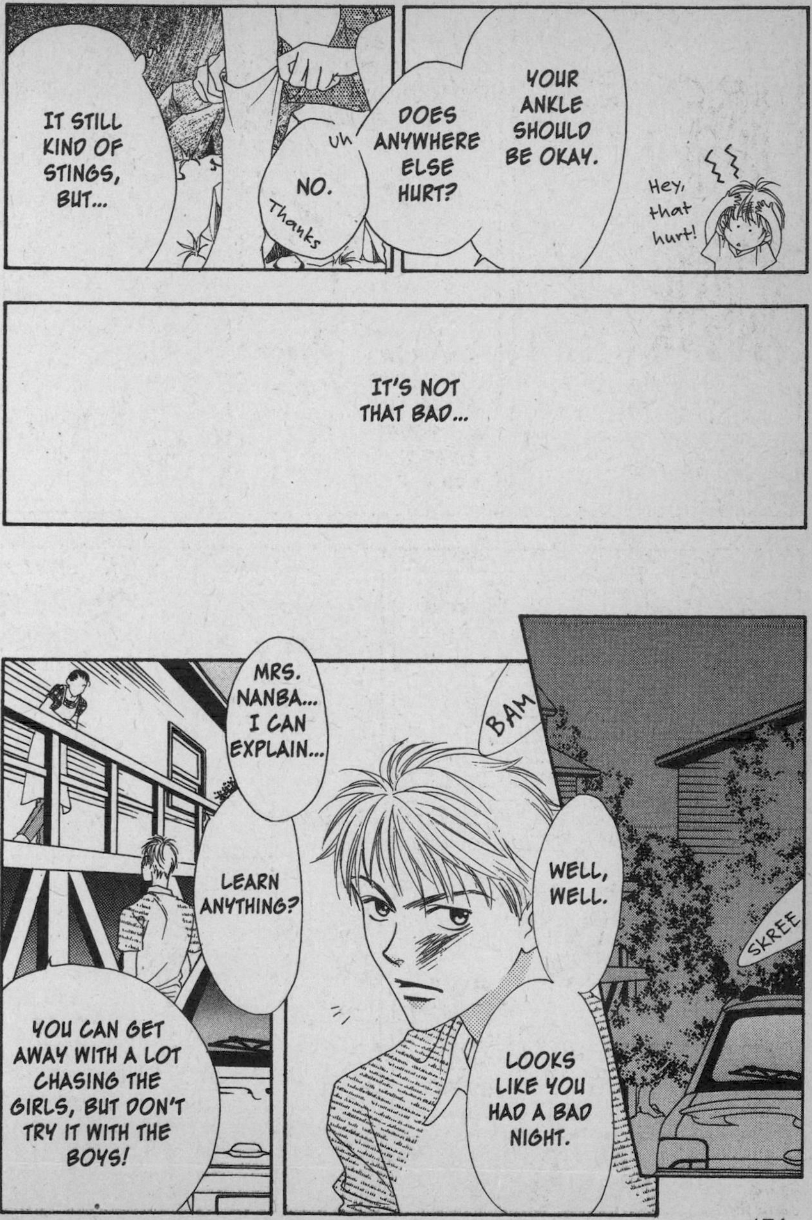
YOUR ANKLE SHOULD BE OKAY.
Hey, that hurt!
DOES ANYWHERE ELSE HURT?
Uh
NO.
Thanks
IT STILL KIND OF STINGS, BUT...
IT'S NOT THAT BAD...
BAM
WELL, WELL.
SKREE
LOOKS LIKE YOU HAD A BAD NIGHT.
MRS. NANBA... I CAN EXPLAIN...
LEARN ANYTHING?
YOU CAN GET AWAY WITH A LOT CHASING THE GIRLS, BUT DON'T TRY IT WITH THE BOYS!

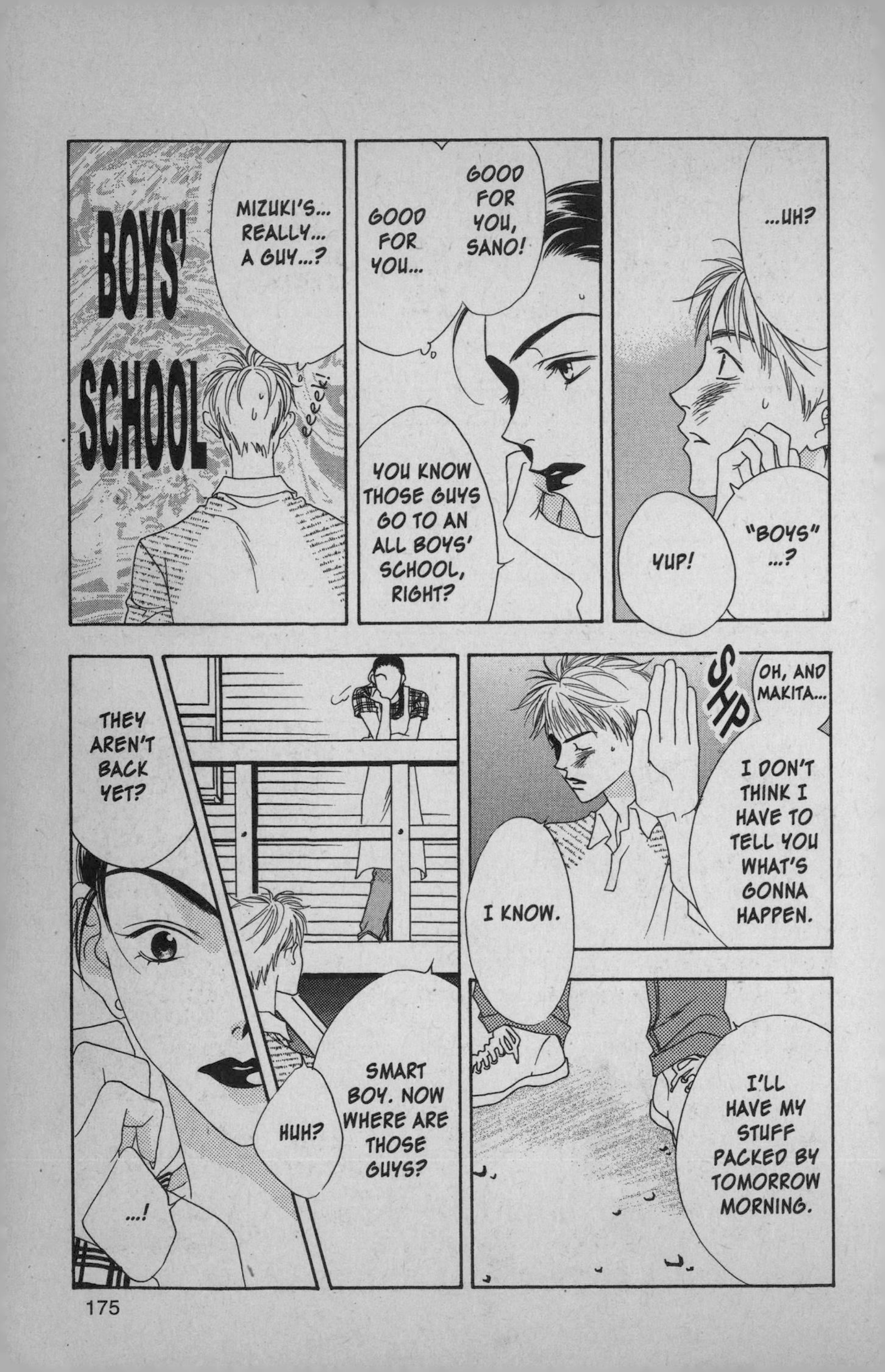
...UH?
"BOYS" ...?
YUP!
GOOD FOR YOU, SANO!
GOOD FOR YOU...
YOU KNOW THOSE GUYS GO TO AN ALL BOYS' SCHOOL, RIGHT?
MIZUKI'S... REALLY... A GUY...?
BOYS' SCHOOL
eeeek!
SHP
OH, AND MAKITA...
I DON'T THINK I HAVE TO TELL YOU WHAT'S GONNA HAPPEN.
I KNOW.
I'LL HAVE MY STUFF PACKED BY TOMORROW MORNING.
SMART BOY. NOW WHERE ARE THOSE GUYS?
HUH?
THEY AREN'T BACK YET?
...!

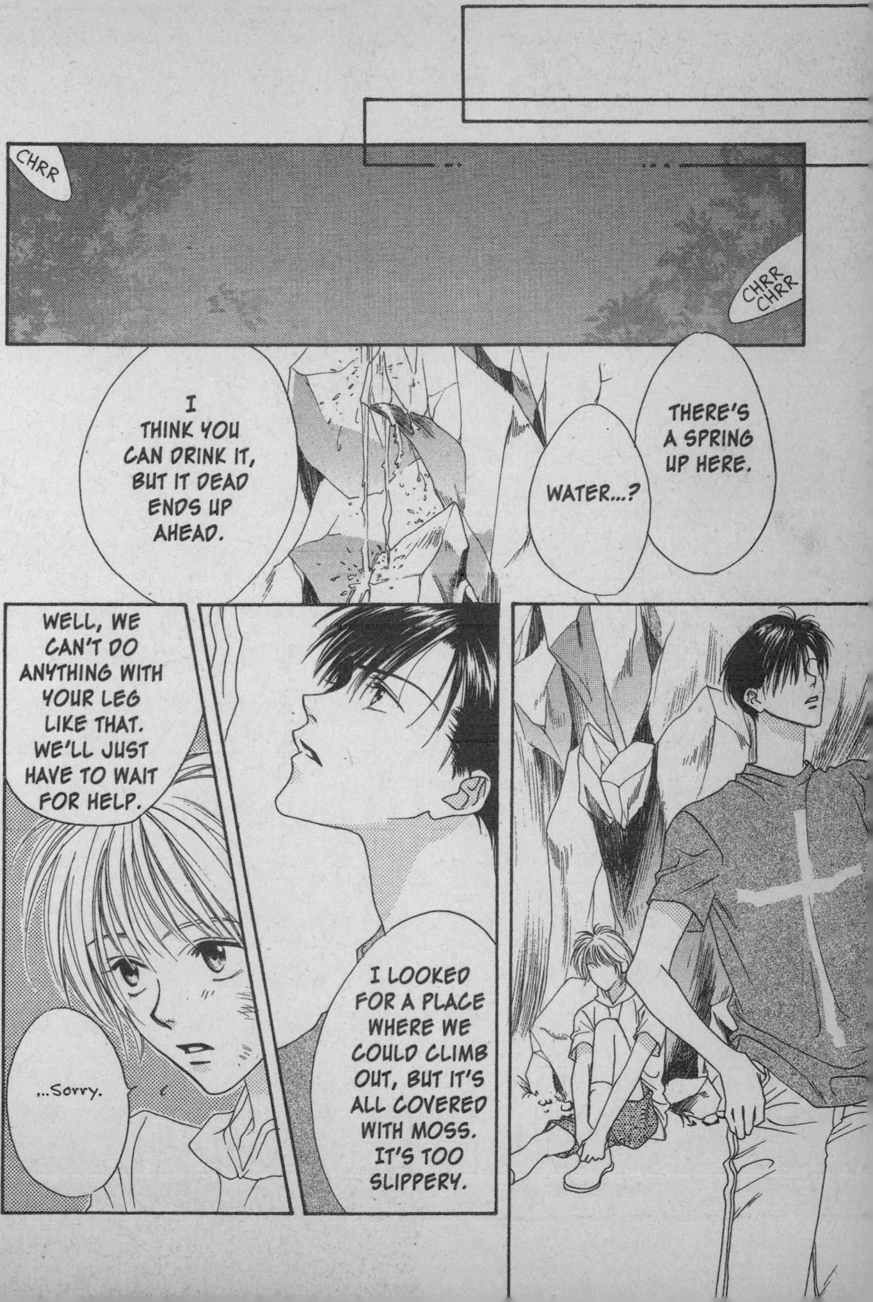
CHRR
CHRR CHRR
THERE'S A SPRING UP HERE.
WATER...?
I THINK YOU CAN DRINK IT, BUT IT DEAD ENDS UP AHEAD.
I LOOKED FOR A PLACE WHERE WE COULD CLIMB OUT, BUT IT'S ALL COVERED WITH MOSS. IT'S TOO SLIPPERY.
WELL, WE CAN'T DO ANYTHING WITH YOUR LEG LIKE THAT. WE'LL JUST HAVE TO WAIT FOR HELP.
...Sorry.

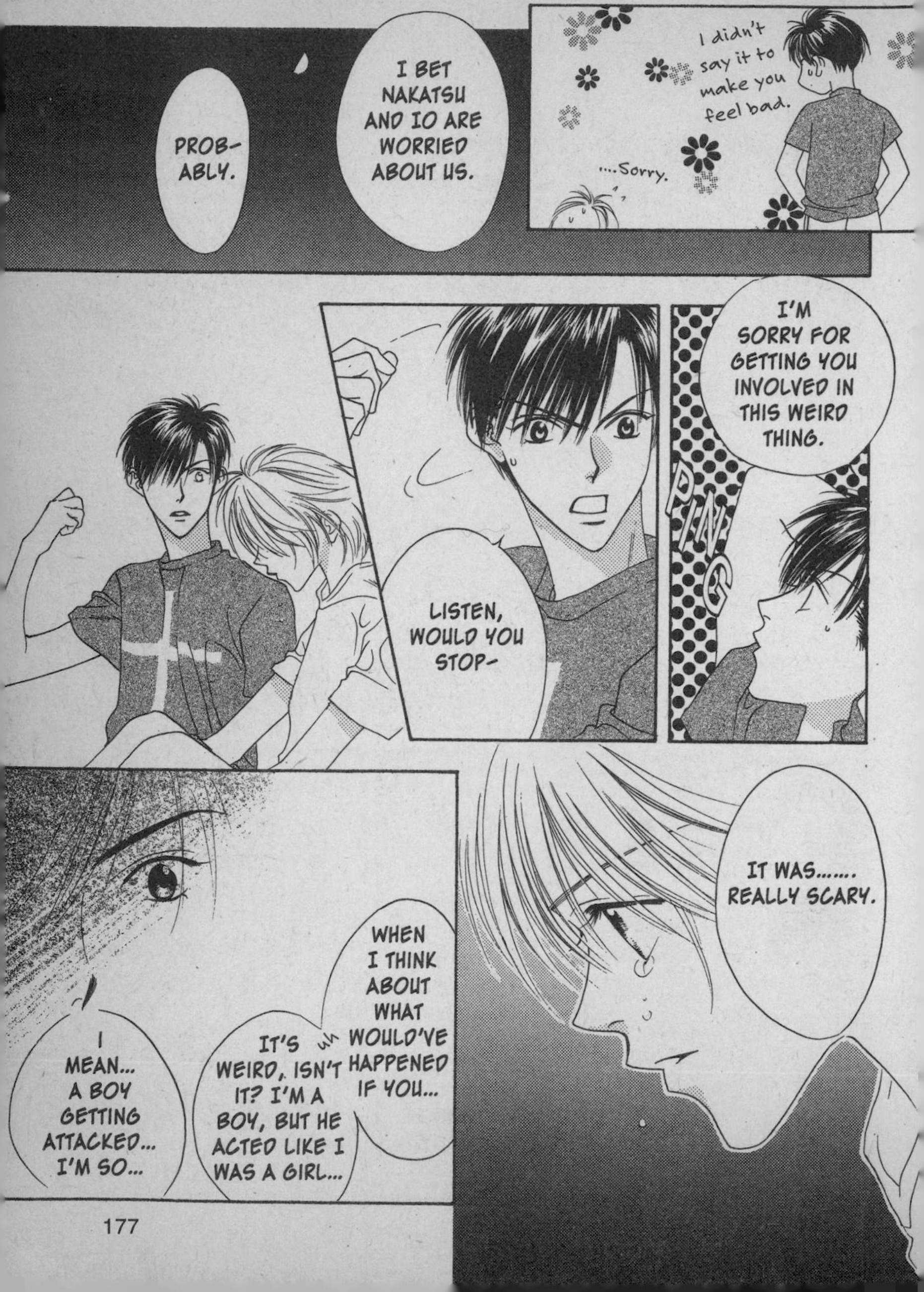
I didn't say it to make you feel bad.
....Sorry.
I BET NAKATSU AND IO ARE WORRIED ABOUT US.
PROB-ABLY.
I'M SORRY FOR GETTING YOU INVOLVED IN THIS WEIRD THING.
PING
LISTEN, WOULD YOU STOP-
IT WAS....... REALLY SCARY.
WHEN I THINK ABOUT WHAT WOULD'VE HAPPENED IF YOU...
uh
IT'S WEIRD, ISN'T IT? I'M A BOY, BUT HE ACTED LIKE I WAS A GIRL...
I MEAN... A BOY GETTING ATTACKED... I'M SO...

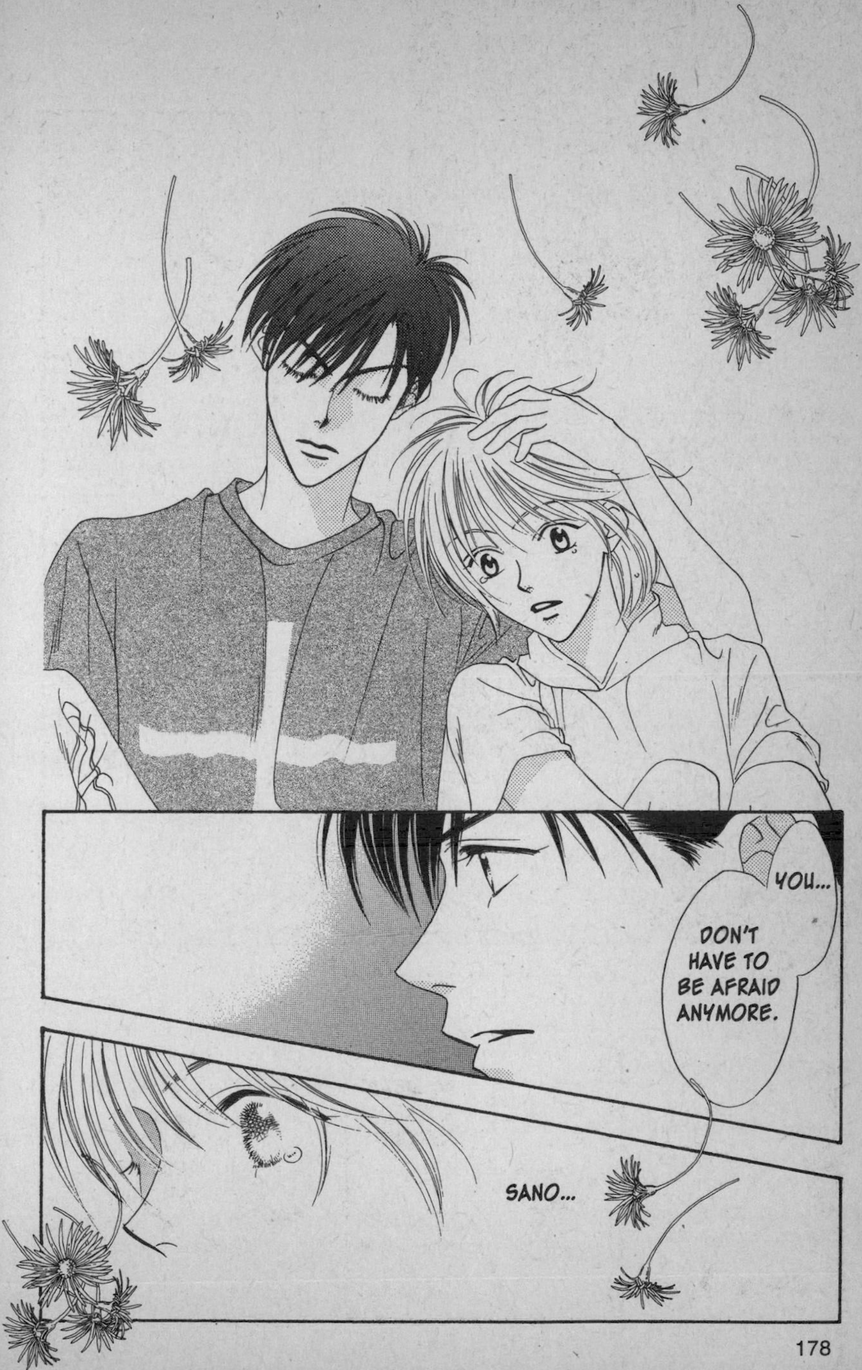
YOU...
DON'T HAVE TO BE AFRAID ANYMORE.
SANO...

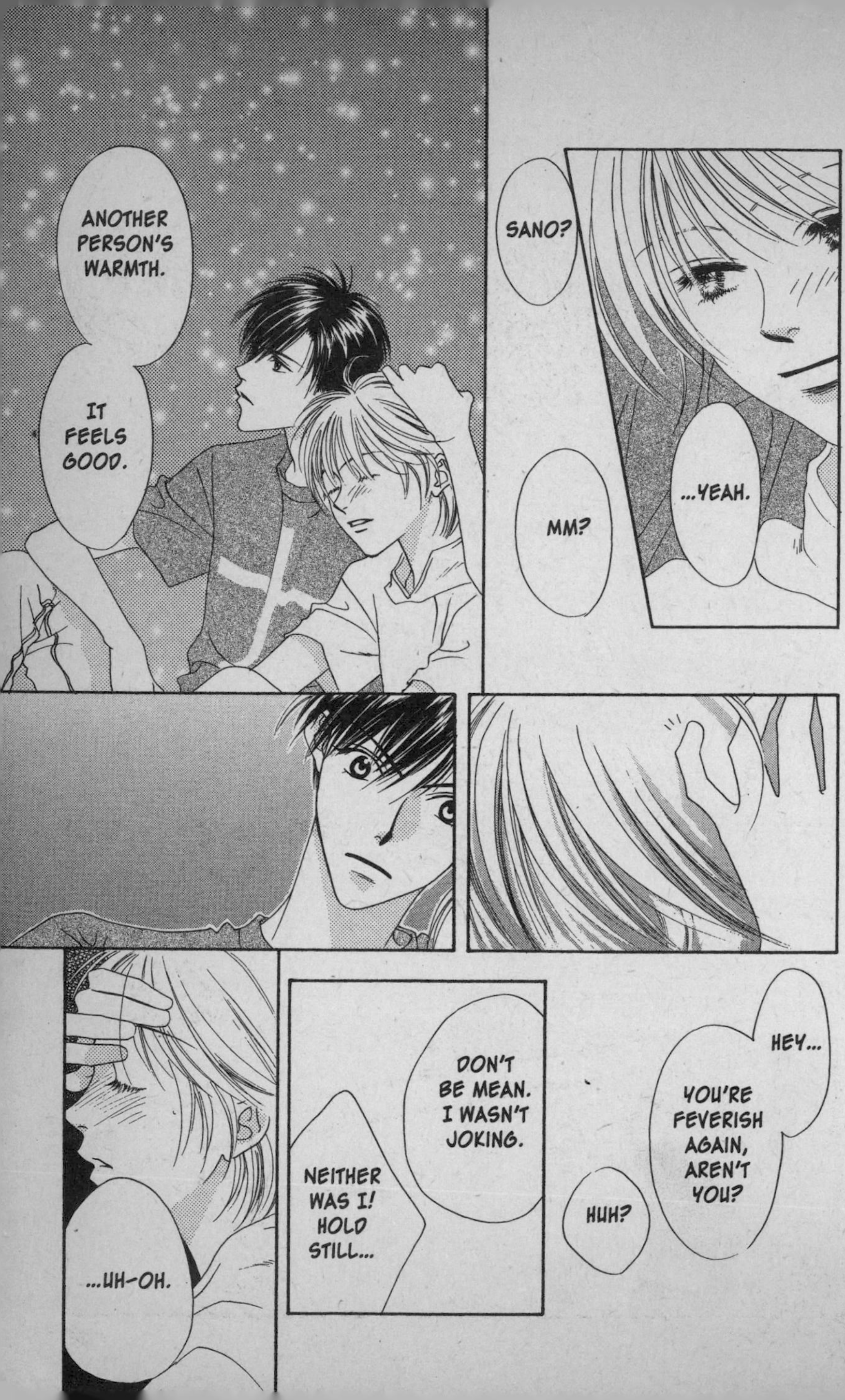
SANO?
...YEAH.
MM?
ANOTHER PERSON'S WARMTH.
IT FEELS GOOD.
HEY...
YOU'RE FEVERISH AGAIN, AREN'T YOU?
HUH?
DON'T BE MEAN. I WASN'T JOKING.
NEITHER WAS I! HOLD STILL...
...UH-OH.

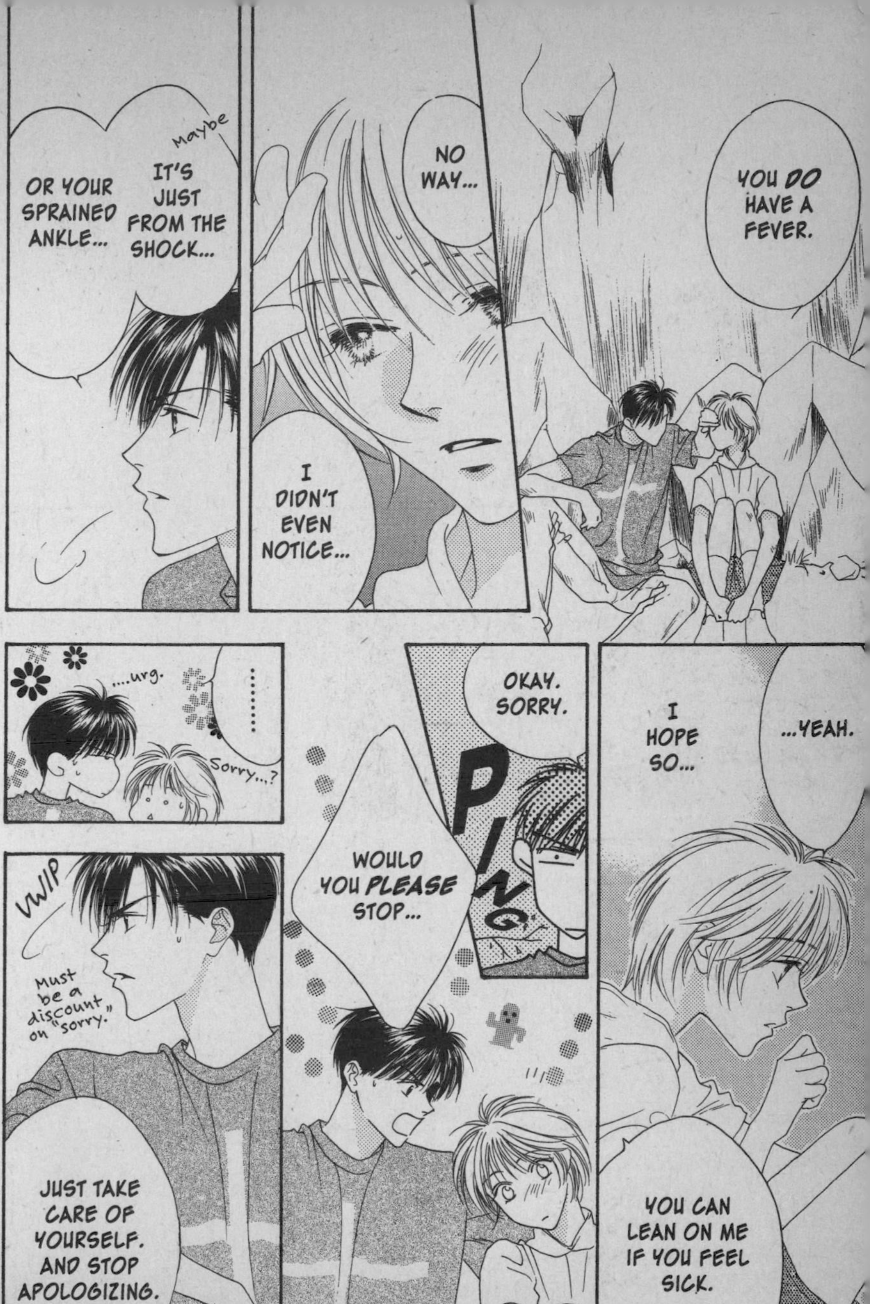
YOU DO HAVE A FEVER.
NO WAY...
I DIDN'T EVEN NOTICE...
Maybe
IT'S JUST FROM THE SHOCK...
OR YOUR SPRAINED ANKLE...
...YEAH.
I HOPE SO...
YOU CAN LEAN ON ME IF YOU FEEL SICK.
OKAY. SORRY.
PING
....
....urg.
Sorry...?
WOULD YOU PLEASE STOP...
VWIP
Must be a discount on "sorry."
JUST TAKE CARE OF YOURSELF. AND STOP APOLOGIZING.

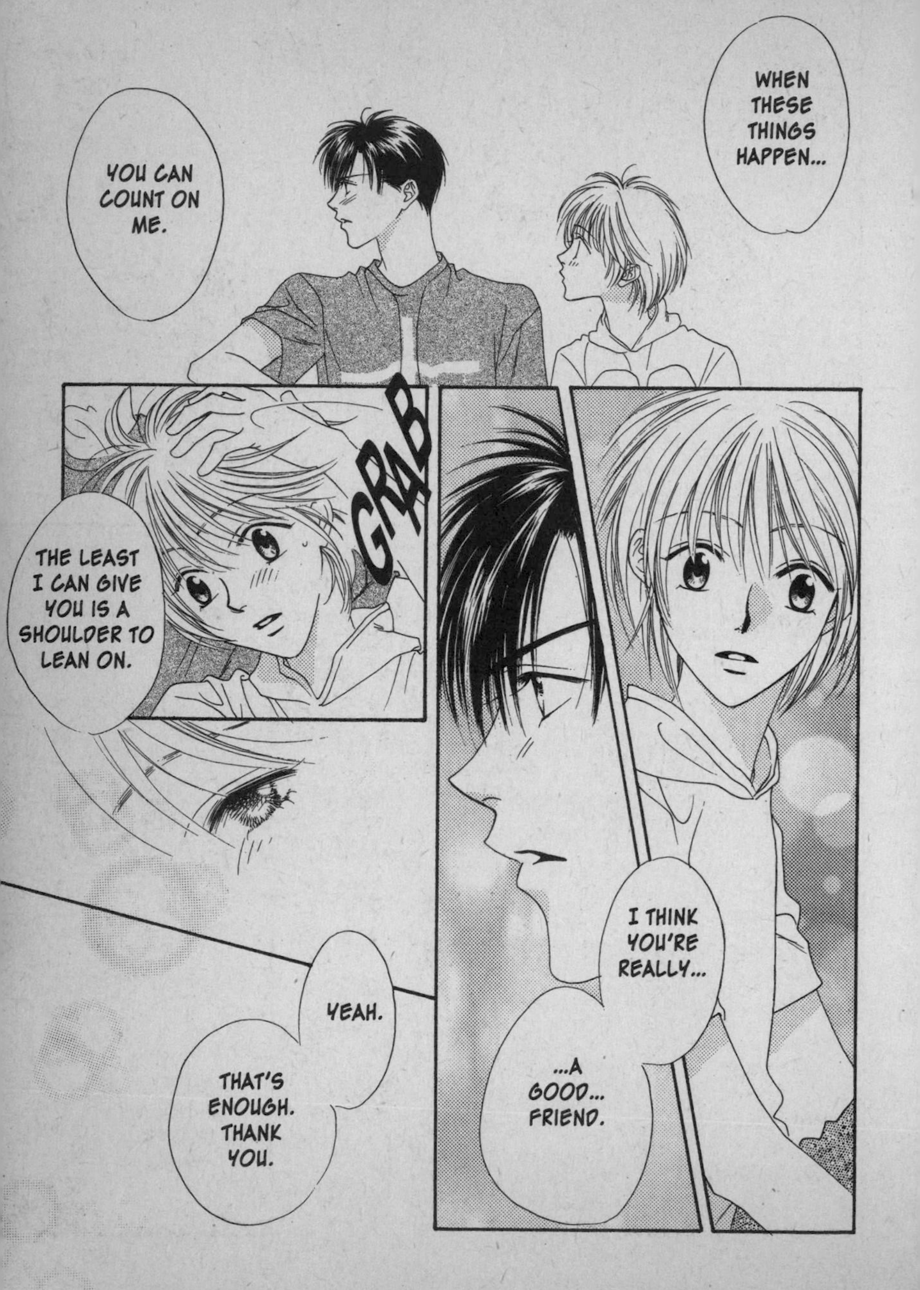
WHEN THESE THINGS HAPPEN...
YOU CAN COUNT ON ME.
I THINK YOU'RE REALLY...
...A GOOD... FRIEND.
GRAB
THE LEAST I CAN GIVE YOU IS A SHOULDER TO LEAN ON.
YEAH.
THAT'S ENOUGH. THANK YOU.

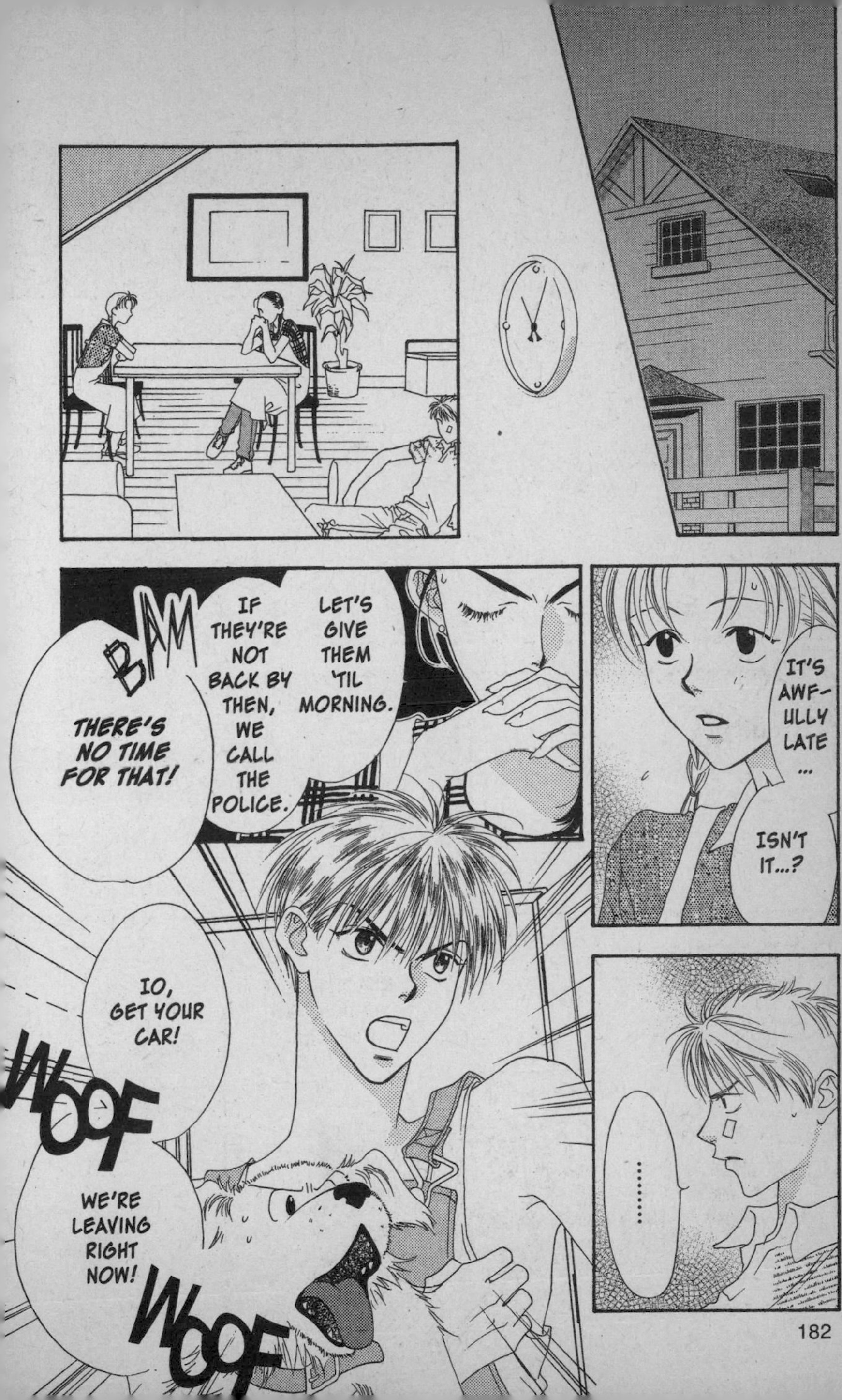
IT'S AWFULLY LATE...
ISN'T IT...?
......
LET'S GIVE THEM 'TIL MORNING.
IF THEY'RE NOT BACK BY THEN, WE CALL THE POLICE.
BAM
THERE'S NO TIME FOR THAT!
IO, GET YOUR CAR!
WOOF
WE'RE LEAVING RIGHT NOW!
WOOF

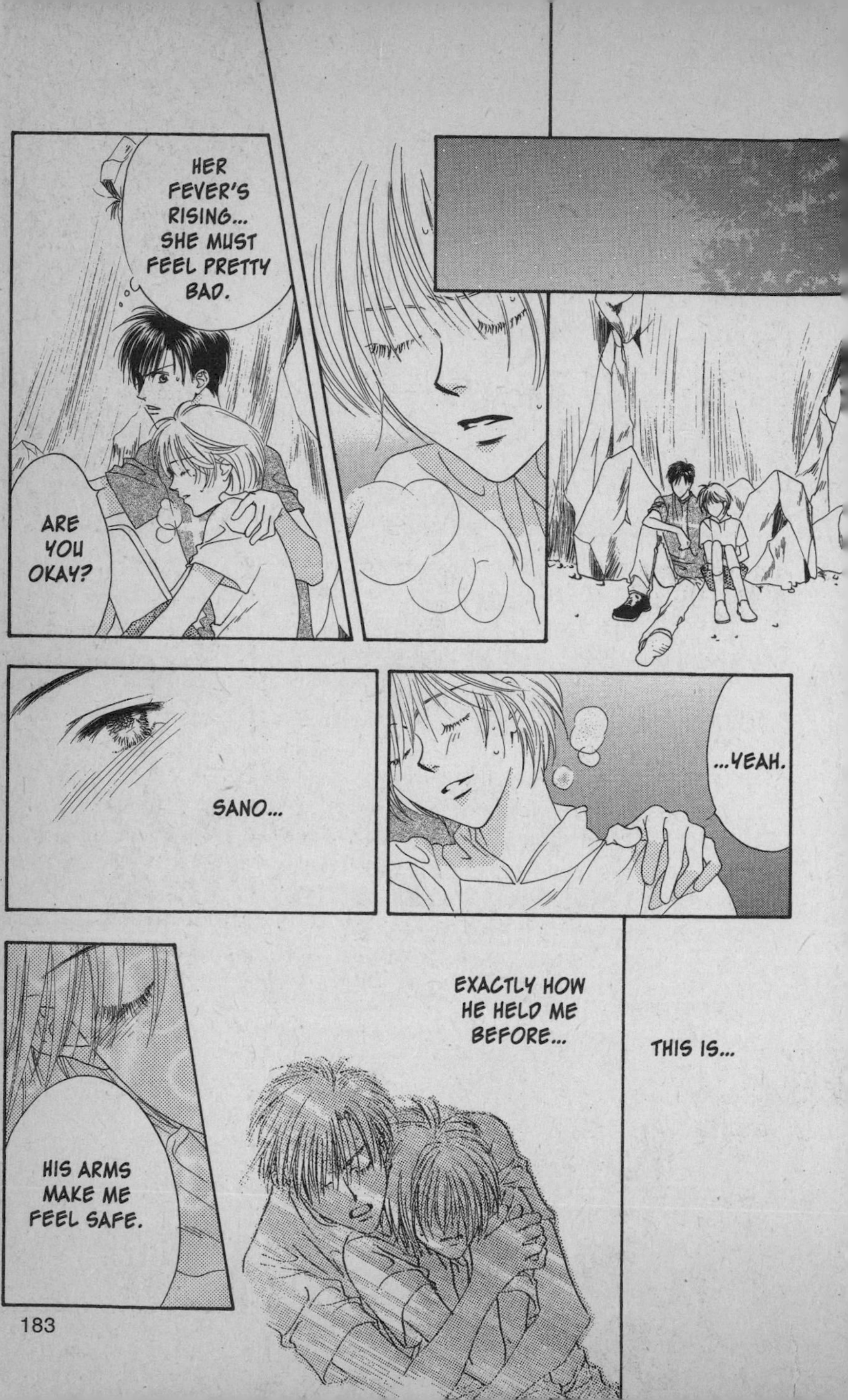
HER FEVER'S RISING... SHE MUST FEEL PRETTY BAD.
ARE YOU OKAY?
...YEAH.
SANO...
THIS IS...
EXACTLY HOW HE HELD ME BEFORE...
HIS ARMS MAKE ME FEEL SAFE.

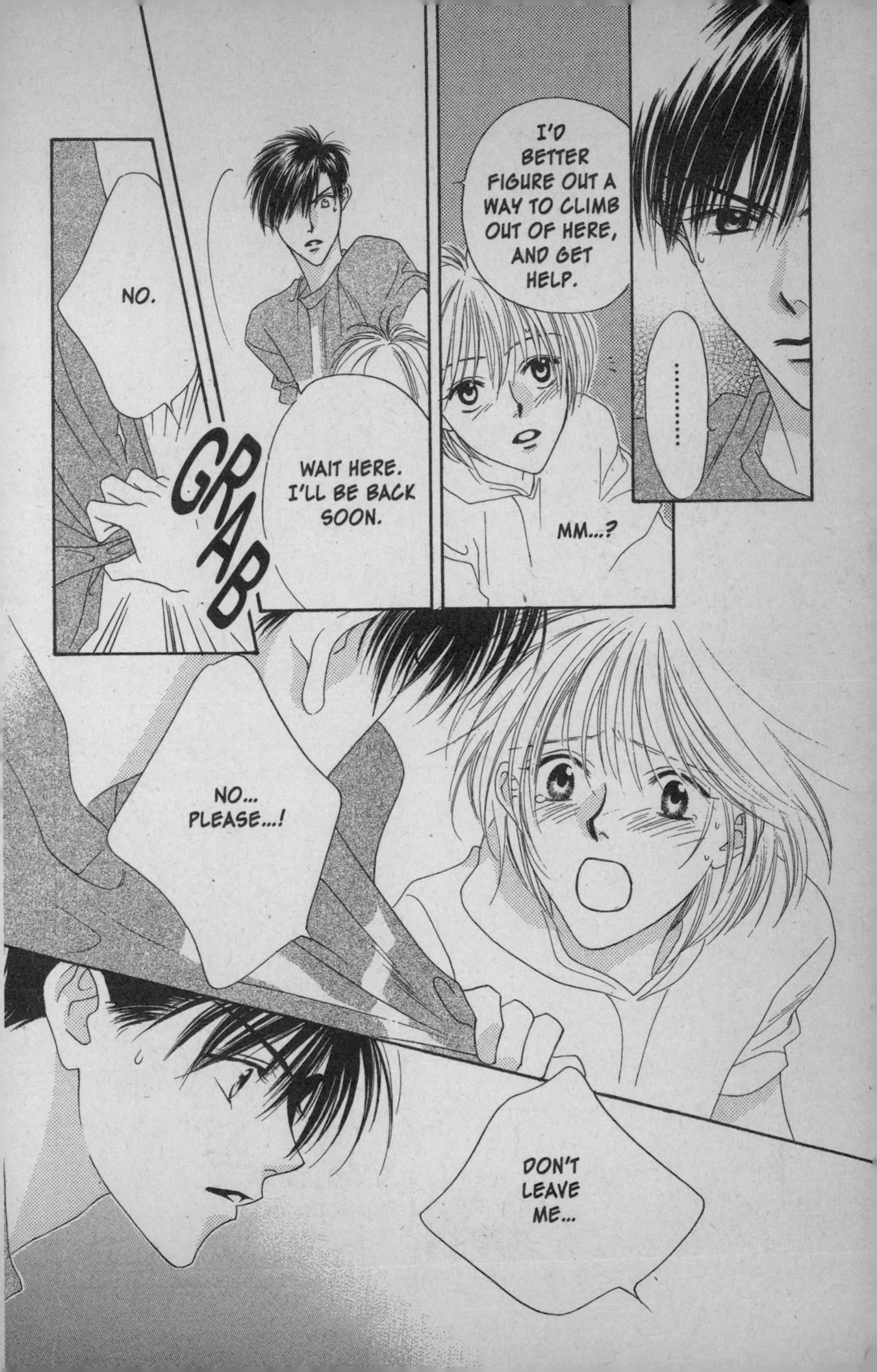
......
I'D BETTER FIGURE OUT A WAY TO CLIMB OUT OF HERE, AND GET HELP.
MM...?
WAIT HERE. I'LL BE BACK SOON.
NO.
GRAB
NO... PLEASE...!
DON'T LEAVE ME...

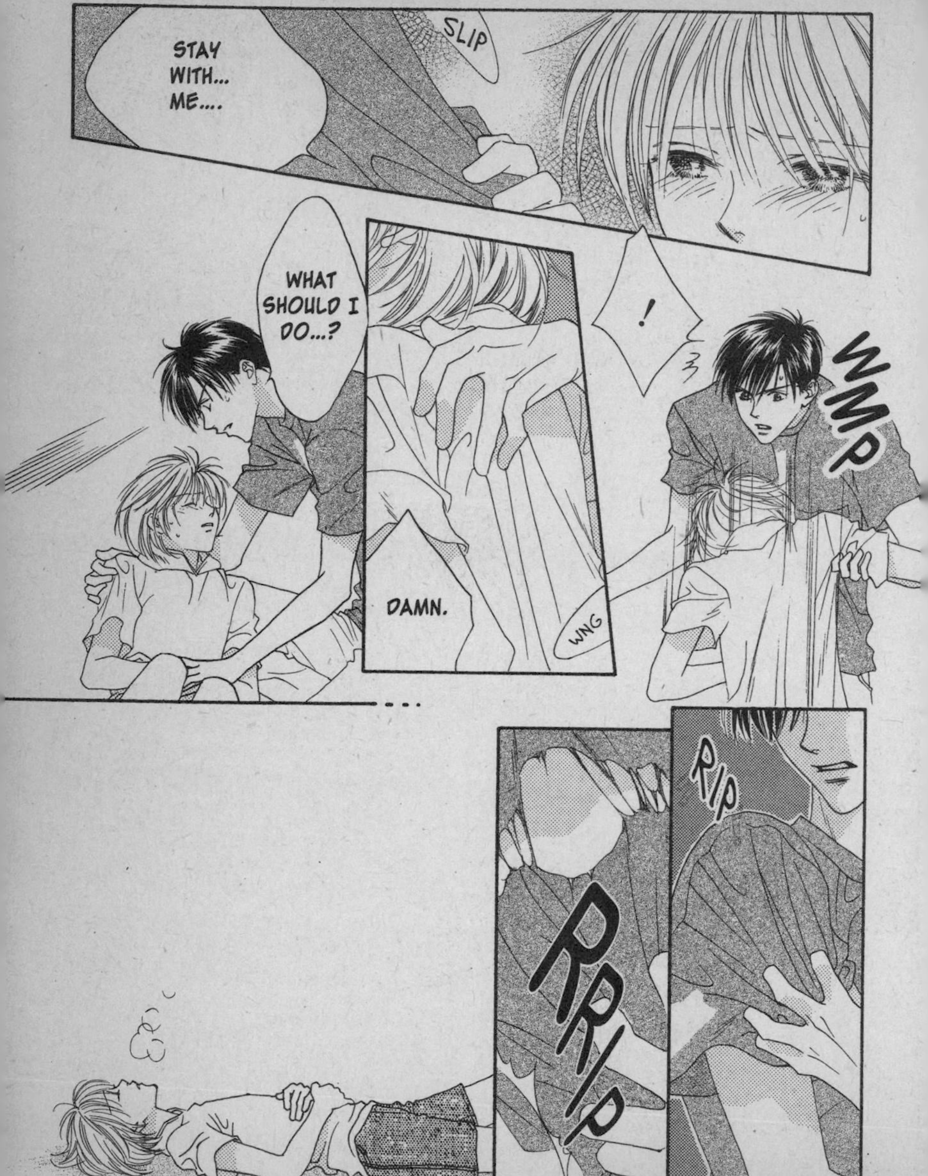
SLIP
STAY WITH... ME....
WMP
!
WNG
DAMN.
WHAT SHOULD I DO...?
RIP
RRIP

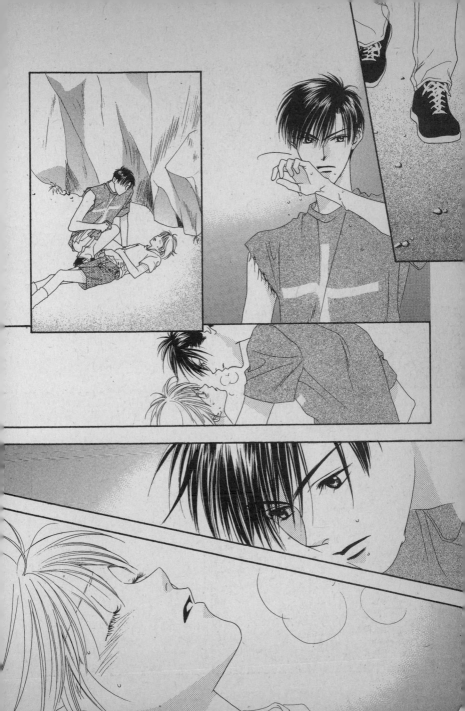

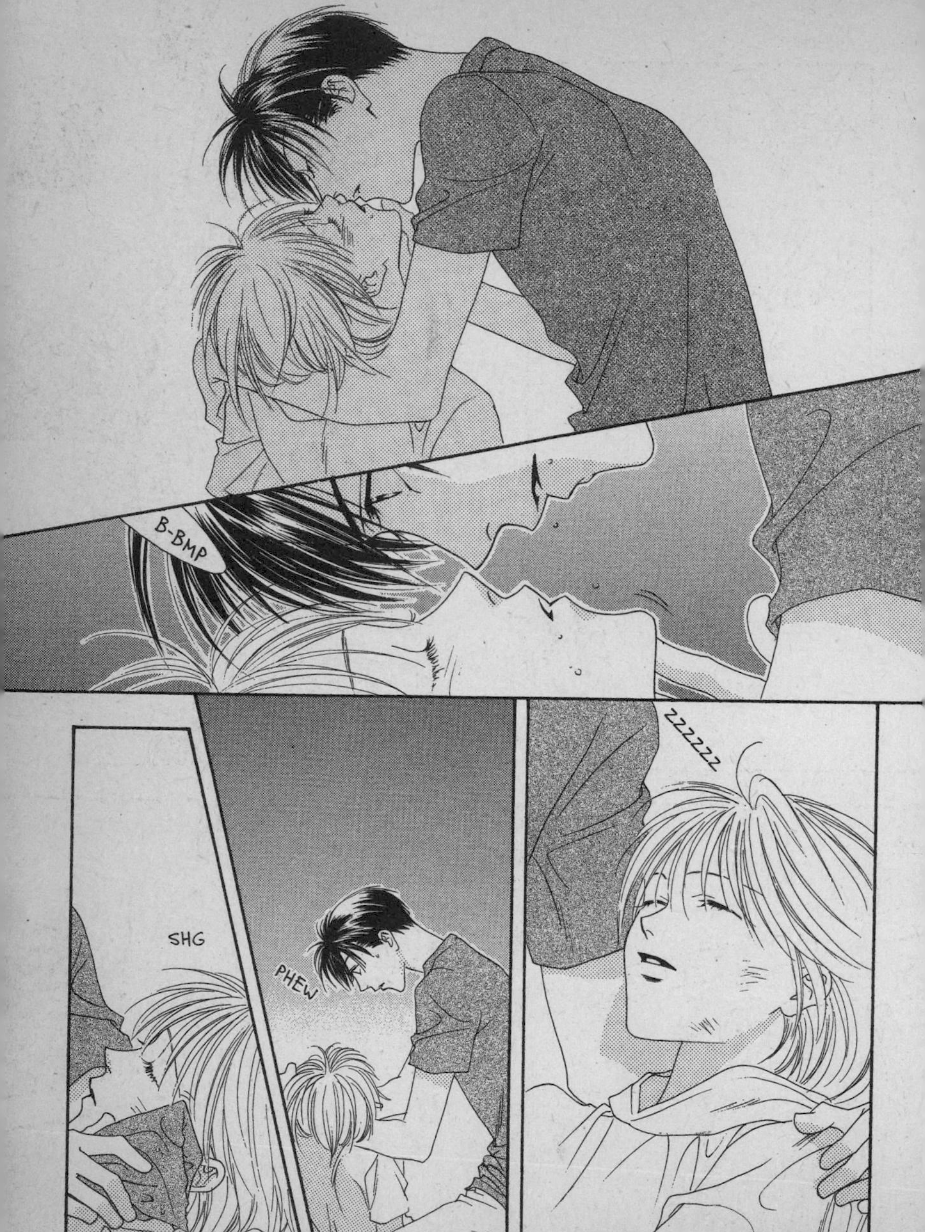
B-BMP
ZZZZZZ
PHEW
SHG

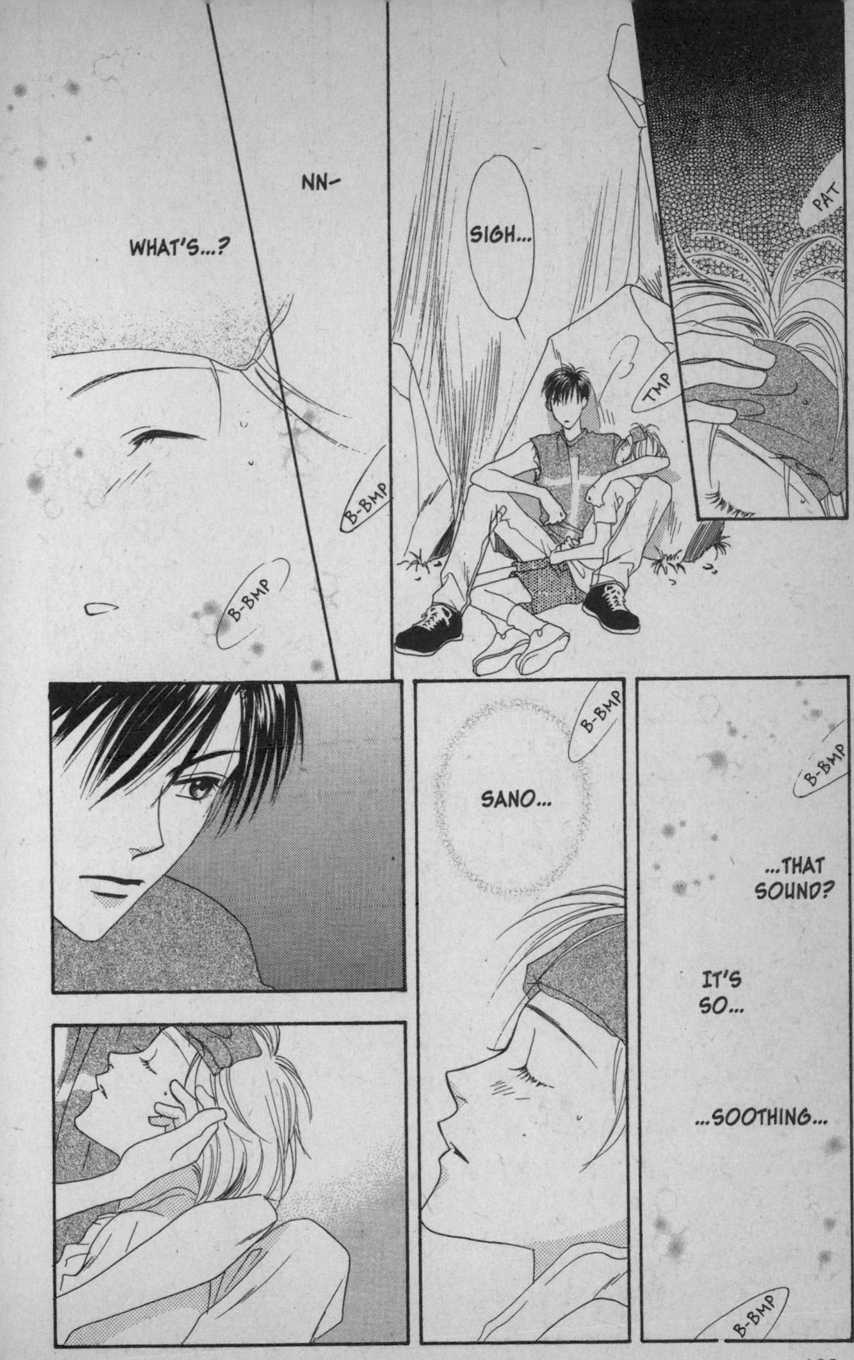
PAT
TMP
SIGH...
NN-
WHAT'S...?
B-BMP
B-BMP
B-BMP
...THAT SOUND?
IT'S SO...
...SOOTHING...
B-BMP
B-BMP
SANO...

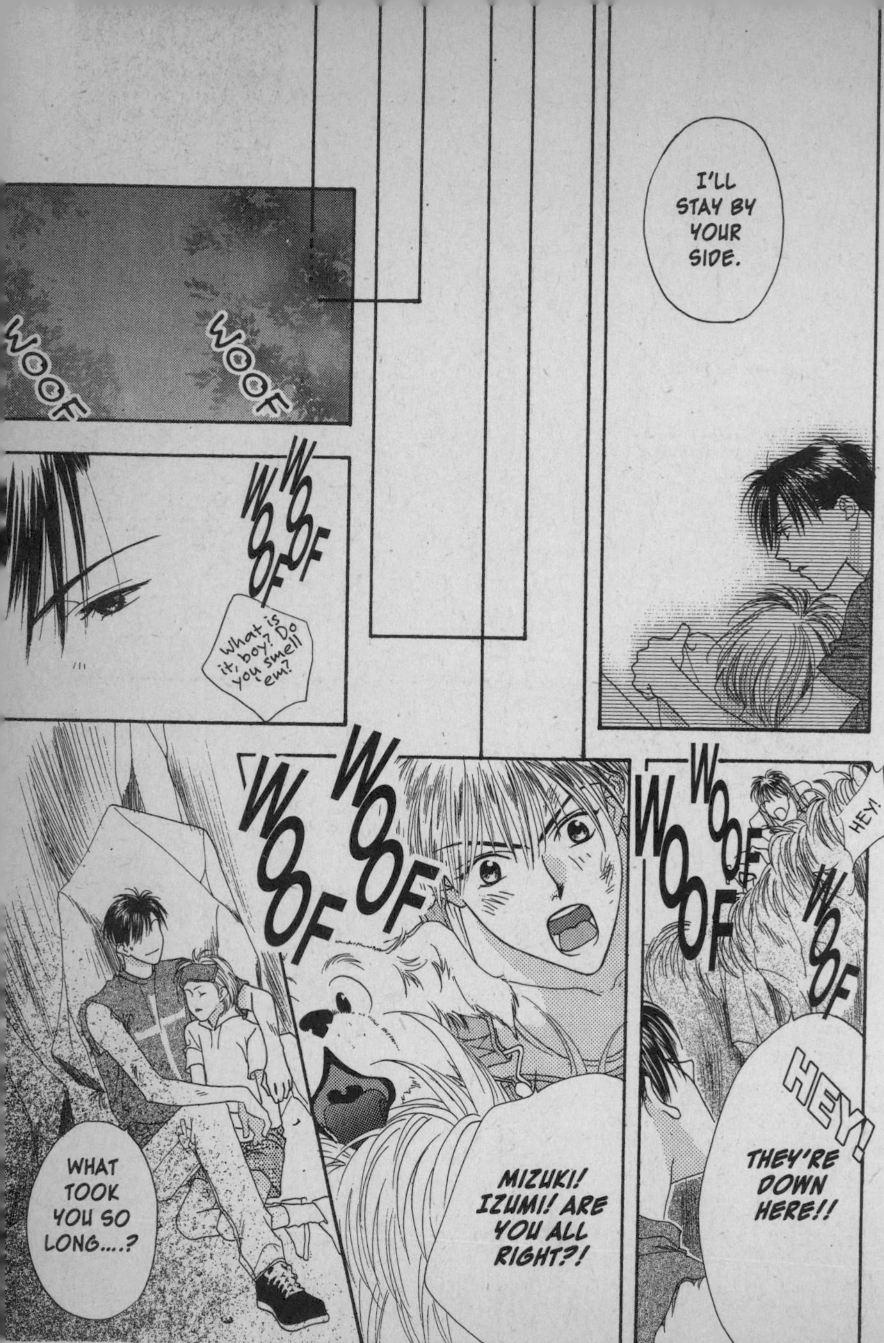
I'LL STAY BY YOUR SIDE.
WOOF WOOF
WOOF WOOF
what is it, boy? Do you smell 'em?
WOOF WOOF
HEY!
WOOF
HEY!
THEY'RE DOWN HERE!!
WOOF WOOF
MIZUKI! IZUMI! ARE YOU ALL RIGHT?!
WHAT TOOK YOU SO LONG....?

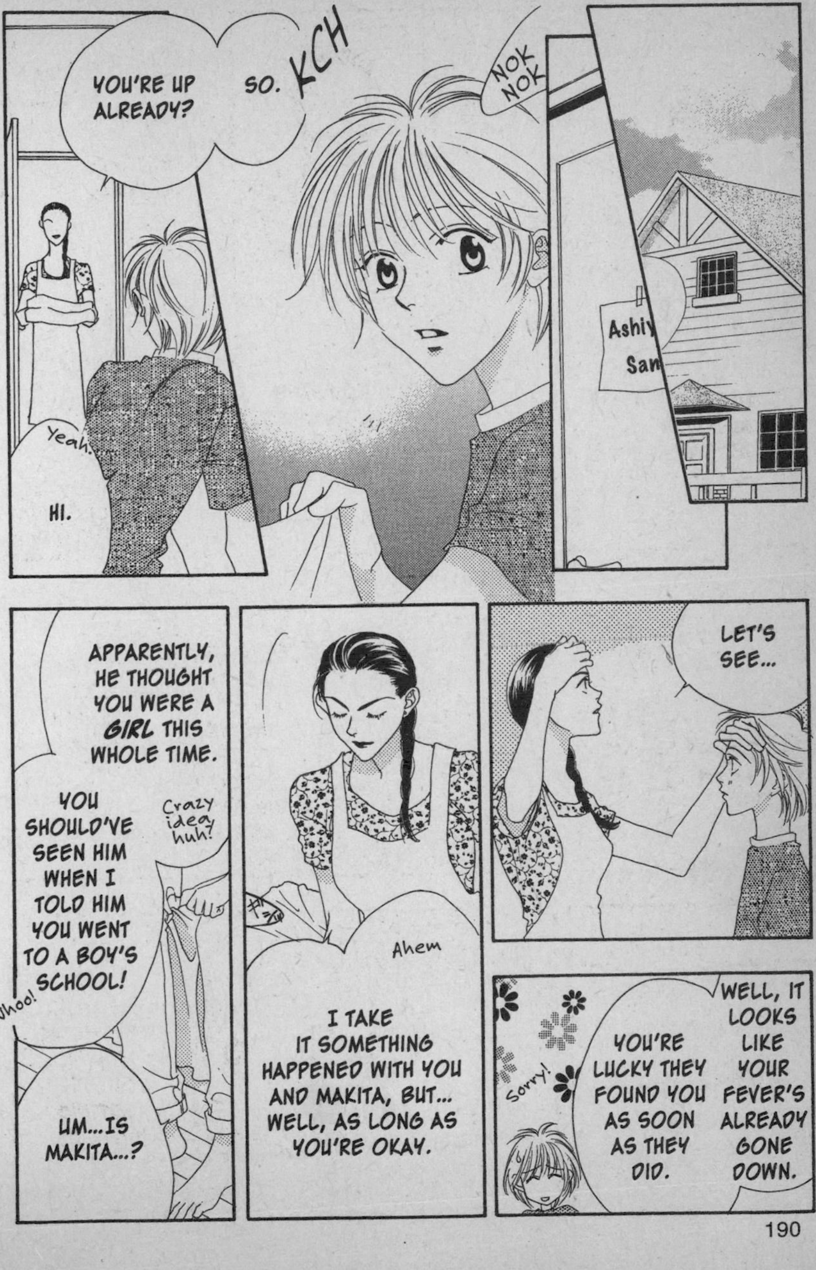
NOK NOK
KCH
SO.
YOU'RE UP ALREADY?
Yeah.
HI.
LET'S SEE...
WELL, IT LOOKS LIKE YOUR FEVER'S ALREADY GONE DOWN.
YOU'RE LUCKY THEY FOUND YOU AS SOON AS THEY DID.
Sorry!
Ahem
I TAKE IT SOMETHING HAPPENED WITH YOU AND MAKITA, BUT... WELL, AS LONG AS YOU'RE OKAY.
APPARENTLY, HE THOUGHT YOU WERE A *GIRL* THIS WHOLE TIME.
YOU SHOULD'VE SEEN HIM WHEN I TOLD HIM YOU WENT TO A BOY'S SCHOOL!
Crazy idea huh!
Whoo!
UM...IS MAKITA...?

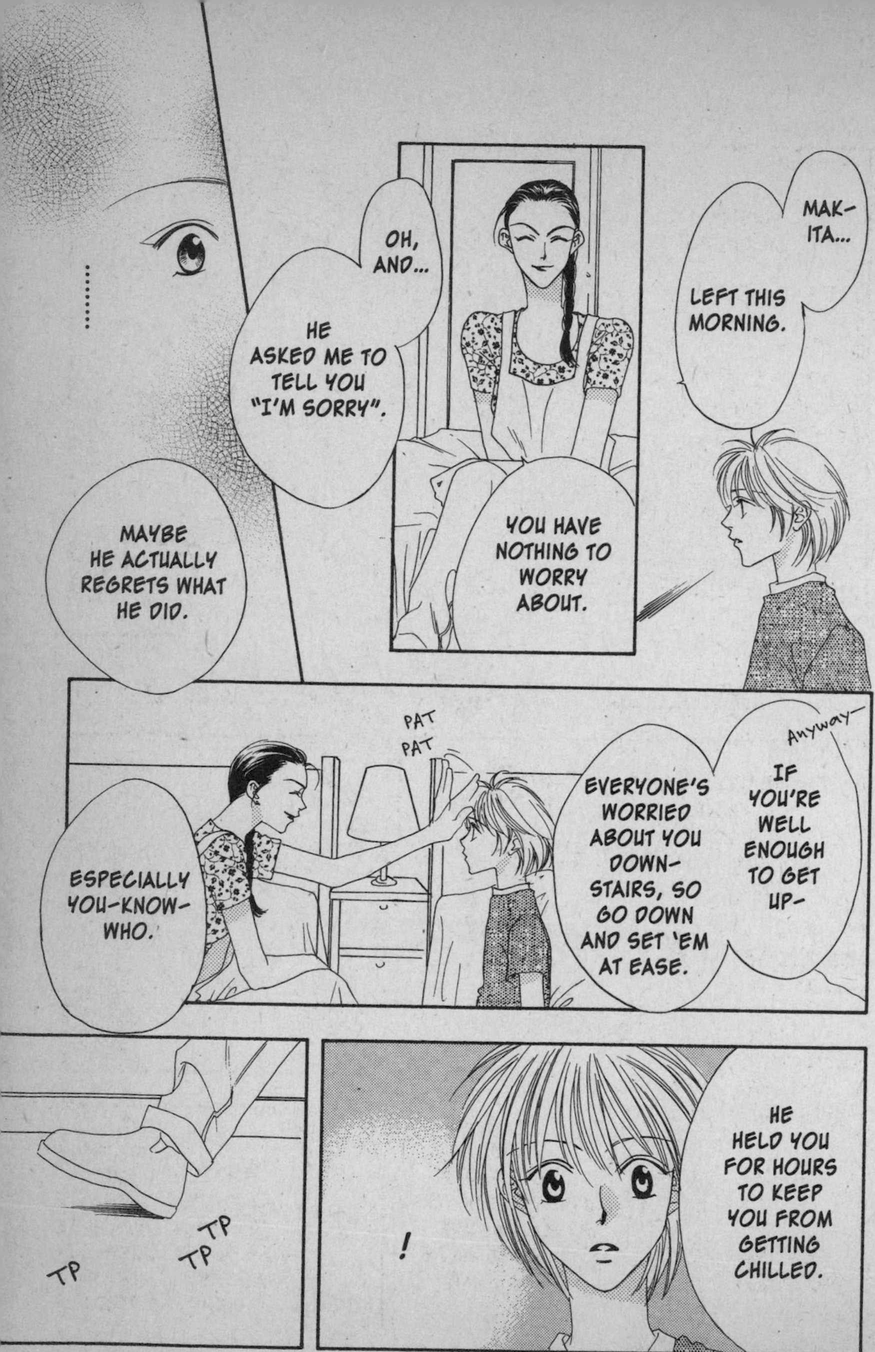
MAK-
ITA...
LEFT THIS MORNING.
OH, AND...
HE ASKED ME TO TELL YOU "I'M SORRY".
YOU HAVE NOTHING TO WORRY ABOUT.
MAYBE HE ACTUALLY REGRETS WHAT HE DID.
....
Anyway—
IF YOU'RE WELL ENOUGH TO GET UP-
EVERYONE'S WORRIED ABOUT YOU DOWN-STAIRS, SO GO DOWN AND SET 'EM AT EASE.
PAT PAT
ESPECIALLY YOU-KNOW-WHO.
HE HELD YOU FOR HOURS TO KEEP YOU FROM GETTING CHILLED.
!
TP TP TP

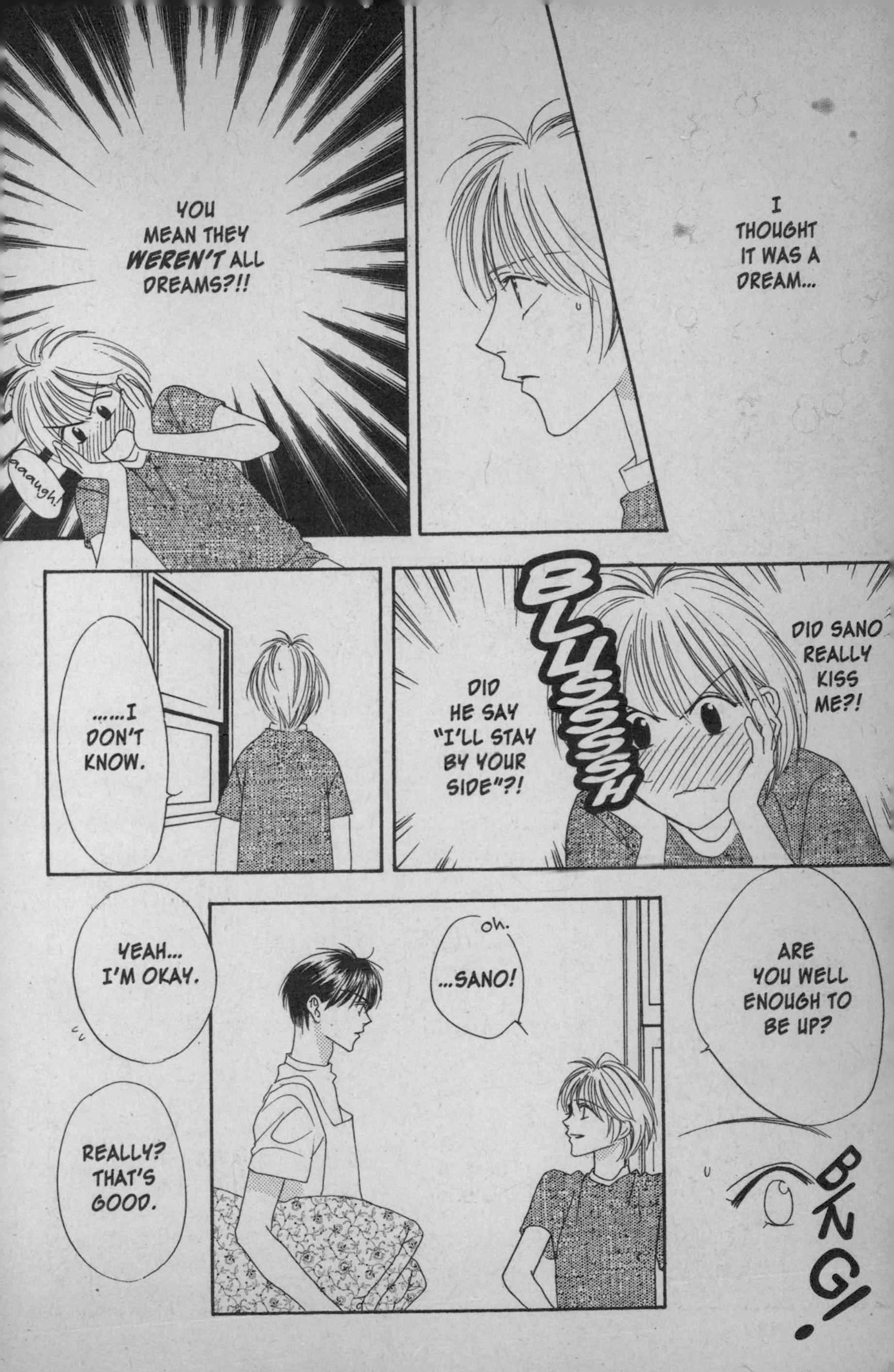
I THOUGHT IT WAS A DREAM...
YOU MEAN THEY *WEREN'T* ALL DREAMS?!!
aaaugh!
DID SANO REALLY KISS ME?!
BLUSSSH
DID HE SAY "I'LL STAY BY YOUR SIDE"?!
......I DON'T KNOW.
ARE YOU WELL ENOUGH TO BE UP?
BING!
oh.
...SANO!
YEAH... I'M OKAY.
REALLY? THAT'S GOOD.

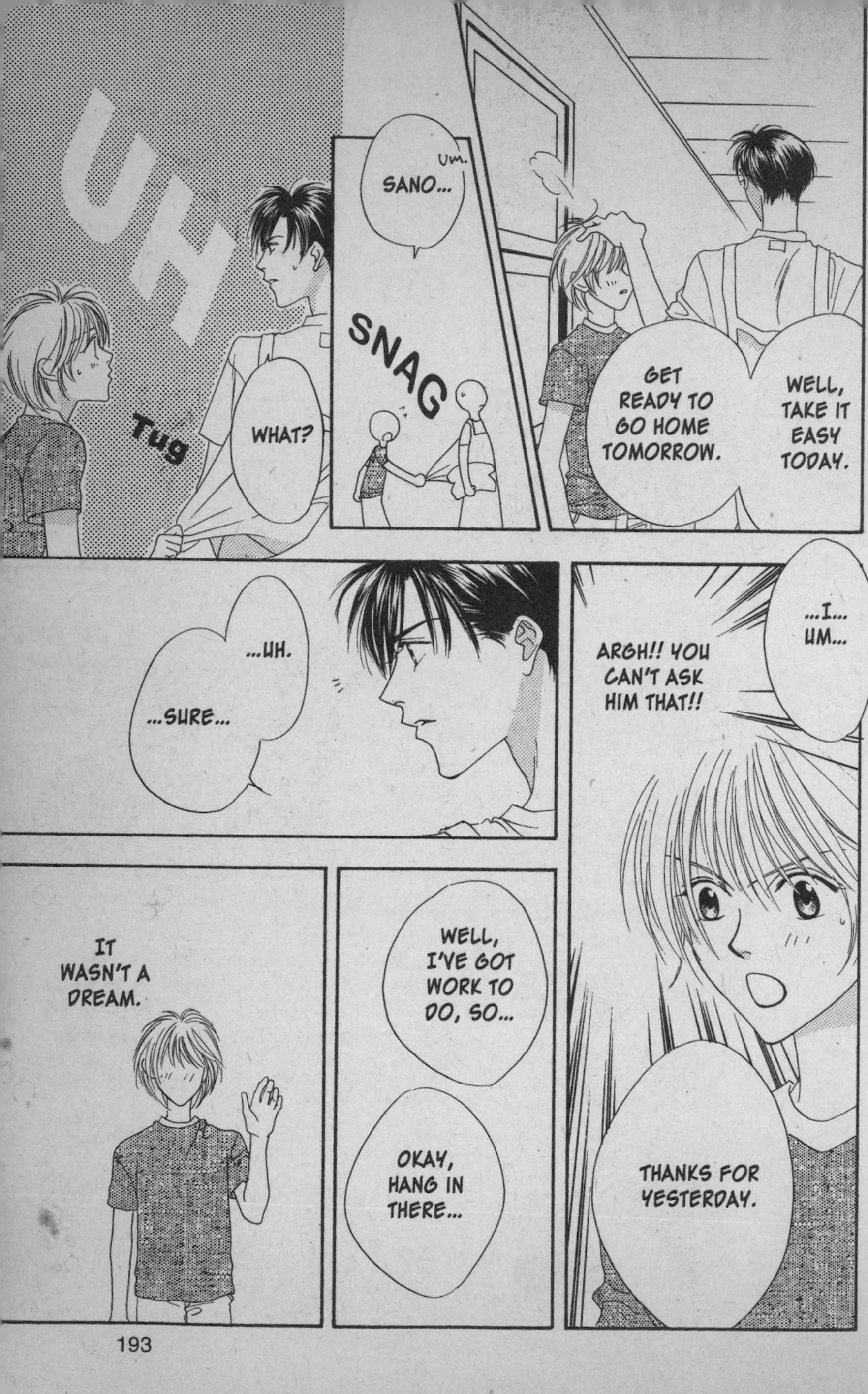
WELL, TAKE IT EASY TODAY.
GET READY TO GO HOME TOMORROW.
Um.
SANO...
SNAG
WHAT?
Tug
...I... UM...
ARGH!! YOU CAN'T ASK HIM THAT!!
THANKS FOR YESTERDAY.
...UH.
...SURE...
WELL, I'VE GOT WORK TO DO, SO...
OKAY, HANG IN THERE...
IT WASN'T A DREAM.

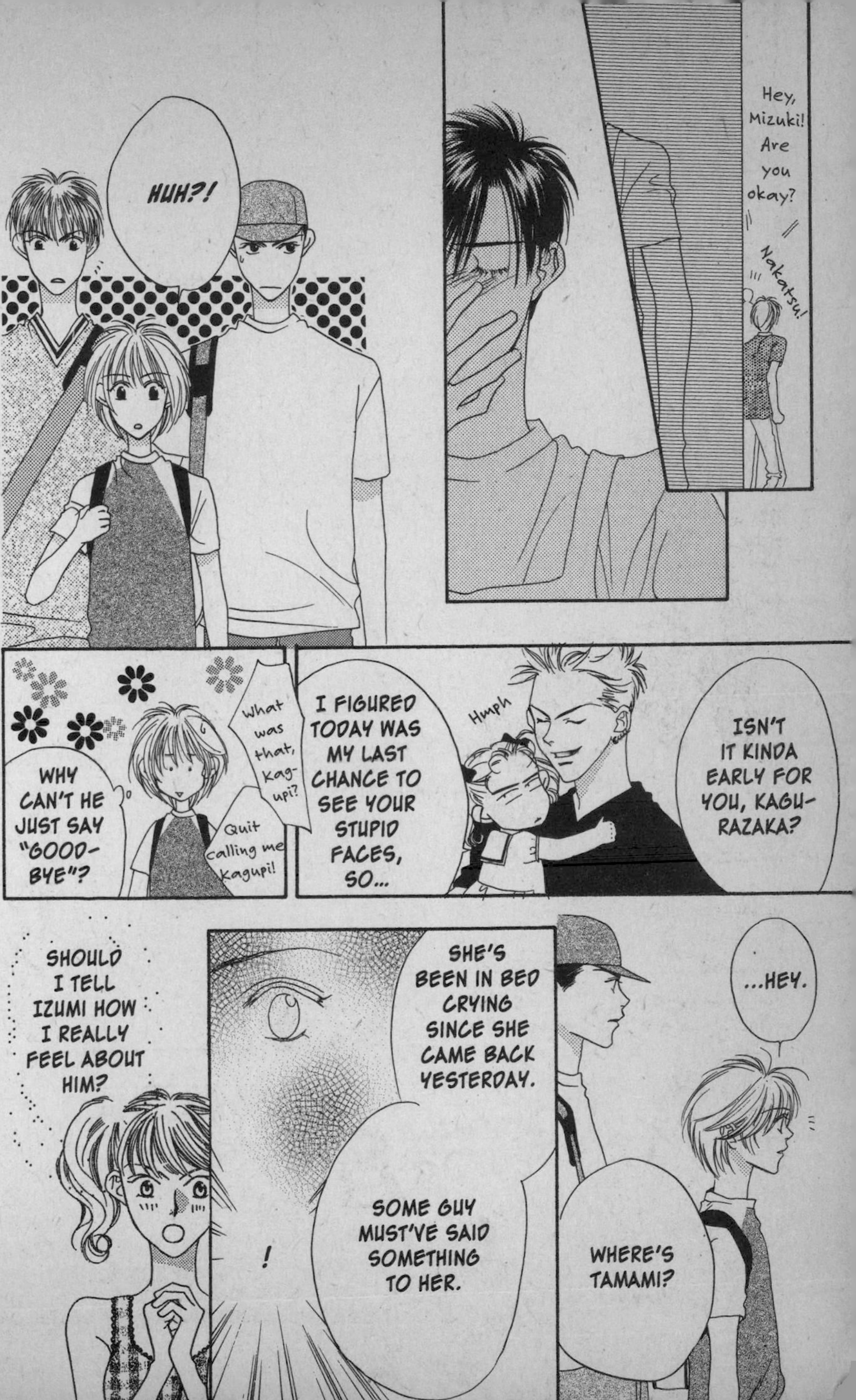
Hey, Mizuki! Are you okay?
Nakatsu!
HUH?!
ISN'T IT KINDA EARLY FOR YOU, KAGURAZAKA?
Hmph
I FIGURED TODAY WAS MY LAST CHANCE TO SEE YOUR STUPID FACES, SO...
What was that, Kagupi?
Quit calling me Kagupi!
WHY CAN'T HE JUST SAY "GOOD-BYE"?
...HEY.
WHERE'S TAMAMI?
SHE'S BEEN IN BED CRYING SINCE SHE CAME BACK YESTERDAY.
SOME GUY MUST'VE SAID SOMETHING TO HER.
!
SHOULD I TELL IZUMI HOW I REALLY FEEL ABOUT HIM?

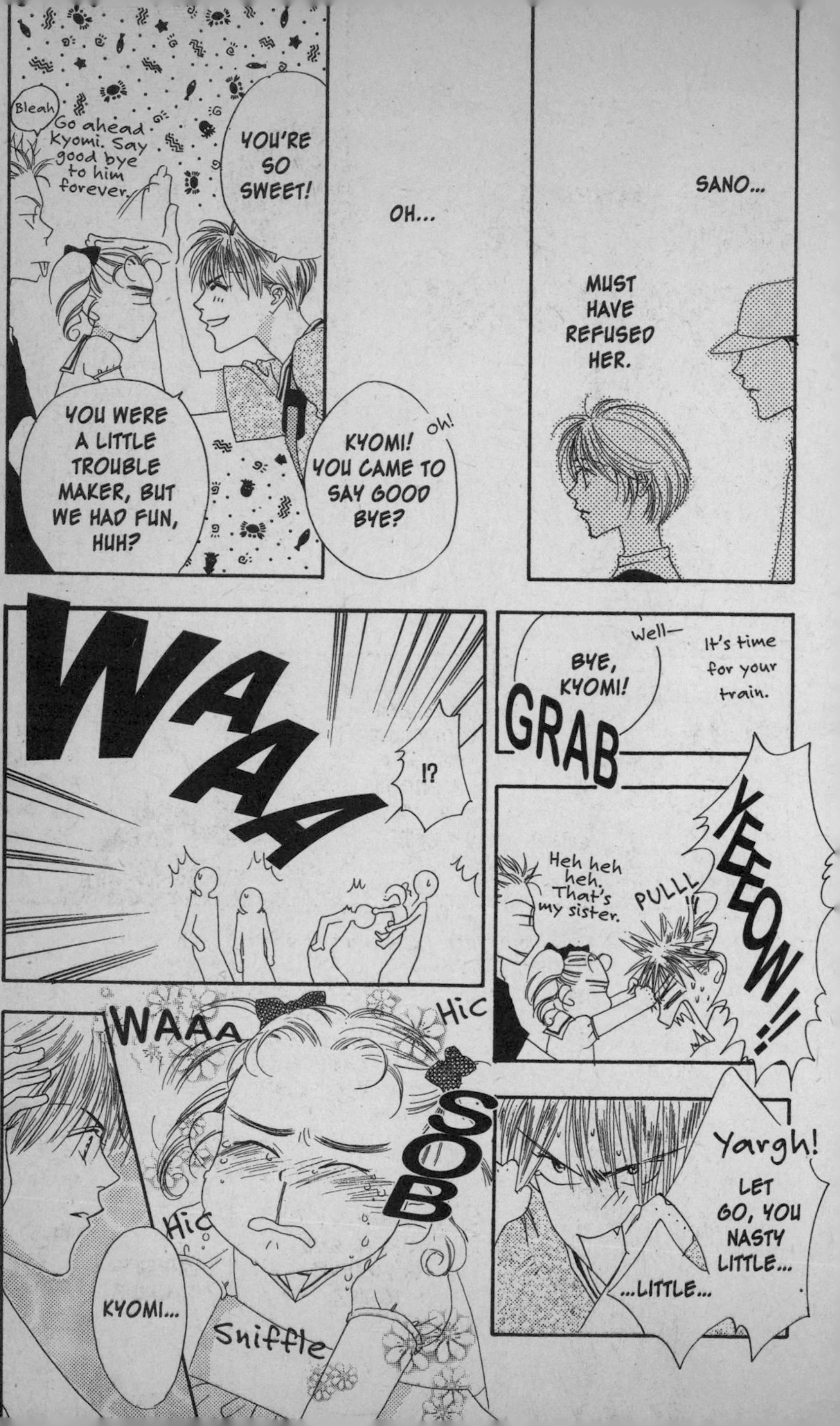

SANO...
MUST HAVE REFUSED HER.
OH...
YOU'RE SO SWEET!
Bleah
Go ahead Kyomi. Say good bye to him forever.
Oh!
KYOMI! YOU CAME TO SAY GOOD BYE?
YOU WERE A LITTLE TROUBLE MAKER, BUT WE HAD FUN, HUH?
It's time for your train.
Well—
BYE, KYOMI!
GRAB
YEEOW!!
PULL
Heh heh heh. That's my sister.
!?
WAAA
Yargh!
LET GO, YOU NASTY LITTLE...
...LITTLE...
Hic
SOB
WAAA
Hic
KYOMI...
Sniffle

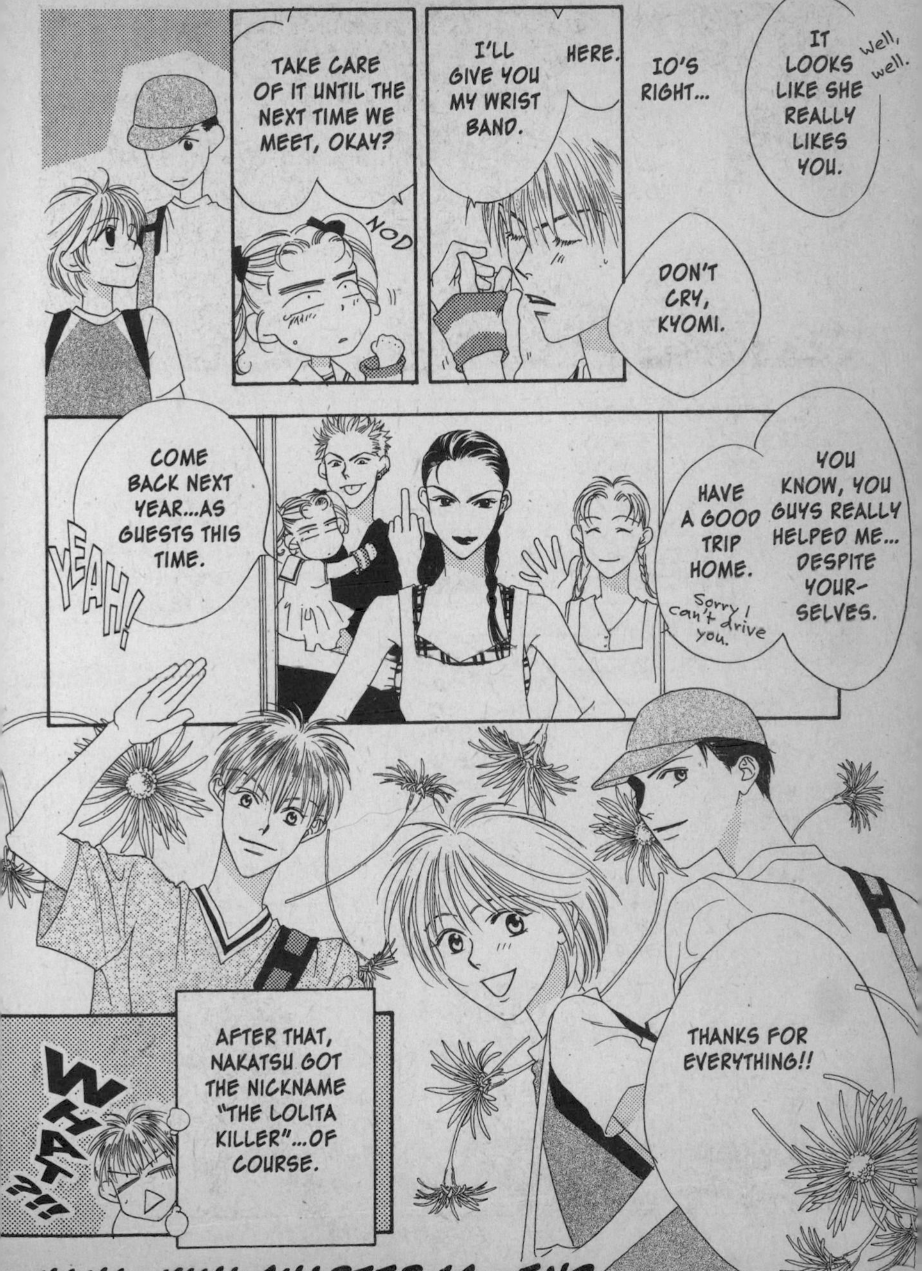
IT LOOKS LIKE SHE REALLY LIKES YOU.
Well, well.
IO'S RIGHT...
DON'T CRY, KYOMI.
HERE.
I'LL GIVE YOU MY WRIST BAND.
TAKE CARE OF IT UNTIL THE NEXT TIME WE MEET, OKAY?
NOD
YOU KNOW, YOU GUYS REALLY HELPED ME... DESPITE YOURSELVES.
HAVE A GOOD TRIP HOME.
Sorry I can't drive you.
COME BACK NEXT YEAR...AS GUESTS THIS TIME.
YEAH!
THANKS FOR EVERYTHING!!
AFTER THAT, NAKATSU GOT THE NICKNAME "THE LOLITA KILLER"...OF COURSE.
WHAT?!!

HANA-KIMI CHAPTER 16: END

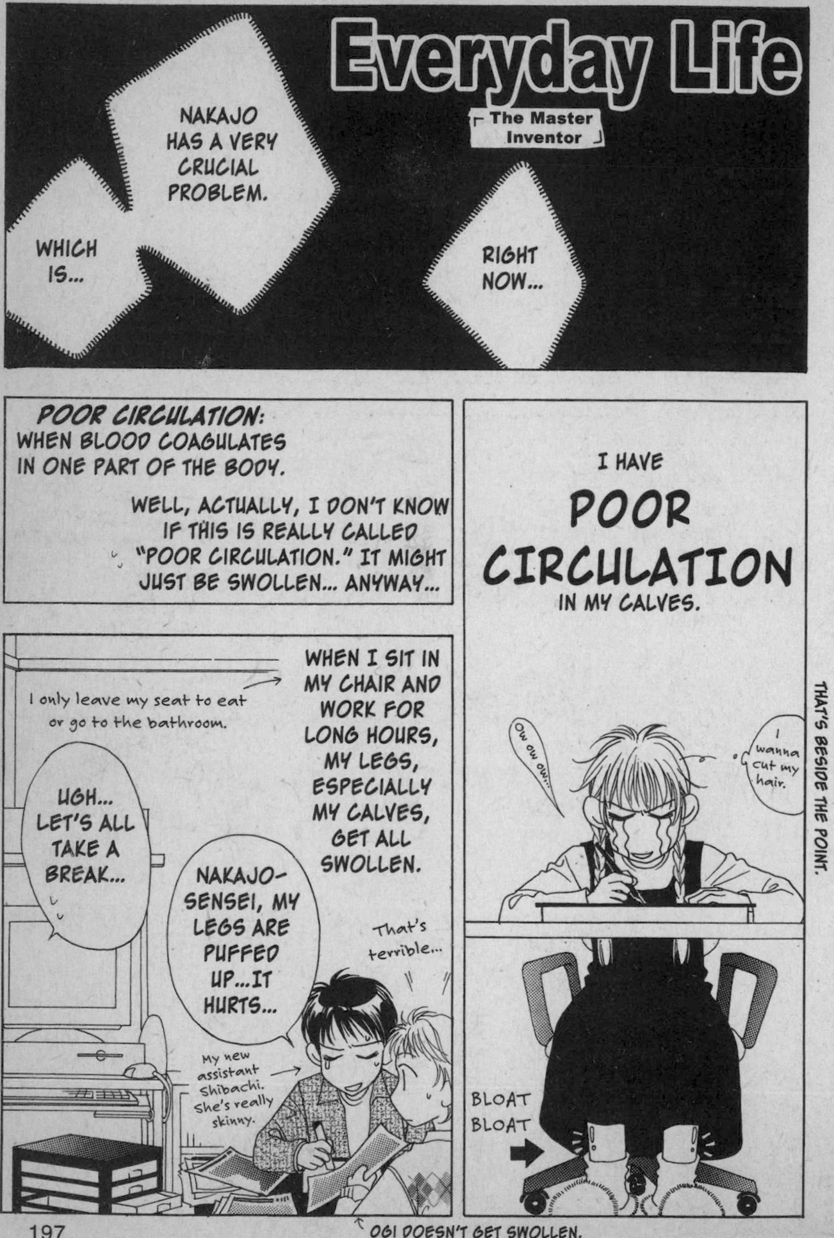
Everyday Life
The Master Inventor
RIGHT NOW...
NAKAJO HAS A VERY CRUCIAL PROBLEM.
WHICH IS...
I HAVE POOR CIRCULATION IN MY CALVES.
I wanna cut my hair.
Ow ow ow...
THAT'S BESIDE THE POINT.
BLOAT BLOAT
POOR CIRCULATION: WHEN BLOOD COAGULATES IN ONE PART OF THE BODY.
WELL, ACTUALLY, I DON'T KNOW IF THIS IS REALLY CALLED "POOR CIRCULATION." IT MIGHT JUST BE SWOLLEN... ANYWAY...
WHEN I SIT IN MY CHAIR AND WORK FOR LONG HOURS, MY LEGS, ESPECIALLY MY CALVES, GET ALL SWOLLEN.
I only leave my seat to eat or go to the bathroom.
That's terrible...
NAKAJO-SENSEI, MY LEGS ARE PUFFED UP...IT HURTS...
UGH... LET'S ALL TAKE A BREAK...
My new assistant Shibachi. She's really skinny.
OGI DOESN'T GET SWOLLEN.

WHEN YOUR LEGS GET SWOLLEN FROM POOR CIRCULATION, YOU HAVE TO ELEVATE THEM. SO I'VE COME UP WITH MANY WAYS TO DO IT.
A blanket folded in half and placed on top.
Stacks of magazines. Not all of them are "Hana to Yume" (ha ha)
BUT IT DOESN'T DO MUCH.
OUCH...
All we can do is laugh.
Ho ho ho
SO I THOUGHT OF SOMETHING.
WHAT WOULD SUPPORT THE ENTIRE BODY AND PREVENT THE BLOOD FROM COAGULATING?
AND I THOUGHT OF ...
ONE OF THOSE CHAIRS IN A DENTIST'S OFFICE!
POINTY CUSHION THAT REDUCES THE PRESSURE ON YOUR BACK.
WIDE SEAT
IT SPINS, TOO... OF COURSE!
YOU CAN BEND IT TO ANY ANGLE.
FOOT REST
THESE ARE THE ONLY TWO FEATURES THAT ARE REALLY HELPFUL.
AH HA HA
HEE HEE HEE
PERFECT
OH, HOW I WANT ONE!
NAKAJO-SENSEI, YOU KNOW THEY HAVE SPECIAL NYLONS THAT PREVENT SWELLING.
...

THEN ALL THE WEIGHT GETS PUT ON YOUR HEELS, SO *THEY* START TO HURT.

WHO'S *THIS* SUPPOSED TO BE?

SHIBACHI IS TOTALLY CRAZY ABOUT HYDE.

THAT'S THE END!
SEE YOU NEXT TIME!

OGI IS CRAZY ABOUT KATSUYUKI MORI AND MAI HOJO.

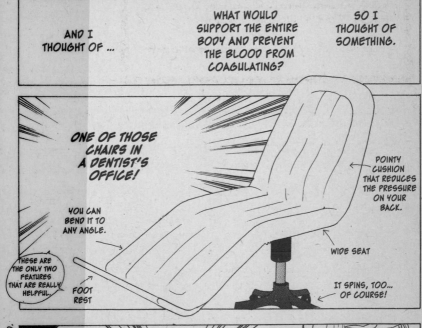

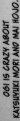

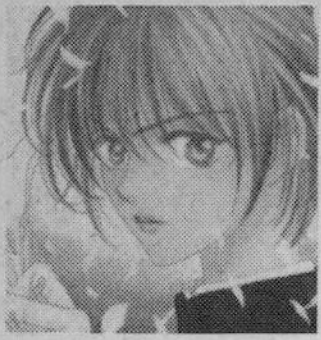

ABOUT THE AUTHOR

Hisaya Nakajo's manga series **Hanazakari no Kimitachi he** ("For You in Full Blossom", casually known as **Hana-Kimi**) has been a hit since it first appeared in 1997 in the shôjo manga magazine **Hana to Yume** ("Flowers and Dreams"). In Japan, a **Hana-Kimi** art book and several "drama CDs" have been released. Her other manga series include **Missing Piece** (2 volumes) and **Yumemiru Happa** ("The Dreaming Leaf", 1 volume).

Hisaya Nakajo's website: **www.wild-vanilla.com**